THE CONSERVATIVE DECADE

EMERGING LEADERS
OF THE 1980s

THE CONSERVATIVE DECADE

EMERGING LEADERS OF THE 1980s

JAMES C. ROBERTS

WITH A FOREWORD BY
GOV. RONALD REAGAN

ARLINGTON HOUSE PUBLISHERS
WESTPORT, CONNECTICUT

**For My Mother
and My Wife, Patti**

Library of Congress Cataloging in Publication Data

Roberts, James C   1946–
    The conservative decade

    Includes index.
    1. United States–Politics and government–1945–
2. Conservatism–United States.   I. Title.
E839.5.R565   320.5'2'0973   80–15663
ISBN 0-87000-462-X

Manufactured in the United States of America

P 0 9 8 7 6 5 4 3 2 1

TABLE OF CONTENTS

Part IV Strategy and Politics

FOREWORD

A little while back, Jimmy Carter took to the airwaves to speak to the American people about what he perceived as a growing "national malaise." In retrospect, it seems likely that he mistook the malaise among his own advisors, and in the Washington liberal establishment in general, for a malady afflicting the nation as a whole.

For decades, liberalism has presented itself as the ideology of hope from Americans looking for a better life. Did we want a more prosperous economy? Help for the poor and downtrodden? Better education for our children? Government of the large but definitely not the economy size was ballyhooed as the answer.

Today, liberalism has had its day in court, and the jury is about to return with the verdict. The American people know we're in trouble, and intuitively, they know it's the blind faith that too many have placed in Uncle Sam that has gotten us into such a mess. The ideology of hope has now turned to one of despair. To a country suffocating under the burdens of rampaging inflation, stifling governmental overregulation, and taxation, Mr. Carter offers more economic controls, higher taxes, and the glum news that the nation will just have to swallow a lot of bitter medicine for a period of years before things become any better.

The extreme form of liberalism championed by Senator Edward Kennedy offers us an economic nostrum that is even worse: wage and price controls, which would create shortages of things we now have in abundance and bring a basically sound, though troubled, economy to its knees. Messrs. Kennedy, Carter and their minions tell us we'll have to change our lifestyles, to start getting along with less, to accept a decline in our standard of living.

In short, the bankruptcy of liberalism is complete. Confronted with the most severe economic crisis of the postwar era, a crisis of its own making, liberalism is devoid of ideas for setting things aright. Confronted with threats of unprecedented gravity from abroad, it offers only weakness and indecision.

For the average American, the message is clear: Liberalism is no longer the answer—it is the problem.

Conservatives offer another direction, one in which the excesses of big government can be replaced by the inventiveness, creativity, and energy of the individual. By cutting taxes instead of raising them incessantly, by encouraging initiative and hard work rather than creating welfare dependence, by working for peace through strength and preparedness, we believe we offer hope for a revitalized America.

There seems little doubt that Americans are increasingly receptive to this message. Polls show ever-greater numbers of people are fed up with crushing taxation and inept and wasteful government. But translating that gut feeling into real political change is no easy matter.

Nevertheless, the change is coming, thanks in large part to a growing and diverse group of individuals often collectively known as the "conservative movement."

As a rule, you won't find references to the conservative movement in the *New York Times* or the *Washington Post*. But with few exceptions, the people involved—whether they're members of Congress or congressional staffs, whether they write for conservative periodicals or the general mass media, whether they work in "think tanks" or universities or the many issue-oriented conservative organizations—view themselves as being part of a movement.

Perhaps the most interesting thing about the conservative movement today is that many of its leaders—perhaps a majority of them—are members of a generation most frequently identified with violent antiwar demonstrations, the drug culture, Jane Fonda and Jerry Rubin, and the high-water mark of radical leftist activism. But somehow, while others were burning flags and conducting sit-ins, they managed to get an education at colleges and universities where liberal and radical orthodoxy were taught with evangelical fervor. What's more, they emerged tempered by adversity on the campus and with a deep dedication to the values and institutions the radicals had sought to subvert.

In this book, Jim Roberts, himself a member of that postwar "baby boom" generation, tells the stories of scores of bright young conservatives who form the vanguard of the most exciting political movement of our times.

Their influence can hardly be overstated. They have given conservative efforts on Capitol Hill a structure, competence, and effectiveness where previous generations had settled for futile gestures of loyal opposition. They are beginning to show up in journalism, which, until recently, has seemed monotonously liberal in outlook. They include economists who are now the talk of the business world, and of politicians who are suddenly discovering the virtues of common sense and devotion to the free market. They are political specialists who have learned how to wage successful election battles against previously unassailable pillars of liberalism. They are specialists in defense policy and foreign affairs, men and women with a thorough knowledge of the world, a well-reasoned view of our place in it, and a commitment to preserve and expand human freedom everywhere.

Those who despair at the state of affairs in our country can read this book and come away with a renewed spirit and a feeling of reassurance that we are rich in leaders ready to let the creative genius of our people flourish and to make a strong, free, and humane America once again the hope of the world.

RONALD REAGAN

ACKNOWLEDGMENTS

This book would not have been possible without the financial and moral support of the Fund for Objective News Reporting, and I wish to express my thanks to Thomas S. Winter, the fund's president, for his invaluable assistance.

In addition, I would like to express my gratitude to Rep. Robert Bauman, chairman of the American Conservative Union, M. Stanton Evans, chairman of the ACU Education and Research Institute, Kathleen Crow, chairman of the California Conservative Union, Richard Harvey, chairman of the Texas Conservative Union, Dr. Victor Fediay of the Institute of American Relations, and Peter Hannaford for their support and encouragement.

I am also grateful to Tim Engle, Jeff Lupoff and Mike Sullivan for assisting with the research for this book.

I am deeply indebted, as well, to Governor Ronald Reagan for writing the foreword to this book. The election of Governor Reagan to the presidency of the United States in 1980 would be the fulfillment of thirty years of intellectual and political effort by the American conservative movement, and a Reagan presidency is the tacit assumption underlying the prospect of a "conservative decade."

Finally, I would like to thank Karl Pflock, my editor, whose support, suggestions and deftly wielded blue pencil have made this a much improved book, and my wife Patti, for her unfailing support and helpful advice and for her cheerfulness in the thankless job of typing the manuscript. Were they not involved in the making of this book, they would have merited their own place in the text, as both are promising young conservative leaders in their own right.

PART I | THE CONSERVATIVE MOVEMENT

1 | THE CONSERVATIVE REVIVAL

Slowly and sometimes fitfully, yet inexorably nonetheless, America is moving in a rightward direction as the nation enters the 1980s. Such an assessment would have been greeted with unconstrained derision by our *cognescenti* only a few years ago, but it is taken as a given in most quarters today.

In its fifteenth anniversary issue, published in December 1970, the cover of *National Review* featured tombstones with "Great Society," "New Frontier," "Fair Deal," and "New Deal" chiseled on them. The accompanying caption read, "After Liberalism What?" The death knell was undoubtedly a bit premature because, as conservative columnist George Will has noted, liberal policies really reached their apogee in the early 1970s under President Richard M. Nixon. It was clear even in 1970, however, that the patient was in dire straits and eight years later, in a *Newsweek* column entitled "The End of the Liberal Era," Will performed last rites and covered the corpse.

The March 1975 issue of the liberal *Village Voice* took notice of the fact of liberalism's decline as reporter James Wolcott wrote:

As the liberal-Left slides shamefully into a pale-colored Classics-Club-comic-book socialism, the real political action in America is on the Right. In a bureaucratic state which is suffocatingly byzantine, conservatives are the true disturbers of the peace— if they can make their voices heard.

They *are* making their voices heard—a fact that was underscored by the March 26, 1979, issue of the *Voice*. The page one headline asked plaintively, "Is There Hope for the 80s?" The accompanying piece detailed the activities of a number of liberal groups who were preparing desperately for "The Race to Beat the Right"—the right being clearly ascendant in the opinion of the author.

1

Yes, conservatism is resurgent in America today. In both the intellectual and political realms conservatives are on the offensive, liberals on the defensive.

In the intellectual sphere conservatives are, without question, winning the war. In the universities, the media, and among the populace as a whole, the adherents of liberalism are abandoning the creed in droves while those who still defend it do so in a listless manner that bespeaks growing disenchantment.

Amidst this liberal decline conservatives are flourishing. Take, for example the media, typically regarded as the best barometer of trends. As Ben Wattenberg has remarked, "Conservatives used to write articles about liberals. Now liberals write articles about conservatives."

A cursory perusal of the nation's leading general circulation journals reveals a plethora of articles either by conservatives or about conservative personalities or issues. This trend is borne out among the syndicated columnists as well. With the advent of a host of new conservative columnists such as George Will, Patrick Buchanan, John Lofton, and others, a majority of the nationally syndicated political columnists, including most of the most popular ones, is now conservative. Among the periodicals, leading publications such as *Harper's, The New Republic,* and *Commentary,* which were formerly staunch advocates of liberalism, have all moved rightward while such neoconservative publications as *The Public Interest* are growing in number and prestige.

In the universities, faculties which were once almost the exclusive domain of liberals are beginning to sport a fair number of conservatives. The most dramatic manifestation of the change can be seen in the economics departments where the Keynesianism that reigned unchallenged ten years ago has been thoroughly discredited by a growing number of young free-market economists. Meanwhile, students themselves are growing more conservative, both attitudinally and politically.

Most important, the populace as a whole is moving to the right. Increasingly disillusioned with the results of the federal spending programs ballyhooed by liberal policy-makers, angered by the social costs of such programs as busing, quotas, and subsidized abortions, and burdened by the economic hardships imposed by a tangle of bureaucratic regulations, the electorate continues to move to the right according to the major opinion polls. As one might suppose of such a sustained change in the electorate's mood, the impact has eventually come to be felt on the electorate's ostensible servants in government, yea, verily even into Washington, the very citadel of the liberal corporate state.

A convincing demonstration of this was made by the 95th Congress during the first two years of President Jimmy Carter's administration. Due primarily to the ravages of Watergate and the lackluster campaign of Gerald Ford, the Republican Party—the country's conservative party—was virtually prostrate at the beginning of 1977. The Democratic Party—the country's liberal party—controlled the presidency, the Congress by a two-to-one margin, the governorships, 38–12, and the state legislatures by more than two-to-one. The stage appeared to be set for a binge of new liberal programs unmatched since the first two years of the presidency of Lyndon Johnson. And, indeed, President Carter and the congressional leadership moved to make such a scenario a reality, proposing a host of bills demanded by liberal interest groups.

Miraculously, when the dust settled two years later, most of the president's program lay in ruins. Far from huddling in desperation in the Carter catacombs, conservative congressional and organizational leaders and conservative activists at the grass roots level displayed a militancy, ingenuity, and organizational savy of unprecedented degree, managing in the process to derail much of the president's legislative agenda. Proposals such as the public financing of congressional elections, instant voter registration, the consumer protection agency, common situs picketing, the cargo preference bill, and a costly welfare "reform" plan were defeated. The misguided energy bill was radically transformed, and the Humphrey-Hawkins "full-employment" bill was essentially gutted.

Even more surprising, conservatives went on the offensive, pushing a whole array of economic initiatives such as the effort to mandate the drafting of a constitutional amendment to balance the federal budget, the bill proposed by Rep. Jack Kemp and Sen. William Roth to effect a sizeable cut in federal corporate and personal income tax rates, and the amendment proposed by Wisconsin's Rep. William Steiger to cut the capital gains tax rate. Most dramatic of all was the Proposition 13 initiative placed on the ballot in California by career curmudgeon Howard Jarvis. Though attacked by most of California's media, Democratic establishment, and powerful labor unions as a nostrum that would wreak fiscal disaster on the state, Proposition 13 was overwhelmingly approved by California voters, a devastating blow that sowed panic among liberal politicians and pundits from coast to coast. And now, for the first time in fifty years, conservatives have the initiative in the area of domestic affairs. In the face of the conservative tide the expansionist government express had stalled, and its captains were fighting desperately just to minimize the damage.

The impact of all this activity was made manifest in the elections of 1978. The Kemp-Roth bill was adopted as policy by the National Republican Party and very nearly passed by an overwhelmingly Democratic Congress. Its principal proponent, Republican Rep. Jack Kemp, a conservative 44-year-old former Buffalo Bills quarterback, was so popular in his largely Democratic district that he had no opposition for reelection, and hence was able to spend his time stumping the country for the GOP, nearly all of whose candidates supported Kemp-Roth. By year's end, Kemp had become one of the four or five most popular speakers in the Republican Party.

Meanwhile, the Steiger bill to cut capital gains tax rates was passed by the Congress over the bitter opposition of President Carter, who had sought to *increase* the rates. Across the country in the fall campaign, the predominant issues were runaway government spending, excessive bureaucracy and regulation and proposals to cut taxes. Tax-cut initiatives were on the ballots in twenty-four states.

In November a badly emaciated Republican Party found itself substantially revived. The party had picked up 319 state legislative seats, six governorships, twelve U.S. House seats, and three Senate seats. There is every reason to believe that these gains, healthy though they were, would have been even more impressive had not the Democrats become so adept at coopting the tax-cutting issue. Time after time, Republican challengers to life-long addicts of the welfare state found these incumbents advocating their own tax-cut plans.

The most spectacular reversal of position had to be that of Gov. Jerry Brown of California who had entered office as a rather eccentric yet economically orthodox liberal. When Proposition 13 was placed on the ballot, Brown fought it tooth and nail predicting the standard dire consequences if it passed. But about two weeks before the election it became apparent to Brown that it would pass, and he began to soften his opposition in anticipation. When the measure did win overwhelming approval, he embraced it with fervor and from then on touted it with such enthusiasm that by the November election he had become identified with Proposition 13—a misconception that was crucial to his reelection by a margin of over a million votes. By April, he was touting the cause of a balanced budget amendment to the U.S. Constitution—an issue which he has adopted as the centerpiece of his candidacy for the presidency.

In his eccentric, eclectic philosophy of government, Brown typifies a state long famous for eclecticism and eccentricity. But California is also deservedly famous as the harbinger of national trends, and its current governor has a hair-trigger sensitivity to those trends. In many ways, Brown is the most interesting politician in the country today. As a Democrat advocating limited government and private sector expansionism, he is the augury for the decade of the 1980s. Brown is symptomatic of the times for another reason: at 41 he is a relatively young man.

Just as the salient political datum of our day is the move to the right, the salient demographic datum of the day is the "baby boom" generation that came on the scene at the close of World War II. The 10 million babies of that era strained the resources of their parents who were struggling to adopt to civilian life; they strained the inadequate capacity of the grammar schools, then the high schools, then the colleges, then the job market. A large blip on the nation's demographic chart, the postwar generation's sheer numerical size made America a youthful country in the literal sense. As it grows older, the average age of the population will go up as well. More significant, the "boom babies" will become increasingly influential in our national life.

This wave is just beginning to crest. The postwar generation has been at work now for ten years or more. Its members are gaining positions of responsibility; in the 1980s, they will occupy a majority of those positions. It would seem at first glance that the coming of age of this generation would have a liberal impact. After all, we are talking about the generation of the flower children, dropouts, communal lifestyles, civil rights activists, antiwar demonstrators, counterculture advocates, New Leftists, Black Panthers, draft card burners, campus rioters, folk singing protestors, Beatle-crazed frenetics, and—in Jonathan Winters' phrase—"long-haired, dope-crazed, hippie, weirdo freaks." This is the Woodstock Nation generation, is it not? The generation of Baez and Dylan, the Beatles, Rolling Stones, Julian Bond, Ralph Nader, the Chicago Seven, Cesar Chavez, the Berrigans, and all the rest.

Yes it is—or at least, yes, it was. But the forces that animated the leftist-counterculture wave of the late sixties and early seventies have largely burned themselves out and, in any case, only a minority of the postwar generation was ever involved in any significant way with the activism that the sixties connotes.

To be sure, the influence of the sixties still endures in more permissive sexual and social mores, but the moral and spiritual principles that have traditionally supported the American nation are still largely in place. A review of the statistics shows that the divorce rate has leveled off and may actually be starting to decline. Church attendance is on the upswing, with the largest gains being scored by the most theologically and socially conservative denominations. The Equal Rights Amendment has stalled, the pro-life movement is growing stronger every year, and private school enrollment is skyrocketing as parents seek an education for their children that emphasizes basics, discipline and hard work.

Moreover, several leading magazines have done "Whatever Happened to the Class of '68" studies and come to the surprising conclusion that the generation of the sixties is an extremely aggressive, hard-working one that is moving quickly up the ladders of corporate success.

My impression is that the sixties generation, having been beguiled by the seductive spirit of libertinism and the romanticism of social revolution, discovered that instead of utopia they found anomie, anarchy, and despair. Chastened by the experience, they have developed a truer perspective on life that encompasses a genuine respect for the enduring values, as well as a realistic perception of human limitations. This perspective, I believe, will do much to shape the nature of public policy in years to come.

I will go further to say that I think history will record the main legacy of the postwar generation as a conservative (or even reactionary) one, reasserting the dominance of the private sector over the public sector, restoring the United States to its role as guardian of freedom in the world, and reorienting the American people back to a personal morality that balances privileges with duty. The people will accept responsibility personally for their own affairs and those of their families and communities instead of surrendering that responsibility to anonymous functionaires in remote seats of government.

It has become a hackneyed expression to say that we live in challenging times, but today it is certainly true as perhaps never before. These are challenging times and dangerous times as well. At home we have seen the gradual dissipation of the vitality that once characterized our country. Abroad, U.S. foreign policy displays a lack of will at a time when the Soviet Union continues its maniacal, implacable plan of conquest and subversion. The hour is very late, for, as Solzhenitsyn warns us urgently, "the forces of evil are gathering for their climactic offensive."

It is a fact that 1984 is not far off, and it is not unreasonable to state that Orwell's 1984 is not far off either unless something is done to halt and reverse the prevailing trends of the times. The task before the postwar generation is quite simply and quite literally to save their country. Can the generation of Woodstock nation accept—let alone carry out—such a task? I believe so.

And one of the reasons I have hope is the fact that, while the counterculture advocates and New Left activists were receiving the lion's share of the media's attention, another movement had been born and was coming into its own. Although its roots go back at least thirty years, and although it has been sustained intellectually and otherwise by previous generations, the fact is that the bulk of the men and women in the ranks and the leadership of the conservative movement were born since the end of World War II.

Gaining intellectual underpinnings from such groups as the Intercollegiate Studies Institute (ISI), organizational savvy from groups like Young Americans for Freedom, and political experience during the Goldwater campaign of 1964, this generation is making itself felt in the state legislatures and the Congress, in the media and in the professions. In the multitudinous conservative organizations old and new, the young conservatives occupy a majority of the leadership and staff positions.

This book profiles some of the most outstanding of these young leaders in government, media, professions, clergy, higher education, and political and intellectual groups. It should be emphasized at the outset, however, that this is not intended to be a comprehensive cataloguing of "young conservative leaders." It is intended rather to be illustrative, to focus on a few of the outstanding people in a given area and thereby to illuminate the activity in that area. For every ten people highlighted in a chapter, there are hundreds, or, in some cases, thousands more who could have been added.

A couple of caveats are in order before proceeding with this narrative. One of them has to do with the "New Right" versus "Old Right" split that has been much reported in the press. Having moved in Washington conservative circles for the past six years—three of them spent as executive director of the American Conservative Union—I feel eminently well qualified to comment on this phenomenon, although my evaluation, alas, does not make very exciting copy.

To the extent that *Old Right* and *New Right* have any meaning at all, it is only in purely chronological terms. The term *Old Right* can be seen to refer to those established groups and publications, including the American Conservative Union, Young Americans for Freedom, the Conservative Victory Fund, the ACU Education and Research Institute, ISI, *Human Events,* and *National Review,* that are led by established figures such as William F. Buckley, Jr., former ACU Chairman M. Stanton Evans, and *Human Events* editor Thomas Winter. The New Right groups and organizations include the Conservative Caucus, the National Conservative Political Action Committee, the Committee for the Survival of a Free Congress, the Heritage Foundation, and *Conservative Digest* and tend to have been founded by, or are at least associated with, fundraiser Richard Viguerie. They came into existence only in the last five years or so. Such differences as exist between these two factions—and they are numerous enough—tend to be personal or to issue quite understandably out of a competition for fame and fortune. A criticism often heard in New Right circles is that the Old Right groups had become complacent, sluggish, and insufficiently aggressive. The most prevalent criticism heard in Old Right circles is that the fundraising costs of the New Right groups are exorbitantly high, leaving little money for action. I think there is an element of truth in both observations.

The point to be made, however, is that on matters of principle and policy there is no *major* difference between these groups and individuals. Except for columnist Kevin Phillips (who argues that conservatives should embrace

big government as a means of rewarding conservatives and punishing liberals), I know of no conservative leader who does not champion limited
government and individual liberty. Similarly, both Old Rightists and New
Rightists favor a reliance on the market economy and both subscribe to
traditional morality.

On any given issue of national importance Old Rightists and New Rightists will be found to be on the same side.

A definition of terms is also in order. Since this is a book about *young*
conservative leaders, it behooves me to state my idea of what young is. I
have arbitrarily decided that the criterion for inclusion in this book is that
an individual be forty years old or younger. I realize that this is an unsatisfactory demarcation line, in that many people thus qualified are intellectually over the hill while many others who are much older than forty are
agile of mind and young at heart. Unfortunately, some such criterion was
necessary for consistency's sake, and this was the best I could do.

I should also make plain at the outset that the reader should not expect
to find here an insider's exposés of intrigue and scandal within the conservative movement. Both certainly exist—they exist within any large political movement—but I think they are incidental to the overall development
of the movement, which I consider to be positive in nature. Since this book
is a friendly consideration of the conservative movement, it accentuates the
positive. The muckraking I leave to others.

I should point out as well that my scope is intentionally limited to political
and quasi-political areas. There is manifestly a moral, philosophical, and
spiritual dimension that undergirds American conservatism, and there are
certainly many developments in religion, philosophy, and the arts that are
worthy of comment in this connection, but this work is concerned with
conservatism in its political context. To venture beyond that would diffuse
the focus of the book—or require another one.

Though among those described here the reader will encounter brilliant
intellectuals, organizers, and politicians, he will find no utopians advocating
some blueprint for the perfect society. Such plans assign to the temporal
order—or, more concretely, to the political order—capabilities that it does
not have and power that it should not have.

Conservatives do have a concept of the good society, of course, but that
concept is one of a free society where adherence to shared values, not
coercion, is the primary means of insuring order and where power resides
in the individual, the family, the church, and the community—what Albert
Jay Nock called Social Power—rather than in government.

Although conservatives have no single, ironclad ideology to sell and no
social blueprints to offer, the reader of this book will discern certain dynamics at work in the ideas and activities of the people described—dynamics that are reorienting the national agenda.

2 | THE POSTWAR GENERATION

If the 1920s are thought of as the decade of the Lost Generation, the children of the 1960s must some day be seen as the "Lionized Generation." Few generations have lived through so convulsed a period, been at the center of so much change, or been the focus of as much attention as the post–World War II generation that came to the fore in the 1960s.

Looking back more than ten years later, the decade seems a mad kaleidoscope of careening images: of the sublime and the grotesque, of war and death juxtaposed with incredible wealth and prosperity, of vulnerability and innocence side by side with satanic evil, of selflessness and sacrifice on the one hand and self-indulgence on the other. It is difficult to think of the sixties in a sustained fashion without inducing sensory overload; the clash of images is too jarring.

There are of course the political events: the election of Kennedy and the euphoria of Camelot, followed by the tragedy of assassination; the succession of Lyndon Johnson and the resulting flood of domestic legislation; the raw, angry reaction of the Goldwater movement; the murder of Martin Luther King and the outrage which manifested itself in riots and burning cities; the assassination of Robert Kennedy; the civil rights movement with its sit-ins and protest marches and, of course, the war in Vietnam, the central fact of the decade and possibly of our time.

The sustained agony of this inconclusive war exacerbated existing frictions in American society and created fissures in the political institutions of the country that threatened to cause their collapse. Lyndon Johnson, nominated by acclamation by his party in 1964, was denied renomination in 1968 by "antiwar" activists. His designated heir, Hubert Humphrey, was nominated in Chicago against a backdrop of riots and police reprisals that fatally crippled the campaign at the outset.

When the war ended the toll was ghastly to contemplate: 55,000 young Americans had been killed; 350,000 had been wounded (many of them

9

permanently maimed); $110 billion had been drained from the economy, a lesion that contributed to the rampant inflation that has plagued the nation to this day; and, above all, a collapse of civic morale had resulted in a loss of faith in our domestic institutions, a failure of will abroad, and a national turning inward.

In morals and manners, the change was no less profound. Beguiled by unprecedented affluence and leisure time, the nuclear family, the fundamental element in American life, showed signs of disintegration, with parents becoming more permissive and more indifferent to their children, many of whom became alienated from their parents and from all the societal values they thought their parents represented.

The sixties was the decade of militant minorities, the decade of black power, women's lib and gay lib, of the American Indian Movement and the strikes of the Mexican-American farmworkers, developments that broke patterns of behavior long established, challenging the mores and shared values that had long prevailed and, in general, profoundly disturbing the national equilibrium.

Everywhere, it seemed, convention and custom were challenged or toppled outright: women demanded to be accorded the same job privileges and, in some cases, the same roles that men had heretofore dominated, homosexuals came out of the closet by the thousands, not only to demand their civil rights but also to loudly proclaim the superiority of their "sexual preference." With the advent of the Pill, permissive abortion, and the abolition of old taboos, premarital sex became common and casual couplings became routine. "Alternative lifestyles" from communes to Himalayan hermitages, to wife-swapping and open marriages came into vogue; dress codes, once clearly delineated between the sexes and relatively changeless for decades, were abandoned in favor of the ubiquitous working uniform of jeans, sandals, bells, beads, and Peruvian Indian blouses.

In education, the three Rs were displaced by free-form courses chosen by the students, standards and attendance requirements were relaxed and grades dropped in favor of "pass-fail."

The sixties were, of course, the drug era, the time of the electric Koolaid acid trip, of peyote orgies in the desert, of amphetamines, of an explosion in heroin traffic, and, of course, of marijuana, King Cannabis. Over all of the great public events of the decade, the marches, protest rallies, and rock festivals wafts the pungent smell of the reefer.

Then there was the music. Never before has a generation been so saturated with sound: hard driving sound powered by relentless percussion and overpowering bass, music amplified to the threshold of pain and accompanied by the visual dazzle of pulsating strobe lights. Anyone who has been to a rock concert knows that the term *good vibes* is more than a metaphor; vibration quite literally describes the salient sensation. It was music to literally overwhelm the senses, the music of the Grateful Dead, the Rolling Stones, and thousands of lesser, imitative groups.

There was other music, of course: the simple protest ballads sung by Joan Baez, the Donne-like imagery and biting delivery of Bob Dylan, Donovan listlessly plucking his guitar and whispering sweet nothings into the ears of his stoned listeners, and, at the apex, the complex, ever-changing, often brilliant music of the Beatles, the apotheosis of the sixties, whose music embodies every major impulse of the decade from the flower child fantasies of "Yellow Submarine" to the shrill "Helter Skelter" that became the credo of Charles Manson.

In the arts, the sixties saw the courts and public pressure force the abolition of most censorship laws. Film and the stage displayed an unheard of explicitness with nudity and profanity, and the treatment of the most controversial subjects became commonplace. The trend was evident as well in print. In most cities whole areas were taken over by adult book stores, peep shows, and massage parlors, much to the chagrin of citizens groups and the police who found it difficult if not impossible to enforce indictments.

It goes without saying that the phenomena that characterize a decade do not expire at the stroke of midnight when a new decade is ushered in and there is considerable debate over when the ferment that characterized the sixties ended. One observer, Ben Wattenberg of the American Enterprise Institute, goes so far as to say the sixties ended in 1978 with the passage of California's Proposition 13. I have always believed, however, that the sixties ended on May 4, 1970, at Kent State University with the fatal shooting of four students by Ohio National Guardsmen. In the time warp of my mind, it is as though the decade were an ascending spiral of frenzy, a progressively intensifying spiral of louder sound, more frenetic activity, gaudier colors that reached a crescendo in the strident, poisonous atmosphere of the nationwide protests against the Cambodian incursion. Then, at Kent State, it ended. And, as in the Beatles' "A Day in the Life," there seemed to echo a long, reverberating gong.

Many people are still enraptured by the sixties, feeling them to be a magic moment in the nation's history. As Lynda Rosen Obst wrote in her preface to The Sixties, a large picture volume published by Rolling Stone:

To many Americans, the drama of the Sixties is the most they have in common. As in the Second World War, they were seized by an extended American drama that irrevocably affected all who lived through it. At certain moments the emotions were so great that we could tangibly feel what the Germans call Zeitgeist, the spirit of the times. Slowly, we who lived through that time, especially those of us who were coming of age came to see how rare that moment was.

For a paean to the sheer serendipity of the times hear one Mr. "Wavy

Gravy," self-styled "Divine Dodo of the First House of Fun," describing the plane ride back home from the Woodstock rock festival:

On the plane ride back we were ready and prepared, and also ripped out of our collective consciousness, thanks to a friend with six hundred tabs of green acid. The stewardesses made an agreement with us to lock themselves in a little room if we would give them the plane back fifteen minutes before Albuquerque. Meanwhile it was *ours*.

People just freaked out all over the place. A bunch of men and women wore stewardess uniforms and cooked omelettes. There was music and a lot of dope being smoked and I lay on the floor speaking over the microphone, reading a Mr. Natural comic over the plane PA. Some guy came up to me and said, "Hey, man, the pilot says he wants the sitar player in the cockpit because he's bored." Somebody'd dosed the pilot, I thought. I staggered to my feet and made my way up to the front of the plane, and there was this guy, he looked like a pilot. I looked right into his pupils; I don't know what he thought. I was just kind of hovering over him, and I spoke to him right from the hip. I said, "Can I steer?" And this guy was so cool, he was so far out, he said, "Fly any way you want, as long as you Fly American."

For a more serious interpretation of what was taking place in the sixties hear Chris Core, popular young radio commentator on Washington, D.C.'s WMAL:

What '68 was, was a time for searching . . . searching history, searching government, searching the soul for some basic answers to questions about war, prejudice, complacency.

Others, however, took a much darker view of the decade. Novelist Joan Didion, for instance, recoiled in horror at what she perceived to be the pervasive violence and ugliness of the time. Didion gave her desultory assessment of the period in her collection of essays titled *Slouching Towards Bethlehem:*

The center was not holding. It was a country of bankruptcy notices and public-auction announcements and commonplace reports of casual killings and misplaced children and abandoned homes and vandals who misspelled even the four-letter words they scrawled. It was a country in which families routinely disappeared, trailing bad checks and repossession papers. Adolescents drifted from city to torn city, sloughing off both the past and the future as snakes shed their skins, children who were never taught and would never now learn the games that had held the society together. People were missing. Children were missing. Parents were missing. Those left behind filed desultory missing-persons reports, then moved on themselves.

. . . This was not a traditional generational rebellion. At some point between 1945 and 1967 we had somehow neglected to tell these children the rules of the game we happened to be playing. Maybe we had stopped believing in the rules ourselves, maybe we were having a failure of nerve about the game. Maybe there were just too few people around to do the telling. These were children who grew up cut loose from the web of cousins and great-aunts and family doctors and lifelong neighbors who had traditionally suggested and enforced the society's values. They are children who have moved around a lot, San Jose, Chula Vista, here. They are less in rebellion against the society than ignorant of it, able only to feed back certain of its most publicized self-doubts, Vietnam, Saran-Wrap, diet pills, the Bomb.

So vexed was the author by the poisonous atmosphere of the sixties that she had a severe nervous breakdown—an altogether understandable reaction in her view. In an interview with Anne Tyler of the *Washington Post*, Didion says, "I offer only that an attack of vertigo and nausea does not now seem to me an inappropriate response to the summer of 1968."

Comedienne Joan Rivers offers a less cogent, though more pithy assessment of the decade: "I hated everything about the sixties, the fashions, the music, everything. I couldn't wait to kiss '70 on the lips."

My own view of the sixties is ambivalent. On the one hand, I like much of the music of the day and the casualness, exuberance and spontaneity that characterize the period at its best. It was, after all, the era of my generation. One tends to be irrationally attached to such a time. On the other hand, I am fully cognizant of the dark underside of the decade: the mind-destroying drugs, the ugly violence of the campus demonstrations, the reckless relativism, the aimlessness and anomie.

What seems clear to me is that the sixties were a natural reaction to a number of factors. They were, for one thing, an explosion of energy, materialism, and abandon that followed the sacrifice and deprivation of decades of war and depression. The sixties generation was the first generation to grapple with the awesome, almost overwhelming abundance produced by the full flowering of American industry and technology. The America of the 1960s was a colossus astride the world, a nation of totally unprecedented power and plenty. It had become a nation of social and geographical mobility and moral change. The resulting world of affluence and flux became too much for many to cope with. It was an especially difficult time for adolescents, who were given nearly every material thing they desired but found themselves undernourished emotionally by parents intent on enjoying their new-found affluence and freedom.

The salient figures were the young people (primarily college students) who were in the forefront of activity, "the kids," as they came to be called. Never has such a premium been placed on youth as in the sixties. Take, for instance, the now-famous story in a January 1965 *Time* magazine on the high school graduating class of that year, calling it possibly the best educated ever. Focusing on the graduating class at Palisades High near Los Angeles, *Time* surveyed the surrounding opulence and the high level of training of the seniors and pronounced them to be standing "on the fringe of a golden era." It was a time when the traditional obeisance to the wisdom of the old was turned upside down and wisdom was instead ascribed to the young. On campus after campus academic discipline collapsed and divisions between faculty and students were blurred, teachers and students being placed on an equal footing or in many cases students being given credit for having *more* of importance to say than their teachers.

At my alma mater, Ohio's Miami University, I recall a quotation in one of the annuals by a professor, John Weigle, which personifies this sentiment: "There are probably two or three weeks in everyone's life when he sees it as it really is," Weigle said. "Those weeks are between 18 and 25. I have seen that glory in young faces. I am privileged."

Perhaps the high priest of the youth cult worship was Charles Reich, Yale professor and author of *The Greening of America*. Crediting many of his insights to the students at Yale with whom he "rapped" regularly in the dining hall, Reich constructed a comprehensive epistemological framework that encompasses the American experience. The saga of mankind, according to Reich, is divided into three great eras, or "consciousnesses." Consciousness I, formed in the nineteenth century, is "the traditional outlook of the American farmer, small businessman and worker who is trying to get ahead." Consciousness II, formed in the early part of this century, "represents the values of an organizational society." It predominates today. Although Reich gives Consciousness II credit for some undeniable advances, he surveys the present scene and finds it wanting:

America is one vast, terrifying anti-community. The great organizations to which most people give their working day, and the apartments and suburbs to which they return at night, are equally places of loneliness and alienation. Modern living has obliterated place, locality, and neighborhood, and given us the anonymous separateness of our existence. The family, the most basic social system, has been ruthlessly stripped to its functional essentials. Friendship has been coated over with a layer of impenetrable artificiality as men strive to live roles designed for them. Protocol, competition, hostility and fear have replaced the warmth of the circle of affection which might sustain man against a hostile universe.

In short things are pretty grim in modern-day America. But not to worry: there is a "new generation" in America and it will deliver us. This is the generation of Consciousness III:

There is a revolution coming. It will not be like revolutions of the past. It will originate with the individual and with culture, and it will change the political structure only as its final act. It will not require violence to succeed, and it cannot be successfully resisted by violence. It is now spreading with amazing rapidity, and already our laws, institutions and social structure are changing in consequence. It promises a higher reason, a more human community, and a new and liberated individual. Its ultimate creation will be a new and enduring wholeness and beauty—

a renewed relationship of man to himself, to other men, to society, to nature and to the land.

This is the revolution of the new generation. Their protest and rebellion, their culture, clothes, music, drugs, ways of thought, and liberated life-style are not a passing fad or a form of dissent and refusal, nor are they in any sense irrational. The whole emerging pattern, from ideals to campus demonstrations to beads and bell bottoms to the Woodstork Festival, makes sense and is part of a consistent philosophy. It is both necessary and inevitable, and in time it will include not only youth, but all people in America.

The rest of the book is an extended meditation on this patently absurd thesis. What emerges clearly from a reading of The Greening of America is the shameless pandering to the kids by a middle-aged man trying desperately to recapture his youth. Peter Marin, reviewing the book for the New York Times, described it as "simplistic, misleading, presumptuous." Mr. Marin was charitable. The Greening of America is a preposterous rag of pop philosophy, the maudlin musings of an addlepated dreamer. A fraud.

Nevertheless, Reich's book became the number one best-seller and for a long time was, as its jacket claimed, "the talk of the nation." In many colleges it was required reading in political science courses.

Not everyone shared Reich's beatific view of the "new generation," however. For example, George Will speaking at the commencement ceremony at Georgetown University in June 1978, had this to say:

The Class of 1968 was praised for its "imagination" and it did indeed require imagination to think of the seizure of a dean's desk as a "revolution." It was theater; it was opera boufe. Radicals disdaining organization, technology and affluence were demoralized by the knowledge that they remained subsidized students utterly dependent on the benefits of all three.

The politicized students of 1968 are remembered as "activists," but they were essentially passive people. The politics of rightmindedness was a way of feeling virtuous while indicting a society within which the indictors enjoyed conspicuous privilege within academic sanctuaries. The radicalism was a pseudo-political manifestation of a culture of passivity.

The favorite art form was cinema, which requires less active engagement of intellect than literature does. The music amounted to sensory overload, not music for the mind to comprehend, actively, but for the senses to absorb, passively. The recreational use of drugs expressed the belief that people are passive machines "turned on" by chemicals.

Given Charles Reich's apotheosization of the sixties generation as a privileged group of idealistic visionaries and crusading reformers and George Will's excoriation of the same generation as a bunch of selfish punks, it might be interesting to see what happened to the sixties generation.

In an article titled "Report on the Class of '68" published in the February

3, 1978, issue of the *Wall Street Journal,* Peter Drucker notes that the class of '68 was "the most anti-business class in America's history and the most radical of all student generations." That is common knowledge, of course.

What is surprising, however, is Drucker's assertion that the class of '68 has since then become *"the most pro-business class among college generations in many decades"* (emphasis added). It is, says Drucker, "the class that went into business careers more heavily than most of its predecessors, if only because job openings in government and education began to disappear as this class reached the job market. It is this class that marked the sharp upturn in M.B.A. degrees which we have seen in the last decade. And it is the class of '68 that has been more successful in business careers than any of its predecessors since the much smaller classes of the 1920s." Wrote Drucker of the class of '68:

> They tend to cluster in the 'hard areas'—in finance, in accounting, in data processing, in planning, in economic analysis, in market research and product management.
>
> They are not 'conservatives' by such traditional criteria as attitudes on matters of race, creed or sex. But they are not 'liberal' in their attitudes toward government and government programs. There they are ultraconservative cynics . . . The Vietnam scars are still raw and bleeding.
>
> . . . These young executives of the class of '68 have very different attitudes towards their careers from those anyone expected of them when they rioted against the 'system' 10 years ago. They tend to be workaholics. They are excited by their work and expect it to be challenging and demanding. There are very few 'dropouts' among them.
>
> . . . But the greatest difference between the class of '68 and their predecessors is the attitude towards management. They expect, indeed they demand high competence from the boss and genuinely professional management from him.

My view of the sixties generation—my own generation—is that it is not intrinsically superior or inferior to any other. Nonetheless, it is likely to be a generation that has a profound impact on the future of America. The main reason for this is sheer numbers.

As the March 27, 1978 *U.S. News and World Report* noted, "Americans in the 22-to-35 age brackets number 47.5 million or two-fifths of all adults under 65." Moreover, as Drucker notes,

> With the class of '68, the babies of the "baby boom" first reached maturity. And they came on the heels of the very small birth cohorts of the thirties and forties so that they entered what was almost a vacuum. As a result, the graduates of '68, barely 30 or 31 years old today, already are moving into leadership positions as assistant vice presidents and assistant treasurers and directors of corporate planning and directors of market research.
>
> They are not yet by and large in the decision-making jobs. But when I sit down

with the "decision-makers" in my client companies, large or small, we frequently are joined by a member of the class of '68, or at least by a graduate of approximately that era. "Meet Johnny Jones, our assistant vice president, data processing," the "big boss" will say. And it is Johnny Jones who has done the homework, who has worked out the agenda, who writes the report afterwards and who then drafts the policy directive for the "decision-maker's" signature. Increasingly, it is not "Johnny Jones" but "Jane Jones." For the class of '68 was the first class with women in significant numbers going into business as management trainees rather than as secretaries.

Because of sheer numbers the sixties generation will exert a significant impact on events for decades to come. The sixties was the youth decade because the baby boom generation was moving into its teens and early 20s. The seventies has been the decade of health foods, jogging, and fitness as the members of the postwar generation reach their stride in their late twenties and early thirties. The focus of national attention is likely to continue its shift as the postwar generation ages.

Another reason for the extraordinary influence of the postwar generation is the fact that is has been exposed to a wider range of experiences than any other generation. Better educated, wealthier, healthier and better traveled than previous generations, at the center of the most tumultuous decade in American history, more skeptical and hard-nosed for the experience, the generation of the Sixties has come through its passage into adulthood tempered, tough, and resilient. Finally, the sixties generation is special because fate has placed it at a watershed in our national life. At home America faces the collapse of the liberal order. Abroad our nation nears a potentially decisive confrontation with the Soviet Union, a super power increasingly bellicose and relentlessly expansionist. A great national drama will surely unfold in the 1980s, and the men and women of the sixties generation will be at stage center.

3 | THE CONSERVATIVE YOUTH MOVEMENT

On August 15, 1979, the Young Americans for Freedom convened at the Shoreham-Americana hotel in Washington, D.C., for their biennial national convention. For those who have attended YAF conferences, the 1979 gathering was hardly a remarkable event. It offered pretty much the same smorgasbord of activities that past YAF conferences have provided: the election of candidates to the National Board, panels on domestic and foreign policy issues, workshops on organizational tactics, speeches by celebrities such as Ronald Reagan, Congressmen Phil Crane and Bob Bauman, and a keynote address by YAF's "godfather," William F. Buckley, Jr. Attendance was between 400 and 500, about average for a YAF conclave.

In a more fundamental sense, however, the ninth national YAF Convention was remarkable, a fact recognized by Buckley in his speech. "Political organizations are notoriously ephemeral," he said. "They come and they go and are forgotten. This one has lasted." The remarkable thing about Young Americans for Freedom is that a political youth organization—a *conservative* youth organization—under its own management, responsible for its own sustenance, should have survived and flourished for twenty years.

The point was made even more telling by the ironic coincidence that the convention convened on the 10th anniversary of the Woodstock Festival, the high-water mark of the counterculture movement of the 1960s. As former YAF executive director Frank Donatelli noted, "Woodstock Nation was a very short-lived nation." He meant by that that the whole organizational infrastructure that had sustained the counterculture—groups such as SDS, the Student Non-Violent Coordinating Committee, the Yippies, and others— had long since withered away. The activists had abandoned the cause and dispersed, and the vision of a new order, which Woodstock symbolized, had disintegrated. Meanwhile, YAF, founded nine years before Woodstock occurred, is still going strong ten years after Woodstock passed into history.

19

The New Left movement of the sixties was much larger in its heyday than
YAF has ever been, but its support was ephemeral. Students in the 1960s
were, for various reasons (idealistic notions, rebellion against their parents,
a desire for excitement or whatever) attracted to the New Left and its whirl
of rhetoric, sit-ins, picket lines, and protest rallies. Their participation in
those activities tended to be intense. But it also tended to be brief. After a
frenzied flurry of words and action most New Leftists moved on to other
things.

This was not the case with YAF, however. YAF members were fewer in
number than their leftist counterparts, but their commitment was, and remains, deeper. Their rhetoric has been quieter, their style more subdued,
but their stamina greater; their resolution stronger. This distinction, I submit,
will prove to have important consequences in the 1980s. The prize of the
decade ahead—the opportunity to set the nation's agenda—will go to the
steadfast minority who had the determination to stay the course. And it has
been a long course, indeed. If one steps back and looks at the burgeoning
activity on the right it becomes evident that it is no momentary flicker but,
rather, a flame that has burned for a long time—sometimes perilously close
to being snuffed out by buffeting winds—but a flame that is now burning
with a steadily growing intensity.

The young conservative activists who are coming into their own now did
not appear ex nihilo with innate wisdom and prowess (a claim that Charles
Reich made for his Consciousness III generation). Rather they are the flowering of seeds sown decades ago, in the 1940s, by a small group of isolated
but grimly determined intellectuals who rejected the intellectual trends of
the postwar era and decided to challenge them. For the most part, they
would be unfamiliar to Americans today, men such as Professors Richard
Weaver of the University of Chicago and Willmoore Kendall of Yale, Frank
Meyer, one of the founders of National Review, Professor Peter Viereck of
Mount Holyoke, Frank Chodorov, editor of The Freeman. These intellectuals, brilliant all, were also frequently eccentric and cantankerous; they
frequently squabbled among themselves. But out of the intellectual ferment
they generated grew the conservative political activity of today.

The achievement of these men has been splendidly chronicled by George
H. Nash, a brilliant young scholar who graduated from Amherst College
and received his Ph.D. in history from Harvard. In his book, The Conservative Intellectual Movement in the United States Since 1945, Nash bril-
liantly highlights the major achievements of the disparate conservative intellectuals following World War II and synthesizes their thought into a
unified whole. In a terse, tightly written introduction, Nash comes out
swinging:

   The focus of this book is on a "movement"—a movement of ideas, but one with
   visibly nonacademic and political aspirations. Conservatism in America after World

War II was not closet philosophy or esoteric sect, at least not for long. It was a decidedly activist force whose thrust was outward toward the often uncongenial America of the mid-twentieth century. An intellectual movement in a narrow sense it certainly was, yet one whose objective was not simply to understand the world but to change it, restore it, preserve it.

Nash then takes aim on the obscurantists and liberal pendants who have sought to undermine the legitimacy of American conservatism:

There are, to be sure, a number of definitions which are inadequate and tendentious. Thus, on occasion conservatism is equated with mindless defense of the status quo, *any* status quo; under such a usage even Stalinist Russia, Maoist China, or any other revolutionary state could be called "conservative" once the revolutionaries had managed to entrench themselves. Sometimes conservatism has been blandly defined as an attitude toward "change"; under such a usage even Fabian Socialists who believed in the "inevitability of gradualness" might be labeled conservatives. Such definitions seem superficial and undiscriminating. On the other hand, some are unduly restrictive. Thus, intellectual conservatism has sometimes been confused with the Radical Right. Frequently, it has been associated with European experiences, such as feudalism, aristocracy, and the Middle Ages—a device often used to explain away conservatism (Mr. X is not conservative, he is "really" something else; America has no conservatives; we are "really" all liberals). Attempts to define conservatism abstractly and universally or in terms of one peculiar set of historical circumstances have led many writers into a terminological thicket.

Nash makes plain that modern American conservatism is not a monolithic ideology whose purity is maintained by some dogmatic synod of philosophers. It is rather a multifaceted philosophy characterized by many strains of thought and the eccentricities of its diverse champions. But if it is not monolithic neither is it hydra-headed. While its many proponents may favor different emphases they share certain assumptions, assumptions that give an underlying unity to the whole. Nash identifies three major components in postwar American conservatism:

In 1945 no articulate, coordinated, self-consciously conservative intellectual force existed in the United States. There were, at most, scattered voices of protest, profoundly pessimistic about the future of their country. Gradually during the first postwar decade these voices multiplied, acquired an audience, and began to generate an intellectual movement. In the beginning one finds not one right-wing renascence but three, the subjects of the first several chapters of this book. First, there were "classical liberals" or "libertarians," resisting the threat of the ever expanding State to liberty, private enterprise, and individualism. Convinced that America was rapidly drifting toward statism (socialism), these intellectuals offered an alternative that achieved some scholarly and popular influence by the mid-1950s. Concurrently and independently, a second school of thought was emerging: the "new conservatism" or "traditionalism" of such men as Richard Weaver, Peter Viereck, Russell Kirk, and Robert Nisbet. Shocked by totalitarianism, total war, and the development of secular, rootless, mass society during the 1930s and 1940s, the "new conservatives" urged a return to traditional religious and ethical absolutes and a rejection of the "relativism" which had allegedly corroded Western values and produced an intolerable vacuum that was filled by demonic ideologies. Third, there appeared a militant, evangelistic anti-Communism, shaped decisively by a number of influential ex-radicals of the 1930s, including Whittaker Chambers, James Burnham, Frank Meyer, and many more. These former men of the Left brought to the postwar Right a profound conviction that the West was engaged in a titanic struggle with an implacable adversary—Communism—which sought nothing less than conquest of the world.

Having identified these components, Nash goes on to make the important point that there is a working consensus that unifies them:

Perhaps, on closer inspection, the divergent emphases of the movement were more intimately related than some realized. Both libertarians and traditionalists evinced, for instance, a strong distrust of "intellectuals"—a point on which everyone from Hayek to Kristol could agree. Hayek and Kirk both preached the gospel of humility and opposition to presumptuous rationalism. All shared a revulsion against "gnosticism" and utopian "social engineering" and a sense of the complexity of the social order. None worshiped the State, although their formulations and policies differed. Libertarians reacted against the State as a threat to individual liberty and economic progress. Traditionalists, sharing much of this critique, also reacted against the total State as an expression of the collapse of the moral and spiritual authority. "Society," said Burke (and traditionalists echoed him), "cannot exist, unless a controlling power upon will and appetite be placed somewhere; and the less of it there is within, the more there must be without." Anti-Communists reacted against the State in its most despotic and ominous contemporary forms, the Soviet Union and China.

One could go on, but the point is clear. There was a fascinating heterogeneity in conservative thought, yet most right-wing intellectuals readily agreed on certain fundamental "prejudices" which they articulated and refined in many different ways: a presumption (of varying intensity) in favor of private property and a free enterprise economy; opposition to Communism, socialism, and utopian schemes of all kinds; support of strong national defense; belief in Christianity or Judaism (or at least the utility of such belief); acceptance of traditional morality and the need for an inelastic moral code; hostility to positivism and relativism; a "gut affirmation" of the goodness of America and the West. These were but a few constituent elements of the working conservative consensus.

This working consensus is so obvious that it is all too frequently forgotten by conservatives. Indeed, most conservative activists don't even know it exists, but they nonetheless naturally subscribe to its key assertions. That is, most conservatives just naturally believe in God and Judaeo-Christian morality. Most believe in the efficacy of the market economy; most believe in traditional values and are concerned about their erosion in recent years. Most believe in the primacy of the individual and in limited government.

Most believe that communism is the main threat to Western civilization and subscribe to a vigorous opposition to it.

To hostile critics conservatism may appear a web of contradictions, but to the average conservative—and indeed, I would argue, to the average American—there is nothing at all contradictory about the key elements in this consensus. For most it's just a matter of common sense.

The spadework done by the conservative intellectuals in the 1940s and 1950s has begun to bear fruit. Looking back on three decades of growth, Nash sums up conservative progress this way:

In 1945 "conservatism" was not a popular word in America, and its spokesmen were without much influence in their native land. A generation later these once isolated voices had become a chorus, a significant intellectual and political movement which had an opportunity to shape the nation's destiny.

As Nash points out, from the very beginning of the postwar conservative revival, its progenitors have seen themselves and their efforts as part of a movement, a movement with sound intellectual groundwork that would eventually result in action in the political arena. This concept was visualized most explicity in *Ideas Have Consequences,* a book published in 1948 by Richard Weaver, a professor at the University of Chicago and one of the most influential intellectual godfathers of the modern conservative movement. Weaver and other architects of the movement had closely studied the growth and development of the Fabian socialist movement in England and America in the latter part of the nineteenth and early part of the twentieth century. The success of that movement had been dramatic indeed. What had at the turn of the century been the fulminations of a small rag-tag clique of students and intellectuals had by the 1930s become public policy in Britain and the United States.

Most closely scrutinized was a group called the Intercollegiate Society of Socialists, an organization founded in the 1920s by a group including Walter Lippmann, who was later to become the most influential columnist of the day. The ISS had set out consciously to proseletize on college campuses around the country, believing that a focus on the academy would pay dividends in the future as the students who had been won over became the leaders of the establishment. A determined effort was made to get socialist literature into the hands of students, to provide articulate socialist speakers to campus groups, and to mobilize students in the socialist political efforts. The ISS's efforts were, over time, enormously successful, resulting in the accession of hundreds of socialist-oriented college graduates to key positions in government, the courts, college faculties, and the media.

It is not surprising then that when conservative columnist and editor Frank Chodorov decided to found a national college conservative organization, he patterned it after the ISS. Founded in 1953, the Intercollegiate Society of Individualists (now the Intercollegiate Studies Institute) has become the leading conservative intellectual organization in America. Much like the old ISS (which later melded into the Student League for Industrial Democracy and then, in the 1960s, metamorphosed into the SDS), ISI sustains a vigorous publications program, including four main journals: the *Academic Review,* the *Intercollegiate Review, Modern Age,* and the *Political Science Reviewer.* ISI also sponsors a graduate fellowship program, a summer school, seminars, and a book and cassette distribution program. The organization now has some 30,000 active members, including about 400 representatives on the campuses of 350 colleges and universities.

As ISI's first president, Chodorov chose a recent graduate of Yale University, William F. Buckley, Jr. who, in 1951, had rocked his alma mater to its foundation with his *God and Man at Yale,* a book that accused the faculty and administrators of Yale of inculcating its students with socialism and atheism in violation of the university's heritage and the wishes of its alumni. Buckley's book produced a storm of controversy on college campuses and in the press and made its author a national figure overnight. *God and Man at Yale* was indisputably one of the opening shots of the conservative movement, and Buckley became the movement's intellectual guru.

The year 1953 was a particularly important one for conservatives, seeing as it did the publication of Russell Kirk's *Conservative Mind.* A young scholar and disciple of the eighteenth century British philosopher and statesman Edmund Burke, Kirk traced the development of conservative thought from Burke's time to the post–World War II period, focusing on such figures as Hawthorne, James Fenimore Cooper, John Randolph, John C. Calhoun, and T. S. Elliot. In so doing, he made a strong case for the existence of an ongoing conservative tradition in America, demolishing the contentions of those who loudly proclaimed that no such tradition existed. *The Conservative Mind* was widely and favorably reviewed and was of enormous importance in establishing the legitimacy of the conservative intellectual movement in the United States.

Another important year was 1955, which saw the founding of *National Review,* by William F. Buckley, Jr., providing a fortnightly forum for the farflung network of conservative intellectuals. In its early years particularly, *National Review*'s pages were the battleground for opposing factions on the right and Buckley and his magazine went far toward facilitating the development of the working consensus among conservative intellectuals mentioned earlier. *National Review* also gradually assumed the role of arbiter on what was outside this consensus, and over the years its editors have excommunicated the John Birch Society, Liberty Lobby, Ayn Rand's objectivism and, more recently, the radical libertarians from the ranks of responsible conservatism. For twenty-five years, *National Review* has maintained its primacy as the flagship journal of American conservatives, and its circulation has grown from a few thousand to approximately 100,000.

In 1960 conservative activity showed a marked increase in tempo largely because of the vacuum left in the Republican Party by the defeat of Richard Nixon and with him the eastern establishment that had controlled the GOP for many decades. The most noteworthy sign of the upsurge in conservative activity followed the nomination of Richard Nixon as the presidential candidate of the Republican Party in the summer of 1960. A group of 100 young conservatives, most of them active in the Young Republicans, decided there was a need for a national conservative youth organization that would be solidly grounded in conservative principles yet activist-oriented. A September meeting of this group at the Buckley family estate in Sharon, Connecticut, led to the founding of Young Americans for Freedom, adopting a charter and approving a statement of principles drawn up by M. Stanton Evans. The document came to be known as the Sharon Statement, and stands today as one of the best distillations of conservative thought ever written. The founding of YAF was, in retrospect, probably the most important organizational initiative undertaken by conservatives in the last thirty years. As Evans later wrote, YAF confounded the liberal establishment in whose view conservatism was supposed to be "the gospel of the old and weary, leftism of the young and energetic. YAF confronted the establishment with a seeming anomaly: young people committed to conservative ideas and hostile to the banalities of the liberal left."

Immediately upon the founding of YAF its directors were blessed with the arrival of a hero and a cause: Senator Barry M. Goldwater and the effort to obtain for him the Republican presidential nomination. In 1960 Goldwater had written *The Conscience of a Conservative*, which became a sensational best-seller, making the senator a national figure in the process. Short, tightly written, and eminently readable, *Conscience* distilled conservative philosophy into a highly readable primer easily digested by the average citizen. The success of this small volume was phenomenal, and sales soared into the millions. Over 100,000 copies were bought by YAF and used to good effect as recruitment aids on the nation's campuses.

It wasn't long before the Goldwater bandwagon was rolling. YAF was in the forefront of the activity in March 1961, organizing a rally for the senator in New York City which filled the 3,000-seat Manhattan Center auditorium to capacity, leaving 3,000 more people standing on the street. A year later, YAF was able to fill Madison Square Garden with 18,500 cheering, screaming fans—this time turning away 10,000.

As the pace of Goldwater's activity quickened, the press began to take note of the phenomenon. In June 1963, both *Time* and *Newsweek* ran cover stories on the senator. On July 4 of that year, YAF held a Goldwater rally in Washington's National Guard Armory that attracted 10,000 people. Throughout this time, Goldwater had declined to declare his candidacy, so YAF spearheaded an effort to draft him. *National Review* publisher William A. Rusher, then in his early thirties, persuaded his friend F. Clifton White to organize a Goldwater for President Committee, and YAF members played crucial roles in its offices around the country.

In 1963, Donald E. ("Buz") Lukens, a YAF member, was elected chairman of the Young Republican National Federation, besting a Rockefeller candidate in the process. The victory was an augury of what was to come in the senior party. In 1964 Goldwater was nominated for president, bringing the GOP under conservative control, a control that still prevails. As Lee Edwards, a founder of YAF, noted, "Barry Goldwater made YAF but YAF also made Barry Goldwater—made him a national political figure and then the Republican nominee for president in 1964."

Goldwater was defeated by Lyndon Johnson, of course, but he brought (in the words of *Time* magazine) a "new thrust" to American politics, a thrust that has endured. It is almost impossible to overstate the profound effect that the Goldwater movement had, especially on the youth of the time. Goldwater has said frequently that the most gratifying compliment is for a young person to tell him that he or she became involved in politics because of his campaign. For literally thousands upon thousands of young people that was the case and many of them have remained active. I am one of them.

It is difficult sixteen years later to convey the aura of excitement that existed in the Goldwater camp in 1964, especially among the young and restless of the day. For us, the senator was the knight on the white horse, the Lochinvar riding out of the west to do battle with evil, a rugged individualist evoking the great West's heroes who eschewed cant and guile and spoke their minds simply and to the point, a man who rose above the phoniness of the unprincipled politico and the fraud of the backroom bosses, a diamond in the rough who exhibited character (if not always tact), a class act, a handsome man with a beautiful wife. A hero.

Of course, no man could live up to all the expectations that were vested in Barry Goldwater, and the senator, quite understandably, did not, but he provided his partisans with a magic moment that was burnished all the more with the passing of the years as the dreary political procession has staggered by: Lyndon Johnson, broken by Vietnam; Richard Nixon, broken by Watergate; Spiro Agnew's *nolo contendere* plea; George McGovern's invective with a twang; Jerry Ford spouting platitudes in his monotone shout; and, finally, the mindless moralism of Jimmy Carter.

What person who was involved in the effort can forget it? The rally that filled Dodger Stadium, the gold-foil shower at the Cow Palace, the California primary victory over Rockefeller, and, most of all, the acceptance speech at the convention, perhaps the most remarkable of its kind ever given. Today people tend to remember only the "extremism in the defense of liberty" phrase, forgetting such lines as this: "From this moment united and determined, we will go forward together, dedicated to the ultimate and undeniable victory of the whole man. . . . I pledge to you that every fiber of my being is consecrated to our cause. . . ."

My own case is representative of thousands of young conservatives during the period. A freshman at Miami University in 1964, I joined the Young Republicans and was quickly caught up in the Goldwater campaign. I well remember the door-to-door canvassing in Oxford, helping to organize a torchlight parade for Goldwater, hitchhiking a ride to Middletown fifteen miles distant at six in the morning to greet the candidate who was coming in by train on a whistlestop tour . . .

Goldwater lost but his campaign made a lasting impression on me— mainly by making a conservative of me. It was through the Goldwater campaign that I became aware of William F. Buckley, Jr., who had as profound an impact on me as he had on thousands of young conservatives before and since. If Goldwater was our political leader, Buckley was our intellectual godfather, a brilliant thinker, a superb prose stylist, a virtuoso with the English language, a peerless debater, a breathtaking whirl of activity—editor of *National Review*, syndicated columnist, host of a weekly television show, author of a book a year, prolific speaker, and debator. And then there was the lifestyle: gourmet, *raconteur par excellence*, holding forth over brandy and cigars, world traveler, sailing his yacht in Long Island Sound, skiing at Gstaad, dashing about New York City in his sportscar or on his Honda, the tall, beautiful wife, Pat, presiding over the elegant dinner parties in their Manhattan *pied à terre*.

Bill Buckley was as Russell Kirk put it, "like Tailfur riding into the Norman host at Hastings, tossing his sword and laughing." Virtually alone, he took on the liberal legions with a reckless exuberance that totally belied the isolation of his position. Bill Buckley: the infectious grin, the sonorous voice and the big words, the darting tongue and the dancing eyebrows, imperious and frosty when jousting with liberals, warm and friendly in private, all zest and verve and razzle-dazzle. He showed, in the words of a *Time* magazine cover story, that "conservatism can be fun."

Bill Buckley and Barry Goldwater: in the early years of the conservative youth movement, they were the diarchy of the right. A potent combination they were too, attracting thousands of students into the ranks of conservatism.

A third individual whom I single out as an especially strong influence on the conservative youth movement in America is M. Stanton Evans. A leader of the Party of the Right at Yale and managing editor of the *Yale Daily*

News, author of the Sharon Statement and later tapped to be editor of the *Indianapolis News,* chairman of the American Conservative Union for six years, and now a syndicated columnist and radio commentator and chairman of the ACU Education and Research Institute, Evans has devoted his whole life to furthering the conservative cause. Despite a crushing schedule of writing and broadcasts and various administrative duties, Evans has always made himself available for speaking engagements to conservative groups around the country, frequently for no fee. I venture to say that very few of the thousands of conservatives who have come up through the ranks through organizations like YAF, the Young Republicans, ISI, or whatever have not come into contact with Evans at some point, either hearing him speak or joining him at the nearest watering hole to down a little bourbon and dance the night away. An incredibly versatile man, he is both thoroughly versed in metaphysics, history, economics, and the classics and an unabashed celebrant of the Middle American values of cheeseburgers, cokes, french fries, fifties music, football games, and fast cars. A learned man with a keen sense of humor, brilliant yet unpretentious, dedicated to the cause and generous in his time and energy in supporting it, Evans has been a model for thousands of young conservatives—myself among them—and will continue to be so.

Yet a fourth individual who merits inclusion in this small group is Ronald Reagan. Although he did not come to the attention of most conservatives until 1964 (when he made his famous speech in behalf of Barry Goldwater), Ronald Reagan has been the dominant figure in the conservative movement since then. Reagan, more than any other person, represents the political maturing of the movement. Having been elected governor of the nation's largest state, where he defeated an incumbent Democratic governor by a million votes despite a three-to-two registration edge, Reagan proved that a conservative could appeal successfully to the general electorate. Having been a popular and effective chief executive for eight years, he demonstrated that a conservative could govern.

Moreover, Reagan turned out to be interested in implementing new approaches consistent with his conservative philosophy, and with his welfare reform program and his advocacy of mandated government spending limitations, he proved to be an impressive innovator and a man ahead of the times.

Today, the times have caught up with Reagan, and he is involved in a campaign that could well lead him to the White House.

Given Reagan's close association with the conservative movement, it should come as no surprise that a majority of the leading operatives in his campaign are young conservatives who came up through the ranks as Reagan fans. It is quite probable that a Reagan administration would draw on these and other young conservatives to fill its ranks, and many of them are profiled in this book.

Goldwater, Buckley, Evans and Reagan were certainly the gurus of our small reactionary cell at Miami University. Never more than a hundred strong, we nonetheless made our presence known, supporting a lively program of speeches, seminars, debates, and films.

I confess that I was at the time a rather shameless imitator of the Buckley style, and the rather forced prose gyrations I perpetrated on campus must have been cloying, even to those who were sympathetic to my point of view. Nevertheless, I flayed away in the regular column I wrote for the student newspaper and in *On the Right,* the quarterly magazine that I edited, excoriating professors, administrators, and liberal and radical students. It was all great fun, but the sparring, especially with the liberal professors, also gave me close contact with the liberal mindset. It was a jolting experience. A few vignettes of the liberal mentality:

—One professor when asked about the concept of states rights laughed and said, "Hold on for a day and I'll demolish states' rights tomorrow."

—Another professor asked what all the fawning over the Constitution was about. After all, he pointed out, it was only a piece of paper with little intrinsic value. (By this reasoning, a murderer should be required only to pay the victim's family $4.76, since that is what the average human body would be worth today if it were broken down into its principal constituents and sold on the market.)

—A third professor, having attended a lecture by *National Review* editor Frank Meyer, wondered aloud in class why Meyer would want to be a conservative. He could understand Buckley being a conservative, he said, because Buckley was a wealthy patrician, but Meyer was obviously Semitic.

This last statement is a variant of the general misconception about conservatism, that holds it to be a creed for the wealthy, WASPS, and the elderly.

That this is not the case was demonstrated in a study done by University of Maryland professor Richard Braungart and published in the July 1971 *American Journal of Sociology.* Braungart compared YAFers with SDSers and concluded that YAFers were, for the most part, the product of non-WASP middle- or lower-middle-class homes, while the SDSers tended to be from the upper or upper-middle class. I can certainly testify from personal experience that at Miami University we had a lively conservative group and that the overwhelming majority of us were members of the middle- or lower-middle class. This has on the whole consigned young conservatives to the fringes of fashion and respectability.

Christopher Buckley, son of William F., made this point about YAF in an article in the February 4, 1977, issue of *National Review:*

They are not, by and large, the sons and daughters of oil barons, Ford Motor Company vice presidents, or Remington Arms executives. They're kids who work very hard in school, maybe bring home a National Merit Scholarship. Most YAFers I've met are bright. They get good grades at college, they like cops, they don't mind singing the "Star Spangled Banner"; as Nicholas von Hoffman says, "the kind who'll make good, dependable employees." During the late Sixties they put up with a lot of grief while they marched around with "Tell It to Hanoi" placards, calling on school administrators to tell it to those punks holding open house for Abbie Hoffman and Angela Davis in classrooms they had caused to be shut down.

Of course YAFers seemed weird. They *were* weird. So weird they announced early in 1972 they would support Agnew—Agnew!—over Nixon because Nixon had sold out America, mom, apple pie and Taiwan over drinks in the Great Hall of the People, beneath grand oils of Marx, Lenin, Engels, Stalin, and the Chairman. And while all this was going on, Ms. Jane Fonda, herself socially conscious, was touring college campuses, including my own, where she received a standing ovation when she got to the refrain about "the U.S. war of aggression." Meanwhile, YAF had organized "Project Appreciation" sending out letters over Martha Mitchell's signature, asking people to contribute money that would go to disabled Vietnam vets in the form of toothpaste, pens, writing paper, reading material, friendship—things the VA couldn't provide. Is that social consciousness? Maybe not, but years from now when you meet St. Peter at the Pearly Gates and he asks you where you were in '72, listening to Jane Fonda or selling "appreciation kits" for GIs who'd had their legs blown off, what answer would you like to give?

YAF's problems are aesthetic, not philosophical. There's a saying about the late Sixties: "A lot of people joined the Revolution to get laid." Exactly! Quick, name me one beautiful person from the ranks of the counterrevolution. I mean someone young, someone with karma, pizazz, *class!* Someone who told it to the mad dogs and told it well. Well? Well? Okay, so name a few beautiful people from the other side. Easy: Dylan, Baez, Phil Ochs, Abbie Hoffman (in an odd sort of way), Angela Davis, John Kerry, Mark Rudd (borderline beautiful), Julian Bond, Allen Ginsberg, Bobby Seale, Eldrige Cleaver, Tim Leary, Joni Mitchell, Janis Joplin, Gil Scott Heron, Jane Fonda (most of all!). *You* may not think they were so beautiful, but they were, they were. When Ramsey Clark launched against Jack Javits in 1974, his campaign staff put together a fund-raiser at Madison Square Garden and by God talk about Beautiful: Paul Newman, Helen Reddy, Harry Belafonte, Phil Ochs, Dick Shawn, Harry Chapin, and a rock band playing "What's a Nice Country like You Doing in a Place Like This?" Troubadors and minstrels from the good old days at the barricades . . . the guest list read like *People* magazine's table of contents. If that had been a fundraiser for Jim Buckley, know who would've been there? Pat Boone.

There's more to conservative philosophy than Pat Boone (no offense intended; I like the guy), just as there's more to Ramsey Clark than Shirley MacLaine (thank God). But consider for a moment a typical YAF dinner function. A sea of faces; upper lips mustachioed in peach fuzz, Ronald Reagan pomade hair swirls, powder blue denim leisure suits, screaming pink cravats, ruffled magenta evening shirts under mauve tuxedos, chain pendants, awful cologne, white patent leather pumps with yellow laces, purple sportscoats with exposed stitching, burnt Sienna sportscoats with exposed stitching, dacron doubleknit flare-bottom slacks (two sizes too small) with white socks peering out; Naugahyde food: tangy roast beef, cold baked potato, waxen broccoli; Anita Bryant singing the "Star Spangled Banner" on a scratched record through a Korean War–issue PA system; a blind priest stumbling against chairs on the dais trying to get to the podium to read a beautiful benediction; people in the back tittering about it; Bronx cheers for Agnew! Reagan! Joe McCarthy! Ashbrook!; moist eyes, mascara running every time the speaker mentions Goldwater; good speeches (always too long); a "rock band" brought in from lower Bergen County; and J. Daniel Mahoney, sitting at the dais, arms folded, head bent forward, asleep.

So rotten was the karma of the average YAFer, Buckley wrote, that he had never joined the organization founded on his family's estate. Far from it:

I'm thinking back to a time six years ago, the YAF's tenth anniversary at Great Elm, my grandmother's house in Sharon, Connecticut. A blue and white tent was pitched on the lawn, people milled about the superstars: my father, my uncle, Al Capp, Stan Evans. It was a beautiful September day, clear and cool. The old house, huge and cavernous, rumbled with echoes of glasses clinking and voices laughing. Allie, aged 15, and I, age 17, clambered up to the attic, where we huddled in a bathroom deserted long ago by some French governess, and smoked a few bowls of hash, laughing. Not wanting to descend, not wanting to have to deal with all those ... people, you know, out there on the lawn—our lawn—we found Aunt Priscilla's scope-mounted Savage 7 mm. and romped across the roof tiles, hunkering down beneath a gable, lining up people in the cross-hairs. Bang bang bang.

But do not despair. Redemption commeth anon. In the six years between the party at Sharon and the time Christopher Buckley sat down to pen his *National Review* piece, much had happened: the process of national disintegration had accelerated and time was running out. YAF's aesthetic shortcomings paled in the face of the monstrous challenge that faced America. With the barbarians at the gate, the beautiful people lounged in stoned bemusement in the town square while Young Americans for Freedom manned the barricades. They might have been attired in tacky leisure suits, but they were there when and where it counted.

Thus, the final act of expiation:

That was six years ago, that hour on Great Elm's roof spent picking off the nation's leading conservative spokesmen and their assorted followers, and in six years maybe I've learned there's too little time for leisurely bang bang banging through the cross-hairs. . . . And that's why tomorrow, after I hand this in to Aunt Priscilla—who's mad because it's one week late—I'm going to write the Young Americans for Freedom and ask them to send me an application form.

Yes, YAFers—and most young conservatives—are middle class, but the middle class is the great strength of the nation. In the last analysis, the cause of national revival and, indeed, the answer to the question of whether the nation will survive depends on the broad mass of middle America. That is where our leaders will be found, and many of those leaders will be alumni of Young Americans for Freedom and similar youth organizations—middle class to be sure but for the most part men and women of intelligence and determination.

In addition to the tens of thousands of YAF members who have gone on to successful careers in business and other fields, hundreds are already in positions where they can affect public policy. Here are just a few:

—Robert Bauman, YAF's first chairman, now a prominent Republican congressman and chairman of the American Conservative Union.

—Jeffrey Bell, a former political director of the ACU, later a research director of the 1976 Reagan campaign, and most recently, after defeating Clifford Case, GOP candidate for the U.S. Senate in New Jersey.

—Charles Black, a former YAF state director, later special assistant to Sen. Jesse Helms and field director of the Republican National Committee, and most recently field director of the Reagan campaign.

—L. Francis Bouchey, former YAF activist, now executive vice president of the Council for Inter-American Security.

—John Buckley, former YAF chairman, now a state representative in the Virginia legislature.

—Douglas Caddy, first YAF executive director, now a successful author and president of the Energy Consumer Coalition.

—Jameson Campaigne, former YAF board member, now president of Green Hill publishers, one of the nation's leading publishers of conservative books.

—Ronald B. Dear, former YAF board member, former executive director of the ACU, and now assistant to the County Judge of Harris County, Texas (Houston), and executive director of Reagan's Texas campaign.

—Donald Devine, former YAF board member, now a professor at the University of Maryland, a member of the state Republican Central Committee, and twice chairman of the Maryland Reagan campaign.

—John T. Dolan, a former YAF activist, now chairman of the National Conservative Political Action Committee, one of the leading conservative PACs.

—Anthony Dolan, a former YAF activist, now a journalist who, in 1978, won the Pulitzer Prize.

—Bruce Eberle, former YAF board member, now president of Bruce W. Eberle and Associates, one of the nation's largest direct mail companies. (Eberle did Ronald Reagan's fundraising in 1976.)

—Lee Edwards, former editor of *New Guard,* now president of Lee Edwards and Associates, a Washington public relations firm.

—M. Stanton Evans, a founder of YAF, named as editor of the *Indianapolis News* at 26 (making him the youngest editor of a major paper), later served three terms as chairman of the American Conservative Union, now a columnist for the *Los Angeles Times* syndicate and a commentator on the CBS radio network.

—Fran Griffin, former Illinois YAF chairman, now media director of the American Conservative Union.

—John Gullahorn, former YAF board member, later served as assistant to the speaker of the Texas House of Representatives and now head of a leading lobbying firm in Austin.

—David A. Jones, former YAF executive director, now director of development at Vanderbilt University and a leading advisor to GOP National Chairman Bill Brock.

—Daniel Joy, former editor of *New Guard,* later head legislative director for Senator James Buckley, now a member of the ACU board of directors and a prominent attorney in Sarasota, Florida.

—David A. Keene, former YAF chairman, later political affairs assistant to Spiro Agnew and James Buckley, now number-two man in the presidential campaign of George Bush.

—Donald Lambro, former YAF board member, now the author of three books and a leading reporter for UPI in Washington, D.C.

—Donald E. ("Buz") Lukens, former YAF activist, later national chairman of the Young Republicans, two-term member of Congress, and chairman of the American Legislative Exchange Council, now an Ohio state senator.

—Patrick Nolan, former YAF board member, now an assemblyman in the California legislature.

—Howard Phillips, one of YAF's founders, later director of the Office of Economic Opportunity, now head of the Conservative Caucus.

—Thomas Phillips, former YAF board member, now president of Phillips Publishing, a multi-million-dollar newsletter publishing firm.

—Daniel Rea, former YAF board member, now weekend anchor man on Boston's WBZ-TV.

—James Sensenbrenner, former Wisconsin YAF chairman, now a member of Congress.

—Arnold Steinberg, former YAF activist, later special assistant to Sen. James Buckley, now head of a successful political consulting firm.

—Herbert Stupp, former New York YAF Chairman, head of New York Youth for Buckley, now editorial director of WOR-TV in New York.

—Kathleen Teague, former YAF activist, now executive director of the American Legislative Exchange Council.

—Randall Teague, former YAF executive director, later administrative assistant to Rep. Jack Kemp, now an executive with Cabot Corporation in Boston.

—Michael Thompson, former YAF board member, now president of Thompson and Associates, a Washington-based direct mail firm.

—Wayne Thorburn, former YAF executive director, later executive director of the Arkansas Reagan campaign, now executive director of the Texas Republican Party.

—R. Emmett Tyrell, former Indiana YAF chairman, now an author and editor of the *American Spectator,* named by *Time* one of the nation's fifty outstanding young leaders.

—Richard A. Viguerie, former YAF board member, now president of Richard A. Viguerie Company, the largest conservative direct mail house, named by *Time* one of fifty promising leaders of the future.

—John A. Von Kannon, former YAF board member, now publisher of the *American Spectator.*

—Huck Walther, a former YAF activist who came to the Right to Work Committee in 1973 and worked in the direct mail operation, now vice-president of the committee and head of public relations and field work, credited with increasing the organization's membership from 40,000 to 125,000 and raising an estimated $25 million through direct-mail solicitations.

Commenting on the importance of Young Americans for Freedom, David Broder, the *Washington Post's* leading political affairs reporter, said, "YAF has unquestionably been the primary breeding ground and training ground for the new generation of conservative leaders. . . . What struck me is that the YAF alumni have profited from the losing battles they have been engaged in. I'm sure some got discouraged and dropped out along the way, but those who survived have been toughened by the experience and have put the lessons they learned to good use." Broder also mentions that there is no analogous organization on the left. "There are factions and groups that come and go but there is no institutionalized organization like YAF."

In 1962 the conservative youth movement had grown to the point that M. Stanton Evans wrote a book, *Revolt on the Campus,* that chronicled its development and successes. Eighteen years later, commenting on the movement's development, Evans said,

I've taken my share of kidding for allegedly predicting, back in 1961, that a wave of conservatism was about to sweep the campuses, when in fact we were on the brink of the "new left" phenomenon.

What I sketched out in *Revolt on the Campus* was a somewhat more modest projection of conservative opportunities: The development of a "creative minority" of conservative students, where there had been none before, which would eventually make its impact on the intellectual and political life of the nation.

I think this modest prediction has been pretty well borne out by events. The work of ISI, YAF, the YRs, and the campus conservative groups has had significant effect. Together with other developments, it has helped create a new conservative climate in the United States. It has supplied us with a new generation of scholars, activists, and political leaders.

If you take a look at the conservative organizations and publications of the present day—ACU, *Human Events, National Review,* Heritage, the Viguerie and Eberle groups—they are for the most part staffed and run by products of the conservative movement on the campus. The same is true for conservative campaigns and conservative activities on Capitol Hill.

The main difference between conservatism in the early '60s and conservatism of the present day is that we now have senior people who are graduates of the movement working to promote the cause in the real-world political arena, with large numbers of new recuits continuing to advance from the ranks of campus conservatism.

Lee Edwards, a founder of YAF and now a public relations consultant, reinforces Evans's observation: "I would say that just in the last fifteen years the movement has grown four-fold. When I began working in Washington fifteen years ago I knew almost everybody who worked for the conservative groups that existed. Now I don't even know all the people working for one organization, the National Right to Work Committee, one of my clients."

There has been an explosion in conservative activity with new organizations coming on the scene almost daily. More conservatives than ever before are teaching in universities, working in the media, running for office, and influencing the course of public affairs in many other ways. Significant among them are young people who have come up through the ranks of the conservative youth movement. The following chapters detail the activities of some of the most prominent.

PART II | THE CONSERVATIVE INFRASTRUCTURE

Staff members of the American Conservative Union, "the nation's premier conservative organization" *(left to right):* Jeffery Hollingsworth, legislative director; Ross Whealton, executive director; William Keys, Public Monitor director; Becky Norton Dunlop, political director; Fran Griffin, media director

4 | ORGANIZATIONS

In no other area can the growth of the conservative movement be seen more clearly than in the burgeoning number of conservative organizations. Twenty years ago "conservative" activity, such as it was, was almost entirely the province of the Daughters of the American Revolution, the American Legion and the Chamber of Commerce—organizations staffed by patriots to be sure, but, nonetheless, organizations whose political experience was limited and whose political goals were all too often vague and unfocused. Some will argue, of course, that the conditions then did not warrant a militant conservative establishment; that in 1960 America's economic health was much better than it is now, the nation's institutions sounder, its position in the world infinitely stronger. A militant conservatism is only called forth, those people maintain, when the nation's equilibrium is upset—and they have a point. It is unquestionably true that perilous times for the nation evoke a strong conservative response. And it is unquestionably true that in recent years we have been living through perilous times. But that explanation does not adequately explain the growth that has ensued. And "growth" does not suffice to define what has happened on the right at the organizational level. An "explosion" of activity is a more apt description. Twenty years ago there was a handful of conservative groups employing a few dozen people at most. Today there are literally dozens of conservative organizations employing thousands of people and disbursing budgets of tens of millions of dollars.

This plethora of conservative groups is remarkable for another reason: most of these organizations are managed by young conservatives under forty. A good example of the phenomenon is the American Conservative Union (ACU), the premier conservative organization today. The ACU is the largest, wealthiest, and most prestigous of the conservative "action" groups and the one most often cited by the press as providing a barometer of conservative sentiment and activity in the country.

The ACU was founded in December of 1964, in the aftermath of the Goldwater. A meeting, organized for December at the Statler hotel in Washington, was attended by more than 150 conservative leaders. man (now a congressman and the organization's current chairman). This group was concerned that the organizational and recruiting successes conservatives had made in the Goldwater effort would be lost in the demoralized atmosphere that prevailed following the senator's defeat. This group concluded that, to prevent this from happening, it was necessary that a national "umbrella" organization be created to bring together the conservative leaders and the heads of the diverse organizations that had supported Goldwater. A meeting was organized for December at the Statler hotel in Washington which was attended by more than 150 conservative leaders. Out of this meeting the ACU was born. The organization grew steadily in size and influence for its first ten years and in the last five years has seen a very rapid growth in both these respects. The Board of Directors consists of thirty-five prominent conservatives, among them four U.S. senators and five members of the House, the editor of *Human Events,* a representative of *National Review,* the chairman of Young Americans for Freedom and numerous other conservative luminaries. The advisory board, chaired by former Secretary of the Treasury William Simon, boasts almost 200 prominent Americans including about 100 members of Congress.

Working under the direction of Congressman Bauman, executive director Ross Whealton, 37, and a young staff of twenty conduct a wide-ranging program funded by a budget of $3 million (up from $350,000 in 1974).

Probably the ACU's best known activity is the Conservative Political Action Conference (CPAC), held in Washington and cosponsored by Young Americans for Freedom. An annual event now seven years old, CPAC has become a traditional gathering for conservatives, regularly attracting more than 1000 activists from all parts of the country. The attendees listen to speeches by dozens of leading conservatives, attend workshops and seminars on issues and tactics, and renew old friendships. The conferences are covered extensively by the media, who look upon CPAC as a barometer of conservative sentiment. Under Jeffrey Hollingsworth, 27, and a legislative staff of four the ACU also maintains an active lobbying program on Capitol Hill. The organization has scored a number of successes including the defeat of the so-called Child Development Bill and the Family Assistance Plan during the Nixon administration and the passage of airline deregulation under Carter. The ACU led the fight against the legal services bill and the Panama Canal treaties—both ultimately unsuccessful efforts, but efforts waged with such skill and tenacity as to inspire enhanced respect and notoriety for the organization. The ACU Forum, a speakers program run for the benefit of members of Congress and their staffs, has been a popular

Heritage Foundation directors *(left to right):* Willa Johnson, Resource Bank director; Edwin Feulner, president; Phillip Truluck, vice president

PAC leaders *(clockwise from top right):* Paul Weyrich, president, Committee for the Survival of a Free Congress; Gregg Hilton, executive director, Conservative Victory Fund; John T. ("Terry") Dolan, president, National Conservative Political Action Committee; John Brasington, president, National Defense PAC

Lobbyists and politicos *(clockwise from top right):* James Dale Davidson, director, National Taxpayers' Union; Charlene Baker, president, Americans for Constitutional Action (with Sen. Paul Laxalt); Michael E. Baroody, director of research, Republican National Committee; Wayne Thorburn, executive

director, Texas Republican Party; James U. Lacy, Jr., YAF chairman; Edward ("Chip") Dent, president, National Voter Initiative Amendment Committee; YAF executive directors: past, Frank Donatelli *(left)*, present, Ron Robinson *(center)*, and designate, Robert Heckman *(right)*

program on Capitol Hill drawing crowds as large as 500 people to hear such speakers as William F. Buckley, Jr., William Simon, Irving Kristol, Herman Kahn, former Rhodesian Prime Minister Ian Smith, Secretary of Defense Donald Rumsfeld and others.

In recent years, the organization has become active in funding class action suits in the federal courts. The ACU was a coplaintiff, for instance, in *Buckley* v. *Valeo*, a suit challenging the constitutionality of the Campaign Reform Act that had been pushed through Congress largely at the behest of Common Cause. Of the total cost of $60,000, the ACU contributed about $30,000. The suit was in large measure successful, with the Supreme Court striking down several provisions of the law. The ACU's STOP OSHA Project achieved an equally significant success in the Supreme Court. The organization filed an *amicus curiae* brief in the *Barlow* v. *Marshal* case charging OSHA with violating the constitutional proscription on unreasonable searches, a view in which the court concurred. The ACU contributed approximately $100,000 to defray the cost of this case, more than half of the total.

The OSHA suit was taken on as part of ACU's Public Monitor program, which functions as a watchdog on bureaucratic malfeasance. Among its activities, Public Monitor publishes a regular newsletter that alerts subscribers—primarily businessmen—to federal regulations that may be damaging to the private sector. The Public Monitor staff also lobbies on Capitol Hill to effect the modification or amendment of undesirable regulations.

The ACU's publications program has also expanded at a rapid rate. *Battle Line,* the monthly house organ, has tripled in size from eight pages in 1974 to twenty-four today, and its circulation has doubled in that time. Under Media Director Tom Faber, 25, the organization also maintains an expanding publication program of issue briefs and monographs, publishes a weekly column that goes free to several hundred newspapers, and has entered the television documentary business in a big way by producing and marketing films nationally on SALT and the Panama Canal treaties.

The ACU's increased activity on the Washington front has been paralleled by equally noteworthy activity at the state level. Organization in the states has been emphasized in recent years and under the direction of Political Director Becky Norton Dunlop, 28, chapters have been organized in most states, many of them with permanent offices and full-time executive directors.

Also affiliated with the ACU are the Conservative Victory Fund (CVF) and the ACU Education and Research Institute. CVF, a political action committee, supports candidates for the House and Senate. Under its 25-year-old director Gregg Hilton (recognized as one of the sharpest political analysts on the right), CVF has become one of the best of the conservative PACs. In 1978, the organizations raised $410,000 and distributed $263,000 to ninety-eight candidates, perhaps the best ratio of dollars raised to dollars spent on program of any conservative political action committee. With the assistance of two staff aides and several interns, Hilton also manages an extensive program of research into the voting records of incumbent House and Senate liberals, information which is made available to conservative challengers.

The ACU Education and Research Institute (ERI) is a tax-exempt foundation associated with ACU. ERI conducts a wide-ranging publication program of monographs and issue briefs and maintains the popular and extremely successful National Journalism Center under the direction of executive director Kathleen Kilpatrick, editor Walter Olson and project director Fred Mann. The organization's budget has grown from $100,000 in 1976 to over $300,000 in 1979.

One of the great growth industries on the right is the tax-exempt foundation—foundations accredited under the 501(c) (3) section of the IRS Code which are eligible to accept corporate grants and contributions from individuals which they can then deduct from their federal income taxes. The IRS directory lists thousands of these foundations and hundreds of new ones are added each year. These foundations are required by law to be nonpartisan and to refrain from political activity. They are forbidden from devoting a "substantial" part of their resources to lobbying activities. These are fairly broad confines, however, and they do nothing to preclude the articulation of a point of view. And, in fact, most of the great public policy research foundations—such as the Ford Foundation, Rockefeller Brothers Foundation, Mellon Foundation, and the Brookings Institution have, in recent decades, been articulators of the liberal approach which favors more centralized government, increased regulation of the private sector, and the redistribution of income. So far has this process gone that two years ago, Henry Ford II was compelled to resign from the board of the Ford Foundation in protest against the liberal thrust of the foundation's activities.

In recent years, however, the imbalance in the "think-tank" realm has begun to shift. At the urging of former Treasury Secretary William Simon, Irving Kristol, and others, money flowing from corporations has altered course dramatically. Simon has urged businessmen to treat their contributions as they would their investments; that is to contribute to organizations that seek to strengthen the private sector rather than the public sector. More and more have been taking this advice, and the result has been a windfall for right-of-center foundations. A prime example of this is the American Enterprise Institute for Public Policy Research (AEI) in Washington. Directed by the Baroody "dynasty" since 1954, the 36-year-old AEI was, until the late 1960s, a small but steadily growing think tank with a generally pro-business outlook. With the advent of the Nixon administration, however, growth began to spurt. AEI President William J. Baroody, Sr., began adding academic "stars" such as Milton Friedman to the organization's board, the scope and number of publications was increased, and fundraising was pursued more aggressively.

Since 1972 the growth has been spectacular. AEI's budget has tripled to more than $7 million, just behind the $8 million budget of the Brookings Institution, a left-of-center think tank that for decades has dominated the Washington public policy arena. Having pulled alongside Brookings in annual budget, Baroody is now out to match his rival in endowments. As of the beginning of 1978, Brookings had an endowment of $35 million while AEI had none. At that time William, Sr., turned over the presidency of the foundation to his son, William, Jr., and devoted his energies to amassing a $60 million endowment for AEI. In terms of staff and program, AEI's growth in the last five years alone has been nothing short of spectacular. Among the luminaries recruited in the past few years are former President Gerald Ford (an AEI Distinguished Scholar), former Solicitor General Robert Bork, former Treasury Secretary William Simon, former Federal Reserve Board Chairman Arthur Burns, and a bevy of academics such as Irving Kristol, Ben Wattenberg, and Herbert Stein.

Simultaneously AEI's output has soared. The organization puts out more than 100 publications a year, covering all aspects of public policy, and produces a Public Affairs Broadcast series that is carried by more than 700 television and radio stations. More than 400 colleges and universities now receive and place its publications in their libraries. Although the Baroody's decline to call AEI a "conservative" foundation, pointing out that many of its publications present both sides of an issue and that the staff contains Democrats and even some liberals, the decidedly conservative tilt of the staff as a whole does produce a generally conservative tone to its publications. Indeed AEI scholarship is credited by many with having a marked effect on national affairs, being responsible among other things for scuttling the $100 billion energy program pushed by Nelson Rockefeller, engendering the debate on airline deregulation, demonstrating that the FDA was blocking the introduction of many safe new drugs, making the case against the Naderite Consumer Protection Agency, and preparing the groundwork for the tuition tax credit bill introduced by Senators Packwood and Moynihan.

Surveying the AEI empire in *Human Events*, columnist Nick Thimmesch wrote:

AEI has come into its own—indeed is "hot" these days—because it is at the right place at the right time—in Washington when this city is reacting to a nation firmly moving to starboard. In a word AEI has become the liveliest "think tank" in town and finds itself in the awkward, but satisfying position of being intellectually fashionable.

AEI is likely to become hotter yet as the climate of opinion shifts still further to the right. Indeed, it bodes well to become the nation's leading public policy research foundation in the 1980s—supplying a new administration with an abundance of ideas and personnel.

One of the Baroody family's most significant contributions is the leavening influence it has had on the Republican Party. A sizeable number of the best minds in the Ford administration were associated with AEI, and today a number of former AEI staffers occupy prominent positions on the staffs of the Republican candidates for President—particularly those of Reagan and Bush.

Michael E. Baroody, 33, plays a direct role in Republican affairs. As director of research for the Republican National Committee, Baroody is responsible for compiling research on issues to aid Republican candidates and for assisting the party chairman and national committee in formulating positions on important policy questions. In 1978, Baroody founded a quarterly magazine called *Commonsense*. Billed as "a Republican Journal of Thought and Opinion," *Commonsense* has quickly established itself in the front ranks of the genre. The inaugural issue featured the following articles: "Mediating Structures" by sociologist Peter Beger; "Federalism" by former Senator James Buckley; a "Prescription for Republicans" by Michael Novak; "Partisan in Foreign Policy" by Fred Ikle, former head of the Arms Control and Disarmament Agency, and "The Accessible Dream: Financing Educational Needs" by Senator Bob Packwood. Subsequent issues of *Commonsense* have maintained the same high caliber and Mike Baroody's journal shows promise of becoming an enduring source of thoughtfulness and creativity in an organization traditionally lacking in intellectual vitality.

Another think-tank success story, in some ways even more dramatic, is the Heritage Foundation. Founded in 1974 with financial backing by the Coors brewing company, Heritage has grown in five years from a staff of five to a staff of almost fifty and from a budget of $250,000 to one totaling almost $3 million. Unlike AEI's Baroody, Heritage's president, Edwin J. Feulner, Jr., 38, pulls no punches about his organization's philosophical predisposition. "A new breed of lawmakers, scholars, and a growing number of think tanks are producing conservative ideas likely to shape U.S. policy for decades to come. The Heritage Foundation has become one of the recognized leaders of this historic new movement," Feulner says.

Under the direction of Feulner and Vice-president Philip Truluck, 32, Heritage supports a wide-ranging program, most notably in the research and publication areas. In 1978 alone, Heritage published 100 policy papers in five areas: "Backgrounders," short analytical papers on specific policy issues; "Issue Bulletins," pro and con analyses of policy options of legislation introduced in Congress; the *National Security Record*, a monthly newsletter focusing on problems in the national defense and foreign policy areas; the "Institution Analysis," information on other Washington-oriented organizations (mainly liberal); and "Critical Issues," lengthier monographs dealing with complex issues such as energy policy. Heritage also publishes *Policy Review,* a quarterly journal only two years old but already widely acclaimed. Edited by Dr. Robert Schuettinger, *Policy Review* has featured articles by Milton Friedman (on tax limitation), Winston Churchill II ("Saving the West"), Senator Daniel Patrick Moynihan (on tuition tax credits) and Senators Barry Goldwater and Edward Kennedy (on the president's power to unilaterally abrogate a treaty).

Heritage also maintains a "resource bank" under the direction of Willa Johnson, 37. The resource bank has surveyed the ranks of academe and come up with a list of more than 1,000 professors who have volunteered to give their expertise on issues within their range of competence in testimony before Congressional committees, in consultation with members of Congress and members of the press. A program of "special projects" is maintained, including the "Washington Briefing Series," speeches, briefings and luncheons for members of Congress and their staffs featuring well-known authorities in various policy fields and a congressional staff training seminar for new congressional assistants.

To get its message out, Heritage conducts a vigorous public information campaign. Eight-hundred-word condensations of *Policy Review* articles are mailed to editors of opinion pages, for instance, and "Heritage Foundation Forum," a weekly column, is distributed to more than 450 newspapers. Although comparatively new on the scene, the Heritage Foundation has already attracted a great deal of notice. Its monographs and articles from *Policy Review* are widely quoted by the media around the country. As the activity has increased so has the critical acclaim. Typical of the huzzahs greeting Heritage's work are the following: "Heritage has already left its mark on major public policy debates, including energy and social spending issues . . . it should continue as a supplier of research articles for conservative allies even as bridges are built towards non-rightist intelligentsia." (*Foundation News Magazine.*) "*Policy Review* contain[s] some of the most thoroughly researched articles published anywhere today—the magazine is must reading for anybody interested in governmental affairs." (Chuck Stone, columnist, *Philadelphia Daily News.*) "[Heritage is] the newest and, in many ways, the best of the Washington think tanks." (William Murchison, *Dallas Morning News.*) A few years ago critical acclaim like this would not have been heard for a conservative think tank, but then, a few years ago, think tanks like Heritage did not exist.

One of the most momentous developments for conservative in this field could be the advent of a foundation called the John T. MacArthur Foundation, named for John T. MacArthur, a self-made billionaire (he founded Bankers Life and Casualty) and conservative activist (he was an active supporter of the Florida Conservative Union). MacArthur died in 1978, leaving behind a trust fund of more than $500 million to sustain his foundation. MacArthur did not stipulate the way in which the earnings of the trust fund ($25 million or more per year) should be spent, but he left the foundation in the hands of a conservative board that guarantees that much of it will go to right-of-center causes.

According to the *Wall Street Journal*, the MacArthur Foundation will be among the largest four—along with Ford, Mellon, and Rockefeller—in the country. As it gears up to start making grants, the leaders of conservative groups around the country can be heard smacking their lips in anticipation.

Budgets and Staffs of
Representative Conservative Organizations (1978)

Organization	Budget	Staff
American Conservative Union	$2,800,000	19
ACU Education & Research Institute	350,000	5
Americans for Constitutional Action	100,000	4
American Council for World Freedom	175,000	5
American Enterprise Institute	7,000,000	150
American Legislative Exchange Council	600,000	4
American Security Council	1,961,285	19
American Tax Reduction Movement*	5,830,000	15
Christian Voice	1,000,000	7
Citizens Committee for the Right to Keep & Bear Arms	1,021,703	15
Citizens for the Republic	2,000,000	20
Committee for the Survival of a Free Congress	1,175,000	12
Conservative Caucus	2,000,000	14
Council for Inter-American Security	750,000	5
Conservative Victory Fund	392,000	3
Heritage Foundation	2,220,641	50
Institute for American Relations	800,000	6
Intercollegiate Studies Institute	750,000	12
National Conservative Political Action Committee	1,500,000	7
National Legal Center for the Public Interest	1,600,000	12
National Right to Work Committee	7,000,000	90
National Right to Work Foundation	3,500,000	45
National Taxpayers Union	1,192,000	18
Pacific Legal Foundation	3,000,000	55
Washington Legal Foundation	800,000	7
Young Americans for Freedom	800,000	12

* Precise figures for ATRM, a group headed by Howard Jarvis, are not available. The figures listed in this chart are extrapolations from data provided by ATRM.

A relatively new conservative activist group is The Conservative Caucus (TCC), founded in 1975 by Howard Phillips, 38, former head of the Office of Economic Opportunity under President Nixon, and the man who tried, unsuccessfully, to abolish the agency. Phillips is convinced that the real objective of conservative efforts should be control of the Congress and to that end TCC is designed to foster organizational activity at the congressional district level—ideally in every district. Phillips has traveled tirelessly around the country organizing in an attempt to make that dream a reality. While perhaps too sanguine about the possibility of making such an enormous enterprise succeed, Phillips has had a number of successes and the Caucus roster currently lists eighty district chapters. The organization has also succeeded in applying pressure on members of Congress on a wide range of issues. Perhaps most important of all, TCC has brought a number of talented political novices into the mainstream of conservative activity. Senator Gordon Humphrey of New Hampshire got his start in politics as a TCC state director, for instance, and Tony Campaigne and Dale Bell, GOP U.S. Senate candidates in New Hampshire and South Dakota respectively, were also TCC state directors.

The oldest of the established conservative groups is, paradoxically, one explicitly oriented toward youth—the Intercollegiate Studies Institute (ISI). Robert Schadler, 33, ISI's director of publications and a man who has been with the organization for ten years says, "ISI's impact has been considerable although our means of communication are more low keyed than those of the left. Conservatives are just not given to demonstrations, rallies, and so forth as much as the left is, so our work tends to be less noticed." This is especially true with ISI, he says, because of its academic orientation. "Ours is not a mass movement psychology," he says. "Rather, like the old ISS, we concentrate on reaching bright students who are likely to be leaders in government or the media." Although ISI's intellectual focus necessarily means a low profile, Schadler believes the organization is having considerable success. "Our publications now go to 30,000 subscribers in the academic community," he explains, "of which about 18,000 are undergraduate students, 2,000 are graduate students, and about 10,000 are faculty members. Ten years ago we had only about 5,000 faculty on our list."

Schadler also sees an improved general climate for conservatives on the nation's campuses. "The Nuremburg rally spirit of the sixties has clearly gone," he says, "and now you see much more openness to the conservative point of view. I've also noted that there are many, many more conservative professors than before. It used to be that we had to depend on a very small circle of academics for our events, but now we are finding a growing number of good conservative professors all across the country. The competition for our fellowships is very keen."

The other major conservative youth organization is, of course, Young Americans for Freedom. Although not as active now as at some times in the past (due in large part to the relative quiesence of the left on the campus), YAF is still going strong at twenty. In August 1979, the organization held its ninth biennial convention in Washington, attracting an attendance of 400 delegates who, in addition to disporting themselves at delegation parties and local bars, heard a number of big-name speakers, and attended seminars, the traditional keynote address by Bill Buckley, and a "roast" of columnist James Jackson Kilpatrick (former victims: Buckley, William Simon, and M. Stanton Evans). Under the direction of executive director Ron Robinson and chairman Jim Lacy, YAF continues to support an ambitious program, including a campus speakers series, various lobbying and legal action efforts (the organization played a major supporting role in behalf of Alan Bakke in his celebrated reverse discrimination suit), and publications. Similarly, Young America's Foundation, YAF's tax-exempt affiliate, conducts a major book distribution effort funneling conservative books to college students and libraries and hosts a series of regional conferences. Its director is Clifford White, 25.

Another major conservative youth group is the 60,000-member Young Republican National Federation (YRs). Although the YRs are not an explicitly conservative organization, they have been a resolutely conservative force ever since 1963 when Buz Lukens, a Goldwaterite, was elected national YR chairman, defeating a Rockefeller partisan. The Lukens victory presaged the nomination of Goldwater a year later and signaled the conservative dominance of the Republican Party which has prevailed since. The YRs, in fact, are the conservative shock troops within the party—more militantly conservative and more aggressive than the party rank and file. In 1968, the YRs split between Nixon and Reagan, but they were frequently critical of such liberal feints as wage and price controls and detente and, for the last few years, their hearts have belonged unabashedly to Ronald Reagan. The current YR president, Richard Abell, is a backer of Reagan. Roger Stone, 27, president from 1976 to 1978, is currently Northeast field director of the Reagan campaign. Stone was the subject of a full-page article in the November 5, 1979, issue of *Newsweek*, which commented favorably on his work for Reagan. He is a typical product of the YRs, which, like YAF, have served as a spawning ground for future Republican, and usually conservative, leaders. Among the ranks of YR alumni are Congressmen John Ashbrook, John Rousselot, political strategist F. Clifton White, Republican National Committee chairman Bill Brock, and dozens of other people who are prominent in GOP affairs.

A newer but highly visible organization is the National Taxpayers Union (NTU), founded in 1969 by James Dale Davidson, 31. The NTU had 220 affiliated chapters around the country at the end of 1979 and is still growing. The NTU has been a highly effective opponent of government waste and of high taxes in general but really came into its own with its guidance of the movement to call a constitutional convention to draw up an amendment to require the federal government to balance its budget. As the effort gained steam, Davidson became an overnight celebrity appearing on national talk shows, writing articles for publications around the country, and testifying before state legislatures. To date, thirty states have passed resolutions calling for the convening of the convention, just three short of the necessary thirty-three. If the effort succeeds, Davidson will have accomplished at age 31 what no one else in the history of the Republic has been able to do.

Another organization that is beginning to make headway with a national drive to enact a constitutional amendment is Americans for the National Voter Initiative Amendment (ANVIA). This amendment would allow issues to be placed on the national ballot upon the petition of 3 percent of the number of registered voters who voted in the last presidential election. Signers of the petitions would have to come from at least ten states and the drive would have to be completed within eighteen months. A majority yes vote in the ensuing election would make the measure law.

The provision would also place some limits on the initiative process. For instance, constitutional amendments, calling up the militia, and declarations of war could not be addressed by initiative, and any measure passed by the procedure could be amended or vetoed by a two-thirds roll-call vote of Congress during the first two years after passage and by a majority vote of Congress thereafter.

The drive to enact a national voter initiative amendment was initiated in 1975 by Edward A. ("Chip") Dent, 36, an aggressive, savy businessman who had parlayed his wits and small savings into a small fortune in real estate by the time he was 30. For several years, Dent sustained his drive, which was first called "Initiative America," with his own funds and worked without pay to advance it, writing memos and lobbying members of Congress on behalf of the idea. The first break came in 1977 when Senator James Abourezk (D.-S.D.) introduced an initiative bill in the Senate. A day later, Representative Guy Vander Jagt (R.-Mich.) introduced a similar bill in the House. In February 1974, Dent founded Americans for the National Voter Initiative Amendment and signed on Representative Jack Kemp (R.-N.Y.) as chairman. The drive has recently begun to pick up important endorsements and widespread financial support from conservative activists.

Not surprisingly, many conservatives do not support the initiative idea, believing that it undermines the representative democracy established by the Founding Fathers. Dent points out some compelling arguments in the idea's favor, however. First, he notes that it would take a relatively large number of signatures to put an initiative on the ballot (based on the figures from the 1976 presidential election, it would take 2.45 million), a fact that would tend to keep the number of initiative efforts low. "For those concerned that the process might threaten our republican, representative, deliberative form of government," Dent says, "experiences at the state level show that petition signature requirements are not easily met. Only one in five petition drives succeed in qualifying for the ballot. Of those qualifying, only one in three measures are passed. In making their decisions the voters exercise considerable discretion." Dent also points out that in the twenty-three states that have the initiative process, actions by the state legislatures still account for 99.5 percent of all laws passed. He feels that the initiative process provides a method of last resort for an electorate that is becoming increasingly cynical, despairing of its ability to affect the actions of the huge national bureaucracy.

Dent also argues that experience with the initiative process at the state level underscores the essentially conservative nature of the electorate, which has demonstrated a far stronger inclination to cut taxes and spending than to raise them. The success of Proposition 13 is but the most obvious example of this. As the December 18, 1978 *Fortune* points out, in the three years since Switzerland instituted the initiative process "the Swiss, by margins generally exceeding 3 to 1, have decided in referendums *not* to cut the work week from forty-four to forty hours, *not* to levy special taxes on the rich and high-salary earners, *not* to grant Swiss workers a say in the management of Swiss industries, *not* to reduce the qualifying age for admission to Switzerland's generous old-age pensions, *not* to allow the central government to raise funds to counter domestic economic downtrends, and finally *not* to allow the central government to run deficits. Instead, the Swiss voted to raise taxes on themselves, so that the federal government could operate on a pay-as-you-go-basis. In the archconservative mountainous cantons of Appenzell and Schwyz, the majority in favor of these measures often ran as high as 18 to 1."

Writing in favor of the initiative amendment drive, conservative columnist Pat Buchanan wrote,

For years now my right-wing brethren have been talking about a natural conservative majority "out there," whose will is frustrated by an elitist establishment ensconced in the bureaucracy, the judiciary, the Congress, and the media—an establishment with a game plan all its own for America, over which we exercise little control.

Well, the Abourezk amendment offers the people an unimpeded end-run around that liberal establishment. Now is the time for the brothers to put up or shut up.

Though impatient with the slowness of conservatives and Republicans to take to the initiative idea, Dent is still optimistic. "Overnight, Proposition

13—an *initiative*—did more to change the fiscal philosophy and policy of this country than all the efforts of Republicans combined over the last ten years—legislative or otherwise," he says. "All Republicans need to do is to realize the political dynamite the initiative holds for Democrats. If Republicans have political savvy, they will make the national initiative the point issue for 1980. And if they keep on it, and don't let up, they will have the Democrats totally on the defensive."

It is just possible that conservatives will realize the opportunity presented in 1980. As chairman of policy development for the Reagan campaign, Jack Kemp will have an opportunity to push the initiative plan and, indeed, Reagan has already endorsed the idea. GOP chairman Bill Brock has also stated his general support. Thus, ironic as it may seem, in 1980 the old radical slogan "Power to the people" may turn out to be the conservative battle cry.

Two other new organizations of importance work within the framework of the U.S. Congress, the House Republican Study Committee and the Senate Steering Committee. Headed by executive directors Richard Dingman and Margo Carlisle respectively, the study committee and the steering committee with staffs totaling approximately twenty people, prepare position papers, develop legislative strategy, and conduct "whip calls" for the conservative members of both houses. The existence of these organizations has proved of inestimable benefit to conservatives in both houses who were often out of synch with the elected leadership. In addition, the committees have been valuable sources of information for conservative organizations, apprising them of the likely timing of the introduction of important legislation and giving them advice on how to lobby particular members most effectively.

Another fast-growing area for conservatives has been the political action committees (PACs) which have mushroomed around the landscape in the wake of the 1976 "campaign reform" law passed by Congress. While hardly a reform, the new law has had a major impact on the way in which federal elections are held. First of the main changes the law wrought was setting a limit of $1,000 on the amount an individual could give to a candidate in an effort to eliminate influence buying by "fat cat" contributors. An individual could, however, give up to $5,000 to a political action committee. Thus, although he could not earmark money given to a PAC for a specific candidate, the contributor could, by contributing to a conservative PAC be reasonably sure that at least part of his money would be going to the candidate(s) of his choice. Second, the law allowed the employees of corporations to form their own PACs, heretofore prohibited, an invitation they accepted with relish. The net result of all this was to effect an explosion in the number of political action committees. To be sure, the directors of the business PACs tended to be rather inexperienced on the whole and their efforts tended to be counterproductive. (In 1978 business PACs showed a tendency to support incumbents, a double misuse of money since most incumbents are relatively well entrenched and able to raise their money locally, and since most are Democrats, many of whom vote against the interests of business.) Having sustained a good deal of criticism in the conservative and business press for this practice, many corporate PACs have since reviewed their contribution criteria, however, and the 1980 elections should see a much higher percentage of business PAC money going to conservatives, and in particular to conservative challengers.

The effect on contribution limits, moreover, has resulted in a whole array of conservative political action committees, which, utilizing direct mail, have built up lists of over 100,000 names in some cases, lists that allow the PACs to give out millions of dollars in congressional election years. The largest of these PACs is Citizens for the Republic (CFTR), chaired until recently by former Governor Ronald Reagan. Starting with Reagan's 1976 campaign contributor list, $1 million left over from the campaign, CFTR amassed a war chest that allowed it to hire a staff of twenty people, publish a monthly newsletter, hold dozens of regional training conferences all over the country, and in the 1978 Congressional elections to give $571,013 to 259 candidates.

In Washington, D.C., probably the main conservative PAC figure is Paul Weyrich, 36, president of the Committee for the Survival of a Free Congress, an organization that, despite its relative youth (founded in 1974) and cumbersome name, has already played a major role on the Washington scene. In 1978, CFSC financial assistance totaled $240,000 to 150 candidates. Weyrich is known as a leader of the New Right—mainly organizations affiliated with the Richard Viguerie "axis"—and is the presiding officer at the "Kingston meetings," the informal get-togethers held each Friday at the CSFC offices at which the heads of New Right organizations and other conservative groups gather to discuss strategy on Hill legislation and to trade political intelligence and evaluations of candidates.

Morton Blackwell, 40, special assistant to Senator Gordon Humphrey and former editor of the *New Right Report,* also chairs a biweekly luncheon meeting of PAC representatives and interested conservative leaders to discuss conservative prospects in key congressional races around the country.

In addition to the Conservative Victory Fund other leading conservative PACs include:

—The National Conservative Political Action Committee, headed by John T. ("Terry") Dolan, 28. Founded in 1974, NCPAC made financial contributions to 200 conservative candidates in 1978 and contributed $440,000 worth of in-kind contributions.

—The Fund for a Conservative Majority (the political action committee of Young Americans for Freedom). Founded in 1969 and headed by Robert

Heckman, 26, FCM made contributions of $260,000 to candidates in 1976.

—The National Defense PAC, which contributes to candidates favoring a strong U.S. military posture. Founded in 1977 by John Brasington, 29, former executive director of the Young Republicans, the National Defense PAC made contributions of $20,000 to 40 candidates in 1978.

—LifePAC, a prolife PAC headed by Ohio State Senator Buz Lukens. LifePAC was founded in 1979 and hence will be active for the first time in 1980. The first PAC to seek to draw on the support of the growing prolife movement, it should be a potent force in future elections.

The existence of these and other conservative PACs and the steady addition of others to their ranks is already having a major impact on Congress. The major change is to elect more staunchly conservative candidates to Congress, men and women who are also more aggressive and independent when they get there. This trend is seen clearly in the Republican class of 1978, both the youngest and most conservative GOP freshman class in many years (see chapter sixteen). In future elections the Republican Party is likely to gain more seats and the new congresses are also likely to be more outspokenly conservative.

As the federal government has grown the conservative community in Washington has grown also, to the point that there are now dozens of organizations located in and around Washington employing several thousand people. Not surprisingly, there is a considerable amount of interchange and communication between these people, and there are several forums in which representatives of the organizations get together regularly. Typical of these is the Monday Club, a luncheon group of congressional staff aides and leaders of conservative organizations that meets on alternate Mondays at the Hawk and Dove, a Capitol Hill watering hole, to listen to guest speakers and trade reports on legislation and activities of the member conservative groups. The Monday Club is sponsored by the ACU Education and Research Institute, and its agenda is set by ERI staffer Dave Williams and Ronald Docksai of Senator Orin Hatch's office.

A similar function is filled by the Kingston meetings and Morton Blackwell's weekly series of luncheon group, both mentioned above. Yet another conservative meeting ground is provided by the Conservative Club of Northern Virginia, founded by James Hinish, an analyst with the Senate Republican Policy Committee. The organization of more than 200 dues-paying members from the Washington area meets once a month in Alexandria, Virginia, to hear leading conservative spokesmen from the Congress, the media, and other organizations.

Direct mail mogul: Bruce Eberle, president, Eberle and Associates

5 | KEEP THOSE CARDS AND LETTERS COMING: THE DIRECT MAIL REVOLUTION

Along with the rapid growth of conservative organizations (some would say preceding it) has come a corresponding growth in direct mail fundraising operations, the primary means by which most of these groups are sustained. It is, in fact, in direct mail that conservatives have perhaps made their biggest technological breakthrough, developing a whole array of sophisticated techniques—indeed a whole new technology—that has raised hundreds of millions of dollars for conservative candidates and organizations, a feat that the liberal groups cannot come close to matching.

Stephen Winchell, a leading conservative fundraiser in Washington, pegs the conservative donor base nationwide at "perhaps 3 million" and that of the liberal counterpart at only 250,000. Another leading conservative fundraiser, Michael Thompson, estimates the nationwide conservative contributor pool at "6 to 7 million" and that of the liberals at "less than a million." Although it is impossible to quantify the donor base of liberals or conservatives with precision, it is universally acknowledged that the right is far ahead.

"Technologically, I'd say we're ten years ahead of them," says Winchell, "and politically I'd say we're fifteen years ahead. There is so much inbreeding among the liberal groups that it inhibits their fundraising effectiveness. Also, they tend to rely more on union dues and government patronage and thus have been less interested in the potential of direct mail."

When it comes to conservative fundraising one name stands out above all the rest: Richard A. Viguerie. Often referred to as the "Godfather of the New Right," Viguerie has become the subject of fear and loathing on the left as his growing empire has spawned new organizations, his fundraising letters have bankrolled a growing list of candidates, and his constituent response mailing have inundated Congress with millions of postcards, letters, and petitions.

59

No slouch at self-promotion, Viguerie has also made sure that his story has gotten to the press and they have responded with fascination, sending reporters to interview him and photographers to capture him posed by the magic reels on which are recorded the names of 5 million contributors—reels that are under perpetual watch by an armed guard.

Viguerie, a native of Texas, is in many ways the Horatio Alger of the right, a man who has risen from nowhere to the status of multi-millionaire in fifteen years' time. In 1961 he went to work in John Tower's senatorial campaign, doing mainly fundraising work. In 1963, he took a job as executive secretary of Young Americans for Freedom, a then-struggling conservative youth organization that was headquartered in New York. Viguerie's main preoccupation in those days was to keep YAF from the financial collapse that seemed always to be imminent, and in this effort he relied heavily on phone calls to wealthy supporters. Hating the anguish of repeatedly begging donors for funds on the phone, Viguerie began to rely more and more on mailings and, in time, the effort became increasingly successful, so much so that Viguerie hired David Jones to take over his duties as executive secretary while he concentrated on fundraising. In a development that became quite common in the saga of YAF, Jones and Viguerie had a falling out in 1965, and Viguerie found himself out of a job. With assets of $400 and the help of Marvin Liebman, then the main fundraiser for conservative organizations, Viguerie set up his own direct mail business, and the rest, as they say, is history.

Since then, Viguerie has done fundraising for literally hundreds of organizations and candidates. Today, his operation, based in Falls Church, Virginia, includes five separate companies involved in direct mail, list rentals, book publishing, and public relations, employing a total of over 200 people and raising over $35 million a year for more than two dozen clients.

"As impressive as Richard's own success is the tremendous number of fundraising professionals he has spawned," says James Minarik, 35, creative vice-president at the Viguerie Company. "They're all over the place." Indeed they are, and most conservative fundraisers will acknowledge their debt—in one way or another—to Viguerie.

"I think Richard Viguerie is an important man in conservative movement history," says fundraiser Bruce Eberle. "He was a real pioneer, and he introduced a lot of the concepts we are using now." Eberle, 37, is another striking conservative success story. A member of the YAF national board, Eberle and his wife Kathie began Bruce W. Eberle and Associates in 1974, working out of their home in northern Virginia, utilizing a single phone line. Five years later, things have changed. "We now have 7,000 square feet of space, thirty-two employees, and fifteen phone lines," he says. The big breakthrough for Eberle came in 1976 when he landed the fundraising

Richard Viguerie executives *(from left):* James Minarik, vice-president; Ann
Stone, account executive; and colleagues

Direct mail entrepreneurs *(from left):* Stephen Winchell; Alan Gottlieb

contract for the Reagan campaign. By the time the primaries were over, Eberle had raised over $6 million for Reagan and—of even greater significance—had amassed a contributor list of over 150,000 names, which he could rent as well as using to mail appeals for his clients. Building on this base, he has acquired some fifteen clients and the list is still growing. In 1979, Eberle expanded his operation with the addition of a sophisticated computer facility, and in 1980, he will expand his office space by about 2,000 additional square feet. Eberle estimates the gross receipts for his clients at $10 million for 1979.

Not surprisingly, Eberle speaks enthusiastically about the virtues of direct mail. "It allows us to go over the heads of the media and to present our case directly to the people," he says. "And through polling and petition drives and letter writing campaigns, it allows the guy at the grass roots level to participate in the national debate."

In addition, Eberle says, "Direct mail has allowed the conservative leadership nationally to galvanize the people on the issues, and it has given our people a real sense of being part of a movement."

Asked about complaints that the conservative direct mail market has become saturated and that the competition for dollars is hurting conservative activity, Eberle says, "It's a self-regulating market. I believe in the free market and that the best candidates and causes will succeed and that the inferior ones will not. It's that simple."

In Eberle's opinion, the new opportunity for conservatives is in television advertising. Leading the way to a conference room, he turned on a video cassette player and ran sixty- and ninety-second spots of senator Jake Garn, urging people to support his effort to defeat the SALT treaty. "It's fantastic," Eberle says, "In Salt Lake City alone, this brought 4,700 responses. Television marketing is virgin territory. It's where direct mail was fifteen years ago when Richard [Viguerie] started."

Eberle says that the half-hour Reagan programs in the 1976 primaries and the American Conservative Union half-hour films against the Panama Canal treaties shown in 1978 were groundbreakers. But he thinks the real promise is in shorter spots that get people to respond by writing in for information. These people then receive solicitations for funds.

Given the success of his short spots against SALT, Eberle is very excited about the prospects for television funds solicitation. "I think we've made a real breakthrough," he says contentedly.

Although Eberle is probably the most successful conservative fundraiser after Viguerie, the distinction would go to Stephen Winchell, 39, president of Winchell and Associates, if gross receipts for his Republican clients were counted as "conservative." Among his other successes, Winchell managed to land the Republican Party as a client—an extraordinarily lucrative contract by anyone's standards.

Like many of the other conservative entrepreneurs in Washington, Winchell got his start in YAF, serving as YAF's Michigan director for the Youth for Goldwater campaign in 1964. Shortly thereafter, he went to work for the Viguerie Company and he remained there, learning the secrets of the trade, until 1975, when he set up shop on his own.

Since then, Winchell has signed contracts with the Republican National Committee, the Republican Senatorial Campaign Committee, and the Republican Congressional Campaign Committee—the three main GOP organizations at the national level. Subsequently, Winchell has been extremely successful, doubling the party's number of contributors to 1.5 million as well as doubling its revenues.

In addition to his GOP clients, Winchell also does fundraising for the Heritage Foundation and a small number of candidates. Gross receipts for Winchell's clients are estimated at $25 million for 1979.

Like Eberle, Winchell is bullish about conservative fundraising prospects. "It's a dynamic market," he says. "The conservative groups and the Republican groups have been able to grow and prosper on direct mail and without hurting each other."

This is possible, he says, even though he concedes that the Republican fund appeals are almost always based on conservative issues. A moderate-to-liberal pitch tends to do very poorly, he admits—a fact that dictates conservative-oriented letters for the GOP committees, even when the chairman of the committee is an unabashed liberal, as is the case with Republican Senatorial Campaign Committee Chairman John Heinz.

According to Winchell, the demographics indicate a continuing expansion of conservative opportunities. "The pie continues to grow," he contends. "The number of elderly people continues to grow both in absolute numbers and as a percentage of the population, and it's older people who tend to give more to causes and campaigns. Theoretically, there is a saturation point for direct mail," Winchell says, "but we are far from reaching it."

Mike Thompson, 34, is another YAF alumnus who has become successful in the direct mail business. His firm, Thompson and Associates, handles fundraising for such organizations as the American Legislative Exchange Council, Committee for a Free China, the Fund for a Conservative Majority, and the National Defense PAC. The Thompson firm, founded in 1975, currently employs eight staff members.

Thompson believes that in the future, conservative groups will have to develop new means of selling their programs to increasingly sophisticated donors. "We have got to do more personal fundraising, and we have to learn to stay in touch more with our contributors and to explain to them just how their money is being spent," Thompson says.

Among other young conservatives who have made it big in the direct mail field is Philip Wiland, president of Wiland and Associates, a Culpepper, Virginia-based firm that does computer work and mailing operations for conservative organizations and fundraisers. Wiland, 34, was a classmate of Thompson's at the University of Missouri, a member of YAF and the Young Republicans. He began his firm in 1971 and now employs more than 100 people and manages a multi-million dollar budget doing work for such groups as the National Right to Work Committee and the national Republican groups.

Alan Gottlieb, 32, and his wife Julie, 26, own and manage another new and thriving conservative direct mail operation. Unlike the other entrepreneurs in the business, however, the Gottliebs opted to locate their operation outside the Washington, D.C., area, selecting Seattle as a base. Gottlieb founded his company in 1974. Since then it has grown into an enterprise employing thirty-five people and providing a complete line of direct mail service including copywriting, computer work, printing, mailing operations, and list rentals. The Gottliebs have four organizations of their own for which they do the direct mail fundraising—the Citizens Committee for the Right to Keep and Bear Arms, the Second Amendment Foundation, the Right to Keep and Bear Arms Political Victory Fund (all firearms-oriented groups), and the Center for the Defense of Free Enterprise.

The company also does direct mail fundraising for a number of candidates, organizations, and commercial establishments, and a considerable amount of subscription mail for publications. In addition, the Gottlieb company produces two radio programs a week, which are syndicated nationally: "Economics 101 on the Air," carried by 187 stations, and "On Target," carried on 136 stations.

The Gottlieb company's business for 1979 exceeded $4 million. Gottlieb's increasing success and his growing political clout in the Seattle area have caught the attention of the media, and in November 1979, Gottlieb was the subject of a cover story in the *Seattle Sunday Times* magazine.

In addition to running all-out to keep abreast of the conservative competition, Gottlieb strives to stay on top of new trends in the liberal camp. "I'm on many of the liberal groups' lists," he says, "and there's much more inbreeding there than there is among conservative groups. The liberal groups have fewer names, so they are more anxious to trade names than conservatives are. If you get on Common Cause's mailing list, for instance, you're likely to be deluged with mailings from all kinds of groups, from the NAACP to the Coalition to Ban Handguns to the Nader groups."

Like all his competitors, Gottlieb is optimistic about the future of conservative direct mail. "We're now into the production of television and radio spots which are working well," he says. "As conservative fundraising becomes more sophisticated and as we start focusing on new kinds of issues, we're bringing new people into the movement and expanding our base."

Constance Brennan, executive director, National Food Machinery
Corporation Foundation

6 | TAKING CARE OF BUSINESS: EFFORTS TO PRESERVE FREE ENTERPRISE

In his book *Two Cheers for Capitalism*, "neoconservative" thinker Irving Kristol takes businessmen to task for their failure to "think politically," by which he means their failure to look beyond the bottom line of the profit-loss confines of their personal enterprise to the larger realities that shape the environment within which exists the free enterprise *system*. There is a lot to admire in the capitalist mentality, Kristol emphasizes, such traits as thrift, industry, self-reliance, self-discipline, and so forth, but being practical men, businessmen are too often unable or unwilling to compete in the struggle of ideas that will ultimately determine whether the system that sustains them will survive. "The simple truth," Kristol says, "is that the professional classes of our modern bureaucratized societies are engaged in a class struggle with the business community for status and power." Unfortunately many businessmen do not understand that this battle is in progress; worse, not only do they not realize that the battle is joined, all too frequently they unwittingly subsidize the enemies.

Michael Joyce, 37, director of the John M. Olin Foundation, is familiar with this problem. "Of the 26,000 grant-giving foundations in the country," he says, "ninety percent of them are small family foundations with assets of less than a million dollars. Of the remaining 2,600 the majority are liberal. I know of only about ten aggressively conservative grant-giving foundations. Among the giant foundations such as Ford, Rockefeller, Carnegie, those that are on the cutting edge of corporate philanthropy, are all liberal." Joyce contends, "Schumpeter was correct. The second and third generations of successful capitalist families are less conscious of the value of the system than is the first generation." In the establishment of corporate foundations, he says, a pattern emerges: "Typically the founder of the corporation sets up a foundation to perpetuate the values he believes in, and then he establishes a board to govern it. The board, often including heirs of the founder, chooses a president who is slightly to their left. The president then picks a director and staff who are to the left of him, and before long the foundation is pursuing ends totally at odds with the founder's intentions."

A big part of the problem confronting business, Joyce says, is that "businessmen don't understand how public opinion is formed. It's not a question that confronts them in their day-to-day activities. They tend to want quick results from their efforts. Molding public opinion takes time, and businessmen frequently don't have the patience. They also tend to have an aversion to intellectual combat and this makes them sitting ducks for the New Class types." Another problem, Joyce believes, is that of image. "The New Class people have all the imagery and all the love on their side. They present themselves as being altruistic. On the other hand, capitalism, for all its merits, is a fairly prosaic system. It's hard to make heroic figures out of businessmen. Ayn Rand tried for a time but she didn't succeed very well."

One corporate philanthropy program that avoids the pitfalls pointed out by Joyce is that of the Food Machinery Corporation (FMC) of Chicago. FMC gave $1.5 million to a wide variety of causes and organizations in 1978 and projects $1.8 million in such contributions for 1979. FMC's philanthropic activities are administered by a board of five and an executive director, Connie Brennan, 38. Brennan's job is to screen in-coming applications and to select those she thinks merit the board's approval. She also travels the country looking for organizations and programs she thinks are deserving of FMC support. Many of FMC's contributions go to charities such as United Way and to local schools and colleges; and in this, the company's program is not particularly unique. It *is* out of the ordinary, however, in that the company is also making a concerted attempt to direct a large part of its grants to conservative causes that are perceived to be trying to strengthen the free-enterprise system. "I see an incredible lack of philosophical understanding on the part of most corporate chief executive officers," Brennan says. "If you look at the massive amounts of money given away by corporations, you see very little giving that is intelligent from the corporation's perspective." She adds, "Typically management does not have the time—or at least doesn't take the time—to supervise the philanthropic activities of the company. So an individual is hired to do this. In many instances, this individual begins to immerse himself in the activities of potential recipients in the community and before long he has become a captive of the charitable groups seeking money and loses his ties to the company. His first loyalty becomes to the donee and not to the company."

Brennan proffers the statement by Ken Mason, president of Quaker Oats, as symptomatic of the problem with corporate philanthropy: "I know of no greater disservice to American business in my lifetime than Milton Friedman's assertion that business' only reason for being is to generate profits for its shareholders." Brennan agrees with Friedman and emphatically disagrees with Mason's contention that business owes something to society. "Communities owe something to the businesses located there," she says. "They provide the jobs and the financial base that makes the community possible in the first place. Most of the corporate giving I see does the company involved no good. You never do enough. Whatever you do seems to foster the belief that you should be doing more and it is absurd to think that by contributing to elements that are hostile to business you are going to make them pro-business. They merely escalate their demands for more support."

Brennan believes in corporate philanthropy but also believes that corporate largesse should benefit the company giving the money—even if only in an indirect way. "FMC is quite generous in its charitable contributions." We want to help the handicapped and other needy people. And we want to support good causes. But we try to be discriminating in our contributions so that we are not subsidizing people who are on the other side. We try to contribute to causes that are probusiness, not progovernment, and we endeavor to make sure that our contributions are not going to underwrite the growth of an interest group that is going to lobby against us."

In 1978, FMC, under Brennan's direction, created a "Public Issues/Economic Education" program that seeks explicitly to support conservative, free-market-oriented groups. Fifteen percent of the company's charitable giving is earmarked for this effort. Brennan states that FMC recently completed an exhaustive study of corporate philanthropy including a survey of conservatives' criticism of corporate giving. "We have compiled the thirty main criticisms, and tried to come up with solutions for each one. Our basic conclusion is that corporations should seek to support groups that have leverage and that means, in general, leverage with academics, politicians, and the media. We subscribe to the trickle-down theory that if we can influence the thinking of these opinion molders the effect of this will gradually seep down to the grass roots level. Our Public Issues/Economic Education giving, which will be about $270,000 in 1980, is governed by this concept. FMC gives to groups that champion free enterprise, that advocate limited government, and that subscribe to traditional values." It is a philosophy that more businesses would do well to emulate.

Under the leadership of its president, former Treasury Secretary William Simon, and of executive director, Michael Joyce, the John M. Olin Foundation has gained a reputation as one of the most politically astute of the conservative foundations. "We made 83 grants in 1978, totaling about $3 million in all," says Joyce, "and all of these went to organizations defending the free enterprise system."

Among the major recipients of Olin funds are the Hoover Institution at

Friends of free enterprise *(left to right from top):* Catriona Tudor and Stuart
Smith of World Research, Inc.; Harding Jones, president, The Atlantic Group;
Michael Joyce, executive director, Olin Foundation; Steve Ritchie, special
assistant to the president, Adolph Coors Company

Stanford, the American Enterprise Institute, the Heritage Foundation, the Law and Economics Center at the University of Miami, and the Center for the Study of the Economy and the State at the University of Chicago. Because of its high profile as a major underwriter of conservative think tanks, the Olin Foundation was singled out for unfavorable reportage in the October 22, 1979, issue of the *Village Voice*. Olin, the article insinuated, was guilty of questionable activities because the foundation gave tax-exempt funds only to organizations it agreed with.

"This is part of the neo-Kantian ethic that you see on the part of liberal critics of corporate philanthropy," Joyce says, "the belief that you should do good without thinking about the consequences." The trouble with this attitude, Joyce explains is that "the liberals and the Naderites and others designed an idea of the public good that coincides pretty closely with what they're interested in and what they're doing. When corporate money goes to support liberal causes that's good. When it goes to support conservatives, that's special interest money and it's tainted. It's a totally skewed perception, and one that has to be exposed for what it is."

The Naderites *et al.*, Joyce says, far from being disinterested in matters of financial gain, frequently have a vested interest in the program they advocate. "Basically the New Class has a vested interest in the growth of the public sector, and one reason for this is that bigger government means more employment opportunities for the New Class members." Joyce contends that the Nader class is also trying to insinuate itself directly into the corporate philanthropy process. "If you read about the press conference held in Washington in April by the new Naderite group, the National Committee for Responsible Philanthropy, you remember that one of their complaints was that there were not enough minority group representatives, women, or disadvantaged people on the corporate committees that are earmarking the grants. This is an attempt to increase New Class influence on corporation giving."

Joyce's criticism of business's feeble performance in the battle of ideas is shared by Patrick Maines, 36, director of public affairs of the National Distillers Corporation. "Corporations exist to make a profit," he says, "and it is difficult for the directors to see the efficacy—or at least the short-term efficacy—of funding programs to further the cause of the market system." In most cases, he states, "corporations tend to spend their advocacy efforts on lobbying efforts trying to influence legislators and regulatory policy in Washington and the state capitals." These efforts, he believes, are in the end insufficient: "Business can lobby until the end of the world but unless the climate of opinion is altered significantly, those efforts will be unavailing."

Another problem of corporations, Maines believes, is that of image.

"Corporations want to present a positive image, not a complaining image," he says, "and the fact is that today it is conservatives, ironically, who are dissatisfied with the status quo. Thus, support for conservative activities can be controversial."

An additional factor working to conservatives' detriment in Maines's view is that in many corporations the public relations types, who tend to have a significant impact in the grant allocations, tend to be graduates of journalism schools. "These people tend to graduate as liberals, and they continue to carry around the wrong kind of ideological baggage."

Despite Maines's gloomy view of most corporate philanthropy, it is clear that the wrong-headed approach he describes is not prevalent at National Distillers. "We have a unique program here, and I was very lucky in being given the broad mandate I have. I was given the mandate to monitor the socio-political environment and to come up with innovative programs to affect it in a conservative way." Under Maines's direction, National Distiller funds a three-pronged program to promote the conservative/free-market viewpoint. One is a traditional grant program under which the corporation gives contributions to a number of conservative foundations (among them the American Enterprise Institute, the National Legal Center for the Public Interest, and the Heritage Foundation). The second is the National Public Policy Syndicate, under which the company publishes a monthly magazine of policy commentaries that should be of interest to corporate leaders. The magazine goes out to a list of paid subscribers in the business world. The Public Policy Syndicate also maintains a speakers bureau that arranges, for a fee, for prominent conservative scholars and public figures to lecture the management personnel at companies participating in the program.

"One of our most innovative programs," he says, "is our National Policy Fellows program. In this effort we go to colleges and universities near our plants around the country and we seek out talented conservative professors in the social science departments." These professors are given grants and in return they are asked to do two things: (1) come to the plant once a month for nine months and hold a seminar with the management personnel of the plant on some aspect of public policy, and (2) the second year, write something for publication based on one of the seminars. This program is in its fourth year, with six to eight policy fellows being chosen per year. "For a relatively small amount of money, this program has had significant benefits," Maines says. "It is informative for our employees who participate in it and it is of real benefit to the professors involved." Many of these conservative professors feel quite isolated, he says, and the fellows program gives them a sense of belonging to a community, plus it also frequently helps their careers by making them more prominent within their profession.

"I do not believe there is any conspiracy involved in the liberal dominance of the foundation world," Maines says. "It's just that liberals work harder at it and there are more liberal organizations active in the field." He feels, however, that "a lot of factors are converging to oblige conservative improvement in this area." One corrective step that should be taken is for business schools to require their students to take public relations courses so that, once out in the corporate world they will be better able to present their company's case—and the case for capitalism—to the public.

He also believes that conservatives must overcome their tendency to write business off as hopeless. "Business is the last best hope for turning this country around. Businessmen have the right mind-set on the issues, though they may not be very good at projecting their viewpoint, and businessmen have the assets necessary to do the job if they are just mobilized. Business can win the fight, but it will take a lot of hard work."

One organization designed specifically to help business cope in the prevailing inhospitable climate is the Atlantic Group, a firm founded in 1977 by T. Harding Jones, 29. "There is a significant strain of guilt evident in many corporate executives," Jones states. "They have been made to feel defensive about the role of business and for many of these executives the purpose of corporate philanthropy is to attempt to assuage their critics." The typical corporate executive, Jones says, "is usually not well-schooled in economic philosophy. He has no real philosophical grounding, no grasp of what the free market is all about. He doesn't see the system in its large context and appreciate its virtues. His main concern, understandably, is making a profit for his company, but in the climate that exists he is made to feel guilty about that." The corporate public relations people, Jones says, are usually worse still, typically being "New Class" liberals who have little understanding of the free market and little desire to defend corporate interests.

The purpose of the Atlantic Group, Jones says, is to "educate corporate executives about the intellectual environment that they exist in, to equip them to deal with it and to guide them in making corporate contributions so that they help strengthen the free enterprise system rather than undermine it."

Although only 29, Jones already has considerable experience battling the "New Class." As a student at Princeton, he became disenchanted with the pronounced liberal/secularist tilt of the university administration and its total disregard for the views of the alumni whose largesse helped sustain the university. Jones decided an antidote was necessary and thus founded *Prospect,* an alumni magazine that was designed as an alternative to the magazine published by the university. The purpose of *Prospect* was to uphold Princeton traditions and to resist efforts by the faculty, students, and administration to undermine them. The journal met with instant and widespread support and is still publishing eight years later, sustained by alumni funds.

Now, with the Atlantic Group, Jones is seeking to transfer this expertise gained at Princeton to the corporate world. Jones's clients at this point include four corporations which he advises on matters of communication and corporate philanthropy and he is optimistic about the future. "A few years ago, most businessmen didn't understand the threat they were facing. Now there are a growing number of corporate executives who realize that American business faces an ideological foe and that it needs to act aggressively to counteract it by contributing to academics, organizations, and political activists and candidates who share their views."

Another firm with a creative program to advance free enterprise is the Adolph Coors Company of Golden, Colorado, brewers of the famous Coors beer beloved of actor Paul Newman and millions of other American beer connoisseurs. In recent years, Coors has pushed a program called "Project Confidence," an effort to educate the company's employees and members of the local community about the importance of the free enterprise system and how it works. One of the leading figures in this effort is Steve Ritchie, 37, special assistant to Joseph Coors, president of the company. Ritchie, at age 32, was already a genuine military hero, one of the few to win public recognition from the Vietnam War. He attended the Air Force Academy, where he was a starting quarterback, and, after graduating, served as a fighter pilot in Vietnam, where he volunteered for two tours of duty. During the war, Ritchie logged more than 800 hours of combat time in the F-4 Phantom and became the war's only Air Force ace when he shot down five North Vietnamese MIG jets. When he resigned his commission in 1974, he was one of the most decorated officers in U.S. military history.

Ritchie has displayed the same energy and stamina in civilian life as he did as a fighter pilot. As the Coors company's unofficial ambassador for free enterprise for the past four years, he has logged over a half-million miles making more than 800 speeches to civic associations, schools, churches, and service clubs. He echoes the criticisms of business made by many conservative critics. "Business is all too often unwilling to become involved in the political battles of the day," he says, "but if the free enterprise system is to survive, it is essential that business stand up and be counted."

Prominent in the Ritchie demonology are what he calls the "sunshine capitalists." "They talk a good game about the importance of preserving the market system, but these businessmen are the first ones on the plane to Washington to look for government favors and protection for their business. If you look at the contributions of the business political action committees, their record is a disgrace. They give as much to one side as the other. What they want is access to members of Congress to get special favors. They don't care if a congressman votes against business in general as long as he provides them with the favors they want."

The public's negative perception of business is also partly the fault of business itself, Ritchie contends, pointing out, "Frequently companies inflate their profits by misrepresenting depreciation and other means in order to impress their stockholders and potential investors." The cumulative effect of this, he adds, is to give the public an inflated view of corporate profits. "The corporate profit figures for the fourth quarter of 1978 were a good illustration of this. The media reported corporate profits had increased by 26 percent over a year before. This was true, but profits for the fourth quarter of 1977 were only 4 percent. A year later, they had risen to 5 percent. That rise was essential if business was to take steps to modernize plant facilities that will make American business more competitive and efficient." He points out that most Americans think corporate profits are at least 50 percent, instead of the 5 percent or so that really exists. "If we could just get across to the public the true size of profits and the vital role they play in maintaining a healthy economy we would be a long way towards solving our economic problem," he contends.

To this end, Ritchie criss-crossed the country speaking about the challenge to the free enterprise system and the necessity to work to preserve it. On many of these trips, he is accompanied by his wife, Sherye, a beautiful and talented woman who pursues her own highly successful career as an artist and interior designer. "People always ask me 'What can I do?' I tell them they must work to inform themselves by reading the right kind of publications and that they must seek to work within their sphere of influence, whether it be their church, civic association, or whatever to encourage their friends to think the right way and vote the right way." The Coors company program is a prototype for other companies in the field of economic education, Ritchie believes. "We hold seminars for our employees and we encourage our 200 distributors to do the same. We provide them with educational materials, and we urge them to become active in civic affairs in the communities and to try to influence events there."

Ritchie sees a need for a rebirth of entrepreneurial activity in America. "Most top executives are not entrepreneurs." They are not rugged individualists. Most are professional managers who have worked their way up the corporate ladder through committees by using the art of compromising. They don't want to rock the boat because they are afraid they will endanger their perks. We need more entrepreneurs, more people with faith in themselves and in the system, more people willing to take a risk."

One of the most thoughtful analysts of the problems confronting American capitalism is A. Lawrence Chickering, 38, executive director of the Institute for Contemporary Studies (ICS) in San Francisco. Under the direction of

Chickering and President H. Munroe Browne, the ICS maintains a large and growing publications program featuring works by a host of top-flight scholars, many of them treating various aspects of the plight of capitalism in present-day America. In 1979, the Institute published twenty books running the gamut of subjects from taxes to foreign policy. The majority of these focused on the pitfalls of government planning and the superiority of market solutions. Among those were *Bureaucrats and Brainpower* (a study of the growing government regulation of higher education); *Federal Tax Reform; New Directions in Public Health Care; Parents, Teachers and Children;* and *The Politics of Planning and Regulating Business.* The institute publications display a uniformly high level of excellence and enjoy a wide readership among public policy analysts around the country. As the ICS's prodigious output grows, as it surely will, the organization can be counted on to become a major power among the nation's think tanks.

Chickering has observed that one of the problems that free-market advocates have in defending the capitalist system is that most people tend to equate the corporation with capitalism, an erroneous assumption in Chickering's mind. He remarks the anomoly that many business types laud the free enterprise system in general but work assiduously to undermine the system by seeking government favors and protection for themselves. He notes, on the other hand, that there is the irony of the "counterculture" which tends to attack "the system" in the abstract while forming a nearly pure system of capitalism among themselves through the sale of handicrafts, organic foods, hand-made clothing, and the like. "Businessmen (and their shareholders) have a primary stake in defending corporations," Chickering writes, "while consumers' dominant concern is with the market system." Another problem, he says, is that the enemies of capitalism have made the system synonomous with materialism and greed. Writing in *Reason* magazine, he notes,

Opponents see materialism everywhere they look, and they attack the system of free exchange for the corruption of motive, while appealing to the 'higher idealism' of social systems that seek goals loftier than the accumulation of material riches and class distinctions.

This attack makes businessmen uneasy, and they usually respond with Chamber-of-Commerce slogans about how "profit is not a dirty word." There is great and pathetic irony in such responses, which only show how ill-equipped businessmen are to defend capitalism. In fact, most conservative businessmen do not begin to be as materialistic as the intellectuals who attack them, but businessmen often believe caricatures about themselves.

Chickering believes that far from being a corrupt system of institutionalized greed and plunder, capitalism is a moral system, a system that provides a structure of liberty within which the individual can pursue his quest for self-fulfillment, moral as well as material.

Addressing the problem of how to preserve the free-enterprise system in the hostile environment that obtains, Chickering writes:

> The great challenge facing those who wish to arrest the decline of capitalism is to restore the "capitalist ideal" the possibility and prospect of virtue and of commitment to the good life. An economic system of free exchange is one which leaves people in it free to exchange whatever they individually choose to value—material or nonmaterial. Those proponents who bind capitalism to man's lowest instincts and aspirations—and even celebrate that use of freedom—only encourage the myth that capitalism is intrinsically materialistic, and thereby collaborate in its demise. Freedom of exchange and freedom to choose—indeed, by its nature, freedom itself—encompass the whole range of human possibilities and potentialities, the highest values as well as the lowest. The overwhelming idealism in liberal capitalism lies not in appeal to lower values, but in aspiration to higher ones. It lies in the possibility that a purely capitalist society, based on individual exchange of values freely chosen, could one day become a community dedicated to virtue and idealism.

Although all of the young executives interviewed for this book expressed disillusionment with corporate America's lack of political acumen, all of them also professed to note some encouraging signs that things might be improving. One such augury is the accumulating evidence that the idea of capitalism is enjoying something of a restoration to grace by the nation's intellectual illuminati. Symptomatic of this attitude is the November 1978 issue of the *Washington Monthly,* a small (circulation 30,000) but influential publication that is widely read by the power elite in Washington. The cover story, titled "Putting America Back in Business," advertised articles such as the "Case for the Entrepreneur," causing Robert Samuelson to remark in the *National Journal* that the unwary reader might mistake the November *Monthly* for the "house organ of the Chamber of Commerce." The article noted that "William Simon . . . must have written the table of contents. The first article lionizes the independent oilman, the second castigates the United States for excessive trade concessions and the third extols the virtues of overseas corporate payoffs." Other examples of the surprising new attitude exhibited by *Washington Monthly* could be easily documented by casually perusing other liberal journals.

Another positive development was documented in the May 10, 1975, *Wall Street Journal.* The story, "Programs to Teach Free Enterprise Sprout on College Campuses," discusses the blossoming relationship between business and the nation's colleges, and especially the growing number of free enterprise chairs being endowed by companies in college economics departments. The article reports that about 100 such business-sponsored programs are now underway on the campus and that many more such are on the way. Some of them, such as the Goodyear Tire and Rubber chairs at Akron University and Kent State University, represent commitments of $250,000 apiece. The *Journal* also reported on the efforts of National Leadership Methods, a consulting firm that has established regional private enterprise contests in which 200 colleges compete for grants from companies. Students then compete for the grant money by devising creative projects to promote free enterprise in their local communities. Also popular, the *Journal* reports, are "executive-in-residence" programs in which companies send executives to lecture to college classes on free enterprise. The article notes further on that a Harris poll taken at 150 colleges revealed that 77 percent of the academics questioned indicated that they favored more contacts with the corporate world, and no one wanting less. A surprising finding to most, I venture to say.

Yet another encouraging development is the growing advocacy of capitalism by blacks and other minorities. The *Washington Post* reported on this phenomenon in a July 25, 1978, piece entitled "A New Black Vanguard," with the subtitle, "Corporate Conservatism is Voiced." The full-page article noted that a growing number of black "neoconservatives" had already become an articulate minority that was "being heard in public forums, at Congressional offices, in private strategy meetings where blacks from the corporate world are pushing a free-market line of argument, one that says private industry can deliver the jobs if only government will get out of the way."

The article quoted black Congressman John Conyers as saying black oil riggers had been in to lobby him to change his hostile attitude toward the oil industry and that "every black manager" of a MacDonald's franchise in Detroit had urged him to vote for a special lower minimum wage for young people so that MacDonald's and other companies could afford to hire more young black workers. The article also mentioned the NAACP's surprise opposition to President Carter's energy policy, which featured more controls on the oil companies, and quoted NAACP chairman Margaret Bush Smith as reminding the delegates that "new jobs come from economic growth in the private sector."

A dramatic example of what can be done to promote free enterprise is provided by Robert Chitester, the young manager of television station WQLN in Erie, Pennsylvania. Chitester viewed the "Age of Uncertainty," the series produced for public television featuring John Kenneth Galbraith, and drew back in horror, both from the series's poor technical quality and the faulty economic theory it portrayed. Chitester mulled over the possibility of doing a series superior on both counts and hit upon the idea of one starring Milton Friedman. He took the idea to Friedman, who rejected it. Undaunted, Chitester developed the idea further and secured some initial pledges of financing, then went back to Friedman. This time Friedman consented. Chitester then went to work to raise the necessary funds and eventually raised $2.5 million from such firms as Olin, Coors, Pepsico, and General Motors. The series was produced. Called "Free to Choose," it features Friedman on location in countries around the world discussing the virtues of capitalism versus other economic systems and using the developments in the countries visited as illustrations of his point. The series—ten segments in all—was aired on national public television starting in January 1980, and Chitester is now hard at work endeavoring to raise the necessary funds to have it shown on one of the commercial networks.

One of the best of the free-enterprise groups is a San Diego-based foundation, World Research Incorporated (WRI), which is staffed by twenty-one bright young free marketeers. The WRI made the national scene in 1975 with the publication of *The Incredible Bread Machine*, a slim volume written by six WRI staffers, Susan Love Brown, Karl Keating, David Melinger, Patrea Post, Stuart Smith, and Catrina Tudor. The book sketches an economic history of the United States, touching on the "robber barons," the causes of the Great Depression, the New Deal antitrust legislation, monopolies, social welfare legislation and a host of other matters under engaging rubrics such as "The Bread also Rises," "The Sun Sinks in the Yeast," and "Better Bread than Dead." To the authors, capitalism is the "incredible bread machine," and government interventions such as regulations and price controls constitute a "no-dough" policy that produces "burnt toast."

Despite the whimsy of the chapter headings, the economics is solid as a rock, as witness these passages on government price supports:

> Years ago the federal government undertook to subsidize cotton farmers. But then it was discovered that the persistently high price of American cotton was hurting cotton exports. So the government subsidized exporters. But then American mill owners pointed out that foreign mills were getting American cotton cheaper than American mills could get it. So now the American mills are being subsidized. And so the growers, the exporters, and the mills are now all indebted to the State for assistance. And what the State subsidizes, to an appreciable extent it controls. "The old trick is to turn every contingency. . . ."
>
> The bureaucrat will force rates higher and then demand greater power in order to force them down again. Or, he will seek to "protect" the farmer and as a result generate a mountain of rotting surpluses, then he will demand still great control over agriculture in order to cure the problem he himself has created. Or, he will regulate the railroads nearly into bankruptcy and then urge a program of government loans to "help" them.

Equally devastating is this analysis of AMTRAK's modus operandi:

> AMTRAK, the government subsidized corporation which operates all passenger service crossing state lines, prints this on the back of tickets:

Times shown on time tables or elsewhere and times quoted are not guaranteed, and form no part of this contract. Time schedules and equipment are subject to change without notice. Carrier may, without notice, substitute alternative means of transportation, and may alter or omit stopping places shown on ticker or time-table. Carrier assumes no responsibility for inconvenience, expenses or other loss, damage or delay resulting from error in schedules, delayed trains, failure to make connections, shortage of equipment or other operating deficiencies.

In other words, you may not get where you want to go, and you may not get there on a train, and you may not stop where you thought you would stop, and the railroad is not responsible for inconvenience or injuries resulting from its own ineptitude. The only thing that you can be sure of when you ride the silver streak known as AMTRAK is that your chances are high that you will arrive on times. Why? Because AMTRAK has re-defined "on time." From the *Wall Street Journal* of March 14, 1974:

In January 1973, AMTRAK reported that 66.2% of its trains arrived on time. By December, 1973, the figure was down to 51%, so AMTRAK, a great fan of Newspeak, re-defined "on time." Under the new definition it may be up to a half hour late. Thus AMTRAK was able to announce an improved "on time" rating of 61.7% for January, 1974.

The authors, to be sure, do not believe that capitalism is a perfect system or a panacea for all humanity's ills; rather, they believe that it provides a framework within which mankind can gradually increase its material well being: "Capitalism will not provide human beings with happiness, if they do not know what will make them happy; it will not guarantee justice, if they do not know why justice is necessary; it will not protect them from the throes of materialism if they wish to place products before people. These things fall within the scope of individual prerogative. What capitalism will do is provide human beings with the material means of survival and the freedom to improve their lives in accordance with their own wishes."

Bread Machine has enjoyed a phenomenal success going through seven printings in five years. Heartened by the success of the book, the World Research staff produced a very clever film version of the book which has proved enormously popular with audiences at hundreds of high schools and colleges.

Since the production of the *Bread Machine* film two other films have been produced. One titled *Libra,* was released in 1978. A futuristic film set in the next century, *Libra* describes a space colony between earth and the moon inhabited by a group of ambitious free marketeers. The Libra colonists discover a way to produce and transmit cheap solar power back to earth. The earth, however, is under the control of a world government which fears the Libra energy plan as a threat to its energy monopoly. *Libra* cost WRI about $280,000, and the foundation has just finished another film—*The Inflation File*—a droll number which spoofs the old Humphrey Bogart mystery flicks. The film traces the adventures of bumbling detective, Avery Mann as he moves through historical epochs and farflung regions of the globe in an attempt to solve the mystery of what causes inflation. It will hardly compromise the appeal of the film to say that our sleuth hits pay dirt in Washington.

In addition to its films, World Research publishes the bimonthly magazine *World Research Ink,* containing articles, interviews, and film and book reviews (circulation: 50,000), as well as *The Occasional Review,* a semi-annual scholarly journal that features longer pieces on the humanities, arts, and social sciences. The organization also publishes an "Educational Series," issue-oriented pamphlets that employ imaginative graphics and playful prose as well as sound economics to make the case for the free market. According to Stuart Smith, WRI's director of marketing and development, the pamphlets go out to approximately 250,000 students a year. Also part of the WRI effort are a student opinion survey program and a "dialogue" program that gives interested students recommendations for further reading and study in free market economics.

In view of the phenomenal success of the World Research program, especially at high schools and on college campuses, it is heartening to note that the foundation is receiving substantial support from U.S. companies such as the Mobil Foundation, Hewlett-Packard and others. Using humor, deftly marshalled facts, and youthful exuberance, the blithe spirits of World Research Inc. have done something the captains of industry could never have done themselves: They have made capitalism not only respectable but exciting to American young people.

Directors of Christian Voice *(from left):* Rev. Robert Grant, chairman; Rev. Richard T. Zone, executive director; Gary Jarmin, Washington representative

7 | THE MORAL MAJORITY

The fundamental Christian attitude on church-state affairs was, appropriately, enunciated by Christ himself: "Render, therefore, unto Caesar what is Caesar's and unto God what is God's." This makes plain that there are two distinct spheres of authority, the temporal and the spiritual, and Jesus makes clear in His ministry that He considered the spiritual to be the more important of the two. This doctrine was developed further by several church fathers, among them St. Augustine, who held that the state was incompetent to govern the transcendent matters of the spirit and that it should leave these areas alone. It was brought to its fullest expression during the Middle Ages with the articulation of the sun-moon analogy, the sun being the church, the moon the state. Each offers light to man, but the role of the sun is manifestly more important.

This separation of church and state and, further, placing limits on the power of the state, is one of the glories of Western civilization and has been a major factor in fueling the West's rise to preeminence. In the United States, it has been codified in our constitution and embraced by most American Christians. Throughout our history, it has served us well. The clergy have not interfered with the government's prerogative to provide for the common defense and promote the general welfare—to deploy the armed forces, deliver the mail, administer the public school system, and administer justice in the courts, etc. The state, meanwhile, has refrained from infringing on the Church's right to conduct services, operate seminaries, train the clergy, fund and administer parochial schools, educate the children of the faithful, and support mission work at home and abroad.

The separation between the temporal and spiritual realms does not mean the exclusion of religion from the national life, however. Far from it. As the late William O. Douglas says, "We are a religious people whose institutions presuppose a supreme being." Our earliest national document, the Declaration of Independence, invokes "the laws of nature and of nature's God" in behalf of the colonists' cause, and ever since the nation's leaders have called upon the Almighty to sanctify their efforts. "In God We Trust" is the nation's motto, a sentiment enshrined in the national anthem, the pledge of allegiance, and stamped on every coin issued. Every session of Congress, the Supreme Court and the state legislatures begin with a prayer and every civil trial requires witnesses to swear an oath—to tell the truth "so help me God." Moreover, the state has always granted special prerogatives to the churches. Church property is not subject to taxation, for instance, and donations to the Church are deductible from the donor's income tax. Persons whose religion forbids them from bearing arms are exempted from service in the armed forces.

Throughout the history of the Republic, church and state have managed to coexist in relative harmony. In the last fifteen years, however, that harmony has been badly strained. The central government has burgeoned in size and with that growth has come a concomitant increase in power as court edicts, laws passed by Congress, executive orders of the president and regulations promulgated at a growing rate by the federal bureaucracy have placed more and more areas under federal control. In 1964, the Supreme Court, overturning more than 180 years of precedent, invoked the first amendment to bar prayers and Bible reading in the public schools—a prohibition that was soon expanded to preclude manger scenes and Christmas pageants in the schools—which injunction is, in turn, gradually being expanded to include all public places. Nor did this enforced secularization stop there. Values antithetical to parents, such as secular humanism and permissive sexual ethics, have been enshrined as part of the curriculum of the public schools.

Simultaneous with the secularization of public life has come the great liberalization of the churches themselves. In the Catholic Church, the change was, of course, begun with the "aggorionamento" of Pope John XXIII, the pope's attempt to renew the ancient church by opening the windows and letting in some fresh air. The mechanism for effecting this renewal, the ecumenical council known as Vatican II, brought together the church's bishops from around the world for two years of wide-ranging deliberation on matters of faith, morals, and the liturgy. The council accomplished a number of positive changes in the church's centuries-old and somewhat creaky structure, but the reforms carried a heavy price. A whole schema of change—the placing of the mass into the vernacular, the modification of dietary restrictions, the loosening of regulations governing convents and monasteries, the new emphasis on collegiality—was promulgated so rapidly that it left many of the faithful dazed and demoralized. An inescapable by-product of this change was the lessening of the church's authority and a

Gary Potter, founder and
director, Catholics for
Christian Political
Action

loss of respect and devotion on the part of the laity which was reflected in
sharp declines in the number of men entering the priesthood and monastic
orders and of women entering convents, and an equally sharp drop in the
number of Catholics attending mass. In the Protestant churches a similar
dislocation took place as the traditional emphasis on scripture and sermons
based on scripture gave way to a new emphasis on secular concerns such
as civil rights, labor relations, the Vietnam War, ecology and—in the case
of the National Council of Churches—energy. Ministers increasingly forsook
the pulpit for picket lines and talk shows; congregations became divided
and, as in the Roman Catholic Church, attendance at church services
dropped.

The trend towards social activism could be seen at its most virulent in
the hierarchies of the churches which tend, as is the case in the secular
world, to be staffed by a professional elite who are insulated from the rank-
and-file communicants. Perhaps the most bizarre example of this is the case
of the Society of Friends, or Quakers, a sect founded in England in the
seventeenth century which has been resolutely nonviolent over the centu-
ries, with its adherents refusing to join the armed forces or to support military

activity of any kind, even to defeat Adolf Hitler. In recent years, however, this philosophy has been perverted by the church's hierarchy.

Writing in the June 9, 1979, issue of the *New Republic*, Stephen Chapman noted, "From the founding of their religion, Quakers have stood against all war and violence. . . . An unyielding pacifism is not the only distinctive feature of the Quaker faith but it is the one that most clearly distinguishes them from most of their fellow Christians." Since World War II, however, this stance has changed considerably. Focusing on the American Friends Service Committee (AFSC), Chapman writes, "In recent years, the AFSC has shown an increasing disillusionment with the capitalist democracies of the West and a preference for Marxist governments and political movements, particularly in the Third World. In this shift, it has allied itself with any number of explicitly violent movements, making only the mildest demurrals about the means such movements employ."

Among the causes the AFSC has championed are those of North Vietnam during the Vietnam War, the Palestine Liberation Organization, and the "liberation movements" of Africa. Similarly, the AFSC has supported the government of Marxist Mozambique and spoken glowingly about conditions in North Korea. Indeed, Chapman states, "In nearly a dozen interviews with AFSC staff people, I never heard any of them say anything critical of any government that might be regarded as left wing." Instead, the organization's enmity is directed exclusively at right-wing governments. When Chapman perused an AFSC brochure on human rights, he noted that the only countries singled out for violating human rights were Argentina, Brazil, Chile, Ethiopia, Indonesia, Iran (under the Shah), Nicaragua, the Philippines, South Korea, Thailand and Uruguay. All except Ethiopia were right-wing governments at the time, and Ethiopia was in the process of becoming a Marxist state.

A similar situation obtains in the United Methodist Church, which has staked out a number of leftist political groups in Washington. One of them, the Indochina Resource Center (IRC), worked aggressively on behalf of Hanoi's cause during the Vietnam War, and even long after the war had ended and the governments of Vietnam and Cambodia were coming under growing criticism around the world for their killings, repression, and torture, IRC spokesmen Don Luce and Gareth Porter resolutely defended the regimes. The United Methodist Church also underwrites the activities of the Washington Office on Latin America (WOLA), a far-left think tank that has consistently supported leftist groups such as the Nicaraguan Sandinista Liberation Front, while apologizing for leftist terrorist groups and Fidel Castro's subversive enterprises.

Typically these political groups have only tenuous ties with the religious inclinations of the churches that are supporting them, and most members of these denominations are not even aware that their churches are funding these groups. I recall an interesting illustration of this anomaly occurring in the spring of 1975 when the House Armed Services Committee held hearings on aid to South Vietnam. One of the people testifying was IRC's Gareth Porter, who identified his group as being a project of the United Methodist Church. After a considerable amount of testimony in which Porter defended Hanoi and attacked the evils of the Thieu regime, one congressman asked him if it was really true that the IRC was supported by the United Methodist Church. When Porter assured him that that was the case, the congressman said, "Well, if that's true I'm going to have to change denominations."

The subversion of denominational principles can be seen on a larger scale in the actions of the National Council of Churches (NCC), the organization that purports to represent thirty-two Protestant and Orthodox denominations with a ,total of over one million members. Over the years the NCC has garnered a great deal of controversy by such actions as supporting the World Council of Churches' move to send $2 million worth of grain to North Vietnam in the spring of 1978—at a time when the Hanoi regime was coming under increasing attack for its systematic repression of its people. The NCC also supported the decision of the world body to give the Zimbabwe Patriotic Front a grant of $85,000—despite the fact that the Front has publicly claimed credit for shooting down a civilian airliner and massacring the survivors and despite the fact that the front has attacked Christian missions in the Rhodesian hinterlands, killing nuns and students. Nor is this action of the World Council an aberration: total aid to African liberation efforts in the last decade total some $1.5 million.

The WCC mindset is analyzed with characteristic precision by columnist George Will who writes, "The World Council of Churches, a purportedly religious and relentlessly political organization is famous for both the intensity and selectivity of its indignation. It is quite polite in dealing with communist governments but catalogues 116 varieties of 'repression' in Latin America, including a form of 'cultural repression' described thus: 'Distraction of public opinion by means of football, sports events, etc., to inhibit attention to the grave problems of the community.' " Will contrasts this attitude with a WCC document's assessment of the Soviet Union: "From the day of its inception the Soviet state has attached great importance to the question of political rights . . . [which are] guaranteed by the right to vote and the right to stand for election."

Despite such outrageous propaganda, the National Council of Churches has been consistently supportive of the WCC's positions. Meanwhile, its own record, while less flamboyantly perverse, is outrageous in its own right. The Rev. M. William Howard, the NCC's new president, has, for instance, admitted to a "tremendous respect" for "liberation" theologians and has stated that there are political prisoners in the United States. The NCC itself has gone out of its way to condemn human rights violations under such regimes as that of former Nicaraguan president Anastasio Somoza while being noticeably reticent to criticize communist regimes. At its last convention, the NCC endorsed the Equal Rights Amendment (ERA) and the plan to deny convention business to those states that have refused to ratify the ERA—the latter a spiteful move that will have its most devastating impact on the waiters, busboys, taxi drivers, and other working people of the states involved.

Complementing the activities of the NCC church organization were the highly publicized actions of the leading religious personalities, men like the Berrigan brothers, the Rev. William Sloane Coffin, and Bishop Pike, most of them liberals or radicals. A good example is the Rt. Rev. Paul Moore, Episcopal bishop of New York, who ostentatiously ordained a lesbian as a priest. The bishop was meanwhile making his cathedral, the Cathedral of St. John the Divine, the nation's largest, available to all sorts of radical political groups, most of whom had nothing to do with Christianity and most of whose activities were in large part *antithetical* to Christianity. Reporting on one such event, the *Washington Post*'s Sally Quinn wrote, "The air inside the enormous cathedral was redolent of incense and marijuana. 'Anybody got any rolling papers?' someone yelled as Bishop Moore, in long purple robes and a cross of peace, stepped out between Charlie Mingus's amplifiers to speak."

Writing in the October 1978 issue of *Harper's*, Paul Seabury described an event at another Episcopal cathedral, Grace Cathedral in San Francisco, this way: "In 1971, during one nature ceremony in the cathedral, a decidedly ecumenical audience watched reverently as the poet Allen Ginsberg, wearing a deer mask, joined others similarly garbed to ordain Senators Alan Cranston and John Tunney as godfathers of animals (Cranston of the Tule elk and Tunney of the California brown bear). The cathedral dean was dimly seen through marijuana smoke, wrestling atop the high altar to remove a cameraman, while movie projectors simultaneously cast images of buffalo herds and other endangered species on the walls and ceilings, to the accompaniment of rock music."

Needless to say, such activities did not reflect the beliefs of the vast majority of the members of the churches involved. Feeling increasingly estranged from, and betrayed by, the hierarchies of their churches, the laity began to show their disapproval. Membership in most of the mainline denominations fell perceptibly, as did contributions, as the laity turned their allegiance elsewhere. For millions of Protestants "elsewhere" turned out to be the evangelical churches of "born again" Christianity, the Southern Baptists and other fundamentalist denominations. While membership in the

mainline denominations plummeted, the evangelicals were attracting converts by the millions. As the strength of these denominations increased, so
did their potential political power. One of the first people to realize this
was Phyllis Schlafly, long one of the nation's leading conservative activists
and the woman who almost single-handedly put together a coalition that
stopped the Equal Rights Amendment in its tracks. In her frenetic efforts to
organize anti-ERA forces in key states around the country, Schlafly cast
about for allies and workers. In state after state she found that her best
volunteers were the profamily members of the conservative, fundamentalist
churches. By 1976, Schlafly had formed a truly impressive grass-roots organization, and in the fall of 1977, when the International Women's Year
Conference, chaired by Bella Abzug, met in Houston, Schlafly staged a
counter rally across town whose 20,000 participants dwarfed the turnout
of the government-sponsored gathering. While there were isolated success
stories such as Phyllis Schlafly's, for the most part, the political potential of
the conservative churches was not realized. Such is not the case any longer,
however. Since the beginning of 1979, there as been a revolutionary change
in the political awareness among the evangelicals, a change manifest in a
host of new Christian political action groups.

Gary Jarmin, 31, the Washington representative of Christian Voice, one
of the largest of the new groups, pegs the birth of the new movement to the
IRS effort to make a religious school's exemption from federal income tax
contingent on the school's providing proof that it did not discriminate on
the basis of race. Jarmin, who was the legislative director of the American
Conservative Union (ACU), arranged for the ACU to mail a legislative alert
on the new regulation to the contributor list of the National Christian Action
Coalition. The mailing resulted in hundreds of thousands of letters of protest
being mailed to the IRS and members of Congress with the result that on
July 13, 1979, the House voted 297–63 to overturn the regulation. On
September 6, the Senate followed suit by a vote of 54-31. "This was a
landmark victory for Christian activism," according to Jarmin. "It is the one
issue which has done more to ignite the Christian community to get involved
than anything in the past ten years. That was the issue that woke up the
evangelical community because they are the ones who stood to lose the
most."

Since this demonstration of clout, Christian political action groups have
been springing up like mushrooms. Two organizations stand out above the
rest, however: the Moral Majority, headed by Baptist evangelist Jerry Falwell, pastor of the 16,000-member Lynchburg, Virginia, Baptist Church,
probably the largest in the nation. Falwell reaches an estimated 15 million
people per week via his "Old-Time Gospel Hour," a radio and television
program carried across the country. Executive director of the Moral Majority

is the Rev. Robert Billings, head of the National Christian Action Coalition which joined with the American Conservative Union to successfully oppose the IRS regulations regarding the public schools. Between them, Falwell and Billings have over 2 million names on their lists of supporters, and they are determined to bring them into the political arena to act against abortion, homosexuality, pornography, and in behalf of prayer in the schools, quality education, and other social issues of interest to practicing Christians. The other major organization is Christian Voice, a new group whose humble one-room headquarters in Pasadena, California, belies the extensive impact the group has already managed to have on the national scene. Formed late in 1978, Christian Voice already has more than 100,000 paying supporters and the support of some 1,500 clergymen including 300 Catholic priests. Christian Voice is essentially managed by a triumverate: the chairman is the Rev. Robert G. Grant, 39, a Baptist minister who runs tours to the Holy Land; the executive director is the Rev. Richard T. Zone, 29, a Baptist pastor; and the Washington representative is Gary Jarmin. Assisting the directors is an advisory board that includes some fifteen members of Congress, including Republican Representative Robert Dornan of California (a Roman Catholic) and Republican Senator Orrin Hatch of Utah (a Mormon). Although the fledgling group is struggling to get off the ground, its directors possess an infectious faith and optimism supplemented by considerable political savy that will stand them in good stead. Says Grant, "If Christians unite, we can do anything. We can pass any law or any amendment. Everywhere we turn, Christian values are in retreat. As Christians we are not going to take it any more." Jarmin agrees. "The climate is right. The Christian community is up in arms much more today than five or even two years ago. The government is so much more involved in our affairs—gay rights, abortion, pornography, drugs, sex, violence—people have become concerned about these things. Moral decadence is a very serious problem today, and politics is a big reason for these problems."

To reverse this situation, Christian Voice has launched an ambitious program. The budget for 1979 was $1 million and that projected for 1980 is $3 million. The Christian Voice directors hope to enlist a minimum of one million members including 7,000 members of the clergy. From the organization's office in Washington, Jarmin will monitor legislation moving through Congress that he feels should be of interest to Voice members. Once a month legislative reports will be sent to the participating clergy covering those pieces od legislation asking the ministers and priests to urge their congregations to write their Congressmen indicating their support or opposition to the bill in question. Emergency alerts will also be sent out when important legislation comes up on short notice. Christian Voice will also maintain a publications program including a newsletter which will be sent to members. Also planned is a political action committee which will make contributions to Congressional candidates that Christian Voice supports.

The program with the most potential impact (and the one with the greatest potential for controvery) is a moral rating of Congress which will rate each congressman and senator on his or her vote record on issues such as abortion, gay rights, education, and foreign policy issues such as aid to communist countries. According to Voice's Grant, millions of these ratings will be mailed around the country in the weeks before election time. Liberal congressmen are already upset by this and other plans of Christian Voice, and howls of protest are already being heard on Capitol Hill from Congressmen who feel themselves vulnerable to such an attack. Other critics of Christian Voice have sought to discredit the group or to pooh-pooh its appeal. For instance, Tom Gettman, chief legislative aide to Senator Mark Hatfield (R.-Ore.) opines that, "Their eclecticism will do them in. I'm confident they will have a difficult time coming up with a Christian consensus on any issue. They won't last long." Gettmen explains that "the gut issues today are stewardship of energy resources and disarmament."

Wes Michaelson, managing editor of the evangelical monthly *Sojourner,* is even harsher in his denunciation: "These people are leading thousands into the belief that God's purposes are identical to the purposes of ultra-conservative politics," he says, adding dispassionately that, "these programs are those of . . . violence, prejudice, war, militarism . . . and ultranationalism." He concludes that the conservative evangelists are members of a "shrinking minority."

The statements of Gettmen and Michaelson are symptomatic of the crisis that besets the Christian establishment in America today: Its hierarchy is riddled with leftist ideologues who are isolated from the thought of most practicing Christians. These are the types who will support a Rhodesian Marxist guerrilla who slaughters Christians, but will not support a black Methodist bishop who had the temerity to try to work with the white minority, a position that strikes most Christians as illogical at best and sinful at worst. Tom Gettmen's boss, Senator Hatfield, applauded President Carter's recognition of the Peking regime—a regime that has over the years executed hundreds of thousands of Christians, tortured and imprisoned millions more, and zealously persecuted Christianity along with all other religions—and the president's severing of diplomatic ties with the government of Taiwan, a regime under which Christianity is flourishing.

In January 1979, the National Religious Broadcasters had a convention in Washington following by a few weeks President Carter's decision to break diplomatic relations with Taiwan. During the luncheon the representative of the Taiwan Christian Radio station was introduced. The 2,000 delegates gave the man a five-minute standing ovation. Gettmen would probably have been surprised, but millions of American Christians would have instinctively understood and approved the action. And these millions of American Christians are the constituency that Christian Voice and other like-minded organizations have available to tap.

As Christian Voice's Jarmin explains, "The potential is just enormous. According to a Gallup poll taken last year, you have 50 million people who describe themselves as 'born-again Christians,' eighteen years or older. If you included children of these families, it would be far in excess of that. These 50 million people have traditionally not been very active politically. This is our primary constituency. These are the people we are trying to reach and activate. Traditionally, this group has one of the lowest voter turnouts at elections. To succeed, I think we only need to activate 10 percent of that group to have an enormous political impact. That's the potential. The key thing is that we have the most unique asset of any political group in the country and that is a Christian media network. Polls show that 47 million American people listen to some form of religious broadcasting every week, either on television or radio. There are 1,300 Christian radio stations; thirty-six TV programs; people like Jerry Falwell, Jim Baker, and Pat Robertson who attract a weekly audience of from 15 to 20 million. The great value in having this audience is that it is a very unique one. It is not your Johnny Carson crowd. You're getting people who have a very intense religious belief and interest. If inspired from a religious belief to do something political, they can accomplish tremendous things."

As Jarmin points out, one of the great assets of the conservative Christian cause is the well-developed media network that evangelical Christians have in place. One effort alone, the Rev. Pat Robertson's Norfolk, Virginia-based Christian Television Network reaches an estimated 15 to 20 million people. These efforts, moreover, are becoming increasingly sophisticated, utilizing satellites and other forms of advanced technology. The evangelicals have also shown an admirable determination to reach out to like-minded members of other faiths, and to avoid a narrow sectarianism. As a *Conservative Digest* cover story on Jerry Falwell's Moral Majority pointed out, Falwell's advisors include conservative leaders such as Paul Weyrich, an Eastern Rite Catholic, and Howard Phillips, a Jew. "All in all," the *Digest* points out, "there may be nearly 100 million Americans—50 million born-again Protestants, 30 million morally conservative Catholics, 3 million Mormons and 2 million Orthodox Jews—from which to draw members of a pro-family, Bible-believing coalition. . . . Overcoming age-old suspicions among Catholics, Protestants and Jews won't be easy, but threats to religious freedom make it necessary."

As conservative Christians have overcome their deep-seated reticence about engaging in political activity, scores of politically oriented organizations have sprung up. Among them are publications such as *Christian School Alert* (Washington, D.C.), *Intercessors for America Newsletter* (Elyria, Ohio), *Call* (Memphis, Tennessee), and *Christian Inquirer* (Buffalo, New York), and organizations such as the Rev. Dan Wildman's National Federation for Decency. Complementing Christian Voice and other new Protestant political action groups is Catholics for Christian Political Action, an organization founded in 1977 by Gary Potter, 40, a conservative Catholic layman.

The purpose of CCPA, Potter says, is to "educate grass roots Catholics on the important social issues of the day and to activate them so their voice will be heard and heeded." The organization has no connection with any official Catholic agency, and was founded for the benefit of the laity, although at present an estimated 500 priests are members. CCPA has intentionally steered clear of any involvement with the church hierarchy, Potter says, because "the bishops are undependable on political issues. They have taken stands in favor of the Panama Canal treaty and the SALT Treaty and in favor of sanctions against Rhodesia and the D.C. Voting Rights Amendment. Things like that are contrary to the views of conservative Catholics." Another difference: "The bishops tend to be accommodationists; we're not. We see two Americas developing. One is a moral America which rejects such things as abortion, homosexuality, government interference in family life, and efforts to weaken the natural bonds, the principles and beliefs that enable us to live civilly together. There is another America that is in favor of these things. We are actively encouraging the development of the Moral America. We are encouraging Catholics to act politically as Christians."

Potter says the focus of the group is on those issues that affect the family, issues that quite naturally include abortion, homosexuality, the movement towards secular humanism in the schools, etc. "But in the end, there is very little that doesn't affect the family. "Even matters like peace and war ultimately affect the family. We try to advance Christian interests wherever we find them, at home or abroad."

Thus, while CCPA has been active in the battle against abortion and for tuition tax credits at home, the group has also sought to focus public attention on Equatorial Guinea, a country which is 95 percent Catholic and whose Marxist dictatorship has been responsible for killing 50,000 people and making refugees out of 150,000 others. CCPA has already participated in an ecumenical day of prayer held in conjunction with Christian Voice and several other conservative Protestant groups on October 14, 1979, the day of the national gay rights parade in Washington, and Potter sees many more such joint efforts in the future. These new groups are working increasingly closely with the large number of "profamily" organizations and leaders that have come on the scene in recent years—organizations such as Phyllis Schlafly's STOP ERA and Eagle Forum, Rosemary Thomson's Family America, and Jo Ann Gaspar's *Right Woman,* a Washington-based newsletter focusing on family-related social issues.

It is, in fact, the threat to the nuclear family—posed by the abortion lobby, militant gay rights groups, and the permissiveness and moral relativism characteristic of the public schools—that has surfaced as the salient issue that has galvanized millions of traditionally apolitical Christians into action and into a new alliance with political conservatives. Reflecting on this phenomenon in *Conservative Digest,* New Right strategist Paul Weyrich writes, "I would go so far as to predict that the family will be to the decade of the 1980s what environmentalism and consumerism have been to the 1970s and what the Vietnam War was to the 1960s." If Weyrich is right—as I believe he probably is (at least insofar as domestic affairs are concerned), the 1980s will be the years of the social counterrevolution and the decade's leading activists will be conservatives.

Mid-American Mencken: R. Emmett Tyrrell, editor, *The American Spectator*

8 | COLUMNS RIGHT: CONSERVATIVE GAINS IN THE PRESS

In the salons of the illuminati, the state of Indiana is generally consigned to the nether regions of Yahooism, written off more or less as a vast cornfield peopled by unreconstructed bumpkins whose only cultural activities are church socials and grange meetings or cheering on the local basketball team or junior's prize-winning hog at the county fair. In these circles Hoosiers are seen as hayseeds who venture into the city (if one can call Indianapolis a city) perhaps once a year to take in the state fair or to attend the Indianapolis 500—the latter a tasteless and *declassé* spectacle featuring mind-numbing orbits around a track by noisy, souped-up jalopies driven by unsavory ruffians. In truth, even Indiana's champions make no claim of sophistication for their state. Columnist M. Stanton Evans, former editor of the *Indianapolis News* and himself a tireless celebrant of the "Naptown" lifestyle, describes a typical Saturday afternoon's diversion as "lying on the couch dressed in baggy pants and a sleeveless T-shirt devouring a package of Wonderbread washed down by a bottle of Big Grape while watching 'Roller Derby' on T.V."

Given all this Yahooism it comes to the continuous surprise of the elite that Indiana boasts one of the sprightliest, best-written journals in the nation. A miracle has transpired: In benighted Bloomington, like concrete pushing through the vast fields of impenetrable alfalfa, a mighty journalistic edifice has arisen called the *American Spectator*.

The magazine, originally named *The Alternative,* was founded twelve years ago by R. Emmett Tyrrell, Jr., then a graduate student at Indiana University in Bloomington. A native of Chicago, Tyrrell came to Indiana on a swimming scholarship. A young man of vaguely liberal views, he became progressively more disenchanted with the nihilistic shenanigans of campus leftists, and eventually he and a few friends decided to found an opposition magazine which they dubbed *The Alternative.* Unlike most of the other ephemeral student political journals that came and went during the sixties, the magazine has survived. Tyrrell remains at the helm as editor, and two of the original staff are still with him: John A. ("Baron") Von Kannon, 30, and Ronald Burr, 30, both of whom are styled "Senior Publisher."

Originally a sporadically published twelve-page magazine with a small circulation limited largely to Bloomington, the *American Spectator* has come a long way in twelve eventful—and sometimes perilous—years. It is now a 44-page monthly with a national paid circulation of over 20,000. Its success has been much greater than this relatively small circulation would suggest. Among its readers are such luminaries as Ronald Reagan, former Secretary of the Treasury William Simon, and Senator Daniel Patrick Moynihan. The list of contributors is no less illustrious, including such "eminentos" (Tyrrell's word) as Tom Wolfe, Irving Kristol, Nathan Glazer, and William F. Buckley, Jr., to name but a few. These writers and others of their caliber plus a host of new highly talented young journalists attracted to the *Spectator* have graced the magazine's butcher-paper pages with some of the best writing to be found in America today.

The growing prestige of the journal has also served to enhance the reputation of its editor who, at the tender age of thirty-five is in danger of being buried by more accolades than even he bargained for. He has received, among other awards, the American Institute for Public Service's 1977 award for the "Greatest Public Service Performed by an American 35 Years or Under" at a ceremony in the U.S. Capitol; he was chosen in 1978 as one of the U.S. Jaycees "Ten Outstanding Young Americans of the Year"; and in 1979 he was touted by *Time* magazine as one of "Fifty Faces for the Future" in a special issue on leadership.

Tyrrell's fame and talent have also opened up journalistic worlds far afield from Bloomington, and his articles appear with frequency in such publications as the *New York Times,* the *Washington Post,* the *Wall Street Journal, Harper's, Newsweek,* and *National Review.* He has written one book, *Public Nuisances,* a volume of essays excoriating a host of particularly offensive public figures (mostly liberals) from Bella Abzug to Walter Mondale, and edited another, *The Future that Doesn't Work: Social Democracy's Failure in Great Britain.* Bob Tyrrell would merit a special accolade just for the quality of writing he has brought the *American Spectator,* but his great contribution to the conservative cause has been in creating an aura of excitement and irreverent humor that has made his enterprise attractive to young journalists.

Tyrrell's headquarters outside Bloomington is a large old house named "The Establishment," and it has become famous over the years. For a while the house served as combination home for Tyrrell and his wife Judy, dormitory for the transient staff, and corporate headquarters for the magazine.

Staff of the National Journalism Center: *(seated, from left)* Kathleen Kilpatrick, Walter Olson; *(standing)* David Williams, Fred Mann

Columnists *(from left):* John Lofton, George Will, Patrick Buchanan.

More media men *(left to right from top):* Patrick Korten and Michael Kelly, founders of the *Badger Herald;* Herbert Stupp, editorial director, WOR-TV, New York; Brien Benson, editor, *Conservative* Digest; Anthony Dolan, Pulitzer Prize–winning reporter; Tom Bethell, Washington editor, *Harper's;* Daniel Rea, weekend anchorman, WBZ-TV, Boston

The "old Fogies" at *National Review (left to right from top):* Kevin Lynch, Chilton Williamson, Joseph Sobran, Linda Bridges, Paul Gigot

The editor and his wife (now the parents of two children) have since moved out, but The Establishment remains, its mystique enhanced with the passing of time, and no visitor to the *American Spectator* would dream of going to Bloomington without making the obligatory pilgrimage to the house, with its famous celebrity rooms. There is, for instance, the Gen. Douglas MacArthur Dining Room, the John F. Kennedy Bathroom, and a rat-infested cellar appropriately dubbed the Franklin D. Roosevelt Room. As I say, Tyrrell no longer lives in The Establishment, he and his wife having moved to a more commodious eleven-room house two miles away. With them live son Patrick Daniel (named after Daniel Patrick Moynihan) and their bulldog "Irving Kristol." The lure of The Establishment still remains, however. It is reported, for instance, that Senator Moynihan, who was the guest of honor at a cocktail party in the Tyrrells' new home, was not content until he had seen it.

Tyrrell's hero is clearly H. L. Mencken, the "Sage of Baltimore," a word stylist without peer, master of the putdown, and self-appointed scourge of those he tagged the "booboise": the small-minded busy-bodies everywhere who conspire to impose their intolerant views on the citizenry as a whole. In his magazine the *American Mercury*, Mencken flayed away with gusto at these national pestilences. Mencken's was a jaunty, irreverant, brawling, impudent kind of journalism—a free-swinging style appropriate to this self-styled "free spirit and child of the gods." Mencken and his era are gone, and it is unlikely that we will see their equivalent again. But the *Spectator* does the next best thing. What Tyrrell has done is to recapture Mencken's spirit—the joy of battle, the scathing put-down, the delight in skewering his foes. He has mobilized Mencken's arsenal and trained it on the booboise of today.

As *Dallas Morning News* critic William Murchison has perceptively noted, Tyrrell probably does not match Mencken's stylistic gift ("Mencken," he says, "could spin a sentence in the sunlight and make it glitter and sparkle like a Tiffany's bracelet"), but he improved on Mencken in a more important respect: Mencken's targets were selected totally at random, without the guidance of any coherent philosophical framework. Tyrrell, on the other hand, has trained his sights on the decadent liberal elite of the nation, a far more powerful and pernicious group than Mencken's bumbling booboise.

In 1979 Tyrrell published *Public Nuisances*, which brought together 27 critical essays (let us charitably call them) on the leading nabobs of liberal jerkdom. The temptation to quote is irresistible, and I hereby succumb:

—Bella Abzug: Her autobiography "suggested the collaboration of a J. Walter Thompson ad hack and a mass murderer."

—Teddy Kennedy and the "Camelot Buncombe": "Camelot is the pornography of American politics, always promising the unattainable and rendering those who participate inflamed, infantile and ludicrous."

—Andrew Young: "A popinjay of nigh unto constant fluency."

—And finally, my favorite, John Kenneth Galbraith: "It is suggestive of the rich times in which we dwell that America's preeminent boomer of socialism, egalitarianism and an end to hypocrisy in high places is a millionaire economist and *bon vivant*, an erstwhile Harvard prof who winters in the Alps midst the rich and powerful. When at home, he upbraids 'The Establishment' for an honorarium that would make Norman Thomas blush, occasionally harangues students, and otherwise devotes himself to huckstering flyblown treatises that are snickered at by all serious economists even as they are snatched up as Book of the Month Club selections. . . . He is to economics what Harold Robbins is to the novel."

Tyrrell also is adept at exposing institutionalized hypocrisy. Consider for instance this description of a United Nations conference:

My own favorite moment came in 1974, when the worthies of 130 countries gathered in Rome for a World Food Conference, urgently called to rescue 500 million people from imminent starvation in India, Bangladesh, Pakistan, and sub-Saharan Africa. At the conference's initial briefing, one of the first questions asked was "Where do we eat?" So vigorously did the delegates discuss international hunger at their first session that within an hour of its adjournment they had totally exhausted the cafeteria's supply of plates and silverware. Soon there was even North-South confrontation. Two African delegates, suspecting exploitation by the Italian waiters, marshaled support from Third World allies and led a valiant effort to force the neocolonial waiters to fill coffee cups to the brim rather than halfway, as is Roman custom. According to press reports, the delegates divided their time about equally between quibbling and haranguing, sight-seeing and eating. They devoured vast quantities of Scotch smoked salmon, fettuccine with truffles, prosciutto with melon, and Chateaubriand. The posted menu at the conference center offered gastronomes a choice of four kinds of pasta, four kinds of meat, two vegetables, dessert, plus wines, beer, mineral water, and cola. And when the last anti-Western tirade had been delivered, the mob jetted homeward, the United States sent wheat to the famished areas, and eventually it rained.

Even many liberals confess to a morbid fascination with Tyrrell's "piranha mind" (Robert Novak's term), but occasionally the tolerant facade collapses. For instance, Frank Getlein, reviewing *Public Nuisances* for the *Washington Star,* is driven to mimic Tyrrell's over-hyperbolic style in order to express his contempt adequately: "R. Emmett Tyrrell Jr. is a semi-professional lout, oaf, bumpkin and buffoon who beats on his betters in his sleazy little far-right rag presumptiously called *The American Spectator.*"

Getlein's outrageous verbiage does serve to make his point, however, namely that Tyrrell's sledgehammer approach constitutes rhetorical overkill, a cloying tendency at times and one that tends to sometimes create sympathy for his victims. Yet, as Aram Bakshian pointed out in the *Wall Street Journal*. "In an age when the very conventions are excessive and public figures tend to shallowness, vulgarity and absurdity, delicate satire is a near impossibility."

Another minor flaw is Tyrrell's subordination of substance to style, a tendency that makes him fawn over such neoconservatives as Irving Kristol, who once belonged to the ranks of the fashionable liberal elite and who still have clout with them. It is style over substance when Tyrrell pants over the thought of a presidential candidacy by Senator Moynihan, a man of Gaelic charm and marvelous wit and rhetoric, but whose record (especially in the Senate) has been one of ADA-style liberalism.

These are small potatoes, however, beside Tyrrell's very real accomplishments. More than any journalist since Bill Buckley, Tyrrell has injected a note of hope and excitement into a movement all too often numbed by defeat and disappointment. A whole gaggle of successful conservative journalists received their training, and in many cases their philosophical orientation, in the shabby yet lively office of the *American Spectator*. And the process goes on.

It is manifest that the conservative supporters of the *Spectator* realize its importance because year after year they heed the pleas to bail the magazine out of its financial crisis (the annual deficit is usually $150,000 or more). American conservatives read Tyrrell's magazine and see in it an oasis of hope in an otherwise dreary media landscape.

Another publication of great importance to the conservative movement is *Human Events*. Founded in 1944 by Felix Morely, William Henry Chamberlain and Frank Hanighen, *Human Events* was published for some years as a modest weekly news sheet concentrating on foreign policy. Gradually the publication was broadened to include domestic policy and politics, and by 1960 it had become a respected and influential fortnightly "house organ" of the conservative community.

Human Events really began to come into its own in 1965, however, when it was purchased by Thomas S. Winter (now editor), Allan Ryskind (now Capitol Hill editor) and Robert D. Kephart (formerly publisher). Under their direction, the publication's size was increased and its coverage made more comprehensive. Since the years of the Nixon administration, *Human Events* has been the most important conservative publication of record for the Washington political community.

Human Events and its editors have also filled all manner of auxiliary roles on the right over the years, one of the most important being that of providing a training ground for young conservative journalists and a forum in which conservative leaders could publicize their activities. *Human Events* has in a sense been the work horse of the conservative movement, tirelessly fighting its battles and reporting its activities week after week for thirty-six years. It is safe to say that most conservative leaders, including most of those mentioned in this book, have at one time or another been assisted in some way by "the national conservative weekly."

American conservatives have always had a complex about media bias, and, on the whole, with good reason, since the media is generally agreed to be to the left of the populace and in many cases—certainly in the television networks and the leading newspapers—this leftward tilt is quite evident. The hostility towards the press that had long seethed below the surface broke out into the open at the 1964 Republican convention in San Francisco when a surprised Dwight Eisenhower touched off a mini-riot with a passing remark in his speech about media types "who couldn't care less about our party." Television commentators sitting in their booths high above the convention floor watched bug-eyed and trembling as thousands of delegates and Goldwater partisans leaped to their feet shaking their fists and jeering at the august ladies and gentlemen of the Fourth Estate. This antipathy deepened during the campaign as conservatives bridled at alleged media mistreatment of Goldwater, and it simmered along at a lower level during the Nixon campaign of 1968 as Nixon tried hard to suppress his hostility towards a press he felt had been against him from the beginning of his political career.

The real explosion, however, came in 1970 when Vice President Spiro Agnew made his famous speech in St. Louis charging the press with being biased. That did it. Commentators from the Olympian Erik Sevareid on down palpitated with indignation. Editorial pages across the nation seethed with invective, charging Agnew and his "master," the malevolent Nixon, with perpetrating a fascist campaign to intimidate and throttle freedom of the press in America. Although Agnew unquestionably laid it on a little thick, he quite clearly had a point, and the press, moreover, tacitly admitted this by changing its ways. Although no liberal editor, publisher, newscaster, or reporter worth his salt would admit that Agnew's criticism was valid, there was a noticeable attempt thereafter to be more fair to conservatives.

Since the Agnew speech, many more news programs feature conservative spokesmen on the issues under discussion. Op-ed pages of the *New York Times* and other major papers are more open to conservative writers, and many more opportunities are available for conservatives to debate with liberals, including programs such as "The Advocates" on public television, "Face Off" on ABC's "Good Morning, America," NBC Radio's "Confrontation," and CBS's "60 Minutes."

To some extent the increased conservative visibility in the media is an attempt by the media moguls to be fair to conservatives in response to the attack by Agnew and others, but perhaps more fundamentally, it is a function of there being more articulate, talented conservative journalists around. As Edith Efron (herself a critic of media bias in her books, *The News Twisters* and *How CBS Tried to Kill a Book*) points out, the main reason the liberals have a stranglehold on the media is that so few conservatives choose to make the media a career.

Like Agnew, Efron has a case but there is, I think, a deeper reason for liberal dominance of the media. Most journalists, despite disclaimers, have a very high opinion of their profession—and of their own importance. Despite all the rhetoric about being guardians of the people's right to know and all that, the press has managed to apotheosize itself into a kind of select institution with privileges and immunities no other sector of society—except university professors, perhaps—would ever claim. This privileged position exists because the press is engaged in performing a sacred duty: giving the people the facts they must know if they are to make democracy work. Like all such sweeping claims of virtue, this one is overblown, of course. The truth is that publishers, editors, and reporters are human, and like everybody else, they have biases and prejudices. Despite protestations to the contrary, these biases and prejudices are reflected in the programs designed, in the subjects that are covered and not covered, in the facts a reporter chooses to use, and in the tone of an article or news clip.

Since media people tend to be somewhat to the left of the populace as a whole, it is to be expected that this bias will be reflected in their work. The mistake conservatives make is to attribute liberal dominance in politics to liberal dominance of the press. In reality, the press in a free society is a mirror not only of the news of the nation but also of the intellectual spirit of the times. Reporters do not create that spirit; they merely reflect it.

Prior to the New Deal, the press in this country tended to be conservative. Since the triumph of liberalism in the early years of the Roosevelt administration, the press has tended to be increasingly liberal as well. With conservatism increasingly dominant in the intellectual sphere, it is reasonable to expect that the press will start to become more conservative, and in fact, that is what is happening. As Washington-based UPI reporter Donald Lambro puts it, "There are unquestionably more conservative columnists, commentators, writers, broadcasters, editors, publishers, etc., but I've also noticed among my own colleagues, most of whom consider themselves liberals, that their views have become increasingly conservative in many areas."

It is a fact that the press is becoming more conservative, and in making this case I offer as Exhibit A the ferment at the *New Republic,* the flagship publication of American liberalism for the past fifty years. In a January 8, 1979, piece titled "New Republic Seen Shifting Liberal Outlook," the *New York Times* took a look at the changes at the magazine. The conclusion:

> Long regarded as an apostle of liberalism, The New Republic has in the last four years under a new editor made some pronounced shifts, mostly—in the views of many of its readers—to the right.
>
> The shift is most evident in coverage of foreign affairs, where the publication's current cornerstones include a strong defense against Communist governments and staunch support of Israel. But it is also noticeable on domestic issues, where the magazine has substituted what might be called a "critical liberalism" for its previous defense of old-line liberal institutions.

The *Times* reporter attributed much of the change to Martin Peretz, owner and editor of the publication for the past four years. Peretz, the article said, had had a "progression of views which in the past embraced such groups as Students for a Democratic Society but which now seems more allied with such Democratic Senators as Daniel Patrick Moynihan of New York and Henry Jackson of Washington."

Commenting on the *New Republic*'s metamorphosis Peretz says, "The liberal consensus has clearly broken up. We're not moderating our views to cope with realities, we're changing them."

Such talk is eminently disturbing to the associates of *The Nation*, the *New Republic*'s erstwhile confrere: "On domestic issues any definition of liberalism can't include the *New Republic*," says Blair Clark, a former editor of *The Nation*.

One of the reasons for Clark's chagrin must be Stephen Chapman, a young graduate of Harvard and self-professed libertarian who was hired as a staff writer in early 1979. Although a libertarian rather than a conservative, little that Chapman has written in the *New Republic*—or elsewhere—would be uncongenial to conservatives. In recent months, Chapman has blasted the Quakers for subverting the nonviolent principles of their sect by under-writing the activities of violence-prone revolutionary groups, recommended the abolition of the federally funded public broadcast corporation, and called for an end to subsidies to the deficit-ridden Amtrak system.

An equally profound change has come over the prestigious monthly *Harper's*. Though never as explicitly political as the *New Republic*, *Harper's* nevertheless was for many years a forum for the concerns of the liberal literary elite. Under the stewardship of editor Lewis Lapham that has changed, and the pages of *Harper's* now resonate with the incisive exposure of the foibles and prejudices of the elite inhabiting the Boston–New York–Washington axis. Although more iconoclastic than conservative, *Harper's* is now open to conservatives from critic Hugh Kenner to Senator S. I. Hayakawa and Governor Ronald Reagan. Washington editor Tom Bethel is an avowed conservative, and month by month his withering prose is focused on subjects such as the burgeoning wealth of Washington's bureaucratic potentates to the malefactions of the Department of Energy.

In the general circulation press, the conservative perspective has perhaps reached its zenith on the editorial page of the *Wall Street Journal*. Under the direction of editor Robert Bartley and a young aggressive staff, the *Journal*'s editorial page is arguably the best in the trade. Wide-ranging and incisively written, the *Journal*'s editorial page offers day-by-day the most cogent analyses of public affairs to be found today. Featuring a mélange of crisp editorials, movie and book reviews, regular columnists, and guest appearances by a wide range of writers and public figures, the *Journal*'s editorial page maintains a high level of literary excellence and readability which make the generally high quality tone of the *Washington Post*'s editorial page (and certainly the generally drab and numbingly predictable *New York Times* counterpart) pale by comparison.

Along with the *New York Times* and *Washington Post* editorial pages, the editorial page of the *Journal* form the leading triumverate of opinion makers in the country today, those most read by the most influential figures in the government and private sector. Being the page most consistent with the rightward moving spirit in the nation, the editorial page of the *Journal* bids fair to become the preeminent editorial voice in the 1980s.

The rightward shift of general circulation publications has been paralleled by—and in part caused by—the growth in the explicitly conservative media. All the major conservative publications of ten years ago are still publishing. William Buckley's *National Review* (circulation 90,000) is still going strong and continues to be a prime source of young conservative journalistic talent. Editor William F. Buckley, Jr., has always sought to nurture conservative talent, and today at *National Review* a majority of the editorial positions are filled by people under forty. Among them are senior editors Richard Brookheiser, 24, Joseph Sobran, 33, assistant managing editor Linda Bridges, 30, articles editor Kevin Lynch, 33, and book review editor Chilton Williamson, 32. They are all editors and writers of exceptional ability, and their prose contributions and deftly wielded blue pencils do much to make *NR* one of the best-written, best-edited journals in the country. *National Review* also boasts the services of contributing editor D. Keith Mano, 37, whose "Gimlet Eye" column consistently exhibits some of the liveliest and most original prose to be found in any publication.

Also continuing to thrive are *Human Events,* the weekly edited by Thomas Winter and Allan Ryskind (circulation 70,000), *New Guard,* the publication of Young Americans for Freedom (circulation 30,000), *Modern Age* and *The Intercollegiate Review,* the quarterly and monthly publications respectively of the Intercollegiate Studies Institute (each with a circulation of 30,000), and *National Security Record,* published by the American Security Council. All have grown or at least held their own. *Battle Line,* the monthly publication of the American Conservative Union has grown from a monthly eight-page newsletter with a circulation of 30,000 to a twenty-four-page-magazine with a circulation of 60,000.

In the ephemeral world of student publications, the longest-lived conservative publication is the *Badger Herald,* a weekly newspaper published at the University of Wisconsin. The *Badger Herald* was founded in 1969 by Patrick Korten, 33 (now an anchorman with Washington's WTOP radio), and Michael Kelly, 32 (now press aide to Colorado's Senator William Armstrong), as an antidote to the leftist-oriented *Cardinal,* the official university newspaper.

The paper was founded to replace *Insight and Outlook,* a monthly conservative journal founded by Timothy and Richard Wheeler in the early sixties. *Insight and Outlook,* in various incarnations, lasted for several years under a number of editors and frequently ran articles of high literary and intellectual quality. Korten and Kelly, however, felt that it was too highly intellectual to appeal to a broad audience. What was needed was an alternative newspaper that carried campus news, sports, and fine arts, and the *Badger Herald* was the result. Over ten somtimes tumultuous years, the *Badger Herald* has survived, as an oasis of feisty young conservatives in a surrounding desert of rote liberalism.

In the decade since it was founded, the *Badger Herald* has produced a lot of outstanding conservative journalists, says Tom Faber, 25, a former editor of the paper and now media director of the American Conservative Union. "At Wisconsin, the *Herald* was the only alternative to the off-the-wall liberalism of the *Cardinal* and because of that, we attracted a large number of students from the journalism school. I think we made a lot of converts."

The paper has also stirred up a lot of controversy over the years with such editorials as "Tough Commie Bites Dust," the *Badger Herald*'s tender eulogy published to mark the death of Mao Tse-tung, and "The Lavendar Menace," a polemic that prompted a near-riot on the part of the university's gay population.

Under the direction of chairman of the board Robert Rithulz, 26, and editor Mark Huber, 22, the *Badger Herald* is still staunchly conservative and resolutely independent, existing solely on the basis of advertising revenue and refusing even to accept the free office space offered by the university. In October 1979, the paper celebrated its tenth anniversary with a banquet featuring M. Stanton Evans as guest speaker, an event that attracted statewide media coverage and even made the national news service wires. Ten years old and stronger than ever, the *Badger Herald* promises to be around for a long time.

Besides the continued success of established conservative journals, there has been an explosion of new publications. *National Review* and *Human*

Events have been joined by a major new publication, *Conservative Digest* (circulation 80,000), a monthly published by the Richard A. Viguerie Company and edited by Stanford graduate Brien Benson, 37. The *Digest* publishes original material plus reprints of articles of interest to conservatives found in other publications.

Newsletters in particular have proliferated at an amazing rate. Among the larger ones are the *Kevin Phillips Report*, a fortnightly report on political happenings written from a conservative perspective; the *New Right Report*, a fortnightly published by the Richard A. Viguerie Company that gives an inside report on what is happening in the conservative movement; the *Pink Sheet on the Left*, a fortnightly published by Phillips Publishing Company and edited by Phillip Abbot Luce which provides conservatives with information about what the left is doing; the *Phyllis Schlafly Report*, a monthly that gives in-depth coverage to issues ranging from ERA to SALT; the *AIM Report*, a fortnightly published by Accuracy in Media and edited by Reed Irvine which details examples of distorted coverage by the major media; *West Watch*, a bimonthly published by the Council for Inter-American Security that focuses on events in Latin America; *American Relations*, a fortnightly published by the Institute of American Relations that covers foreign affairs; *Policy Review*, a quarterly journal analyzing public policy published by the Heritage Foundation and *Commonsense*, a quarterly public-policy-oriented journal published by the Republican National Committee; and, forthcoming, a fortnightly political newsletter to be published by *Human Events*.

One area of journalistic enterprise in which conservatives traditionally have been deficient is humor. The realm of satire, in particular, has been almost entirely conceded to the left. Of late, however, some promising developments have appeared on the right side of the ledger. One of them is a yet to be named quarterly journal of satire edited by Walter Olson, 25, a graduate of Yale University and now a director of the National Journalism Center, and Steven Masty, 24, a graduate of Hillsdale College and Scotland's Saint Andrews University. Assisting them are a part-time staff of Yale graduates: Richard Vigilante, 23, Lee Liberman, 24, and Charles Bork, 24. Articles in the forthcoming inaugural issue include "A Visit to (George) Bush Gardens" (tasteless food, nonalcoholic beer, colorless plastic flora and fauna); "The Slugs" a hitherto unpublished manuscript about bureaucrats in Athens by the Greek playwright Aristophanes; "Blunt Instrument Control," a piece about new government regulations to handle a "hard-hitting problem" by licensing wooden spoons, rolling pins, sash weights, and small plaster busts of Brahms; an analytic piece about Teddy Kennedy replete with water metaphors; a Li'l Abner–style comic strip about the Carter family; and "Ode to Mary Jo," a country and western ballad in which Senator Kennedy figures prominently.

As significant as the growing number of publications has been the shifting conservative attitude toward the press. A conservative movement formerly skeptical, if not downright suspicious, of the press has come to view the media as a prize to be wooed and won. Richard Viguerie, the "godfather of the New Right," is a prime success story in this effort. Viguerie has a story to sell: the impact he is able to make in elections and on legislation in the Congress by using direct mail appeals to a contributor bank of more than 4 million names. He hired a public relations firm to get this story out, and so far it has been a remarkably effective self-promotion effort. Major articles about Viguerie have appeared in most of the major publications of the country, and he is widely quoted by reporters on a wide range of political subjects.

Other conservatives have been quite successful in utilizing the media. The American Security Council (ASC), for instance, sponsors monthly luncheons for members of the press which feature guest speakers on a wide variety of topics. The ASC has also pioneered the production of television documentaries. These programs, stressing the need for increased national defense efforts, are then sold to hundreds of local television stations around the country—an effort that reaches millions of people.

This tactic has also been used successfully by the American Conservative Union which has produced and marketed two films on SALT II and one on the Panama Canal treaties. The ACU films include an effective appeal asking for contributions, and by using this device, the organization has been able to raise hundreds of thousands of dollars and add many thousands of members to its rolls. The ACU has also led the way in distributing columns expressing its point of view. The column "Conservative Outlook," giving the conservative point of view on a particular subject, is usually written by a member of Congress on the ACU Board. The column is then furnished "camera-ready" to a list of newspapers who have indicated a desire to carry the series. It now goes to over 400 newspapers, many of them small dailies and weeklies, with the result that, for a comparatively small cost, the ACU gets its message out to several million readers. This tactic is also being used successfully by the Heritage Foundation and other organizations.

Another new program of importance to conservatives is the National Journalism Center, a year-round program sponsored by the ACU Education and Research Institute and headed by M. Stanton Evans. The NJC brings college students interested in journalism to Washington for three-month terms. The students are assisted in finding lodging and are paid $100 a week to cover living costs. They are given a major research and writing assignment due at the end of the term, are assigned to cover stories and write them up, to meet once a week for a lecture by a media figure, and are assigned for six weeks to assist a conservative reporter, columnist, or editor in Washington. The program has been hugely popular and, since its inception in 1978, more than 100 students have participated. Moreover, many NJC alumni have gone on to take jobs with conservative publications.

Conservatives are making progress with the media partly because of greater media receptivity to them and their ideas and in part because of the shifting spirit of the times. But more important is the fact that more conservatives are taking Edith Efron's advice: they are entering the media. Nowhere is this more apparent than in the area of syndicated columns. The change has been nothing short of startling: a few years ago conservative columnists were a small minority; now they dominate the genre, and the three most popular political columnists today—William F. Buckley, Jr., James Jackson Kilpatrick, and George Will—are conservatives. Five years ago, there were few conservative syndicated columnists: Buckley, Kilpatrick, John Chamberlain, Ralph de Toledano, Victor Reisel, Holmes Alexander, Morrie Ryskind, and Jeffrey St. John being the most important among them. The intervening years have seen the emergence of George Will (Washington Post syndicate), M. Stanton Evans (Los Angeles Times), John Lofton (United Features), Patrick Buchanan (New York Times), William Safire (New York Times), Phyllis Schlafly (Copley), David Brudnoy (self-syndicated), William Rusher (Universal Press) Michael Novak (Washington Star), R. Emmet Tyrrell (Washington Post), and Joseph Sobran (Los Angeles Times). Two of these writers have been awarded the Pulitzer Prize for commentary in recent years: George Will (1977) and William Safire (1978).

Will is probably the best of the new conservative columnists, and indeed many would claim that he is the best columnist on the scene today, period. A gifted stylist, he seems to have been born to the metier of the column. To be sure, he has his detractors among conservatives—the result of his hauteur, his disdain for conservative-movement activists, and the fact that in 1976 he plumped for Nelson Rockefeller while panning Ronald Reagan, a more successful governor than Rockefeller and a man whose views are more in tune with Will's. Recently, however, Will's views have come to reflect a toughened conservativism and on most of the issues of the day he is likely to be on the front lines. Speaking of Will's gifts, colleague James J. Kilpatrick has predicted that he will be this generation's Walter Lippmann, a view that pays Will a high compliment in view of the influence Lippmann had and one that says much about the changing intellectual temper of the times.

Two other young conservatives are likely to become journalistic powers in their time: Pat Buchanan, 39, and John Lofton, 37. Buchanan has a gift for the tart phrase (Jimmy Carter is "this deracinated little man with his mortician's smile") and a good-natured cambativeness. These qualities have made him a popular columnist and that made his "Confrontation" radio show with liberal columnist Tom Braden so popular that NBC is syndicating it nationally.

Lofton, one of the most outrageous, wittiest men alive, made his mark as editor of "First Monday," the Republican National Committee's publication during the Nixon years. There he lampooned the Democrats (especially liberals) with such gusto that he increased the magazine's circulation from 20,000 to 200,000, making the party millions of dollars in the process. Vintage Lofton is his cure for the energy crisis: "All Department of Energy personnel whose last names begin with A through Z should stay home on odd-numbered days. These personnel should also stay home on even-numbered days." Possessing a quick wit, agile tongue, and a "loutish" disregard for the sensibilities of the poor liberal slob he happens to be opposing, Lofton is one of the best debaters in the country today. As a columnist he is the best investigator of the lot, a veritable bloodhound who ruthlessly pursues his prey by placing person-to-person phone calls to them and demanding that they explain inconsistencies, untruths, and dissembling in statements that have come to his attention. The consternation, hysteria, and profane comments that result frequently make superb copy.

Other examples of conservative successes in the media abound, but let a few suffice to make the point:

—Pat Korten, 33, former editor of ACU's *Battle Line*, is now the number one newscaster on WTOP, Washington's leading all-news station.

—Dan Rea, 31, five years ago a "penniless punk" found rattling around YAF conferences, is now weekend anchorman on WBZ-TV, Boston's NBC affiliate.

—Herb Stupp, also a YAF alumnus, is now chief editorial writer and commentator on New York City's WOR-TV.

—Jeff MacNelly, the 34-year-old cartoonist for the *Richmond News Leader*, is now nationally syndicated and perhaps the country's most popular political cartoonist. In 1977, MacNelly won the Pulitzer Prize for his work.

—Tony Dolan, 33, a former YAF activist and now a reporter for the *Stamford* (Conn.) *Advocate*, was awarded the 1978 Pulitzer Prize for investigative reporting.

—Alan Crawford has at age 26 already been editor of YAF's *New Guard* and a daily newspaper, the *Morgantown* (West Virginia) *Gazette*. He is now the author of a book on the New Right and a highly successful freelance writer whose articles appear in a wide variety of publications.

As I have noted, this list of successes could be greatly expanded, and it is likely to grow exponentially in the future. The media tend to mirror the spirit of the times—and that spirit is increasingly conservative.

Ronald Zumbrun, president, Pacific Legal Foundation

9 | CONSERVATIVES TAKE THEIR CASE TO COURT

The term *public interest lawyer* conjures up images of an ardent environmentalist bent on preventing the construction of a new dam, factory, or military installation. He is the consumer activist at a regulatory hearing striving to insure vigorous regulation of business by government agencies. He is at the forefront of women's rights litigation waging a continuing battle to prevent the erosion of the Supreme Court's abortion decision. He is the civil rights lawyer pushing for increased busing to achieve racial balance in schools or building an affirmative action program calling for strict quotas in employment.

Throughout the 1960s, non-profit legal foundations were a growing bastion of liberalism. Thanks to the activist Supreme Court under former Chief Justice Earl Warren, the judiciary became the primary battleground on which many controversial public policy issues were decided. The courts increasingly took on the role of the legislature, taking actions which were politically too hot to handle by elected officials.

The assumption of this authority by the courts was not without controversy. Constitutional experts argued that the increasing powers usurped by federal judges who are appointed to life terms, and thus never face the pressures of answering to the voters, is not the kind of democracy that the Founding Fathers had in mind. Nevertheless, Congress has been quite content to defer to both the courts and administrative agencies in making unpopular decisions. Administrative officials with imprecise goals given them by elected officeholders have enormous discretionary authority. Similarly, public-policy directives from Congress lose much of their force as they move through the administrative hierarchy. Public interest lawyers exert great influence at administrative hearings which shape many of the decisions. When decisions fail to come out to their liking they are challenged in court.

119

Legal Beagles *(clockwise covering both pages):* Daniel Popeo *(on right, with Sen. Barry Goldwater),* president, Washington Legal Foundation; Spencer Abraham, founder, *Harvard Journal of Law and Public Policy;* John Kwapisz, founder, Law Students for a Free Society; Harrison Fitch, president, New England Legal Foundation; Michael Uhlman, president, National Legal Center for the Public Interest; John Bolton, Covington and Burling.

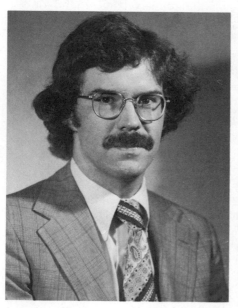

The "public interest," however, is an illusive—and probably illusory—concept. Due to the structure of this new decision making process, well-meaning judges necessarily look not to the electorate for the public's view but to representatives purporting to serve it. Unfortunately, the public interest lawyer has traditionally operated with a distinct bias—the belief that virtually all of society's problems can or should be remedied by government.

Contrast with this viewpoint a public interest lawyer dedicated to the preservation of sound economic growth, free enterprise, private property, and individual rights; one who does not believe that expanded government regulation should be inevitable but that a reduced government role is desirable. This is a widely held position in the United States. In fact, it is probably a majority position. Yet, until 1973, none of the approximately ninety public interest legal organizations operating throughout the United States represented this point of view. Among the civil rights activists, environmentalists, consumerists, welfare rights groups, and other special interest organizations, there was none that represented the perspective of free enterprise, balanced growth, and limited government.

Historically, public interest law was dominated by two organizations: the American Civil Liberties Union and the NAACP Legal Defense Fund. Then, in 1964, along came Ralph Nader. "Nader's Raiders," unchallenged and unbridled, had an immense impact on the growth of federal regulation by fostering the notion that the public interest demanded it. The Nader name is associated with over 100 consumer activist organizations, several of which are in the legal field.

John Bolton, 31, an attorney with the Washington law firm of Covington and Burling, traces the genesis of liberal dominance of the legal system to the famous *Brown* v. *Board of Education* case of 1954:

Ever since the Brown decision in 1954—and particularly during the heyday of the Warren Court—there is just no dispute that the role of the judiciary, particularly the federal judiciary, has grown immensely in America. The courts have departed from long-accepted standards of judicial restraint. They have been willing to decide cases in areas that had previously been left to the political branches of government and they have used their injunctive powers far more than at any point in American history.

In large measure, I think they set out on this course because of the political beliefs of the justices that were liberal activist beliefs. I think that legal doctrines were adopted sometimes with more reason than others to support those political beliefs and I think that the activity of the Supreme Court gave encouragement to a number of lower courts, particularly in the D.C. Circuit, that had similar inclinations to expand their power as well. That expansion of power occurred not just in terms of making new substantive law but in changing the rules of procedure in the federal courts, substantially reducing the effect of legal doctrines like standing, rightness and mootness that had led courts not to decide cases in the past. Standing is whether a person has the right to bring a suit, rightness is whether the suit is fit for adjudication and mootness is whether the controversy is still alive. Throughout the years of the Warren Court, those doctrines became looser and looser and more cases became possible and more decisions became possible.

The principal case that I would point to is Baker vs. Carr and the other reapportionment decisions where the Court, over the very strong objections of jurisprudential conservatives like Frankfuter and Harlan, really got right into the heart of regulating the political process, ordering states to reapportion legislatures, changing systems—for example, where the Senate of the state, like the Senate of the United States, would be apportioned on the basis of counties and ordering those bodies to be reapportioned on the basis of population, requiring very strict mathematical conformity to the one-man, one-vote principle—really writing legislation, I think, rather than constitutional law.

In criminal law, you've got Miranda where the court went so far as to write the little card that policemen carry around with them now—the Miranda warning the policemen are required to give suspects.

In other areas, the Court has not hesitated to suggest very strongly to Congress that legislation has to be worded in certain ways to be acceptable.

The Court has made substantial incursions into the separation of powers. *Powell v. McCormick* is a good case there. That was a case involving Adam Clayton Powell's claim to a seat in the House of Representatives where the Court, in the view of many, carved a substantial hole in the separation of powers by invading the purview of Congress and deciding its membership.

Paralleling this liberalization of the judiciary, and in fact contributing to it, has been the phenomenal growth of liberal "public interest" litigation— "public interest" being litigation brought out of philosophical motives supposedly in an attempt to further the public good, rather than for personal, self-interested motives.

"Obviously, the court can only act when it is confronted with a case," Bolton states.

In the 60s and 70s, there has been a substantial increase in what has been called (erroneously in my view) "public interest law." That covers a broad spectrum from the traditional American Civil Liberties Union-type litigation, to environmental litigation, to litigation under the Federal Communications Act, to litigation under any number of federal regulatory standards where you had groups of citizens with basically ideological goals in mind attempting to use the regulatory process to advance these goals. These were not cases where the regulators were proceeding against the regulated. It's a case of outside groups prompting or forcing the regulators to move in ways the regulators themselves had not contemplated moving.

"In large measure, this public interest law activity started during the civil rights movement—this notion that you could use the courts to achieve social goals. The civil rights movement found itself stymied time and time again in Congress in its attempt to enact civil rights legislation so they went to the courts. Other groups, almost exclusively liberal groups, saw that that type of activity was highly efficacious, and they adopted many of the same strategies and approaches as the civil rights movement. So, it began in the fifties and really came to flower in the mid- and late-sixties and early seventies.

In John Bolton's view, the American Civil Liberties Union has unquestionably been the cutting edge in the field of liberal public interest law:

I think the ACLU has been the principle group responsible for the changes. They are both historically and, I think, at present, the most effective litigators of the so-called public interest groups. They have a network of at least 5,000 volunteer lawyers around the country. They have staff lawyers in only a very few cities with full-time paid employees with offices. They rely on private lawyers who volunteer their time on a pro-bono basis. They are very careful about the cases they take; they screen their cases carefully to make sure they have a good case before they bring it; they have effective lawyers who are able to litigate effectively, and they have been very persuasive and very successful in their litigation. They worked a substantial expansion of first amendment constitutional law, working principally through groups on the fringes of the political process.

Although I support much of the first amendment stuff that they do, I think they have also gotten involved in areas that I don't really see as being at the core of their interest—school busing for instance, which I don't see as having anything to do with civil liberties. I think it's very contrary to the notion of freedom of choice. They've been involved very heavily in women's rights litigation, and I don't see much there in the way of civil liberties. They have moved very extensively in recent years from being just a civil liberties group to being just a liberal group. For instance, they were very actively involved in the movement to impeach Richard Nixon. They just recently got involved in the nuclear power issue, saying that their concern is the civil liberties implications of the need to have guards and things like that for these dangerous nuclear facilities. The end result, of course, would be to prevent the development of nuclear power.

I would put the ACLU out in front. I think they have been the most effective and the most successful. One proof of their fundamentally liberal membership: once they got involved in the effort to defend the American Nazi Party and its effort to have a demonstration out in Skokie Illinois. They received 30,000 resignations from their members and suffered a substantial drop in the funds they were able to raise. Nobody likes Nazis, but then nobody likes the Communists that the ACLU always defends, and nobody resigns when they go to court on behalf of the Communists.

Bolton believes that the ACLU has been successful in part because of its strategy of focusing on the First Amendment and in working diligently to shape First Amendment law to fit its conception: that is, that the amendment provides absolute protection for political speech (which to the ACLU also includes matters of morals by which definition pornography is protected) but does not include commercial speech such as advertising, an area that the ACLU is only too happy to regulate. According to Bolton, the ACLU and its kindred liberal groups have been successful, in part, because they have a clear notion of what they want to achieve and because they have developed specific areas of expertise:

Many of these liberal groups are concerned with FCC; they're concerned with environmental issues—the Sierra Club, Friends of the Earth, etc. and they get to know the administrative agency that they're interested in; they become familiar with its procedures; they become well versed in the facts—if it's environment, they become well versed in the chemical and scientific facts; they participate in rule-making within that agency; they participate in adjudicatory proceedings within that agency; they participate in appeals from that agency; they go up on the Hill and lobby when new statutes that agency would be in charge of enforcing come up. They become totally expert in that field. Conservative groups have not been able to follow that pattern. They all seem to have broad mandates. As a consequence, I think they are spread too thin. As a result, they don't build up that kind of expertise the liberal groups have and as a practical matter, they can't be as effective.

Bolton's achievements in the area of public interest law are a good demonstration of how to put the ACLU lesson into practice. As a junior attorney at Covington and Burling, he approached the partners at the firm in 1975 with a proposal to represent then-Senator James Buckley and former Senator Eugene McCarthy in challenging the Election Reform Act before the Supreme Court. The act, an Orwellian document drafted principally by Common Cause, the so-called citizens' lobby, established individual and organizational limits on contributions to candidates for federal office, limited the amount of money that could be spent on campaigns, the amount of a candidate's personal money he could spend on his own campaign, and prohibited individuals from spending money in independent efforts in support of, or in opposition to, candidates.

Covington and Burling agreed to take on the case *pro bono publico* and a broad-based group of co-plaintiffs (including the New York Civil Liberties Union and the American Conservative Union) was put together. Oral arguments before the Supreme Court totalled almost four hours (a record) and the Court issued a page-long opinion (also a record). While the Court did not completely vindicate the Buckley group, it did strike down a number of the law's most important provisions including the limits on a candidate's personal spending and the prohibition against independent efforts for or against a candidate. It also found that the composition of the FEC violated the separation of powers act in that the members were appointed by Congress, and it ordered the FEC to suspend operations until this situation was corrected. Unfortunately, President Ford passed up a golden opportunity to put the FEC out of business by signing a bill that reconstituted it to meet the court's criteria. Nevertheless, the case represented a signal victory for conservatives, illustrating dramatically the possibilities presented by public interest litigation.

The beginnings of conservative public interest law can be traced back to a controversy in California in the early 1970's. In 1971, the state had a burgeoning welfare system on the brink of bankruptcy. Without some kind of reform, it was estimated that welfare would cost over $3 billion in combined federal, state, and county funds for the fiscal year 1971–72. The situation portended either gigantic state and local tax increases or the diminution of important public programs.

Governor Ronald Reagan appointed a special task force for the purpose of initiating massive welfare reforms. Its objectives included capping the spiralling cost of welfare; reducing the welfare rolls to those strictly entitled to benefits; reforming the state and county system for the administration of the program; requiring those able to work to actively seek employment; increasing assistance to the truly needy; and strengthening family responsibility. Reagan wanted to disqualify those who were not legally entitled to benefits while making grants more equitable and increasing them as warranted, to those eligible.

Accomplishing these goals required a combination of administrative, regulatory and legislative action. At the outset, liberal public interest groups launched a massive effort on all fronts to scuttle the reform proposals. Three separate statewide conferences, with about 150 attorneys in attendance, were held to develop a strategy for blocking the program. As a result of these meetings, eighteen major lawsuits were filed. However, almost two years later the state had prevailed in sixteen of the eighteen major attacks on the program, temporary and preliminary injunctions were overturned, and the legislation moved forward.

By the middle of 1973, there were 785,000 fewer persons on the welfare rolls than predicted in pre-reform projections. Taxpayers saved over $1 billion, benefits to needy families increased by over 30 percent including automatic cost of living increases, and grants to the aged, blind, and disabled were increased substantially following enactment. Yet, Reagan's program was an enormous success that almost never got off the drawing board. Reflecting upon the reform struggle, many legislators, state officials, and others saw that a balance in public interest law was desperately lacking.

Thus, the Pacific Legal Foundation (PLF) was born. It was a stunning twist of form when this public interest law firm opened its office in 1973 and took on the Environmental Protection Agency using the EPA's own mandate as the weapon. Nearly 100,000 acres of prime timber in the Pacific Northwest was threatened that year by the tussock moth. EPA and the U.S. Forest Service decided in the name of the environment that it was better to let the area be defoliated by insect infestation than to use DDT which was the only known agent that would effectively kill the moth. The attorneys at Pacific Legal filed suit arguing that by allowing the destruction of an entire forest, EPA was not following the will of Congress to protect the environment.

Before the case came to trial, the EPA relented; DDT was sprayed and the forest was preserved. More important, however, was the immediate recognition that the case gave to the PLF. Here was a non-profit law firm—serving the public interest—which fought against government controls. The case marked the beginning of conservative public interest litigation.

In 1969, the Congress, perhaps unwittingly, delivered a powerful weapon into the hands of the public interest law movement when it enacted the National Environmental Policy Act, NEPA. Under its mandate, the government is required to assess the "environmental impact" of every "major" federal action. This assessment takes the form of an "environmental impact statement" to be written by the federal agency reviewing the action in question. To organizations such as the Environmental Defense Fund, the Sierra Club Legal Defense Fund, the Natural Resources Defense Council or the Center for Law and Social Policy, these documents are a veritable gold mine of litigation. According to John Bolton, "they can always be challenged in court and when they are rewritten they can be challenged again." The object of the exercise is not to make a certain construction project more environmentally sound but to prevent it altogether. The long delays of a project often become so costly that it must be cancelled.

A newer arrow in the quiver of the environmental groups is the Federal Endangered Species Act used recently to protect the Tennessee snail darter from obliteration by a billion dollar dam project. The partly built dam stands as a lasting monument to the environmentalists' notion of the "public interest."

Much to their consternation, however, laws such as the Endangered Species Act and the NEPA can prove to be two-edged swords that can be wielded against environmentalists as well as developers. The Pacific Legal Foundation recently filed suit in a U.S. District Court calling for rigid enforcement of the Endangered Species Act by the EPA and the U.S. Fish and Wildlife Service. It charged that the EPA's plan to stop ocean dumping through a five mile pipeline of waste materials which dispense nutrients and organic compounds into the Pacific marine environment was taken without regard for resulting harm to the food chain of the brown pelican, the California gray whale, and the El Segundo blue butterfly.

The EPA had wanted to convert the disposal to a land operation, a move that would cost taxpayers over $350 million. Los Angeles officials charged the action would present no appreciable benefit to the ecological system in the ocean. In its suit, PLF charged that the EPA had not ascertained the environmental impact of stopping the ocean dumping, nor did it file an environmental impact statement. It seems that the onshore site chosen by the EPA was near the only known habitat of the endangered El Segundo blue butterfly. Moreover, the EPA proposal would remove nutrients that support a fish population in the area estimated to be ten times normal levels. The fish are a vital food supply for both the brown pelican and the gray whale, the suit alleged, and any action reducing the fish level would jeopardize the two predators.

Environmental groups cried foul. "A clear abuse of environmental laws," grumbled an opposing attorney. But Ronald A. Zumbrun, PLF's director, said that the suit's allegations are no more improbable or unworthy than those made in suits brought by the environmentalists. The suit is now pending in the courts.

Challenging the EPA does not connote an antienvironmental position. According to Robert Best, Pacific Legal's 39-year-old head of environmental law, "The standards adopted by the EPA were done in a hurry. The air and water standards were not badly written, but in other areas, the laws are excessive and scientifically unsupportable." He points out that the politics of environmental law are a hindrance to the EPA doing a credible job. "With the case of the tussock moth," explains Best, "even though it was clearly the right thing to do, DDT was not politically acceptable to the EPA." Best contends that the political climate is changing, with the public becoming more sophisticated over the effects of environmental law: "The average person will not accept the issue from an environmentalist's point of view, and with this people are beginning to notice the trade-offs —the social and financial costs of stringent environmental laws. I think people are going to begin accepting risk-benefit considerations."

Since Pacific Legal opened its doors, it has won an astonishing 120 of the 150 cases it has accepted. The firm now has a staff of forty, including sixteen attorneys, a $1.8 million budget, offices in Sacramento and Washington, D.C., and plans to open another office in Houston in the near future. Critics point to the PLF list of contributors and insist that the foundation is nothing more than a front for big business. However, 65 percent of PLF's budget comes from small individual contributions and charitable foundations, among them the Lilly Endowment and the Hearst Foundation. The rest comes from cattlemen, farmers, progrowth interests such as construction labor unions and real estate developers, corporate law firms, and large corporations such as Southern Pacific Corporation and the Santa Fe Railroad. The same critics fail to point out that a large portion of funding for the liberal public interest law firms comes from business sources including the Carnegie Corporation, the Ford Foundation, and the Rockefeller Brothers Fund. The Ford Foundation alone has contributed over $20 million to various liberal groups. Environmentalist groups receive 54 percent of their income from foundations and so far no one has charged that they are a front for the Ford Motor Company.

Liberals argue that it is they who are outnumbered in the courts since it is often the business community they are fighting. They claim an organization such as PLF merely adds to the imbalance when it argues that business growth and less government regulation are in the public interest. Yet, as Covington and Burling's Bolton sees it, there is a fundamental flaw in this argument. "Individual corporations do not and cannot represent the 'voice' of economic growth," he says. "They represent themselves. The corporate lawyers working for General Motors couldn't care less about the adverse effects on Ford of a legal decision in which they are involved. In fact, if Ford got stuck, then all the better. The lawyer representing the corporate client operates on economic terms and is often willing to compromise a case in the interest of his particular client." Ralph Nader's lawyers, on the other hand, are motivated by ideology and never compromise their views. The corporate lawyer is indifferent if his case sets a precedent which affects those other than his client. The Nader lawyer cares *only* that his case will have a wide impact. The corporate lawyer purports to represent the best interests of the public but is regarded only as an advocate of special interests by judges and juries. The Nader lawyer purports to be a representative of the public interest and is widely regarded as such. The adversary process is perceived as that of the public good versus private interest. But, in the hands of Nader and his allies, the "public good" has become one of no growth, increased regulations, and, inevitably, higher costs to consumers.

PLF readily acknowledges that it represents business but adds that it also represents unions, consumers, property owners, and property seekers as evidenced by the following accomplishments:

It succeeded in striking down a proposed federal limitation on the sale of farm acreage and in California it is seeking to overturn a local ordinance which would deprive owners of beachfront property of their possession.

PLF also sued the powerful White House Council on Environmental Quality (CEQ), the top ecological arbiter for the federal government. Apparently, the CEQ, contrary to the law, had held no public meetings in more than eighteen months, during which time it had issued one sweeping order after another. According to a staff memorandum the CEQ had also fallen into the habit of conducting its affairs without a quorum.

PLF also recently filed suit against the Department of Transportation (DOT) for suppressing evidence on the efficacy and safety of air bags. The Department has mandated the use of "passive restraints" such as air bags on all large model cars manufactured after August 1983, a requirement that would add hundreds of dollars to the price of a new automobile. PLF discovered that when the DOT began thorough experiments on the efficacy of air bags, fatalities in accidents were running higher than official projections for cars so equipped. Moreover, nobody had taken into account the possibility that air bags would cause fewer people to wear seat belts and thus might actually prove counterproductive. Until Pacific Legal used the Freedom of Information Act, DOT had effectively suppressed a document known as the Kahane Analysis (after the government scientist who produced it) which alleged that the Department's claims about the air bags were both inflated and unsubstantiated. PLF has contended that, given the unknown hazards involved, including inadvertent deployment or malfunction, a car buyer should have the freedom to choose whether he wants to pay for air bags. Meanwhile, Ralph Nader's Public Citizen has counter-sued to speed up implementation of the mandate, an action which has been consolidated with that of PLF and is now pending.

In another celebrated case, PLF brought action against the California Department of Transportation for what had become known as the "Diamond Lanes Project." The Department had closed down one-fourth of the traffic lanes on the Santa Monica Freeway in Los Angeles to all vehicles not carrying three or more persons. However, the decision was made without determining the impact on the environment. Traffic had snarled, accidents increased, fuel consumption was up, and pollution abounded. PLF charged that the Department had failed to take into account that there was no public transportation alternative available to commuters. Following a seventeen-day trial, the freeway was put back into full use.

Pacific Legal Foundation, drawing on the Reagan experience, has been actively involved in aiding several states in improving their welfare programs, and has served as a consultant to a number of state governments including Illinois, New York, Pennsylvania, South Carolina, and South Dakota. PLF also instituted a computer checking system for fraud in El Paso County, Colorado, a system that cut welfare costs by 24 percent. The governor of Illinois requested that PLF set up a similar system in Springfield. The first spot check disclosed that of the 200,000 welfare cases examined, over 20,000 were ineligible. When news of the institution of the fraud detection system hit the headlines, 7,500 welfare recipients failed to show up for their checks the next week. In the first year alone, $34 million was saved.

Few who watched the televised presidential debates in 1976 were aware that, without the fast action of the Pacific Legal Foundation, the show may not have gone on. Independent candidate Eugene McCarthy and American Party candidate Tom Anderson had filed suit in a U.S. District Court to prevent televising of the debates unless they were included. PLF entered the suit arguing that the First Amendment's right to free speech protects the public's right to know and receive information about the candidates. Any attempt to prevent the debate would be an unpermissible restraint on the exercise of these First Amendment rights. The court concurred with the brief submitted by PLF and the show went on.

PLF was also an important participant in the famous Allan Bakke case. Bakke had been denied admission to a University of California Medical School because of a quota system set up to admit minorities. The Supreme Court held that, while minority status can be an important factor in the admission process, it cannot be the sole factor which freezes out equally or better qualified nonminority applicants. In effect, the Court held that strict quotas based on race are unconstitutional unless the institution has a clear history of discrimination.

While it remains the largest, PLF is by no means the sole advocate of the conservative point of view in public interest law. Another new entry in the field is the National Legal Center for the Public Interest founded in Washington, D.C., in 1975. President of the Center is Michael M. Uhlman, 39, a kinetic young Virginian who formerly served on the staff of Senator James Buckley, later on President Ford's staff, and who taught in the California state university system.

Uhlman is highly combative and makes no attempt to hide his scorn for the liberal competition. "The notion that liberal groups have some God-given monopoly on the public interest is a myth," he says.

Syndicated columnist James J. Kilpatrick beheld the Center's work in a column and found it highly pleasing:

> In the familiar image, the goddess of justice carries evenly balanced scales. In certain areas of litigation, chiefly those beloved by Ralph Nader, the scales have been out of whack for years. Now things are evening up, and it's good news all around.
>
> The National Legal Center for the Public Interest, headed by a ball of fire named Michael M. Uhlman, is providing a conservative counterweight to the liberal forces exemplified by such organizations as the Consumers Union, the Sierra Club, Common Cause and Mr. Nader's various fronts.
>
> Thanks to the Center, heavy-handed agencies of the federal government are having to meet an opposition with a powerful clout. The Jane Fondas of the anti-nuclear claque no longer have it all their own way.

Rather than being a monolithic national organization, the National Legal Center acts as the hub for several regional centers, providing them with backup services and research, expert witnesses and so forth, but allowing them considerable autonomy in choosing cases to pursue. As the success of the National Legal Center has accumulated, the staff and budget have grown apace. At the end of 1979, the center had a budget of $1.8 million and a a staff of seven. Needless to say, the center's adversaries on the left are incensed by this growth. "I think it's a detestable attempt to hijack real public interest input," the National Resources Defense Council's Richard Ayres complained to the *Wall Street Journal*.

Prudence would suggest that Mr. Ayres and his cohorts batten down the hatches. There is more to come.

The concept of decentralization surrounding the Legal Center led to the establishment of independent regional centers that could devote their full attention to the diverse issues and problems associated with their areas. Local community leaders could thus take an active role in advocating their perception of the public interest, and this would carry more weight in local courtrooms. When important issues arise in the federal sector that affect a particular region, the Legal Center can refer them to the appropriate office for potential litigation.

Currently, there are six regional litigating organizations affiliated with the Legal Center whose areas of activity, taken together, include most of the United States. They include: the Capital Legal Foundation which focuses on activities of key federal regulatory agencies; the Great Plains Legal Foundation; Mid-America Legal Foundation, Mid-Atlantic Legal Foundation; Mountain States Legal Foundation; and the Southeastern Legal Foundation. In the few years of their existence, these groups have become involved in hundreds of separate actions ranging over a wide variety of subjects.

In addition to acting as a back-up service center, the National Legal Center through its scientific and academic advisory boards has been able to provide top-flight expertise when needed at local trials. As part of its educational function, it has also established a legal internship program with the Dickenson Law School in Carlisle Pennsylvania and has sponsored a number of significant conferences attracting some of the nation's leading judges, scholars and commentators on legal affairs.

One of the fastest growing regional offices is the Mountain States Legal Foundation located in Denver and serving states from Montana to New Mexico. Along with the American Conservative Union's Stop OSHA Project, Mountain States was instrumental in raising funds and arguing *Marshal* v. *Barlow,* a case challenging random warrantless searches of businesses by agents of the Occupational Safety and Health Administration (OSHA). Bill Barlow, the owner of a small heating and plumbing firm in Pocatello, Idaho, had, despite threats of jail, refused to allow government agents onto his premises until they secured a proper search warrant from a judge or magistrate. The case argued that the same Fourth Amendment right which prevents government agents and policemen from searching the business of an illegal narcotics trafficker or the home of a terrorist organization should apply to businessmen as well. The Supreme Court agreed in a landmark decision, and ordered OSHA to institute procedures for obtaining warrants or cease operations.

While several cases involving the Mountain States office have had an immediate national impact, going all the way to the Supreme Court, the main thrust of the foundation is directed at more local matters. Thus, when several environmentalist groups brought suit in Washington, D.C., challenging the adequacy of an environmental impact statement concerning the proposed Foothills Water Treatment Facility near Denver, Mountain States was quick to intervene. After three years of costly litigation, the water project will proceed as planned. However, the penalty of hundreds of thousands of dollars in construction costs and attorneys' fees incurred by the state of Colorado as a result of the environmentalists delaying tactics will be passed on to the consumer, according to the Mountain States spokesman.

One of the largest undertakings of the Mountain States Legal Foundation was the filing of a case challenging the Secretary of Interior's right to withdraw 62 million acres of land from public access without the consent or approval of Congress. The suit involves the U.S. Forest Service's RARE II program which would take lands now used for recreation, timber, minerals, oil, and gas and prohibit vehicles of any kind (including the family automobile) from entering upon them. The proposal would quadruple the acreage in the U.S. under such restrictions. The purpose of the case is to shift the decision making from bureaucrats to the Congress which has a broader overview of the nation's interests in jobs, energy, family recreation, and economic development as well as environmental concerns.

Under the Davis-Bacon Act, which has been on the books since depression times, contractors must pay prevailing area rates, as determined by the Secretary of Labor, on federal construction projects and most local projects where federal funds are involved. The 1931 Act was aimed at protecting local construction workers from transients willing to work for next to nothing. Today, however, the Labor Department is notorious for using the Act to mandate top union rates, including fringe benefits, as the "prevailing" rates for construction. As a result, unskilled laborers, happy to work for $5 an hour, must be paid $12.40 an hour in a recent example. The skilled worker, of course, gets similar treatment leading to pay scales that go far afield of the average wage. The upshot of this practice is that potential construction projects become unaffordable and workers become unemployed. For the projects that are built, the inflationary impact of the regulation is enormous. Moreover, by forcing contractors to pay premium wages on government jobs, the Labor Department makes it difficult for those same contractors to pay their crews less on private construction. Estimates are that the law adds $17 billion to the annual cost of construction. The Government Accounting Office has urged its repeal. Even the *New York Times* has denounced the Act as unjustified and inflationary, but efforts to amend the Act have been stymied under pressure by big labor. Ever since passage of the Davis-Bacon Act, Labor Secretaries have insisted—and the Supreme Court seemed to reaffirm—that their determination of wage levels was subject neither to administrative nor judicial review. However, the Southeastern Legal Foundation, together with the State of Virginia, had a different notion, and the authority of the secretary of labor has been successfully challenged for the first time in forty-eight years. In a landmark decision, a U.S. court of appeals held that the decisions regarding minimum wages are reviewable by the courts. The decision means the Labor Department must end its arbitrary refusal to approve standard rates.

The Southeastern Legal Foundation, located in Atlanta, was the first regional office set up under the National Legal Center. Like its sister foundations, Southeastern will accept no payment from the parties it defends. It relies on private contributions and foundation grants. Headed by former Rep. Ben Blackburn, a Georgia Congressman for eight years, Southeastern's casebook reads almost like the headlines of the daily newspaper. Its eclectic selection of legal topics includes environment, nuclear power, discrimination, farming, government regulations, and individual rights to privacy. "Before the Southeastern Legal Foundation participates in a case, its participation must be approved by its board of legal advisors," according to legal director Wayne Elliott. They use a panel of distinguished attorneys from ten surrounding states who serve without compensation. The pattern is one followed by each of the regional public interest firms.

Another sprouting organization is the New England Legal Foundation, formed in 1977 and located in Boston. Its articulate director, Harrison A. Fitch, is a leading area spokesman for balanced economic growth. At age 35, he sees himself pitted in a David-and-Goliath-like confrontation in the public interest legal arena.

"There was a feeling," says Fitch, "that public interest law had been left to the Ralph Naders, the Sierra Clubs, and the Common Causes. We are hoping to erase that bias. We are not hired guns for business and industry. We are thinking about people like the neighborhood store owner, the energy consumer, the taxpayer, the unemployed."

The New England Legal Foundation recently filed a brief supporting the development of a fifty-acre industrial park near Lebanon Regional Airport in Massachusetts. The project also calls for improvements in the airport's runways and moving the terminal to a safer location. Several environmental groups have sued to stop the project. "This is just one instance out of thousands where the antis," as Fitch refers to his opposition, "seek to systematically prevent business development in our area. You have to walk across an active airport to get to your plane at that airport but, if the project represents growth, the environmentalists will try to stop it," says Fitch.

"There's a substantial feeling that business has a lot of money," Fitch continues. "But the finances of the Sierra Club and others make them very powerful and well-financed organizations. And they've been in court without substantial opposition for well over a decade. When we sought a grant from the Ford Foundation, they turned us down flat." Even if the new legal foundations can match the financial resources of their adversaries, they often are at a disadvantage in arguing their position in court, according to Fitch. "It's hard to say we need jobs and profits when someone else is saying you're polluting our rivers," he said. "It's our job to tell the court that you can balance both environmental interests and economic concerns."

Fitch claims that the foundation's most significant contribution to date was in the area of First Amendment rights. The suit involved a Massachusetts law which prohibited corporations from financing campaigns on public referendums. Other groups, including labor unions were exempt from the restriction. In a departure from normal practice, the U.S. Supreme Court cited the New England Legal Foundation's brief in overturning the law. Hailing the high court's decision, Fitch said, "It was certainly a defeat for those who would place prior restraint on the free flow of information in society. I think the reaction from groups which said it was a defeat for consumers is plain wrong. That position assumes that only what consumer advocates think is appropriate is what consumers should hear."

Another bright star on the legal horizon is the Great Plains Legal Foundation (GPLF) headed by former Missouri Governor Christopher ("Kit") Bond. Elected in 1973, Bond, at age 33, was the youngest governor in Missouri history. He finds his new position no less challenging. "The people who founded the Great Plains Legal Foundation saw that many of the important decisions involving government regulations are made in the courts," says Bond. "And that is our entire focus. The judiciary has become an important force in the economic and social policies in this country."

Located in Kansas City, GPLF serves much of the farm belt and is particularly well-suited to fighting the cause of the farmer. "More federal dollars are spent in the regulation of agriculture and agribusiness than any other industry," according to Bond. More than $350 million are spent each year in paperwork done for agricultural regulations. This puts a lot of pressure on the farmer. Bond claims the plight of the farmer is serious. "The number of farmers is decreasing and so their political power is cut. It is up to those of us who know and understand agriculture to do a better job of informing regulators about the burdens that regulatory red tape causes farmers and the costs consumers ultimately bear," he says.

"The area that has been overlooked is the judicial system and the regulatory agencies," Bond contends. "Many of the regulations are passed by the agencies and then reviewed by the courts. Elected officials are not involved in the process. It has been said that the legislature purposely passes bills that are general and leaves it up to the courts and the agencies to battle it out to see who is to get hurt."

A major GPLF victory involved getting the Food and Drug Administration (FDA) to back off its proposal to require a veterinarian's prescription in order for a farmer to add antibiotics to animal feed. Producers use feed with antibiotics to control disease and promote weight gain in the animal. FDA announced its ban because of a theoretical concern that the use of anti-biotics might lead to the development of bacteria resistant to them. Yet, there had been no clinical proof of FDA's suspicion, even though these drugs have been repeatedly tested for the twenty-five years they have been used in animal feed. Representing pork, cattle and poultry producers, GPLF argued that if all antibiotics were banned, it would take substantially more feed and more energy to produce the same amount of meat. In the end, consumers would have paid $1.6 billion more as a result of higher prices for a smaller supply.

In another case, GPLF, among others, was instrumental in battling the sugar industry by getting a postponement of the FDA's proposal to ban saccharin. Called by press accounts the "most singularly potent opponent of the saccharin ban," GPLF contended that the food additive is an essential means of controlling diets of the millions of diabetics throughout the country as well as those with obesity and other sugar-related medical conditions. It was found that even if the FDA's theory that saccharin can cause cancer was correct, the number of deaths caused by an increase in calorie intake alone in the American diet as a result of banning saccharin would be more than ten-fold FDA's estimate of cancer deaths. According to Kit Bond, this is a good example of the "tunnel vision" with which regulatory agencies approach their tasks. "There has been no real effort in agencies to weigh the supposed benefits against the real costs of regulations to the public," said Bond.

An integral part of the law long associated with liberal public interest organizations is the criminal area. Unfortunately, while great strides have been made toward protecting the legal rights of criminals and the criminally accused, the victims of crime are the most neglected in our criminal justice system. Americans for Effective Law Enforcement (AELE) is one of the few nonprofit citizens organizations dedicated to representing the rights of law-abiding citizens and the victims of crime. Operating out of offices in Ev-anston, Illinois, and Virginia Beach, Virginia, AELE is leading the activity in a new and rapidly developing field of law in which crime victims are suing third parties, including government agencies, whose negligence has caused them to be victimized. Frank Carrington, executive director of AELE, gives the following examples:

The warden of a Washington State penitentiary conceives a "take-a-lifer-to-dinner" program without legislative authority to do so. A life termer with a record of some 40 felony convictions and 17 escape attempts leaves the walls to go to dinner with a prison baker, escapes, and murders the plaintiff's husband in the course of an armed robbery. She sues the state of Washington and the warden and recover $186,000.

An Arizona convict with a long felony record is released by the parole board after serving one-third of his sentence, despite a warning from the prison psychiatrist that he is dangerous and will probably commit more crimes. He murders the plaintiff's decedent and wounds another in an armed robbery. They sue the parole board members for negligent release. The Arizona Supreme Court holds that the defendants are not immune and must stand trial on the negligence issue.

A California Youth Authority parolee with a record of violent antisocial acts is negligently placed in a completely unsuitable foster home and is left unsupervised by the parole authorities. He beats the plaintiff's 10-year-old son almost to death. The parents sue the state; the California Court of Appeals rules that the state is not immune from an action for negligent failure to supervise, and the state settles the case for $265,000.

Cases such as these do not necessarily represent "majority" law at this time, according to Carrington. Many courts are reluctant to "second guess" the actions and dispositions of correctional and other custodial authorities on the theory that if liability is upheld, the discretion of custodial officials will be impaired and qualified persons will be afraid to make value decisions. However, there comes a point where the discretion of authorities becomes an abuse of discretion which should not be tolerated. Immunity from the law fosters negligence. Yet many victims' rights lawsuits have been lost because of the doctrine of sovereign immunity afforded government employees and agencies. With the help of AELE some very novel and ingenious legal theories were devised to break through this immunity, bringing success to victims' rights litigators. The result is that officials have been put on notice that unless reasonable care is taken with regard to the release of criminals, they can be held accountable. Third-party victims' rights litigation has built into it the very salutary aspect of preventing future victimization of the innocent by the criminals. It would be redundant to cite statistics demonstrating the intolerable domestic problem of violent crimes repeated by those who were once in custody. A concept which might prevent further victimization thus has important public policy rationale going for it.

Americans for Effective Law Enforcement acts as a clearinghouse of information for attorneys interested in victims rights. It has intervened in several of the leading cases in the area, and staff attorneys have lectured to over 100 different agencies and legislative bodies on the topic. Its data bank of court decisions, briefs, memoranda, trial tactics and empirical data used in victims' rights litigation is available, gratis, to attorneys on request.

Says Carrington, "In the present state of the law, the victims' rights litigator will not find the going particularly easy. Still, the opportunity to serve the two-fold purpose of vindicating the rights of the specific victim via the civil law process and the added feature of preventing future victimization through example should make this area of litigation attractive to the trial bar."

If conservative effort has been missing over the years in the area of public interest law, this is equally pervasive and probably a significant result of a lack of balance in law schools. While law students are mirroring society in a move to the right today, such trends are difficult to find among faculties. Throughout the country, law professors and their associates, many of whom graduated in the sixties and early seventies, are far more liberal than their students. There is a common disdain in academia for the moderate Supreme Court under Justice Warren Burger and a yearning for the activist Court of Justice Earl Warren. The same Burger court which translated the constitutional right to due process into the right to have an abortion and ordered the busing of schoolchildren across towns to achieve desegregation is condemned in our law schools as reactionary.

In the criminal area, the Center for Criminal Justice Policy and Management was established in 1977 at the School of Law of the University of San Diego. The Center seeks to improve legal education through a variety of innovative conferences, publications, seminars, and other special projects. It works closely with Americans for Effective Law Enforcement in assisting victims in obtaining legal representation for litigation, providing research and consultation to attorneys involved in victims' rights cases, and assisting legislators and legislative committees in drafting statutes relating to victim compensation laws.

Though a distinct entity from the law school, the Center's activities include direct participation in the training of law students by staff members and Visiting Fellows and the development of new law school courses. The Center addresses all aspects of the criminal justice system and offers a unique opportunity for conservative scholars and practitioners to meet on common ground. Utilizing their varying experience, knowledge, and perspectives, the participants mutually engage in problem-solving efforts and publish their ideas on a regular basis.

In Washington the increasing conservative activity on the public interest law front indicates that the possibilities in the field are beginning to be exploited although clearly there is a long way to go. Daniel Popeo, 27, the director of the Washington Legal Foundation, says,

There is a tremendous vacuum. The growth of public interest law—as we know it—is too slow. My fondest wish is that there was another 100 organizations like the Washington Legal Foundation. I did a list of organizations that were procriminal, "proconsumer," antibusiness, anti-small-business legal services . . . and there are literally thousands of such organizations. They are at the city, county, state, and national level and they have a great deal of money. Some of them receive a great deal of money from the federal government as well. Ralph Nader is not poor. As you can see, we have a very spartan existence. Yet, we're supposed to be the corporate shills. I don't own one share of stock. I've seen the tax returns on these other organizations and they own blue chip stock; they have certificates of deposit that are quite large. I think they've lost touch with what the real public interest is. I don't think they have any right to say what the public interest is.

Appropos the Nader empire, Popeo comments:

The Nader complex is huge. I could show you organization charts of the regulatory agencies and all of these people were at one time connected with one of the Nader organizations. There are two things that Ralph Nader has never gone after: the tax code, because he loves his tax exempt contributions and direct mail, because he loves to write his own direct mail and he uses it extensively. If you include the people in government jobs who have his seal of approval and the people in organizations that he directly or indirectly controls, I would say that he has an army of 1,000 public interest lawyers, overseers, scientists, etc. He has many scientific organizations that do nothing but test products and harass businessmen. The reason that our country's productivity is at the lowest point since World War II is because a businessman is not going to try something new when he's got a fool like Ralph Nader at his throat. Ralph Nader is accountable to no one. He is less accountable to the public than the bureaucrats who were never elected to public office. The name Nader has come to personify an antifree enterprise, anti-small-business bias.

Although founded only two years ago, the Washington Legal Foundation has begun to make a dent in the Nader public interest law phalanx. Popeo, a stocky, brash, free-wheeling zealot, has at the young age of 27 already displayed a sure command of his profession and a talent for publicizing his organization's work.

"We're going to look the Naderites, the bureaucrats, and the criminals in the eye. And we're going to tell them we've been pushed around enough and now we're going to start fighting back," Popeo told the *Wall Street Journal*. Then taking aim at his favorite target, Ralph Nader, he commented, "I think people are fed up with Ralph Nader. . . . People like Nader and Jane Fonda lead a very rarefied existence. They have no sense of reality."

The taunt succeeded in drawing a response from Nader who professed to be thrilled by the emergence of groups like WLF: "I find them very useful," he told the *Journal*. "Their positions outrage consumers even more than corporations. These guys are so bald . . . so brazen . . . they don't even couch their opposition diplomatically. We're delighted by them."

Nader's followup comments, however, indicated that the delight might be a little less than unqualified. Quoth Ralph: "My idea of a public interest lawyer is someone who isn't funded by special interests and who is guided by their conscience. Not these guys. They're in it for the money." Such reactions, of course, delight Popeo and company, giving them much-needed visibility.

The organization's profile has also been enhanced by some prominent cases it has taken on. One was a suit filed on behalf of Sen. Barry Goldwater and a group of colleagues challenging President Carter's right under the Constitution to unilaterally abrogate the U.S. mutual defense treaty with Taiwan. Arguing the case for the plaintiffs in Federal District Court was Daniel J. Popeo, 27. For the defense, the government of the United States, the chief lawyer was none other than the Hon. Griffin Bell, attorney general of the United States. The Court found the Goldwater argument sound on Constitutional grounds but concluded that the case lacked mootness since the Senate had not expressed itself on the Taiwan issue specifically. This objection was remedied later, however, by a resolution proposed by Sen. Harry Byrd (I.-Va.) and adopted by the Senate, that the Senate must concur in the abrogation of treaties and that this applied to the Taiwan case as well. In the wake of this action Popeo filed for reconsideration and in October 1979 obtained a great victory when Judge Oliver Gasch ruled that the termination of a treaty required the consent of two thirds of the Senate.

The case eventually reached the Supreme Court, which declined a ruling because of lack of mootness. Nevertheless, this was a dizzying brush with success at the peak of the judicial system of the United States, and it has galvanized Popeo to intensify his efforts.

Popeo has also brought suit on behalf of a number of members of the U.S. House challenging the transfer of ownership of the Panama Canal assets to Panama without a vote by the House of Representatives.

These high visibility constitutional cases are only a small part of the WLF case load, however. A main focus of the organization's efforts is in the area of victims' rights. Popeo wants to require parole officers to issue "victim impact" statements when releasing prison inmates, evaluating the impact of their release on society. If the released criminals perpetrated crimes, these "impact" statements can be used by the victims and their families in seeking restitution from the state. Such a regulation, Popeo believes, would make parole officials more cautious in releasing criminals—especially repeat offenders.

Despite its brief time on the scene, the Washington Legal Foundation has already had an impact. The staff—presently three full-time lawyers, two law clerks and two secretaries—is being augmented by the addition of part-time lawyers, and the organization recently moved to offices with triple the space of the old quarters.

One of the brightest conservative lawyers on the Washington scene is

William Olson, 30, an activist for several years with Young Americans for Freedom and the American Conservative Union, a graduate of the University of Virginia law school, and now the head of his own law firm. Though not a public interest lawyer, Olson has given generously of his time doing *pro bono* work for a number of conservative causes and has already handled a number of celebrated cases.

One of these was a suit brought on behalf of the Public Service Research Council (PSRC) against the U.S. Post Office before the Federal District Court for Washington, D.C., in late July 1978. The suit, which also named the AFL-CIO and several postal workers unions sought an injunction against the parties named from carrying out a threatened strike which would have paralyzed the nation's mail service. In his brief Olson noted, "Federal law provides that no individual may accept or hold a position in the government of the United States if he participates in a strike against the government of the United States. (5 U.S.C. 7311) The members of the defendant unions are employees of the United States to whom this statute applies."

Judge Gerhardt Gesell found the PSRC reasoning irrefutable and upbraided the Justice Department lawyer for failing to make such an obvious argument against the unions' right to strike. The judge let it be known to the defendants that should they choose to proceed with the strike, he would invoke the law's prohibition on their holding federal jobs. Under this threat, the unions decided to refrain from striking and a settlement was reached. The story on the Public Service Research Council victory received wide play in the media across the country.

On May 17, 1979, Olson, acting on behalf of the National Journalism Center (a subsidiary of the American Conservative Union's Education and Research Institute) filed suit again in the Federal District Court for Washington, this time against the Commerce Department. For two years, the NJC had been applying under the provision of the Freedom of Information Act to ascertain what American companies were selling what types of sophisticated technology to the Soviet Union. There is considerable evidence that some of this technology is being used in the manufacture of Soviet military equipment, some of which was used against American soldiers in Vietnam. The contention of the National Journalism Center is that the public has a right to know the nature of the technology transfer going on.

The Commerce Department balked at the request for the information, however, contending that divulging such information would be unfair to the companies involved and that such a disclosure was not included within the purview of the Freedom of Information Act. The NJC argued that it is, however, an argument that would appear to be manifestly superior as witness the fact that the Commerce Department subsequently went to Congress requesting a change in the Freedom of Information Act that would specifically exempt the disclosure of trade information. The case is still pending in court.

As is the case with many conservative difficulties, the genesis of the liberal predominance in public interest law can be found in the law schools, where liberals have held sway unchecked for many years. The legal profession, not surprisingly, reflects this imbalance. According to John Bolton, "In a lot of graduate business schools around the country, students are not really taught free enterprise economics. At Yale, there is a perfect example. There's a School of Organization Management, a graduate program specifically designed to train people for careers either in business or government. It's a concession that it's all sort of a bureaucratic, managerial society and that you can float between business and government and not even know the difference. In law school, it's much the same way. There is very little, if any, education as to how the business system works or how to defend it. All they've got are the cases they've learned in school; they don't have any appreciation for the larger issues. In my class in law school, there were about 165 students. About two were conservative; maybe ten were closet Republicans; and the rest were Democratic liberals at best. Some were a lot worse."

There are signs of change, however. Don Toumey, a second year student at the Yale Law School has done an informal survey of the students and faculty at the law school and the results point to something of a conservative trend. For instance, Toumey says that conversations with his fellow students and with professors at the law school have convinced him that students are much less radical than they were in the sixties and more open to the conservative approach, even though liberalism is still the regnant ideology at the campus.

Toumey quotes a liberal professor as saying, "Today it seems that politics is no longer central to students' lives. Students are no longer interested in it the way they once were."

Toumey finds a vague nostalgia on the part of some students for the activism of the sixties, but he feels that today's students are more realistic and skeptical of the radical theories and programs of the last decade.

Professor J. W. Bishop of the Yale Law School faculty recalls that, "The students of the sixties were basically sheep. They'd look at any radical poster that went up and be inclined to agree with it." Today, Bishop notes, "There are no more character wall posters. Students work harder and they're more interested in law. The National Lawyers Guild doesn't cut any ice at all anymore. I guess they're around, but they're not putting out their inflamatory publications. I think law students are behaving the way they did in the forties and fifties. They're studying law."

Toumey agrees: "Students are more career-oriented and less political than they were in the sixties," he says, adding, "while liberalism is still the dominant ideology on campus students are more open to conservatism than they were before."

At some law schools conservative activity is overt, organized, and quite impressive. An example of this can be seen at the Harvard Law School. Exasperated by the realization that no scholarly legal publication in America offered a nonliberal outlook on matters of law and public interest, a group of students at the Harvard Law School recently established what they claim is "America's first conservative law review," the *Harvard Journal of Law and Public Policy*. Its first issue features a broad scope of articles ranging from discussions of national defense and the state of American education to highly cerebral legal analysis of such issues as the constitutionality of using union dues for non-collective-bargaining purposes. Founded in the summer of 1978 by two Harvard Law students, Spencer Abraham and Steven Eberhard, the Journal now has a staff of over forty members of the law school student body. "Working on a law journal is one important way a law student can improve his legal writing skills," said Abraham. "But when the existing publications feature exclusively liberal articles, conservative students are often unwilling to compromise their principles just to improve their talents." Therefore, according to Abraham, "conservative law students are, in a sense, discriminated against when it comes to getting the chance to work on law reviews."

In addition to providing conservative law students at Harvard with a chance to gain legal writing skills, the new *Harvard Journal* provides one of the few scholarly forums in which conservative lawyers and legal scholars can publish their work.

"Prior to the creation of our journal, there was really no place for a conservative legal writer to present his views unless he was really well known," claims Eberhard. "As a result, there is no telling how many good ideas have been stifled over the years just because creative thinkers had no incentive to seek alternative solutions to legal and public policy problems. It is our hope that the *Journal* will provide such a forum and our belief that by doing so we will stimulate conservative writers to produce new alternatives to the liberal arguments we have become all too accustomed to."

According to Abraham, the absence of conservative legal publications has also had a detrimental effect on the attitudes most law students formulate while in school. "Law students tend to leave school familiar only with the liberal perspective regarding the direction the law should take. This problem is exacerbated by the fact that such a significant portion of the people teaching law are themselves liberal. Presenting conservative answers to legal problems will demonstrate that there is a second side to most questions," says Abraham. "If we at least succeed in conveying that message, perhaps we will get new lawyers to think about what the law should be and where it should go rather than blindly following the liberal urgings of our professors."

The fact of the conservative trend among law students is corroborated by Loren Smith, 33, a professor at the Delaware Law School in Wilmington and general counsel of the Reagan campaign. "There is just no question but that conservative values are vastly more popular than they were ten years ago," Smith says. "The radical wave of ten years ago has subsided and the interest in poverty rights, gay rights, etc. is rapidly diminishing."

Instead, Smith says, "You see a new emphasis in the law journals and in the interest of students in issues such as deregulation, individual rights, limiting government power, and restoring the courts to a proper perspective in our Constitutional system rather than looking to them as a cure-all for all of society's problems."

Smith also detects a renewed emphasis on excellence within the legal profession. "In the sixties, the idea of the lawyer as social engineer was in vogue. It was your political beliefs and well meaning intentions that were important, not your competence as a lawyer. Now there is growing concern with being a good lawyer and a growing desire as well to make legal services a superior service to consumers in the private sector."

Smith notes in his students a rejection of ideology that he finds refreshing in contrast to the ideology-surfeited sixties. "When I discuss the severe limitations of government ability to solve social problems there is very little argument on the point," he says. "The inefficiency of government programs is almost taken as a given. Ten years ago, a significant percentage of students would have disputed such an assertion."

Student skepticism does not signal apathy to Smith, however. "My students are energetic, motivated and intellectually stimulated," he says. "The difference is that today their activism tends to be channelled through individual efforts rather than public efforts."

Smith admits that he speaks from a vantage point that is atypical of the nation's law schools in general in that Delaware Law School was founded in 1971 as an explicitly conservative institution dedicated to turning out conservative lawyers. The school no longer articulates such a goal per se, although a majority of the professors on the faculty is conservative. Smith, however, says the trend he sees in the Delaware students is mirrored nationwide, leading him to believe that the legal profession is likely to become more conservative in the 1980s. He has hopes that the profession will once more become the champion of the private sector it once was.

"The American Bar Association was founded in the early 1880s as a means of promoting and protecting a laissez-faire economy," says Smith, "and it was an immensely successful effort. Conservative lawyers argued the case for limiting government control over business, and by 1897 the effort had achieved conservative dominance of the Supreme Court."

For the next thirty years, that dominance prevailed, resulting in such decisions as *Allgeyer* v. *Louisiana* (striking down the state's authority to force the Allgeyer Company to drop an insurance policy negotiated with an out-of-state company not certified by the Louisiana government) and *Lockner* v. *New York* (striking down the state's minimum-wage law as unconstitutional).

In an era of overweening government power, a counterweight to the state is desperately needed, and Smith is hopeful that an increasingly conservative legal profession will provide this kind of force.

At another liberal law school—that of the University of Wisconsin—the beginnings of a national conservative law students' organization can be seen. Founded in late 1979 by John Kwapisz, 33, a second-year law student, "Law Students for a Free Society" has sixty members at law schools around the country. Conservative reticence is the main stumbling block, Kwapisz says, explaining, "Conservative law students like most other conservatives, tend to be private people who are concerned about providing for themselves and their families. They are sound on the issues and they agree that the situation is serious, but they seem to have an ingrained antipathy towards activism."

Despite the handicaps, Kwapisz believes there is a market for his organization and he is pressing ahead with an ambitious program. Among the activities envisioned are: a newsletter providing a survey of legal works that would be of interest to conservative law students; the printing and dissemination of selected law review and magazine articles of interest; the formation of a speakers bureau of good conservative law professors and practicing attorneys around the country; a speakers program subsidized by the organization; an annual conference of conservative lawyers and law students at which they would be able to trade information and develop strategies.

That there is a need for such an organization is beyond doubt but the main problem, as always, is funds. And here once again one runs into the great anomoly of corporate America: business by and large tends to support liberals rather than conservatives. Commenting on this problem, Covington and Burling's John Bolton says, "One of the difficulties is that business is not too likely to contribute to conservative public interest law firms because they don't really see the need for it. Business uses big law firms to defend their interests. The problem is that businessmen, being practical types, are interested in the particular problem or regulation that they face. They are looking for a solution for that specific problem. It's a rare businessman who will be more concerned about principle than about the bottom line. It's certainly understandable from the corporation's own point of view. But it is lamentable that when they turn from their profit and loss statement to their consideration of what the corporation will do to be a good corporate citizen, they give to some foundation that probably supports writers that are against free enterprise as opposed to giving to a group like the Pacific Legal Foundation that tends to support a free market point of view more than they are able to justify in their own litigation concerns."

Even among the ranks of the great corporate foundations, however, signs of redemption exist. The September 14 *Washington Post* reported, for instance, that the Ford Foundation was ceasing its financial support of the ten public interest law firms it sustains wholly or in part. These firms are all liberal, and the *Post* noted, "are frequent intervenors in the complex proceedings that lead to creation or enforcement of government regulations." The paper quoted representatives of the groups as saying that Ford had been the main underwriter of this type of public interest law and that the termination of funding by Ford would jeopardize the existence of the firms. This real possibility was confirmed by Ralph Nader who noted that the termination of support could "well be attributed to the fact that these groups' very successes have made them controversial in the corporate circles that make up part of the foundation world's culture."

This is a euphemistic way of saying that Ford and other companies who are bankrolling such liberal groups are in the end undermining their own positions. It may well be that such an explanation gives the corporate managers concerned credit for too much sagacity, and that the real reason for the decrease in corporate largesse is one of economics. McGeorge Bundy, immediate past head of the Ford Foundation is said to have left the organization portfolio sorely depleted. Similarly it is probably wishful thinking to assume that conservative public interest law firms will now suddenly receive a windfall of Ford money. But even if they do not receive a penny from Ford, the cutoff of funds to their liberal competitors will go a fair way toward evening out the odds.

PART III | ISSUES

Guru of supply-side economics: Dr. Arthur Laffer, University of Southern California

10 | ECONOMICS: THE END OF THE KEYNESIAN ERA

By anyone's reckoning, Arthur Laffer does not look the part of your basic economist. A young man given to natty threads, including alligator-skin cowboy boots, and an afficionado of country music, antique crystal, and exotic cacti, Laffer, in the words of *Newsweek* magazine, "shares quarters with his wife, four children, four turtles, one blue macaw, two sulfur-crested cockatoos, a ferret named Fawn and five parrots." Hardly the stock image of a practitioner of the dismal science. Indeed, Laffer would appear to have more in common with comedian Steve Martin's "wild and crazy guy" than Paul Samuelson. But appearances are deceiving. Laffer is not only an exceptionally brilliant economist; he is arguably, at 37, one of the four or five most influential economists in the country today—an eminence that he has achieved in the startlingly short period of three years.

"When you're hot, you're hot," wrote Richard Reeves in *Esquire* magazine. "And Arthur B. Laffer is hot, has been since June 6"—June 6, 1978, being the day California voted overwhelmingly to adopt Proposition 13. Reeves reported that when Laffer, a professor of business economics at the University of Southern California flew into Los Angeles to vote for Proposition 13, he "was met at the airport by the staffs of state Republican leaders who were looking for his advice on what California should do next. There was a telephone call from the Governor, Jerry Brown, wanting the same thing. Then there were, in rough succession, calls from and meetings with: the *Times* of Los Angeles, New York and London; NBC for a prime-time special; ABC for "Good Morning America"; *Newsweek; Time; Playboy;* fourU.S. Senators, and fifteen Congressmen."

Laffer was not the architect of Proposition 13, but he had supported it enthusiastically as a concrete implementation of his prescription for economic rejuvenation: tax cuts. Laffer burst upon the scene as the flamboyant spokesman for the "incentive economists" who advocated slashing personal

The ''New Conservative'' economists *(counter-clockwise from top left):* Martin Feldstein, Harvard Business School; Michael Boskin, Stanford; Paul Craig Roberts, assistant editor, *Wall Street Journal;* Bruce Bartlett, legislative assistant to Sen. Roger Jepsen; John Gould, University of Chicago; Sam Peltzman, University of Chicago; Warren Coats, International Monetary Fund

and corporate tax rates as a means of increasing economic productivity *and* government revenues. The idea became a *cause celebre* of the influential *Wall Street Journal* and became codified on Capitol Hill through legislation offered by Representative Jack Kemp (R.-N.Y.) and Senator William Roth (R.-Del,). It was later embraced as official Republican policy by the Republican National Committee.

Laffer is representative of a whole generation of young economists who are leading a revolt against the regnant Keynesian orthodoxy. Although they are still relatively few in number, the influence of these conservative economists is growing fast and their ranks are increasing almost exponentially. In fact, nowhere is the success of the conservative revolt against liberalism more pronounced than in the realm of economics. No longer restricted to a few free market-oriented universities such as the University of Chicago and the University of Virginia, the new conservative economists are found on campuses everywhere these days—a phenomenon that threatens Keynsian dominance of the economics profession with imminent demise.

The young John Maynard Keynes once wrote, "The ideas of economists and political philosophers, both when they are right and when they are wrong, are more powerful than is commonly understood. Indeed, the world is ruled by little else. Practical men, who believe themselves to be quite exempt from any intellectual influences, are usually the slaves of some defunct economist. Madmen in authority, who hear voices in the air, are distilling their frenzy from some academic scribbler of a few years back. I am sure that the power of vested interests is vastly exaggerated compared with the gradual encroachmt of ideas."

For fifty years, the acceptance of economic theories of Keynes has validated his observation about the impact of economists. For half a century, the theories enunciated by this brilliant, eccentric little man have held sway over the leaders of the industrialized world and the underdeveloped nations guiding the disposition of vast economic resources affecting the lives of hundreds of millions of people.

In 1926, Keynes wrote a book called *The End of Laissez Faire*, in which he described the increasing difficulty the "classical economists" had in explaining the economic trends of the day. Economists of the classical school operated in terrain that today we call microeconomics—that is, in explaining the way the market allocates scarce resources. They presumed a general stability of prices and employment and a generally steady growth of the economy as a whole. In terms of economic policy, economists of the classical school had little to offer save the general advice that government budgets should be balanced and the market be left unfettered. Governments then, as now, were never able to follow this advice, although some approximated it better than others, and government intervention in the economy, through tariffs, subsidies, changes in banking laws, etc., tended over time to exacerbate the cyclical changes in the economy making recession and inflation more severe than they otherwise would have been.

As has become a familiar pattern since then, the economic difficulties caused or exacerbated by government came to be seen as a failure of the private sector and of the theories of classical economics, whose theories could not explain what was happening.

It was in this milieu that Keynesian economics was spawned, with Keynes' masterwork, *The General Theory of Employment, Interest and Money* providing the theoretical framework previously lacking. Basically, the *General Theory* held that the modern economy is inherently unstable in that it had an innate tendency toward a deficit in aggregate demand, that is, once full employment is reached, people will have an inclination to save rather than invest, hence, demand will slacken and unemployment will result. The maintenance of high demand, therefore, became the primary objective of government policy with deficit spending being the indicated policy in recessionary periods. "Fine tuning" of the economy—government manipulation of fiscal and monetary affairs—would in this scheme of things maintain a felicitous equilibrium. In the Keynesian view, the stimulus of high demand was the all-important imperative. Budget deficits didn't matter, in fact, were seen as a positive good.

Lord Keynes was an aristocrat and an elitist, factors that probably go far toward explaining his deep faith in the ability of the government to manage the economy. As Irving Kristol has pointed out, his *General Theory* "reveals a frank disdain for the traditional bourgeoisie virtues (thrift, industry, diligence) and for the bourgeoisie as a class. There is also a strong implication that ordinary people are just too short-sighted to make capitalism work, and that they needed the likes of John Maynard Keynes to manage the system for them."

This elitist attitude has been a characteristic of Keynes' disciples since. Economics as a profession has grown in prestige, and its practitioners have come to form a new mandarin class of highly paid and powerful figures flitting back and forth between the universities and foundations and the federal government which has burgeoned in conformity with the dictates of Keynesian theory.

For years, the Keynesian approach seemed to work fairly well as the United States experienced a post-War explosion of economic growth. At the federal level, budget deficit followed budget deficit as the Keynesians in control of economic policy primed the pump to keep demand high. Companies hired more workers to meet the increased demand and they in turn spent more. In this heady atmosphere, consumption soared and prosperity increased in an apparently endless upward spiral. By the mid-sixties, however, the revelry began to come to an end. Faced with an escalating war in Vietnam, President Lyndon B. Johnson declined to take the politically unpopular step of increasing taxes to finance it. Maintaining that the nation could have both "guns and butter," he sought to finance both the war and a plethora of existing and new social welfare programs by deficit spending. The result was that an economy already running at full capacity was overheated by billions of dollars of deficit spending. From 1965 to 1969, more than $42 billion in deficit spending flooded the economy with the result that inflation spurted from 2.1 percent to 6 percent.

Another pernicious effect of the spending surge was that people increasingly inclined toward consumption at the expense of savings and investment. Accordingly, capital formation languished, plant modernization was deferred and the U.S. economy began to lose its competitive edge. Meanwhile, inflation continued to push people into higher tax brackets where larger chunks of their income were absorbed by the government while the money remaining bought less and less. Under the weight of all these pressures, the economy began to stagnate so that, by the 1970s, the nation confronted the previously unheard of phenomenon of "stagflation": simultaneous high inflation and high unemployment. By the end of the 1970s, Keynesian economists were forced to confront the glaring anomoly that the doctrine that was supposed to insure economic equilibrium had instead produced wild fluctuations and extreme distortions.

As *Time* magazine put it: "Nobody is apt to look back on the 1970s as the good old days. The economy's most disruptive decade since the Great Depression has borne the stagflation contradiction of no growth amid rampaging inflation, the can't do trauma of receding productivity in the nation that was long the world's cornucopia, the reality of an energy shortage in the land of supposedly boundless resources and the debauch of the dollar that once was 'as good as gold.'"

And, appropriately enough, recriminations were being visited upon those whose policies had brought it all about. As *Time* stated, "Economists, proud and powerful in the 1960s, now look like Napoleon's generals decamping from Moscow."

The John Maynard Keynes who wrote so confidently of the "end of laissez-faire" in 1926 would be a somber man indeed should he return today, because the end of the 1970s appears to signal the end of the Keynesian era as well. Signs of this demise abound. They can be seen at the highest level in the awarding in recent years of the Nobel Prize in economic science to Milton Friedman, of the Chicago "monetarist" school of economics and to Friedrich von Hayek, a leader of the Austrian school, both trenchant critics of Keynes. Another sign of the times is the fact that in 1979 for the first time in many years, *Economics,* the leading economics textbook written by Nobel Prize-winning economist Paul Samuelson is not being used at Harvard. It seems the faculty concluded it is somewhat passé. The replacement, a text written by Richard G. Lipsey of Queens University, stresses "the declining confidence of economists in the possibility of fine-tuning."

The decline of Keynesianism can be seen quite clearly in the remarks of many Keynesian economists themselves—men such as Gardner Ackley, chairman of the Council of Economic Advisors under Lyndon Johnson— who now admit to growing doubts about their creed. But the fall of Keynes can be seen most clearly in the rise of a whole generation of young economists, most of them under 40, who have rejected the Keynesian approach and are formulating exciting alternatives based on the free market approach.

Remarks Rudolph Penner, head of Tax Policy Studies at the American Enterprise Institute: "The exciting ideas are now coming from the under-forty crowd and they are saying government is not efficient." Known variously as "the new conservatives," "supply-side fiscalists," "incentive economists," and "rational-expectation economists," the young economists are having a powerful and unsettling effect on a profession where Keynes had once ruled with impunity. They have been the subject of increasing media attention in recent months including an August 27, 1979 cover story in *Time* magazine which hailed their "rising rebel cry for less government, more incentive and investment."

Among the leading figures in this new movement are about two dozen economists scattered at universities around the country. They include Arthur Laffer, of the University of Southern California; Martin Feldstein and Richard Zeckhauser of Harvard; Rudiger Dornbusch, Stanley Fisher, and Robert Hall of MIT; William Nordhaus and Paul MacAvoy of Yale; Michael Boskin of Stanford; Sam Peltzman and Jack Gould of the University of Chicago; Michael Darby and Armen Alchian of UCLA; and Robert Barrow of the University of Rochester.

Individual quirks and varying emphases aside, most of these economists can be classified in two major groups: the "supply-side fiscalism" school, which emphasizes lower tax rates and other incentives to spur productivity, and the "rational expectations" monetarists who emphasize a steady, predictable growth in the money supply as a means of avoiding inflation and providing for economic stability. Despite the fact that these two groups have their roots in different intellectual traditions, they tend to find themselves in agreement on most policy issues. The new economists all agree, for instance, that government policy has caused people to spend excessively and to save too little and that federal monetary, tax, and fiscal policies have encouraged consumption at the expense of investment. All deplore an excess of regulations which has had the effect of stifling initiative and lessening business confidence. And all decry the chronic federal budget deficits and the Federal Reserve Board's erratic monetary policies. Among the prescriptions for reform that these economists advocate are:

—A reduction of the government's overall intervention in the economy.

—The establishment of a program of consistent moderate economic growth, which would check inflation and give individuals and business the ability to plan ahead on a rational basis.

—Avoid one-shot tax rebates that merely cause bursts of demand and work instead to cut personal income, corporate, and capital gains tax rates in order to provide the incentive for individuals and companies to save and invest.

—Reduce government spending so that an increasing percentage of GNP will be available to the private sector for use in job-creating expansion.

—Eliminate the skein of counterproductive government regulations that hamstring business and retard productivity.

—Strive to balance the federal budget.

Of the multitude of new conservative economists, perhaps the most influential is Laffer. He is a "supply-side fiscalist"—a term coined by his friend and disciple Jude Wanniski, a former assistant editor of the *Wall Street Journal*—who stresses the importance of providing the private sector with incentives as a means of increasing productivity. The son of a wealthy industrialist, Laffer grew up in Cleveland and attended Yale, where he got his B.A. and his M.B.A., and Stanford where he received his Ph.D. An intellectual descendant of Adam Smith, the French classical economist Jean-Baptiste Say, and Leon Walrus, Laffer is a brilliant economist in his own right, having done original work in a number of obscure areas.

His most spectacular talent, however, has been as an alchemist who transforms the abstruse concepts of economics into ideas intelligible to the layman. Summing up his credo, Laffer says, "If you want more of something, you subsidize it and if you want less of something you tax it. In America, we subsidize nonwork, consumption, welfare, debt, and failure while we tax work, productivity, savings, investment, growth, entrepreneurial activity and success."

Laffer has distilled these contentions into two main concepts: the "Laffer curve" and the "wedge." The Laffer curve is essentially a graphic rendering of the effect of the law of diminishing return on government revenues raised through taxation. The bullet-shaped curve shows that the progressive increasing of tax rates will also increase government revenues—up to an optimum level. When this point has been reached, at the apex of the curve, and tax rates are increased further, tax policy enters the prohibitive range. In this area, the rates are so high they actually begin to decrease economic activity which in turn causes revenues to fall. The higher the tax rates in the prohibitive range, the lower will be government revenues. Laffer believes that U.S. personal and corporate income tax rates are now in the prohibitive range. Hence, a tax rate reduction, he contends, would actually increase economic activity *and* government revenues. The wedge very simply is the difference between wages paid to an employee and wages he actually keeps. The difference—the wedge—is comprised of taxes such as social security that are taken out of an individual's base pay leaving him with his "take-home pay." In recent years, the wedge has been growing larger, and Laffer argues convincingly that as it grows an employee's incentive to work is reduced along with the employer's incentive to produce.

Writing in *Tax Executive* magazine, Laffer gives this illustration of the wedge:

Imagine that a person's wages are $100 per week. Under current law, the total cost to the firm of that person is not $100 a week, it is $105.85 a week, which includes the employer's contribution of 5.85 percent for social security. But when you look at wages received, the employee doesn't receive $100 a week. The employee received only $94.15 a week after deduction of the employee's contribution to social security of 5.85 percent. The wages paid are $105.85 but the wages received are $94.15. Looking strictly at the social security system, what you find is a wedge driven between wages paid and received in the amount of $11.70, or 11.7 percent, in this case.

It is easy to see what would happen if the size of the wedge were increased. Imagine that the total contributions were raised to 25 percent, that is 12.5 percent for the employer, and 12.5 percent for the employee. The employer would now find he is paying $112.50, an increase from $105.85. Looking at the market strictly from the employer's standpoint, as the wages paid rise, the demand for employee's services fall.

An employee who had been receiving $94.15 now would receive only $87.50 with his new contribution of 12.5 percent of the social security system. There is a reduction in wages received by the employee. The supply of employee services that are offered to the market place will fall. As the wedge increases, wages paid rise, and wages received fall. This, in turn, causes a fall in the amount of factor services supplied to the market. Essentially, the equilibrium level of output and factor services will fall. An increase in the wedge leads to a reduction in the supply of work effort and in the supply of output.

Laffer first drew a diagram of his curve on a napkin in Washington's Two Continents restaurant one night in September 1974 as he sought to explain the concept to his friend Donald Rumsfeld, then chief of staff to President Ford. Since then he has had occasion to draw it hundreds of more times as have his growing number of followers. One of the most effective of these is Jude Wanniski, a former associate editor of the *Wall Street Journal*. Wanniski sold the *Journal*'s editors on Laffer's supply side economics in 1975, and ever since the prestigious paper has been vigorously trumpeting Laffer's prescriptions.

The results since have been nothing short of electrifying, most notably in such quarters as the establishment of the Republican Party, which is in sore need of a little electricity. The impact on the GOP is owed mainly to Representative Jack Kemp, the four-term New York congressman, former pro-football quarterback, and long-time economics buff. In October 1976, Laffer and Wanniski met with Kemp. Out of this meeting grew the concept of the Kemp-Roth bill—a bill introduced by Kemp and Senator William Roth (R.-Del.) that would slash federal tax rates by 33 percent over three years and institute indexing of the tax rates to prevent individuals from being pushed into higher tax brackets. Kemp and his cohorts agreed that, in conformance with Laffer's theory, such a tax cut would, over the long run, actually increase government revenues rather than decrease them. (The ratio of government spending to total GNP, however, would gradually decline as productivity increased and inflation was curbed.)

In support of this contention, they offered the impressive example of the massive tax cut originated by President Kennedy in 1963. At that time, the highest marginal tax rates (the tax paid on each additional dollar earned) was 91 percent and the lowest was 20 percent. Kennedy proposed cutting these rates to 70 percent and 14 percent respectively. He also cut the corporate tax rate from 52 percent to 48 percent. A great hue and cry went up from the opponents of this proposal, including most leaders of the Republican party who argued that the cuts would balloon the federal deficit. The Treasury Department concurred, predicting a federal revenue loss of $89 billion between 1963 and 1968. What happened instead was a sustained burst of economic growth that produced a revenue *gain* of $54 billion during that five-year period.

Kemp took his case for a tax cut to President Ford, the congressional leadership, and the Republican National Committee, arguing that the GOP had to cease its obsession with balancing the budgets kept permanently in deficit by Democratic spending programs and that the Party should cease preaching the somber message of austerity, offering instead an upbeat message of growth and increased prosperity. The leadership remained skeptical, however. Kemp meanwhile had taken his message to the Republican rank and file in a whirlwind series of speeches to GOP business and civic groups. He shortly became one of the top draws on the Republican lecture circuit, firing up GOP partisans long accustomed to defeat with a message of hope for the future.

At length the Party leadership capitulated and adopted Kemp-Roth as a GOP proposal. During the 1978 congressional elections, the Republican National Committee chartered a plane which carried Kemp and other Party leaders on an airborne whistle-stop tour of major cities where they spread their gospel of massive tax cuts. The proposal became probably the dominant issue in the congressional campaigns as Republican candidates across the country campaigned on a platform of tax cuts. Perhaps foremost among them was Jeffrey Bell, a 33-year old political activist who had formerly served as political director of the American Conservative Union. Bell, a little known figure at the time, campaigned almost exclusively on Kemp-Roth in the New Jersey primary against liberal Republican institution Senator Clifford Case, who opposed the bill. Bell won in one of the major upsets of the year. Given Bell's victory and the landslide triumph of Proposition 13 in California, it did not take the Democrats long to figure out which way the wind was blowing, and before long nearly every Democrat running had formulated his own tax cut plan.

When the results were in, they were seen by many in the media as a defeat for Kemp-Roth. Jeff Bell, the most enthusiastic advocate of Kemp-Roth, had been defeated in New Jersey 56 percent to 44 percent by Bill Bradley, a popular figure in the state because of his fame as a star of the New York Knicks, and the GOP failed to make substantial gains in the Congress (a gain of eleven in the House and three in the Senate). The critics fail to note, however, that several ardent supporters of Kemp-Roth—such as Republican William Armstrong of Colorado, who defeated incumbent Democrat Floyd Haskell—did win races and that the party's gains of three Senate seats, eleven House seats, six governorships, and over 300 state legislative seats were quite healthy ones indeed. The argument fails to note as well that the Democratic adoption of tax cuts proved its popularity and suggests that the real problem was the GOP's failure to make the voters identify tax cuts as a Republican issue—not the repudiation of the concept by the voters.

In the period since the 1978 elections, a number of developments have occurred that confirm the wisdom, both political and economic, of Dr. Laffer's tax cut prescription. In Britain, Margaret Thatcher took the Tory Party to a solid victory over the Labor Party by campaigning aggressively on a pledge to cut taxes and in Canada, Progressive Conservative Joe Clark ousted Liberal Pierre Trudeau by using a similar approach. Thatcher's main economic advisor, Sir Keith Joseph, has worked closely in recent years with American supply side economists, and Clark explicitly acknowledges his debt to Jack Kemp in formulating his economic platform.

At home, the huge slash of property taxes effected in California by Proposition 13 has confounded the critics by creating an economic boom in the state. During the final quarter of 1978 and the first quarter of 1979, personal income rose by 14 percent over the previous year and the private economy in the state had generated 552,000 jobs in the year following Prop 13, enough to absorb all public employees laid off plus a large influx of job seekers from other states, while simultaneously reducing unemployment.

Howard Jarvis, Proposition 13's architect, is now crusading confidently for income tax rate cuts at the state and national levels.

At the federal level, a similar success story has developed with the passage in November, 1978 of the Steiger bill to cut the capital gains tax rate. The Tax Reform Act of 1969 had raised the maximum tax on capital gains from 25 percent to 49 percent and reduced the writeoff on capital losses by 50 percent. As a result, venture capital (the high-risk investments made by adventuresome entrepreneurs which are the cutting edge of innovation in the economy) had almost dried up. In November 1978, however, a bill proposed by Representative William Steiger (R.-Wisc.)—and drafted in part by Laffer—passed the Congress. It cut the maximum tax on capital gains to 28 percent. In the aftermath of the Steiger bill's passage the stock market soared, venture capital levels increased eleven-fold, and a marked improvement in economic enterprise could be noted with firms increasing their budgets for research and development and for new plants and equipment.

It is quite plausible to argue, as many economists including leading conservatives do, that the Laffer approach errs in not advocating a spending cut to accompany the tax cut. But to dwell on this criticism is to ignore the far greater virtue of the approach and that is that, for the first time in many decades, conservatives have been able to effectively take the initiative against the big government advocates who have for so long dominated the dialogue on economics.

Writing in *National Review*, Bruce Bartlett, a former aide to Representative Kemp, summed up the breakthrough of Kemp-Roth this way:

What Kemp, Roth & Co. have accomplished is nothing less than extraordinary. Even before the Jarvis-Gann vote one could see new vigor among Republicans in Congress, as they finally got off the defensive and onto the offensive. There is no question that Kemp-Roth spawned the tuition tax credit bill and the Steiger amendment to slash capital gains taxes. More such efforts will come.

Once the Republicans dropped their dogmatic quest for a balanced budget at any cost and realized that tax reduction is the political answer to the Democrats' spending, then new ideas—politically popular and economically sound ideas—began to flow exuberantly through the GOP. The supply-side fiscalists have nudged the interests of economists away from the Keynesian emphasis on spending, or demand, which has fostered the large budget deficits of past years. And the Republicans have caught the mood of the people, to a point where, for the first time in two decades, it is not unreasonable to consider the possibility of a Republican President backed up by a Republican Congress.

Among the new conservatives Laffer's principal rival for the spotlight is Martin S. Feldstein, 39, a professor of economics at Harvard. Although with his bald head, gnomelike appearance, and staid lifestyle, Feldstein is the opposite of the flamboyant Laffer, he is the unquestioned virtuoso of the new generation of economists, a man who has done brilliant research in a wide range of areas, a man who is, on the one hand a highly cerebral don capable of comprehending the most abstruse mathematical formulas and, on the other, an engaging, unpretentious person who is capable of communicating economic concepts with the average Joe.

Feldstein's most seminal contributions have probably been made in his research into the effects of government programs on the private economy. In this regard, his work is representative of one of the most salient contributions of the new conservatives: through research, using sophisticated computer models, they have been able to analyze the effects of the government's economic interventions. This work has led them independently to the conclusion that government intervention in the economy is counterproductive. Summing up his credo, Feldstein told *Time* magazine, "I do not begin from the ideological position that government activity is inherently bad because it limits individual freedom. Instead, I criticize government policies because they simply do not work or because they have such adverse side effects. Often the best reforms involve a smaller role for government, and less interference with the national working of the private economy."

Feldstein has been dubbed "Mr. Elasticity" by his students at Harvard because of his belief that elasticity describes the effect that changes in price have on supply and demand. According to Feldstein when elasticity is high, a slight increase in price will trigger a large drop in demand. In terms of government programs, Feldstein believes that with a government initiative to provide an incentive to do something, the response depends on the supply and demand elasticity of that activity.

Feldstein's research into government programs has convinced him that these programs almost always have severe side effects that the originators did not foresee and that, in many cases, the net impact of the programs is negative. "A lot of policy is adopted with the lawyers' mentality that all elasticities are zero," he told *Fortune* magazine. "There is a kind of myopia in decision making—an inability to see long range implications, or a tendency to underestimate the long-run effects." Feldstein's study of social security, for instance, has led him to the conclusion that the net impact of the program on the economy has been to cut severely into private savings, thus reducing the GNP and retarding economic prosperity. Feldstein believes that in 1974, the last year covered in his study of social security, capital accumulation would have been $90 billion, or 55 percent greater, and the GNP 14 percent higher had there been no social security program. Feldstein, in fact, goes so far as to contend that social security is the biggest impediment to economic growth because of the devastating effect it has on savings and investment. The solution, he believes, is to curtail the increase in benefits, letting private pension plans and personal savings take up the slack.

Similarly, his research into unemployment insurance has convinced Feldstein that it has the perverse effect of actually increasing unemployment because it encourages employers to lay off workers in slack periods as a means of cutting costs and reducing inventories.

Feldstein's verdicts on other social welfare programs are equally harsh. He believes that the food stamp program has increased welfare dependency and that Medicare and Medicaid have promoted unnecessary hospitalizations and medical tests, thus playing a major part in the skyrocketing rise of medical costs in the United States.

Feldstein does not advocate abolishing these programs outright, believing that that would be politically unfeasible and too violent a dislocation. But, he does feel that the scope of the programs should be reduced and their growth curtailed. He believes, for instance, that Medicare and Medicaid patients should have to pay at least part of their medical bills and that people on welfare be required to pay some tax on their benefits as a means of increasing their desire to seek employment. Feldstein also advocates paying more attention to the "structural" cause of unemployment—the lack of marketable skills by millions of unemployed people. His remedy is to encourage private companies to train these people for specific jobs rather than to rely on government-subsidized jobs. He also favors indexing of the personal income tax and capital gains tax.

Feldstein's conservative views and prescriptions have dismayed many of his more liberal colleagues, but a *Time* magazine survey reports that he is nonetheless regarded by his peers as the preeminent economist of his generation. Their high regard was manifested recently when they conferred on Feldstein the John Bates Clark award, given every two years to the most outstanding economist under forty. (Earlier winners include Milton Friedman and Paul Samuelson.) Feldstein is also president of the National Bureau of Economic Research, a prestigious foundation whose former presidents include Arthur Burns.

He has consistently turned down jobs with the federal government under both presidents Ford and Carter, feeling that he can be more effective as an independent spokesman. He has dispensed advice to both Republican and Democratic organizations, however, and if a conservative wins the White House in 1980, it can be assumed that the new administration will rely heavily on the ideas of Feldstein in the formulation of its economic policies.

Another major center of new conservative activity is the University of Chicago where the influence of Milton Friedman still looms large. Now in vogue at Chicago is the "rational expectations" school represented by professors Robert Lucas, Jack Gould, Sam Peltzman and others. Unlike the Keynesian approach which evidences contempt for the ability of common people to act rationally, the Chicago group reposes a great deal of confidence in the people. At the heart of the rational expectations approach is the belief that people *do* respond rationally to protect their own interest in the face of change and that these sensible responses have an unforeseen cumulative effect of undermining efforts that government attempts to alter the economy by fiscal and monetary interventions.

The Chicago group maintains, for instance, that the repeated monetary expansions of recent years have lost their effectiveness as people realize that the net result is going to be inflation and act accordingly. The University of Minnesota's Thomas Sargent, a rational-expectations theorist, was quoted by *Fortune* magazine as saying, "People recognize the truth and stop making the same mistake. When they do, they eliminate the planned effects of the policy." Chicago's Jack Gould, 39, adds, "A household's inflationary expectations affect the demand for money. That affects the supply and that affects the rate of inflation—and *that* changes the expectations." The rational expectation economists thus have a deep-seated distrust of the computer models that Keynesian economists use to predict the effect of economic policies. These models assume that people will always react the same way and thus fail to take into account the effects that experience has on expectations—changes that perforce invalidate predictions based on past studies.

The rational-expectations people have a deep skepticism about the efficacy of government programs, and a countervailing respect for the abilities of average people, and a deep humility about the limits of economists to understand—let alone manage—a vast economy of over $2 trillion. Instead of economic manipulation, they advocate a slow, steady growth of the money supply and stable government fiscal policies—policies which will create a climate of stability that will enable people to plan ahead with confidence. *Fortune* calls the rational-expectations analysts the "down-to-earth" economists—an appellation that places them in contrast to the haughty manipulators of the Keynesian school. And, in truth, their visions of proper economic policy *are* rather pedestrian compared to the visions of the utopians. Nonetheless, many of the utopian schemes, sustained by nothing but flights of fancy, have come crashing down. Those built on the rock of reality tend to endure. Unlike the Keynesian school and some of the new conservatives who are students of macroeconomics, the rational-expectations economists tend to focus on microeconomics—on how people react to economic changes. Says Chicago's Peltzman, "We can teach students to understand consequences. They can learn how to figure that if you do this, and nothing else happens, you get this result. Micro can tell us, for example, that, if airlines are deregulated, tickets will cost, say, 50 percent less than they otherwise would. Notice I don't say the price of tickets *will* be 50 percent lower. That depends on the possibility of war, on OPEC, and a lot of other things that I don't know anything about."

Among the other leading economists of the new conservative school is

Michael Boskin, 33, of Stanford. He shares the conservative economists' criticisms of Keynesian economics mentioned previously and many of their prescriptions for reform, adding the controversial proposal that the personal income tax should be abolished altogether. As things stand now, Boskin says, people must pay taxes on their total income, including savings. Savings therefore are taxed twice: first when the money is earned and again when it returns dividends. In Boskin's view the government thus acts to discourage savings. He would replace taxes on income with taxes on consumption, thereby creating a powerful impulse to save and invest that would radically enlarge capital accumulation and increase investment, thus creating greater growth and prosperity.

William Nordhaus, 38, of Yale is also highly critical of government intrusion in the economy. According to Nordhaus the cost to the private sector of meeting the myriad government regulations is on "the same order of magnitude as the federal budget—hundreds of billions of dollars each year." Nordhaus, thus, argues for dismantling the complex of tariffs, subsidies, and regulations that increase consumer prices.

Two other economists of note are Rudiger Dornbusch, 37, and Stanley Fischer, 35, both of MIT. The two are authors of *Macroeconomics,* a 651-page text that has become the leading textbook for advanced economics classes. The text reflects the authors' skepticism of computer models as the basis for economic planning, as well as their preference for free trade as opposed to the protectionist edifice that now covers U.S. trade policies.

Yet another young economist of growing influence is Paul Craig Roberts, 40, a former professor at the Hoover Institution at Stanford, later an economist with the House Budget Committee, and now an associate editor of the *Wall Street Journal* and columnist for *Political Economy.* Roberts is both a seminal economist who has done original work in a number of areas (among them the workings of the Soviet economy) and an experienced operator in the rough-and-tumble world of practical politics on Capitol Hill, having served as the staff point man in the original battles over Kemp-Roth.

Roberts has also been one of the most persistent and effective critics of Keynesian economics. "Keynesian economics in this country was based on the assumption that government action would solve all our problems," Roberts says. "It was an emotional thing that was launched and ran its course, immune to evidence. People just sort of got caught up in it and carried along." The decline in Keynesian economics has come about for a number of reasons in Roberts' view, one of them, paradoxically, being the personal success of a number of leading Keynesians. "As time went on, the advocates of a government-managed economy became older and richer. Galbraith and Samuelson became millionaires—and a lot of the idealistic fervor died. It became hard for them to say they were on the outside trying to help the disadvantaged. They became the establishment and had nothing new to say."

The end of the Vietnam War also helped in Roberts' view. "The Vietnam War was used to radicalize economics," he says. "I remember that during the war, there was this Union of Radical Political Economists, about 2,000 strong, that operated at Harvard and other schools. They wanted to completely change the American economic system. They were ideologues rather than scientists. Some went around saying things like public policy had to be used to counteract success—that is, employed as a weapon against merit, ability, and good luck.

"It was worsening stagflation, immune to traditional Keynesian policies, that allowed supply-side fiscalists to challenge the Keynesian contentions on the basis of both theory and fact."

Among Roberts' noteworthy articles is a piece published in the *Public Interest* magazine titled, "The Breakdown of the Keynesian Model." It is an effective demolition of such fundamental Keynesian notions as the belief that the stimulation of demand or spending is the *sine qua non* of economic prosperity. The stimulation is sought at all costs, Roberts notes, thus the policy of higher taxes and government deficits as a means of producing greater government spending and, hence, greater demand. The Keynesians, Roberts notes, totally ignore the adverse effect that higher tax rates have on production, saving, and investment.

Roberts quotes to wonderful effect the testimony of Dr. Alice Rivlin, director of the Congressional Budget Office, concerning the effect of cutting tax rates. Proceeding along an exceedingly peculiar line of reasoning, Rivlin actually manages to conclude that people would respond to a cut in income tax rates by working less, thereby maintaining their present level of income and increasing their amount of leisure time. The implication of this, as Roberts points out, is the absurd conclusion that the way to make people work harder is to *increase* taxes!

Roberts tells how government economists continue to ignore incentives in spite of the enormous pressure he and others had brought to bear in the issue:

Both CBO and OMB realized that the question about incentive effects most fundamentally challenged their concept of economic policy. The comments of Rivlin, Lance, and the OMB staff all unequivocally acknowledged that the econometric models upon which they rely for guidance in the choice of economic policy alternatives do not include any relative price effects of changes in personal-income-tax rates. However, since they believe that the performance of the economy is a function of spending levels, not of production incentives, they expressed no concern over this neglect. They said that economic theory and empirical studies leave it unclear whether the neglected supply-side effects are important; regardless of how the issue is resolved, they questioned the practical importance of supply incentives for short-run policy analysis.

Roberts' exposé of the Keynesian models and his article on taxation published in *Harper's* (a major factor in stopping the Carter administration from increasing taxes under the guise of "tax reform") caused considerable furor on Capitol Hill, with numerous members of Congress calling into question the models usually used to predict economic growth and government revenue. As a result, Chase Econometrics, one of the three large economic forecasting firms used by the federal government for economic forecasting, took steps to alter its econometric models to incorporate supply side factors.

Roberts' other success while on the Hill was in helping to bring Kemp-Roth to the fore. Representative Marjorie Holt's version of the bill actually passed the House at one point (but the Democratic leadership later got enough Democrats to change their votes to defeat it), and a version of it was passed by the Senate. Since leaving the Hill, Roberts has watched Republicans back away from tax cuts at times. "I think many Republicans have dropped the ball on tax cuts," he says. "They are letting things like a balanced budget amendment and tax credits deflect their attention from tax cuts." Roberts says that with the exception of Republican Senators Orrin Hatch, William Roth, and S. I. Hayakawa, the biggest boosters of Kemp-Roth in the Senate were two Democrats—Lloyd Bentsen of Texas and Sam Nunn of Georgia.

To Roberts, the Republican inclination to balance Democratic budgets is futile and, in any case, of little moment compared to the truly revolutionary reform of reducing the level of government spending relative to that of the private sector through a policy of economic growth. "I wouldn't be surprised if the liberal Democrats allow the Republicans to pass a balanced budget amendment as a means of diffusing the tax cut issue," he says.

Reminded that Kemp-Roth would be a major item in a Reagan campaign, Roberts said that should congressional Republicans become budget balancers again and fail to do the spade work on the issue, Reagan could be left advocating a seemingly extreme position. In Roberts' view, Republican members of Congress need to hire smart, tough staffers who can take the initiative on issues away from the liberal Democrats. Without this, he says, even if a Republican President is elected who advocates the correct economic approach, his program will have rough going in Congress.

Although still in the minority these and other like-minded "new conservative" economists are having a growing impact on economics faculties of the nation's universities. Observes Bruce Bartlett, now a staff assistant to Senator Roger Jepsen, "It used to be that they [the new conservatives] were concentrated in a few schools. Now, you see them everywhere. Every economics department has to at least have a token." Indeed, on many faculties, the conservatives are moving into the majority. Writing of the rational expectations school, *Fortune* magazine reported, "As an explicit theory, rational expectations is not yet taught in economics at the college level: formal incorporation of new theories into the curriculum is always slow. But the intellectual moods and attitudes that the thesis engenders—its skeptical posture, its insistence on real-world testing, its suggestion that both economists and government have overreached themselves to society's detriment—all these have penetrated the minds of many teachers. They also show up in incipient form in some of the new economics textbooks. The rational-expectations doctrine is by no means the sole determinant of all these changes, of course, but it is increasingly influential in many of them."

In order to judge the trends at play in the nation's economics departments, *Fortune* polled the professors at 55 American universities mostly in the Southeast, Midwest and Southwest. The questions and the "yes" responses are listed below.

Is there a sense of lost moorings in economics?   66%

Increasing doubt about the accuracy of macroeconomic models?   75

Less confidence in the ability of the government to fine-tune the economy?   82

Less confidence in government programs as solutions to economic problems?   87

Are you teaching economics differently than you did five years ago?   98

In addition to the ferment on the faculties, there is a growing movement towards free market economics discernible among undergraduates, propelled in part by a growing number of national, basically libertarian organizations that do missionary work on the campuses. These young libertarians frequently do not share orthodox conservative positions on such matters as national defense or some social issues such as the legislation of marijuana, but on economic matters they are pure Adam Smith.

With the enormous advances scored by the young free market economists in academe, it was only a matter of time before the effect was felt at the federal level and, indeed, signs are appearing that the impact of the new conservatives is being felt in Washington. One manifestation is the "Midyear Review of the Economy" Report published by the Joint Economic

Committee of the Congress. The report states, "The tax and regulatory barriers to production must be addressed or the average American is likely to see his standard of living decline in the 1980s." The report goes on to say, "The U.S. savings rate has consistently been well below the rates experienced by the other major industrialized countries . . . our growth in production since World War II has lagged behind the rate posted by every one of our major trading partners."

To remedy this situation, the JEC says "we have to take steps to shore up the supply side of our economy." This advice is a startling revelation coming from a committee of Congress, as is the admission from Secretary of the Treasury G. William Miller that "for too long we have focused on consumption and have not invested enough in productive capacity."

Ditto the statement by Jerry Jasinowski, assistant secretary of commerce for policy, that "we must admit openly that manipulation of demand vis à vis public expenditure, taxes, and control over credit does not get to the heart of the problems of the 1970s and 1980s. The source of these problems lies not with the ability to consume but with the capacity to produce."

Warren Coats, 37, a Chicago-trained economist on leave from the International Monetary Fund to work at the Federal Reserve Board, is distressed as are most conservative economists by government policies of the past few decades, but he sees signs of hope. He says, "My colleagues here run the range of political views, yet sitting around the table at lunch time talking about the events of the day, what's going on in the country, and what Carter's doing about this and that, it's been very pleasing to hear people from across the political spectrum agreeing, for example, on the importance of leaving to the price mechanism the allocation of products. Just withdraw the government from all kinds of areas in which it has interfered in the price mechanism—that's, after all, what the vast part of government regulations is about. That's not true in all cases, of course; there are all kinds of regulations, but a good part, one important part of the kinds of regulations the government promulgates, interferes in one fashion or another in the market place's capacity to allocate resources. And it is very reassuring, refreshing to me to hear the extent to which people of most all political points of view are coming more and more to appreciate the importance of leaving that pricing mechanism to do what only it can do so efficiently and sticking to the more direct approaches to income distribution."

Hearing of such advances, conservatives cannot fail to take heart, but anyone who has worked around Washington develops a healthy cynicism regarding the gap between rhetoric and practice. Even if the intellectual revolution has been totally victorious, there exists an inertia-bound bureaucracy in Washington that makes the mere contemplation of the needed reforms a demoralizing task. Administering the distasteful but essential economic medicine that the nation desperately needs will unquestionably be one of the most difficult tasks of a conservative President and Congress in the 1980s. The task, however, is unavoidable, and it is well that conservatives prepare to meet it head-on.

Saving the schools: Paul Copperman, author of the *Literacy Hoax*

11 | THE COUNTER-REVOLUTION IN EDUCATION

The December 7, 1978, *New York Times* ran the following headline on page one: "City Considering Racial Shuffling of Its Teachers." The article stated:

The New York City Board of Education, having abandoned a system of assigning new teachers on the basis of race after a public outcry is "seriously considering" assigning them on the basis of residency to achieve the same goal—a better racially integrated school faculty.

According to sources familiar with the Board's negotiations with the Federal Office for Civil Rights, teachers with addresses in predominantly white neighborhoods would be sent to schools in minority areas. Those with addresses in largely minority neighborhoods would be sent to schools in white areas.

The *Times* quoted one source on the board as saying the new system was being considered because "it was less onerous and demeaning than trying to determine the shade of a person's skin." The article explained that the old "assignment by race system, under which white teachers were told to choose their schools from one box, while black and Hispanic teachers were directed to another box, met a good deal of opposition when it was instituted last year. In a speech from the floor of the United States Senate, Daniel Patrick Moynihan compared the racial assignment with 'the Nuremburg laws of Nazi Germany.' "

The same day of the *Times* story, the *Wall Street Journal* ran a story on its front page under this headline: "No-Nonsense Schools With Christian Ties Tilt With Bureaucrats." The piece, datelined Southern Pines, North Carolina, began:

Six years ago a group of parents who are members of Calvary Christian School here got fed up with the local public schools. They decided their children weren't learning enough and that much of what they were learning conflicted with their religious beliefs.

171

So the 200-member congregation built its own school, in the parking lot behind the church, to teach fundamentalist Christianity and basic subjects like reading, English and math. Today the school is thriving, with twelve teachers and more than 125 students in kindergarten through 12th grade.

Calvary Christian is one of a growing number of such schools, 5,000 by one churchman's estimate, that are gaining strength from the "born-again" Christian movement and a "back to basics" trend in education."

These two articles say a great deal about what has happened in American education in the past fifteen years. Succinctly put, the American public school system, once one of the national glories, has gone through a traumatic revolution so intense and so unsettling that the system is in a downward spiral of deterioration that may end in its collapse.

On one level this would seem to be a great anomaly. Spending on the public schools at the local, state, and federal level totaled about $27 billion in 1977, about two and a half times the amount for 1950, and the number of teachers has shown a corresponding increase, from 914,000 in 1950 to 2,199,000 in 1978. The public school teachers have a powerful union in the National Education Assocation which wields enormous clout with Congress and teacher's salaries have shown a dramatic improvement. School facilities are better and the scope of programs open to students is greater than ever before.

Yet, simultaneously there has been a dramatic and continuing decline in the level of achievement of the graduates of the public school system. Fully 13 percent of all American seventeen-year-olds are now functionally illiterate and the Scholastic Aptitude Test (college boards) administered each year to students seeking admission to college has shown a continuing decline in average scores since 1963, with the average verbal score falling from 478 to 429 in that period and the average math score falling from 502 to 468.

Observers of the nation's high schools (and in many cases the elementary schools as well) find them frequently to be wastelands with high absenteeism rates, apathetic teachers, and listless or unruly students, many of whom are stoned on drugs. Theft and violence are rampant and racial antagonism is high. Millions of parents, horrified at what is happening in the public schools and seemingly powerless to do anything about it, have written off the public schools, removed their children from them, and placed them in private or parochial schools.

One of the most trenchant analysts of what has gone wrong with the public schools is Paul Copperman, a young educator and author of *The Literacy Hoax,* a devastating indictment of the failure of public education and a lucid prescription for reforming the schools. Copperman, a 32-year-old bachelor and the son of Russian Jewish immigrants, grew up in Buffalo in a rough working-class neighborhood.

"I led a gang when I was a kid," Copperman says. "I did a lot of fighting. I didn't know my parents had been to college until I was fifteen years old. Nobody else in the neighborhood had been to college and we weren't raised to be different." Nevertheless, Copperman adds, "We had rigid rules in our house. You did your homework and your chores before you went out to play. There was a very authoritarian, old-fashioned kind of structure."

Copperman's family moved to California in the early 1960s, and he enrolled at the University of California at Berkeley in 1965. There he completed work for a bachelors degree in mathematics and studied linguistics under Noam Chormsky. Copperman says he was uninterested in the "juvenile middle class leftism" prevalent at the university. Rather he began teaching part-time at a private reading clinic in Berkeley out of a desire to see what could be done to help inner-city kids. He was so successful in that endeavor that the school attracted a stream of state and federal grants for programs he designed.

In 1970, Copperman founded his own reading school, the Institute of Reading Development in San José. Today, the institute is the state's largest reading school, with headquarters in San Francisco and branches in six other cities. The faculty is composed of doctoral students trained by Copperman. Twenty percent of the students are children of inner-city or migrant family parents and they are taught gratis. They are also taught successfully. Copperman takes pride and delight in their achievement, not least because it gives the lie to the sociologists who have pinned the blame for low achievement in inner city schools on the students' family life rather than on the schools.

Copperman's book has caused a great furor in the nation's educational establishment—and rightly so. Extensively researched and thoroughly documented, it is a devastating indictment of every major trend in public education over the past fifteen years. Copperman contends that from the early 1800s to the late 1950s, public education in America improved at a rather steady rate: a progressively greater percentage of the school age population graduated from high school and their level of achievement grew correspondingly. In 1958, following the launching of Sputnik by the Soviets, the improvement of American education became a *cause célèbre* in the United States, and swift action was taken to reach that goal. Increased funds were appropriated for education, the curriculum was strengthened (especially the science curriculum), and more demanding assignments were given to the students.

These changes produced an improvement in educational achievement that continued until 1965, when SAT scores began to fall. Because of the greater amount of preschool training and television programs like "Sesame Street," Copperman says, children continue to show achievement improvement through the second grade and a leveling off in the third grade. From the fourth grade on, he maintains, American education is in decline. Copperman provides a number of reasons for this decline, which I summarize here in a necessarily truncated form which, though it touches on the main points of his analysis, nevertheless does not do justice to the depth of it.

(1) *New theories of education and their implementation.* Based on the writing of Alexander Sutherland-Neill *(Summerhill: A Radical Approach to Child Rearing),* Charles Silberman *(Crisis in the Classroom: The Remaking of American Education),* and John Holt *(How Children Fail),* American educators began experimenting with alternatives to the traditional regimen of structured classroom instruction such as the "open classroom" which basically allowed the children to learn in a free form environment in which each child pretty much designed his own curriculum with the teacher present as a mere advisor. The result, as Copperman points out, was disastrous:

The goal of the new math was to teach children the concepts underlying the basic arithmetic operations. The goal of the new science curriculum was to teach children how to think like scientists. The goal of the new curriculum was to encourage each child to think for himself, to set his own learning goals, to pace his own learning activities, and to experience repeated success. The new curriculum attempted to do away with competitiveness, to meet the needs of each individual child, and to structure the school day so that each child's energy, basic curiosity, and zest for life were permitted expression and fulfillment. Virtually all of the curricular changes cataloged at the beginning of this section were developed to accomplish these new goals.

The problem with the new curriculum was that it did not include enough teaching. Recent research implies that the curricular reforms of the past dozen years led directly to the achievement decline experienced by late-elementary school students. Furthermore, there is no evidence of compensating gains in the areas of self-esteem, creativity, anxiety reduction, and general psychological health. As lovely as the goals of the new curriculum sound, it is impossible to escape from the reality of the pedagogical principle with which I started this chapter. The new curriculum sacrificed too much teacher direction, teacher input, and teacher discipline. One of the most serious charges that can be leveled against America's educational leaders is that they encouraged the implementation of wholesale curricular reform before the reforms had been proven successful, and, in many cases, before they had even been tested. What is perhaps even worse, when they were given several billion dollars to develop and test new educational programs, their experiments did not even approach compliance with basic principles of educational research.

(2) *The diminution of authority.* An analogue of the "open classroom" concept was the notion that students are partners with their teachers rather than subordinates to them, a notion that resulted in the disintegration of discipline, a prerequisite for learning, in the classroom. Copperman traces

Critics of the system *(clockwise from top):* author Connaught
Marshner; *Human Events* reporter Joseph Baldachinno; former
director of the California educational tax credit effort William Burt

this to the permissive attitude toward child rearing fostered by the affluence of the post-war era and the desire of the parents of that era to spare their children the deprivation and regimentation they endured. The unfortunate result of this laudable impulse was all too often anarchy in the classroom caused by arrogant, unbridled students and timid teachers. This breakdown of authority, Copperman says, has contributed greatly to absenteeism, poor attendence at classes by students who do come to school, and the frightening upsurge in drug use in the schools and in violence and vandalism. This point is driven home in a most frightening manner by the transcript of an interview Copperman did with a number of students in representative American high schools, which is reproduced in his book.

(3) The loss of local control over the schools. "During the past fifteen years, the governance of American public education has largely passed out of the hands of local communities. The first move in this direction actually occurred during the first quarter of this century, when a reform movement aimed at reducing political influence and corruption in the public schools professionalized the field of education. During this period a significant degree of local control was surrendered to school administrators, their professional associations, and the schools of education where they received their training. The trend toward reduced local control accelerated sharply during the past fifteen years, as a result of the explosive growth in the size and power of teachers' unions and state and federal educational bureaucracies."

Naturally, the education bureaucracy that has developed seeks first and foremost to perpetuate itself and to improve the wellbeing of its members. Higher salaries, longer vacations, less time in the classroom, and fewer outside duties are sought with the predictable result that students are given less discipline, less homework, less instruction and less attention by the teacher. This bureaucracy also has a vested interest in disguising the falling achievement levels of the students and the reasons for them.

(4) Lower standards. Partly because of the laziness of the educators and partly out of a desire to accommodate more children from poor minority families, educational standards have been lowered drastically. Copperman writes that, "The consensus is that the average student is assigned 50 percent less reading and writing than in the early 1960s and that standards for written work are correspondingly low." Or again, "Many traditional and rigorous courses have been replaced with fare best described as educational entertainment. Courses in film literature and science fiction are replacing English composition; courses in contemporary world issues are replacing world history. In these courses the amount of work assigned and the standards to which it is held are considerably lower than in the courses they replace."

Other manifestations of the lower standards are the acceptance of "black English," "Appalachian English," and bilingual education at the expense of standard English. The tragic irony of these initiatives is that they actually harm the students they were designed to help, a point Copperman makes in no uncertain terms: "Minority children need to speak in standard English, so that they can prosper in our society. The authors of this document and those teachers who are attempting to institute its policy are consigning their minority students to another generation of educational and economic poverty. This document and the policy it espouses are a travesty of the most basic principles of education." Summing up his indictment of the lower standards, Copperman writes, "I believe that an overwhelming majority of the nation's parents, black, Mexican-American, and white, would violently disapprove of most features of the new English curriculum if they were aware of them. The dominant principle in this curriculum is to give students what they demand. We have a curriculum without standards, with insipid content, that neither exposes students to their cultural heritage nor trains them in the reading and writing skills they will need to function in society. I am convinced that the deterioration in the secondary-level English curriculum bears a significant share of the responsibility for the achievement decline experienced by America's secondary students over the past dozen years."

(5) *Grade inflation.* A concommitant of lower standards is inflated grades:

While courses were getting easier and reading and writing assignments were being reduced, high-school grades were moving upward. The following graph depicts the percentage of A's and B's, or C's, awarded throughout high school to representative groups of first-time college freshmen from 1966 to 1977. By 1977, over 81 percent of the high-school grades reported by these students were A's or B's, less than half of one percent were D's, and less than .05 of one percent were F's.

Verification of this pattern comes from the two major college entrance testing programs. ACT reports an increase in the average high-school grade-point average from 2.59 on a four-point scale in 1966 to 2.85 in 1976. Grade inflation during this period occurred in each of the four subjects investigated, English, math, social studies and natural sciences, but was most pronounced in English.

This trend is also seen at the college level: "The most important manifestation of the deterioration in academic standards is sharp and continuing grade inflation, which is even greater at the college level than the analogous phenomenon at the high-school level. The faculty survey cited earlier in this section reported that 94 percent of the nation's college and university professors believe that grade inflation is an important problem at their own institutions, and two-thirds admit to assigning higher grades than their students deserve."

Finally, and perhaps most surprisingly, Copperman comes down hard on the compensatory education programs funded largely by the federal government, which were designed to boost the basic skills of educationally disadvantaged students. "A dozen years and $50 billion later we are in a position to evaluate the major compensatory education programs," he writes, and concludes that they have, by and large, been colossal failures.

As proof Copperman cites a 1969 study of the highly acclaimed Head Start program by Westinghouse Learning Corporation and Ohio State University—a study that showed Head Start had virtually no long-term effects on students' learning habits or attitudes toward school. Results for the Head Start summer school program were so bad that Westinghouse recommended that the program be abolished altogether. A number of other evaluations of Head Start, including a 1975 study done by the General Accounting Office, corroborate this finding.

A major problem with compensatory education programs, according to Copperman, is that the legislation initiating the programs stipulates that the funds may not be used to strengthen existing programs, but must, rather, go to pay for auxiliary personnel and materials—part-time teachers, "specialists," and sophisticated machinery, etc. Since, in Copperman's view, "the basic unit of elementary and secondary education is the classroom—one teacher working with a group of students," compensatory programs are at best marginally useful since they do nothing to buttress this central element and, in most cases, the programs have a deleterious effect by undermining the existing classroom situation. Another flaw in the program—although Copperman sees it as intended by the drafters of the legislation—is that the authorizing legislation requires that local parents' committees be established in each school district and that they have advisory, participatory, and planning role in the program. In talks with the heads of a number of major metropolitan school districts, Copperman discovered that approximately 50 percent of the funds allotted to a school district under the compensatory program go to the parents in the form of salaries: "Through the mechanism of the parents' advisory committees, the parents hire themselves as teachers aides, community aides, clerical aides and hall aides!"

Reviewing the decade and more of compensatory education programs, Copperman concludes that

Compensatory education failed, and will continue to fail, because it did not accept the primacy of the classroom unit, and therefore did not recruit good teachers and principals into inner-city schools, or support the good ones already there. Instead, compensatory education focused on secondary services—parent aides, reading and math specialists, teacher-proof programs—all of which denigrate the role and the authority of the classroom teacher, and prevent the principal from being able to fulfill his leadership role. Compensatory programs exacerbate the very severe problems of classroom control and motivation which are at the heart of the educational problems in our inner cities. As a result, the overwhelming majority of teachers and principals in these schools are demoralized, and function very poorly. Competent personnel flee these schools, or they sink to a level of functional mediocrity, or worse, after but one or two years teaching in them. Underprivileged children, who need good, orderly educational experiences, are subjected to a chaotic curriculum taught by the worst public-school teachers in the country.

Copperman recommends a program to reform the public schools, the main points of which are:

—Taxpayers should move to regain control over the local schools by pressing for a "Magna Carta" of education, enacted by the Congress, that would severely restrict the ability of the federal and state bureaucracies to run the local schools.

—Local boards of education should acquire the expertise to evaluate the performance of the local school administrator and faculties by hiring independent, competent experts to review the program and report their conclusions to the boards.

—District boards should require that all students completing the twelfth grade be required to take a proficiency exam in all basic skill areas. Such an exam would help administrators and parents to establish standards and evaluate programs.

—Replace the compensatory education with night classes to train parents in ways to help their children do their homework, develop good study habits, guide their children's course selections in high school, and evaluate their work in school.

—District school boards should develop alternative schools which are highly structured, academically oriented, and focused on basics. Parents would then have the option of sending their children to the open classroom school or to the traditional kind.

Copperman's book caused quite a stir in the education establishment, whose doyens vigorously drubbed him for faulty research and employing sensationalist tactics. The conclusions of The Literacy Hoax found corroboration from many quarters, however. One of the most powerful was a three-hour, three-part series produced by CBS News called, "Is Anybody Out There Learning?" The conclusion at the end of the series was that not many students are learning very much. Anchored by Walter Cronkite who was backed by six correspondents and a large production crew, the series began by focusing on the public school system of Denver, an average metropolitan school system. What did CBS find? Shades of Copperman! Racial antagonism towards white Anglo-Saxon cultural values (standard English, math, etc.), busing, high and increasing absenteeism, falling test scores, permissiveness, and the automatic passing of students regardless of grades. True to the dictates of the "open classroom" types, the system's curriculum has mushroomed to over 700 courses, including many without a trace of academic utility. Achievement levels, meanwhile, have fallen dramatically and continuously during this time. Reviewing the CBS series for the *Wall Street Journal,* Aram Bakshian commented on the tragic decline of the public schools and particularly on the disaster this decline has been for minority groups:

> Yet for all of the major immigrant groups that flooded into the United States in the second half of the 19th and the first half of the 20th centuries, there were two great melting pots—the American private sector, which provided an expanding job market for cheap labor, and our public elementary and secondary schools, which managed to impart a common language, a shared sense of citizenship, and the beginnings of an American ethos for immigrant groups as varied as Irish, Italians, Jews, Slavs, Greeks, Chinese, Germans, Japanese and even the occasional Armenian.
>
> The achievement of America's public education system has been unique. No other society, in any era, has successfully turned millions of disparate, poor and often illiterate immigrants—few of whom had experienced the full rights and responsibilities of citizenship in their countries of origin—into full partners in a new society, sometimes in a single generation.
>
> Yet there are increasingly disturbing signs that, for the two largest and least assimilated of America's ethnic minorities—blacks and Chicanos—the educational melting pot is turning into a slag heap.

The tragic irony, of course, is that the very measures undertaken to help minorities have worked to their detriment instead. Lower standards, huge infusions of money and equipment, alternative curriculum options such as "black English" and bilingual education: these have all had the effect of stunting the acquisition of the basic skills that minority children will need to enable them to cope in the world.

Perhaps the salient example of the idiocy that has characterized this approach is busing. This perverse practice was ordered by the courts based largely on the Coleman Report, a study commissioned by HEW in 1966 and carried out by a team led by Dr. James S. Coleman of Johns Hopkins University. The report concluded that it "appeared" that minority children's skills were improved if they were assigned to classes that were at least 51 percent white. Thus, despite—indeed contrary to—the 1964 Civil Rights Act which specifically forbade the assignment of students based on race, the courts ordered the massive busing of school children in cities throughout the country as a means of achieving thoroughly integrated education. In many cases federal judges totally displaced the role of the local school boards and proceeded to draw up complicated plans based on arbitrary quotas, a tactic that soon had buses criss-crossing cities and townships in a totally crazy pattern, often transporting small children for hours each day to reach the schools assigned to them.

Few practices in modern history have proved so wasteful and destructive as busing. Whole neighborhoods have been swept by violent protest, cities divided, billions of dollars have been wasted in added fuel costs, litigation expenses, and augmented security forces. The practice has increased animosity between the races, accelerated the flight of whites from the cities, resulted in millions of children being pulled out of the public schools and, in many areas, has caused the virtual cessation of educational activity in the local schools. In recent years, it has become increasingly apparent that, if the public schools are to be saved, this pernicious practice must be halted.

Several young conservative educators and journalists have done yeoman service in bringing the plight of the public schools to public attention. Among them is Solveig Eggerz, a Washington-based free lance writer and the wife of conservative columnist Alan Brownfeld. Eggerz's study, "What Went Wrong with the Public Schools?" is a trenchant analysis of the causes of the decline of public education which places much of the blame on the militancy and burgeoning power of the National Education Association (NEA). In an article in the July 28, 1979, *Human Events,* Eggerz presented a condensed version of her indictment of the NEA. "The decline in student achievement is now a familiar story and the NEA—the union representing most of the 2.2 million teachers who instruct our students—is running out of excuses," she writes.

Eggerz argues that the NEA is not only indifferent to the disintegration of the public schools but has also been implacably hostile to all proposals to remedy the decline—measures such as the adoption of standardized tests that would allow parents and elected officials to monitor the skill levels of students and the efficacy of the schools' teaching methods, tuition tax credits, the voucher plan, and virtually all legislative efforts to help non-public education. What the NEA is interested in, as Eggerz makes plain, is in feathering its own nest, increasing salaries and perks for educators, strengthening the predominance of the public schools and making the NEA the nation's sole arbiter of educational standards and, even more objectionable, a domineering force on the political map.

Among the NEA's self-appointed goals, Eggerz points out, are

—Getting the federal government to shoulder "at least one third of the cost of primary and secondary education."

—"To tap the legal, political, and economic powers of Congress."

—"To become the foremost political power in the nation [NEA President John Ryan]."

—Reordering "congressional priorities by reordering Congress."

—Achieving for public school teachers the legal right to strike.

In order to accomplish its mission the NEA has amassed an annual budget of $250 million—ten times that of the AFL-CIO. In addition, the NEA's political action committee has become one of the largest PACs in the nation, pouring over $3 million into federal, state, and local campaigns in 1978.

As the NEA's size and power increase its product becomes ever poorer, its standards even more bizarre, spinning off into such arcana as "leisure skills" and "corporate morals," a trend reaching a macabre nadir with the introduction into some school curricula of "death education," a course in which students take field trips to cemeteries and inspect coffins. Death education, an NEA publication chirps, means "probably the last of the old taboos to fall in the public schools."

As the public becomes more aware of the NEA's complicity in the decline of the schools, signs are beginning to appear that the union's days of wine and roses may be coming to an end. For instance, black leader Rev. Jesse Jackson recently sharply challenged the union's right to strike: "How clear is the right to strike when the union doesn't calculate what it will cost a child whose teacher walked out of the classroom? . . . How clear is the right to strike for more money when the employer—a taxpaying parent—holds tax receipts in one hand and test results in the other that prove he's paying more and more for less and less?"

A particularly effective guardian of the public interest in educational matters has been the weekly newspaper *Human Events*. In addition to the Eggerz article, the publication has run an on-going series of articles on the crisis in American public education, many of them written by senior reporter Joseph Baldacchino. Baldacchino did a particularly effective job in exposing the outrage perpetrated on the public schools called Man, a Course of Study (MACOS), a behaviorist curriculum developed at a cost of $7 million by the National Science Foundation (NSF). As Baldacchino related it in *Human Events:*

After this course was developed by a group called the Educational Development Center, Inc., (EDC) at a cost to the taxpayers of over $6.5 million, it was considered so outrageously controversial that fully 50 commercial publishers refused to touch it. In order to make MACOS commercially available, therefore, the NSF entered into a dubious arrangement whereby it agreed to allow an off-beat publishing outfit known as Curriculum Development Associates, Inc. (CDA) an 80 percent discount on royalties owed to the government.

As for the content, Baldacchino reports:

Materials for MACOS, which include numerous books, films, records, pamphlets and other teaching aids, are full of references to adultery, cannibalism, infanticide, killing of old people, trial marriages, wife-swapping, murder and other behavior practiced by the Netsilik Eskimos studied as part of the course.

The idea, drummed into fifth-grade children day after day, is that such practices are considered all right by the Eskimo culture and, by extension, should be looked upon with tolerance by ours. And this is what bothers parents and other critics of this program. It is not that students should not be exposed to knowledge of other cultures, but there is some question as to whether children should be exposed to such harsh realities at this young stage of their development. In the view of many, this kind of material might better be reserved for college-level anthropology courses.

Such a program would have been outrageous enough if prepared for study by high school students. MACOS, however, was designed for fifth-grade students and at one point was being used by an estimated 1,200 elementary schools.

Thanks in large part to the *Human Events* reporting on MACOS, the program became the subject of heated criticism in Congress. On March 25, 1976, the House reduced the NSF budget for textbooks from the $5.5 million requested to $1.4 million, and adopted by voice vote an amendment offered by John Conlon (R.-Ariz.) that forbade the NSF from designing any program similar to MACOS.

Another extremely effective critic of the performance of the public schools is Connaught Coyne Marshner, 29. In her book *Blackboard Tyranny* (Arlington House) she reviews in detail the cause and results of the public schools' decline and the difficulties parents have in effecting a cure for the problem. Parents, Marshner says,

come in all races, creeds, political affiliations, social classes, occupational categories, and in every other subdivision imaginable. Because of this diversity, parents as parents have been slow to organize themselves as a single interest group. Until recently, the need has not been imperative to do so. But a child is educated only once. If he does not learn what he should during that period, he may never correct the deficiency. A child grows up only once, and if his formation is poor he can be ruined, and ruined permanently.

The duties of parenthood are many, and they are time consuming, demanding, and difficult. Political activism is not usually considered part of parenthood. But if parents—rather than government bureaucrats—are to guide their children's lives, political activism must be added, and added now, to the burdens of parents in the 1970s.

To that end much of Marshner's book is devoted to a detailed blueprint for parental action to improve their children's education. She gives a useful primer on how the education establishment works in the United States from the federal level to the local school including how the NEA works its will on the members of Congress and the state legislatures. Marshner gives as her objective the reassertion of parental control over education of their children. To accomplish this, she recommends parents seek to enforce four primary goals for education: "1. To teach children to read, write and figure;

2. to transmit facts about the heritage and culture of their race; 3. in the process of (1) and (2), to train the intelligence and stimulate the pleasures of thought; 4. to provide an atmosphere of moral affirmation." Specific problems that parents should look for, Marshner says, include: unacceptable textbooks, unacceptable "special programs" of the guidance of psychiatrist's office, sex education, unproductive or harmful programs for "gifted children," harmful classification of students, behavior and attitude modification, "parenthood" classes, drug education, busing, incompetently taught modern math, improper or worthless reading methods at elementary levels, vandalism and physical safety problems, drugs available at school, and unsatisfactory teachers on the faculty.

In order to accomplish her goals the author provides guidance for evaluating the curriculum of the local school district, dealing with teachers and the local school heads, forming parents' committees, editing a parents' newsletter, lobbying the state legislature, organizing to oppose the teachers' unions, and starting private schools.

One of the effects of the decline of the public schools has been the increase in the number of private schools. Since 1970 the number of school-age children has diminished, and the enrollment in the public schools has decreased by nearly 2 million to 43.7 million. Simultaneously, enrollment in nonsectarian private schools has increased by 60 percent to 1.8 million and continues to increase at a sharp rate.

The increase in the number of Protestant parochial schools has been equally dramatic. Traditionally strong supporters of the public schools, Protestant parents have become increasingly distressed by their decline in recent years as prayer has been forbidden, and secular humanism has been enshrined in its place; textbooks and instructors have tended to stress sex education and moral relativism; basic education has been replaced by free form curricula and discipline has collapsed.

Dr. Ona Lee McGraw, educational affairs coordinator for the Washington-based Heritage Foundation, summed up the effect of the decline on its main victims, the children involved. "These children are being so intellectually stunted," she says. "Children need to learn of the beauty of life, of the value of the permanent things. They need to acknowledge the existence of God. They need to read great literature like C. S. Lewis' Narnia or his science fiction trilogy. Instead they are reading pop fiction and trivia."

The result has been a surge in the number of private Protestant schools, many of them operated by the evangelical "born-again" Christians. Precise figures on these schools are hard to come by, but by one estimate they number more than 5,000 with new ones being organized at the rate of more than one a day.

The situation with the Catholic schools is far less healthy—but that may change in the near future. Traditionally, most parochial schools in the

United States have been Catholic, and as late as 1966 educated over 11 percent of all school-age children. Since 1965, however, these schools have suffered a sharp decline. In 1971 and 1973, the Catholic schools were hit hard as the Supreme Court issued rulings that made it illegal for state governments to provide financial assistance to private sectarian schools— rulings that meant sizeable cutbacks in aid to Catholic schools in many states. In addition, funding for the public schools exploded, soaking up greater percentages of taxpayers' money through local property taxes. The simultaneous boosting of public school teachers' salaries and fringe benefits along with improved working conditions helped to make the parochial schools less competitive. As a result, Catholic school enrollment decreased by 28.4 percent—2,158,810 students from 1965 to 1975. There are encouraging signs that this decline may be reversed, however. One such sign is the movement to institute tuition tax-credit systems which would enable parents who opt to send their children to private schools to deduct up to a certain figure from their federal income tax.

One site of considerable tax credit agitation is, not surprisingly, California. There the 22,000-member affiliate of the National Taxpayers Union (NTU) is pushing a drive to put a tax credit initiative on the state ballot. Working under the direction of California NTU chairman Bill Burt, 29, the group aims to acquire 750,000 signatures by December 14, 1979, in order to put the measure on the ballot by June 1980.

"Our plan would allow parents to deduct up to $1,200 per child attending an accredited private school in the state," Burt says. "This plan, if enacted, would put a large dent in the state budget. Of a total state budget of $21 billion between $8 and $10 billion goes to education."

According to Burt, the money remaining in the state education budget would actually provide more money per pupil for those children remaining in the system, as it costs the state more than $1,200 a year per student. "This is going to be a very tough fight, no doubt about it," Burt says. "We're taking on the teachers' union, which is the most effective lobby in Sacramento." Nevertheless, the effort has received some important endorsements, including those of Howard Jarvis and the State Republican Party, and Burt believes that passage of the tax credit plan is eminently feasible. "This is a very significant effort," he says. "California typically leads the way in innovative efforts like this, and if we succeed in passing the tax credit measure it could mean a revolution in American education."

At the national level, the most prominent of these plans is the Tuition Tax Credit Act of 1977 (S.2142) sponsored by Senators Daniel Patrick Moynihan (D.-N.Y.) and Robert Packwood (R-Ore.). This bill would entitle parents to deduct 50 percent of a child's tuition cost (up to a limit of $500) at a private elementary school, secondary school, or college.

Opponents of the bill—including President Carter—vehemently attacked the Moynihan-Packwood bill claiming that it would be a boon to the rich at the expense of working-class taxpayers. Moynihan and Packwood pointed out, however, that 51 percent of the students in private schools come from families with incomes of less than $15,000 per year. In addition, the bill would provide for the remittence of a sum equal to the credit to low income families who pay no taxes.

Nor do the charges that tax credits would hurt minorities stand up under close scrutiny. In fact, once again, the opposite would seem to be the case. A good example of what can be done for minority students outside the public schools was reported in *Time* magazine, which detailed the efforts of Marva Collins, a black Chicagoan who operates a one-room school for inner-city children. She maintains a highly disciplined, no-nonsense regimen, concentrates on the intensive teaching of basic skills—and manages to improve the skills of her students remarkably. *Time* notes that Miss Collins urges the parents of her students to then send them on to parochial rather than public schools.

The case for tuition tax credits is made eloquently by Walter Williams, a black professor at Temple University. Writing in the spring 1978 issue of *Policy Review*, the quarterly publication of the Heritage Foundation, Williams argues that

A state monopoly in the production of a good or service enhances the potential for conflict, through requiring uniformity; that is, its production requires a *collective* decision on many attributes of the product, and once produced, everybody has to consume the identical product whether he agrees with all the attributes or not. State monopolies in the production of education enhance the potential for conflict by requiring conformity on issues of importance to many people.

. . . It is noteworthy to recognize that the flight to suburbia in search of better schooling is becoming less of an exclusively white phenomenon. Blacks are fleeing the cities in unprecedented numbers.

The Tuition Tax Credit Bill would create the possibility of school integration in a way that school integration decrees do not—through people *voluntarily* pursuing what they believe to be in their own best interests. The use of the courts to promote racial heterogeneity and cooperation in our school systems can be called nothing less than a dismal failure.

. . . Test performance scores show that the great majority of black children are three to five years behind the national norm. These facts make meaningless the argument advanced by the critics of the Tuition Tax Credit, that if it were enacted there would be a ground swell of fly-by-night, poor quality schools which would exploit the poor.

Black parents, educated or not, can discern high and low quality education. This is evidenced by the fact that many black (as well as white) parents have given false addresses so that their children could attend better schools outside of their districts.

. . . At the heart of the problem in public education is a system of educational delivery which creates a perverse set of incentives for all parties involved. At the core of the perverse incentives is the fact that teachers get paid and receive raises whether or not children can read and write; administrators receive their pay whether or not children can read or write. Children (particularly minority children) receive grade promotions and diplomas whether or not they can read and write.

The individual parent who is poor is helpless in such a setting. It is quite difficult for the individual parent or group of parents to effectively force the public school system to produce a higher quality education. The benefit of the Tuition Tax Credit is that it enhances the possibility for the individual parent to *fire* the school providing poor services and to enroll his child in some other school providing better services. The Packwood-Moynihan bill promises to give low-income parents at least some of the powers that their higher-income counterparts have, namely a greater role in determining educational alternatives for their children.

The "soak the poor to pay the rich" objection has therefore been pretty effectively disposed of. Other problems remain, however. The main objection of the parochial school advocates is that the Packwood-Moynihan bill contains a clause directing the Department of Health, Education and Welfare (HEW), among other agencies, to report on civil rights enforcement by the IRS and to make "suggestions . . . for enhancing" the IRS enforcement "of public policies against racial discrimination and other forms of discrimination. . . ."

Senator Jesse Helms (R.-N.C.) stated that, although he favored tuition tax credits, this clause made it impossible for him to support the bill. Helms observed that, "it does not take too much imagination," given HEW's record in such affairs, to envision the agency "demanding coed sports programs, coed dormitories, the hiring of homosexual teachers, the availability of abortion counselors, the abolition of male and female choirs, and so forth, all erected on some pretext of public policy."

As it turned out, Helms' worst fears were soon realized as HEW issued new regulations that would in effect find many private schools guilty of segregation until they proved otherwise. Specifically the new procedure would define any private school as a "reviewable school" if it had been formed or substantially expanded at or about the time of the desegregation of the public school system of the community in which the school was located and if the school's enrollment were less than 20 percent of the percentage of minority students in the district, i.e., if a school district's population were 50 percent minority, a private school would have to have at least 10 percent minority students. Schools in this reviewable category would automatically lose their tax exemptions until they proved they were making a "good faith" effort not to discriminate. Such a demonstration, it turned out, would require a school to meet a long list of requirements such as minority recruiting, minority scholarships, minority hiring, etc.

This regulation elicited a firestorm of outrage, with many Christian schools going to court and many of their leaders threatening to disobey the law. The lead in rolling back this regulation came from Gary Jarmin, then legislative director of the American Conservative Union. At Jarmin's urging, the ACU arranged the mailing of a "legislative alert" to the membership of the Rev. Robert Billings' National Christian Action Coalition. The alert informed the recipient of the danger of the regulation and urged him to write to the IRS demanding its repeal. As a result of this effort, the IRS received more than 500,000 letters protesting the regulation. Later, the ACU sent another mailing asking the recipients to write to their congressmen urging them to force the IRS to withdraw its initiative. Again a massive outpouring of letters resulted. This and similar efforts ended in the House voting on July 13 by a margin of 297 to 63 to deny IRS the authority to rule on the eligibility of church schools for tax-exempt status. The Senate passed similar legislation on September 6, and President Carter signed it. This victory may be regarded by future historians as a landmark event in the annals of conservative movement activity.

The situation with regard to higher education closely parallels the decline recorded for the elementary and secondary schools, which is to say a look at the nation's colleges and universities reveals the same doleful litany of massively increased funding on the one hand, and on the other, lower standards, lower achievement levels, grade inflation, and the replacement of core curricula with a growing cafeteria of electives, many of them trivial.

One ominous trend obvious to even the most cursory observor is the tremendous growth in government funding for higher education. The funding has gone to the state institutions, obviously, but to many of the large private colleges as well. By the end of the 1970s, in fact, many of the leading private universities, such as Harvard, Yale, and MIT, were receiving more than one third of their total financial support from the federal government. One effect of this was to put the many hundreds of small private colleges at a severe disadvantage. With their high costs and lack of subsidies, they found it increasingly difficult to compete with lavishly funded state-supported universities with their comparatively low tuition costs. As a result, private schools have been disappearing at an alarming rate. Since 1950 over 350 private colleges have gone under.

Another ominous development is that, along with federal grants to private colleges has come growing federal control with IRS, HEW and other federal agencies and departments subjecting the recipient institutions to a tangle of regulations and quotas based on sex, race, etc.

Reviewing the "affirmative action" program dictated to the University of California, the *Wall Street Journal* observed:

Consider what sins are being committed in the name of education at—or more likely, to—the University of California. University officials and HEW's Office of Civil Rights have agreed on an 'affirmative action' (i.e. quota) plan that calls for eventually replacing 178 of the positions now held by white males in a total staff of 1,489. The New York Times concluded this would mean replacing them with "97 women, 20 blacks, 42 Asians, 10 Chicanos, no native Americans (Indians) and nine others." University officials dispute those specific figures, explaining that the plans call for only 96 women, two blacks and three Asians—as if that makes the concept any less grotesque. All that's missing is that the quotas extend across 30 years, rather than having a 1984 deadline.

As a result, many of the college presidents who had slavered after federal funding, pooh-poohing the warnings about accompanying controls, were at length to be heard from in a growing chorus of complaint.

Kingman Brewster, then-president of Yale, complained, for instance, that the "leverage of the federal spending power" was being used to control private colleges in ways the government could not use directly. Thus it has come to pass that the impossible is happening: the leaders of the big liberal institutions—whose economics courses have instructed generations of students in the beauties of "affirmative government" have begun to shun government funds and to embrace "dat ol' debbil," business.

This turnabout was personified most remarkably in a speech by A. Bartlett Giamatti, the new president of Yale:

Private educational institutions must realize that they are part of the private sector. The ancient ballet of mutual antagonism between private businesses on the one hand and private educational research institutions on the other is not to anyone's interest. That ballet of antagonism must give way to a more mutual dance. There is a metaphor that informs the private business sector as it informs the private educational sector, and that metaphor is the free marketplace. Whether the free marketplace involves the competition of commodities or of ideas, it is a common metaphor and a precious asset.

According to the Wall Street Journal, a poll taken in 1976 showed that 72 percent of all college administrators favored more reliance on corporate rather than on government money. The article reported that in 1977 American corporations gave $206 million to private colleges and universities— 33 percent more than the alumni donated. This figure, however, represents only a small fraction of what corporations could give. Federal tax law allows companies to donate up to 5 percent of before tax profits to charity. But most donate only one percent and of that, less than half goes to private colleges. The bottom line is that there is more than a billion dollars of extra corporate money available. The Journal noted that college presidents were well aware of this and that they were making an unprecedented effort to exploit the opportunity by setting up special offices to solicit corporate contributions.

Speaking on behalf of his tuition tax credit bill, Senator Moynihan stated, "Diversity. Pluralism. Variety. These are valuable characteristics of education as of much else in this society. And perhaps nowhere are these values more valuable than in the experiences our children have in their early years, when their ideas and attitudes are formed, their minds awakened, their friendships formed. Tax credits for school tuitions furnish an opportunity to support these values."

These values that Moynihan cherishes are on the verge of being lost in American education. Yet with tuition tax credits in place and the mutual embrace of private education and private enterprise, there would be good reason to believe the drive towards an all-powerful educational leviathan run by the federal government has been halted and that in the 1980s a new American educational renaissance of diversity, excellence, and creativity might be at hand.

Realists abroad *(left to right):* Chester Crocker, Roger Fontaine *(seated),* Kenneth Myers, all of Georgetown University's Center for Strategic and International Studies

12 | FOREIGN AFFAIRS: TOWARD A NEW FOREIGN POLICY

As serious as the domestic problems of the United States are, a compelling case can be made that the crisis confronting America abroad is graver still, commanding remedial action of the most urgent sort. By almost any criterion one cares to employ, the United States has been in general retreat around the world since the end of World War II, a retreat that accelerated following the trauma of the American involvement and subsequent defeat in Vietnam; a retreat that has assumed the proportion of wholesale flight since the advent of Jimmy Carter, Cyrus Vance, Andrew Young, and company.

To the extent that any sort of coherent foreign policy exists under Carter, its salient characteristics would appear to be accommodation of Communist and Third World countries, erratic dealings with traditional allies and hostility toward authoritarian governments friendly to the United States. This might seem a simplistic and unfair characterization of Carter's foreign policy, but I believe it is a tenable one.

In Asia, Carter sought from the beginning to terminate the U.S. presence in South Korea and reached with alacrity to embrace Peking while coldly casting aside our treaty with Taiwan, a loyal and exemplary ally. And, despite his professed concern for human rights, the President was notably slow in criticizing the barbarities of the Vietnamese and Cambodian regimes.

In Latin America, Carter undermined the Somoza regime in Nicaragua, criticized the governments of El Salvador, Honduras, Guatemala, Brazil, Chile, Argentina, Bolivia, Paraguay and Uruguay—all right-of-center regimes—while attempting a rapprochement with Castro, signing a treaty turning over the Panama Canal to the leftist Torrijos regime, praising the advances made by the Manley government in Jamaica, and facilitating the installation of a Marxist regime in Nicaragua. In Africa, a policy originally

193

orchestrated largely by Andrew Young has sought to encourage the most radical elements, such as the guerrilla forces in Zimbabwe, while undermining the most democratic government on the continent, the biracial government of Zimbabwe. In Europe, the leaders of the NATO countries admit in private to being concerned about the uncertain leadership provided by Washington. And so on.

In this atmosphere of confusion and uncertainty the Soviet Union has waxed triumphal, gathering vassal states with numbing regularity and projecting its power and influence to every corner of the globe. So parlous has the international situation become that many foreign affairs experts are convinced that a period of profound instability and danger awaits the United States in the early 1980s—in the best of circumstances.

Given the awesome challenge facing the United States in the 1980s it seems fair to say that the number one task of a new president will be to rally the American people to face the challenge. Chilton Williamson, book review editor of *National Review* puts it this way:

> Our chief job, it seems to me, is to bring the country around to a just and accurate assessment of global realities, and especially of course to an understanding of the wickedness, unparalleled in human history, of the Soviet Union, and the terrible danger that it offers us. The irreconcilable differences between the United States and the Soviet Union ought not perhaps to be represented on the religious or transcendental level, as Solzhenitsyn is doing: that is like taking an open-and-shut case of coldly premeditated murder directly to the Supreme Court, when it could have been disposed of in one afternoon in a Corn Belt courthouse. It pays the Communist hoodlums entirely too much respect by suggesting that the most elevated arguments are necessary to find them guilty as charged of the most brutal and disgusting crimes, naturally repugnant even to a society of dogs. It is indeed imperative to convince Americans, and the rest of the West, that the Communist regimes are not "just another form of government," as George Kennan likes to say, but a monstrous aberration. Nevertheless, I believe the way to do this is to bring forward the most obvious dangers—aggression in Africa, the arms control hokum, the build-up of the Warsaw Pact forces—and to convince the country that, even at the risk of armed conflict, we must oppose the Communist salients.
>
> I firmly believe that, at least in the short run, the foreign threat is far greater than the threat posed by an overweening and bureaucratic Washington. It is true that there is nothing peculiarly conservative about defending ourselves abroad—as there is in seeking to dismantle big government—but there it is, that is my point: it is probably the major task of conservatives, during the next couple of generations anyway, to succor a variety of causes which are generically less conservative than commonsensible.

Williamson overstates the danger facing the United States a bit perhaps, but not by much. He is entirely correct, to my mind, in concluding that the foremost task confronting the American people is to come to grips with the

Foreign affairs analysts *(left to right from top):* Dale Tahtinen, foreign policy advisor to Ronald Reagan; Stephan Halper, foreign policy advisor to George Bush; Ronald F. Docksai *(left)*, chairman, and L. Francis Bouchey *(right)*, vice-president, Council for Inter-American Security (with Hon. Patrick Wall, Conservative member of the British Parliament); Robert Downen, secretary, Coalition for Asian Peace and Security; Gregory R. Copley, foreign-affairs publishing magnate.

challenge posed by the Soviet Union. That is also the urgent task that will confront a conservative president: to formulate a comprehensive, coherent foreign policy that adequately perceives the totality of the Soviet challenge, that entertains no illusions about the nature of the regime that we are dealing with, and that provides for a strategy that will enable the United States to compete with and ultimately win a struggle with the Soviet Union. A foreign policy suitable for the 1980s must be based on the imperative of furthering the just interests of the United States; it must be a policy that posits the type of world we care to see and that tailors our policies to further such a vision.

Designing and implementing such a policy will not be easy and it must be conceded that in the area of foreign policy, conservative expertise is in short supply. Foreign affairs has always been the nearly exclusive domain of liberals—a condition that obtains in the world of foundations and think tanks as well as in the State Department and other internationally oriented government agencies.

In New York and Washington, and in certain other cities and academic centers around the country, there exists a whole network of liberal foreign policy institutes whose staffs analyze and advocate policies, publish newsletters, monographs, and books, and hold conferences, and who interact with the policy makers in the State Department in Democratic, and, to a lesser extent, Republican administrations. In the case of the Carter administration these organizations—such as the Institute for Policy Studies and the Washington Office on Latin America—have had a profound impact, supplying a large number of recruits to fill the policy-making jobs in the State Department.

Conservative administrations until recently have had no such network of professionals to avail themselves of. In the last three years, however, an inchoate network of conservative foreign policy has emerged. Though still quite small compared to its liberal counterpart, this complex is beginning to provide some effective competition. In his effort to staff the policy-making positions of the State Department and the National Security Agency, a conservative president can be expected to depend heavily on the faculty of Georgetown University in Washington, D.C., especially its Center for Strategic and International Studies (CSIS). To be sure, the CSIS is no monolithic enterprise and its staff members reflect diverse views on the conduct of foreign affairs, but on balance the Center tends to be somewhat right of center, and its ranks contain a number of superbly qualified analysts of a conservative cast.

One of the best of these is Dr. Chester Crocker, 38, a specialist in African affairs. Crocker looks at the conduct of foreign policy under the Carter presidency and finds it appalling in its naiveté and incoherence. According to Crocker:

First, there isn't a coherent liberal view on substantive grounds. That comes across loud and clear when you look at the public relations of the Carter administration. There's no substantive back-up. There's no power, no influence, no suggestion of a strategy for getting from where we are to where we want to be. So, you have initiatives across the board: the Middle East, Southern Africa, U.S.-Soviet arms issues, immigration questions, conventional arms transfers, etc. But, the bottom line is influence. They are somehow uncomfortable talking in terms of influence. It's as if they could somehow charm the world out of its own fears and convictions.

I look at the world as a place in which American influence is in decline, but that might be reversible. They look at the world as a place where American influence is quite properly and appropriately declining and our policy should adjust to that and attempt no more to influence or coerce people but simply get them to agree with us. I agree that there are limits, but I don't agree that you can't have a policy until you've had a Gallop poll to see whether people like it, or until you've asked the Soviets if it's alright.

There is a parallel between Carter's foreign policy and his domestic campaign. You've got Andy Young trying to "Rafshoon" the Third World. There's a sense that if you tell the other person what he wants to hear, you'll be both popular and effective in dealing with him. That's fine when you're campaigning, but not when you are trying to manage day-to-day affairs. You've got to sit down, knock heads together, make bargains, and deliver the goods even when the going gets rough. Soviet propaganda about the neutron bomb should not influence Carter's decision on whether it's a good weapon or not. Carter is really in a no-win position. He doesn't really have a position of his own other than avoiding criticism and hostility.

I look at Carter as a cipher in office. That is, he wants to be in office but he doesn't stand for anything. The people around him do. They stand for very different things which are in conflict.

Concerning the President's misbegotten human rights policy, Crocker says,

I think you can give the Carnegie Endowment for International Peace substantial credit for that. A number of appointments came from that source. There was a lot of work done at places like this emphasizing what was called during the Kissinger years the "forgotten dimension" in foreign affairs, namely the human dimension. Somehow there was a long-standing verity here that we had to have a humane foreign policy and that Henry Kissinger had been inhumane. It is affected by trends in the academic community too: human rights and civil liberties issues, starvation issues. A number of case studies were done and widely talked about in intellectual circles right before the election. For example, the disaster, the drought in west Africa. There was a concern about a lack of sensitivity to the liberation issues in southern Africa. There was a great sense that we had the wrong allies—the Greek colonels, the Brazilians, the South Koreans, etc. These people, who were in exile during the Kissinger years, were very unhappy with the notion that we should keep the allies that we had. One way to question the existing alliances is to find fault with our allies. On human rights grounds, you can do that.

The aversion to Chile, Argentina, South Korea, etc. is based on the feeling that we shouldn't be dealing with right-wing dictatorships. We should be dealing with "progressives"—with people who are forward looking. In my view, that's a kind of double think. Let's just look at some of these "progressives" and examine the human rights record in these countries. That's never been done. It's a double standard. Most of the people that feel the most strongly about human rights are the generation after Kissinger and after Vance. They may be saying, "Look, foreign policy has been handled in insensitive ways before." It's kind of a generation turn-over, a reaction against the past. That may be part of it.

As regards the African policy orchestrated by former U.N. Ambassador Andrew Young, Crocker finds it a naive attempt to make short-term gains with hostile governments at the price of destabilizing the situation on the continent and unnerving our traditional allies there. Crocker says,

I've been quite a shrill critic. There are a number of basic points that I feel are wrong-headed. For the first time, this Administration has a activist policy. But, I would argue that's mostly rhetoric. There hasn't been much in the way of resources behind it—aid resources, military assistance or even political will. As a result, it's been mostly a policy of launching initiatives in southern Africa. But many Africans are confused as hell as to where we stand. Africa is a very fragile continent. And for a government to deal with it, they have to have some sense of where we're going to be tomorrow, not just today. This uncertainty exists in the Ivory Coast, Senegal, Kenya, Zaire, Egypt, and Sudan. Morocco is absolutely climbing the walls. Some of our so-called new friends have also been puzzled as to whether we mean business or not. Yet, the Administration's view has been to come in and almost proclaim guilt for past American sins and then get down to business with black Africans. We've tried to downgrade the role of East-West competition in Africa. We've been ambiguous about the Cubans. On occasion, the State Department has issued statements declaring that we were equally opposed to intervention by the Cubans and by the French.

In Zimbabwe-Rhodesia, our approach was in one sense utopian. We tried to launch the Anglo-American plan in 1977 to provide a transition to majority rule that would please everybody. We had a whole series of principles that had to be met; we would give all parties a stake in the security forces; get the U.N. involved to monitor elections. It was the most enormously ambiguous package that could be conceived. None of the parties in conflict could have any confidence in the outcome. The issue in Zimbabwe is not how good the constitution is; it's who's going to be running the country. We've stuck with the high moral ground—whether or not it's genuine majority rule—we're stuck with the issues of constitutional purity. In effect, the result of our diplomacy has been to drive black moderates and whites together—and then when that happened, to discredit them and give veto power to the guerrillas on the outside. It wasn't until the British election and intervention that you saw us backing off and taking a back seat.

Another prominent Georgetown Center policy analyst is Dr. Roger Fontaine, 38, director of the Latin American Division. Fontaine served as Ronald Reagan's chief adviser on the Panama Canal treaties. He has written for a wide range of scholarly journals and many general circulation publications such as the *Wall Street Journal, Washington Post* and *Los Angeles Times.* Like Crocker, Fontaine is critical of the Carter administration's concept of foreign policy. As regards Latin America, he says, "The Carter people began with a negative and a positive assumption about Latin American policy. The negative assumption was that it is a big mistake to get caught with a theme— a large program like the Alliance for Progress. Carter therefore pulled out of any kind of regional promises; it was all bilateral. We will take care of specific problems in a can-do manner. One example of this was the Panama Canal Treaties. The other was a review of our relationship with Cuba; opening up new, formal relations after twenty years of isolation. The third is to concentrate on human rights: to push Latin America away from military dictatorships to socially acceptable, perhaps left-of-center regimes. That was the mix Carter came in with. Not that Jimmy Carter thought about these things; he didn't. It was the academic feed-in he was getting."

The basic shortcoming with U.S. policy toward Latin America, in Fontaine's view, is "an inability to decide how important" the region is. "Carter's attitude toward the region is sort of a weird synthesis of what's happened before: a misinterpreted synthesis where, on the one hand, we have no slogans, no overarching programs but on the other hand, we pay lip service to a lot of vague high-minded principles."

In Fontaine's view a classic case of the ineptitude of U.S. Latin American policy makers is the disaster in Nicaragua:

The basic lesson to be gleaned from the Nicaraguan tragedy is not to back the wrong side. We pulled the plug on Somoza and had the wrong idea on what would take his place. We felt by pulling the plug on Somoza we could somehow manage the middle. There was, of course, no middle. We should have gone back two years ago and taken Somoza at his word and said, "This is your last term in office. You're going to have an election in 1981 and that election is going to be closely supervised." The Conservative Party—or a faction or spin-off of the Conservative Party— would have won and taken office with our blessing. That would have meant going in there with a fairly heavy hand to teach those guys democracy and to be very clear what the rules were. That's what should have been done. Nicaragua is a country where we have tremendous leverage. If we had used it, 50,000 Nicaraguans would be alive today; the economy would not have been devastated; the Sandinistas would not be in power. It would have meant a long-term commitment on our part— probably ten years. These alternatives were very clear two years ago. The Carter administration was fooling around with gossamer fantasy. It was not based on Nicaraguan history—it was based on nothing.

What is needed, Fontaine believes, is

an assessment of Latin America's importance which is accurate, neither exaggerated nor underestimated, and which is sustainable and based on a clear perception of what we want Latin America to be in the next ten to twenty years. I don't think we've done that. There's no one in the Administration or in the intelligentsia who will come out and say, we'd like to have Latin America democratic with a small "d"; we'd also like it to be capitalist; we'd like to have it developing; and we'd also like to have them oriented toward the United States, Western Europe, and Japan; and, in addition, be anti-Communist. I think that should be the goal and I think we should tailor our policies accordingly. That means trade and commercial policies, aid policies, military arrangements. It also means in areas where things have gone on for too long and too far—in the Caribbean, for instance—that the United States should vigorously assert its self interest.

Probably the OAS is not the place to do it because it is too big, too slow, too clumsy and too stupid. But, you can get some cooperation from states that are close by and are concerned. I'm not just talking about Guatemala, Honduras and El Salvador. I'm talking about Costa Rica, Panama, Venezuela and probably Columbia as well. But, unless the United States asserts its leadership and starts making its presence felt in the area, we're not going to get any support.

In terms of specific policies, Fontaine says,

First, encourage social reform. Second, we should do what we can behind the scenes to encourage a transition to civilian rule without imposing arbitrary deadlines. Bolivia, for example, is afraid we're going to come down on them. They've already botched one election and they'll have to have a third election. This is a classic case of moving too fast. What they've done is totally confused the political situation; they have a very weak civilian government which may or may not last; and third, a ruined economy. It's all because of premature elections. We had no business telling the military government to get out and to do it by July of 1978.

Trade is also very important and the Carter Administration has done nothing in this regard. Their markets in the United States are very important to them although it seems to be a small matter to us.

Economically, many Latin American countries are far more advanced than most countries in Africa and many in Asia. With a little bit of stability and a stable economic policy, they could move very quickly. A lot of them, for example, don't have the energy problems that a lot of non-Arab Third World countries have.

The most important thing is to keep the North American market open. South Korea increases its exports by 30 percent every year, and the growth rate until this year has been between 12 and 15 percent. South Korea is doing it on very few natural resources; they're doing it on human talent alone. Most Latin American countries could do the same thing.

Another key Georgetown figure is Kenneth A. Myers, 35, the director of European and Canadian Studies at the Center. Myers, a graduate of Colgate University, the Johns Hopkins School for Advanced International Studies, and the Free University of Berlin is also an adjunct professor of European Politics at Georgetown University's School of Foreign Service. In recent years, he has done important work on the problems facing the Atlantic Alliance.

In a recent monograph, "North Atlantic Security: the Forgotten Flank," Myers argues that NATO's concentration on shoring up its southern flank is creating a dangerous void on the northern flank which the Soviets are moving to fill. He writes,

> In Soviet calculations, the correlation of forces is moving in a direction favorable to Moscow, while the West is perceived as locked in the throes of economic chaos and political indecision—a loss of a sense of purpose. In the North, the Soviet Union expects to be treated as *the* superpower with global interests. The other superpowers, as well as the indigenous Nordic countries, are expected to recognize Soviet regional preponderance and to readjust their foreign policy calculations in consonance with the vital Soviet interests in the area. In Soviet rhetoric, a state of low tension in the area can be maintained only if the West recognizes the futility of contesting Soviet vital interests in the North.

It is essential, Myers writes, for the United States and the other NATO countries to move quickly to redress this problem before the growing Soviet power in the area becomes dominant.

In addition to the Reagan campaign, the Georgetown Center also has the Bush campaign well covered. Stephan Halper, 34, a CSIS fellow, is policy coordinator for the Bush presidential effort. Halper is a graduate of Stanford and Oxford Universities. He worked at the Ford White House in the Office of Management and Budget and later worked in the Ford campaign preparing policy papers.

Halper's area of specialization is international economics, and he has also done work for Georgetown on Far Eastern affairs and Southern Africa. He shares Fontaine's conservative view of foreign policy and the two collaborated on a column on foreign affairs which has been sold to a number of papers including the *Baltimore Sun, Los Angeles Times,* and *Christian Science Monitor.*

Another individual who is likely to have a good deal of influence in foreign affairs if Ronald Reagan wins the presidency is Dale R. Tahtinen, 34, foreign affairs advisor on the Reagan campaign staff. Tahtinen is a graduate of Northern Michigan University and holds master's and Ph.D. degrees from the University of Maryland. He served for five and one-half years as night editor for the Defense Intelligence Agency's *Daily Intelligence Summary,* then as an assistant to Michigan Senator Robert Griffin and as assistant director of the American Enterprise Institute's foreign affairs and national defense studies program before going to work for the Reagan campaign.

Tahtinen is responsible for drafting many of Reagan's major foreign policy statements and for performing a running critique of the Carter administration's foreign and defense policies. "The tragedy of Carter's foreign policy is that this country no longer has any credibility in the world," he says. "There is no underlying consistency to our foreign policy today; we spend all our time just trying to put out fires."

Tahtinen also believes that unlike the Soviets, Carter does not see a relationship between events that happen in the world; that policy is made instead on an ad hoc basis, dealing with each problem that arises as an isolated phenomenon. "There is also no planning for the period beyond the next election," Tahtinen believes. "That's why you see the cancellation or the cutback of important weapons systems based solely on short-term economic benefits, and totally ignoring long-term implications."

The Carter human rights policy, in Tahtinen's view, has been a disaster. "This is a moralistic policy and very naive one," he says. "Although it was designed to be applied across the board, it has been very selectively applied. A few Communist countries have been criticized, but administration spokesmen have concluded that to criticize them does no good, so as a result we have focused on the shortcomings of our friends and allies." The message this policy has carried has been extremely costly, Tahtinen believes. "What we have told Third World countries is that if they align themselves with the United States they are going to come in for criticism and abuse. The message is: the more hostile towards the United States you are the better you'll be treated."

Tahtinen believes the first task facing a Reagan administration would be to restore credibility. "We have to get the United States back on a positive track; to put out the word that we stand for something and will stick by it," he says. "We have got to make it plain that we will stick by our friends. If they have a problem, we will work with them to correct it, but we are not going to criticize them in public."

Tahtinen argues that the United States must "reassert leadership as the number one power in the western world," that it must develop a strategy based on firmness and strength that will discourage the aggressive designs of the Soviet Union. "We have to make it clear to the Soviets that we will protect our interests," he says. "Now we are far too eager to cooperate with the Soviets."

The Cuban problem, he feels, is indicative of this: "There we totally capitulated over the question of Soviet troops and over the presence of MIG-27s capable of carrying nuclear weapons. After backing down on the question of the troops we turned around and approved a massive grain sale."

Tahtinen also believes it is foolhardy for the United States to help the Soviets build up their strategic reserves through technology transfers and other means. "Any sale of equipment to the Soviets should be based on an assessment that it does not hurt the strategic interests of the United States," he says.

The Council for Inter-American Security (CIS) is another developing source of conservative foreign policy expertise. Under the leadership of its chairman Ronald Docksai, 29, and its director L. Francis Bouchey, 34, CIS has in its two-year existence done some highly professional work in Latin American affairs, an area for too long ignored by conservatives.

Speaking of CIS's role, Bouchey says, "There has been a continuing dramatic deterioration in America's security position in this hemisphere, which has gone little noticed. "The concept of collective security for this hemisphere has been lost in an emotional orgy of self-flagellating rhetoric and hysteria which has alienated our friends and encouraged our enemies. Under the guise of human rights, a small group of leftist policy makers in the Carter administration have gravely damaged the security within our own hemisphere."

According to Bouchey, the objectives of CIS are "to halt the unilateral disarmament of the United States and to encourage the forging of a new cooperative alliance between responsible anti-Communist people and governments from Canada to Argentina that will protect the U.S. southern flank."

CIS publishes a regular newsletter, West Watch, which covers important developments in Latin America, and the organization sustains an expanding publications program of books and monographs. The organization also sponsors a monthly series of dinner meetings on Latin American affairs for members of Congress and their staffs and provides testimony before Congress on matters affecting Latin America.

In 1979, CIS sponsored a symposium on Mexico, Central America and the importance of the South Atlantic nations which brought together prominent speakers from Brazil, Argentina, Chile, Uruguay, El Salvador, Nicaragua, Guatemala, Honduras, and Mexico plus many participants from across the United States. The organization has completed a film on Castro's Cuba and a book on Mexico, and is working on a film on Mexico.

One of the major contributions of CIS thus far has been in strengthening ties between leading anti-Communist leaders—intellectuals, businessmen, and government officials—in the United States and the countries of Latin America. Out of these meetings has come the genesis of a strategy for winning the competition with communism in Latin America.

The Heritage Foundation, located a block away from CIS on Capitol Hill, is also doing some good work in the field of foreign affairs. The director of foreign policy research and analysis for Heritage is Jeffrey B. Gaynor, 34, a well-traveled analyst with an extensive network of contacts around the world. Gaynor's main job at Heritage is in drafting "backgrounders" on foreign affairs topics, concise studies on issues of interest that are distributed widely on Capitol Hill and to editors and publishers around the country. Gaynor's work in this area has focused on issues as diverse as Namibia, NATO, China policy, and Latin American affairs.

Just a couple of blocks away from both CIS and Heritage is the Institute of American Relations, a foreign affairs foundation established in 1976. IAR publishes a fortnightly newsletter on foreign affairs and, like CIS, maintains a variety of activities including a publications program, a program of conferences, and a weekly series of briefings for Capitol Hill staffers. In 1979, IAR sent representatives to places as far-flung as mainland China, Europe, Zimbabwe-Rhodesia and Latin America to evaluate conditions there and to report to Congress. The organization also sponsored the visit to the United States of Doan van Toai, a former Viet Cong supporter who was imprisoned by the Communist government of Vietnam. Toai defected, bringing with him a document called Charter '78, a denunciation of the inhumane Hanoi regime signed by several dozen intellectuals and clergymen now held prisoner by the Communists. Toai traveled to California to meet with folk singer Joan Baez. There he told her of the appalling repression perpetrated by the Communists and of the suffering and dying of tens of thousands of "boat people" who were desperately trying to escape from Vietnam.

Baez was so moved that she took out full-page ads in five major newspapers, cosigned by more than sixty former antiwar activists and denouncing the barbarity of the Hanoi regime. She also began a campaign of concerts designed to bring attention to the plight of the boat people—an effort that has contributed directly to the much increased efforts by government and private groups to aid the boat people.

One of the directors of the IAR is John Carbaugh, 33, an aide to Sen. Jesse Helms (R.-N.C.). In the past few years, Carbaugh has developed into one of the most savvy operatives that conservatives have in the foreign affairs field. With his extensive contacts in the press, the foreign affairs, defense and intelligence communities, Carbaugh has helped Helms, a member of the Foreign Relations Committee, to become a major force in influencing foreign affairs.

On November 27, 1979, Carbaugh had the pleasure, rare for a congressional aide, of being the subject of a half-page article on page two of the *Washington Post*. Writing of Carbaugh and fellow Helms staffer, James P. Lucier, 44, the Post's Kathy Sawyer described them as a "southern-fried Rosencrantz and Guildenstern battling the red meanies of the left."

Carbaugh, wrote Sawyer, "is the baby-faced nemesis of President Carter's foreign policy planners . . . the flamboyant one, a strategist who thrives on action, publicity, personal contacts, even with the liberal press and who, by his own account, never misses a chance to deal directly with a head of state."

In the pursuit of his shuttle diplomacy, Carbaugh has traveled, at the expense of the Institute of American Relations, to Brazil, Argentina, Chile, Uruguay, El Salvador, Nicaragua, Guatemala, Haiti, England, Germany, South Africa and Rhodesia—often visiting the heads of state of these countries or, at least, high-ranking officials.

One reporter quoted in the *Post* story said that Carbaugh is "an intrepid leaker and planter of news stories and the consensus is that he is both honest and effective, if a bit full of himself." According to another, "Carbaugh takes the flak and he tries to take the glory."

Among the accomplishments that Carbaugh and Lucier have to their credit are plotting delaying tactics that stalled SALT II on the Senate floor for at least a day and bringing the fact of the Russian brigade in Cuba to the attention of the Senate. The State Department credited them with almost wrecking the Rhodesia peace talks, going on in London, by almost persuading the Muzorewa side to be intransigent. The British Foreign Office denied this but the resulting publicity in the United States served to vastly enhance the images of the two high-powered staffers.

All who know Carbaugh describe him as a blustering, boisterous, hard-driving, high-rolling operative. In the course of his bouncing from one right-wing cause to the next he occasionally gets tripped up but he also manages to make an impact. Helms, for instance, says that information gotten from Carbaugh's contacts keep him literally weeks ahead of the congressional committees. Sanford Ungar, managing editor of *Foreign Policy,* magazine also paid tribute to Carbaugh: "He is a very engaging character," Ungar said. "He's about 50 percent as effective as he thinks he is—and that's pretty damn good."

The Coalition for Asian Peace and Security, a new organization formed in June of 1979, has as its primary focus insuring that the United States lives up to its commitment to the non-Communist countries of Asia. Chairman is Dr. Ray Cline, director of the Georgetown University Center for Strategic and International Affairs. He is assisted by an advisory committee composed of some forty distinguished Americans including *National Review* publisher William Rusher, Clare Boothe Luce, Edward Teller, Ben Wattenberg, and a number of prominent academics. Staff director of the Coalition is Robert Downen, 28, an Asian affairs specialist and for five years a legislative aide to Sen. Robert Dole (R.-Kan.). Under Downen's direction, the Coalition monitors the situation in Asia, seeking to insure that the United States lives up to the terms of the Taiwan Relations Act and the treaties with South Korea and other nations in the area, and insuring that Peking does not make any attempts—overt or otherwise—to undermine the independence of the free nations in the area. The Coalition regularly reports its findings to the press and the Congress.

Gregory R. Copley, at age 33, is already the potentate of his own mini-empire of foreign affairs concerns. A native of Australia and a resident of the United States for only the last few years, Copley manages a thriving Washington-based enterprise that includes the publication of *Defense and Foreign Affairs* magazine, a monthly with a subscription price of $50 that goes to a select readership of some 2,000, most of them foreign affairs specialists, Defense Department officials, or embassies in Washington. Copley also publishes a host of other publications including *Defense and Foreign Affairs Daily, Strategic Middle Eastern Affairs,* the *Weekly Report on Strategic Latin American Affairs,* the *Weekly Report on Strategic African Affairs,* the annual *Defense and Foreign Affairs Handbook,* and the *Quarterly Strategic Bibliography.* These publications provide a nonstop gusher of fact and opinion encompassing foreign affairs and defense matters in all corners of the globe. To sustain this torrential output, Copley relies on a staff of ten and a network of correspondents around the world.

He does much of the writing himself, displaying a literate style and an encyclopedic knowledge of international and strategic realities as he threads his way through matters as diverse as the coup in Afghanistan and the RAF's newest fighter plane. Surveying Copley's enterprises, it can be said that his activities are as farflung as those of the U.S. State Department and that his grasp of world realities is vastly superior.

Defense policy expert John Lehman climbs into the cockpit of an Air Force F-5 fighter. Lehman is considered by many observers as a likely candidate for a top defense policy post in a Republican administration.

13 | DEFENDING AMERICA: STRATEGIES FOR THE 1980'S

In July 1979, after a number of false starts over the preceding year, the long-awaited Strategic Arms Limitation treaty was finally signed in Vienna by President Carter and Soviet Premier Brezhnev. The ceremony set in motion what was to become probably the most momentous foreign policy debate since the League of Nations ratification debate of the 1920s. Although the Carter administration devoutly wished for the debate to be limited to the terms of the treaty itself, the opponents of the treaty, and many uncommitted Senators as well, insisted that SALT be placed in the context of Soviet behavior around the world and that the treaty be used as a pivot point for a review of the whole framework of U.S.-Soviet relationships. To the administration's chagrin the latter view prevailed with no little thanks due to the belated discovery of a Soviet combat brigade in Cuba.

As the debate progressed through the summer and fall, both sides committed all the resources they possessed to the fray which proceeded on a multitude of levels—from pedantic experts debating the esoterica of theories and armaments numbers to enthusiasts having it out at meetings of local civic organizations.

Before long it was apparent to observers of every sort that one of the star players on the treaty opponents' team was John F. Lehman, 36. Lehman had served under Henry Kissinger at the National Security Council and then was named deputy director of the Arms Control and Disarmament Agency, headed then by Fred Ikle. During his tenure in these two posts, Lehman had helped to formulate the terms of the SALT I agreement, participated in negotiations with the Soviets, and watched the SALT process at close hand for eleven years.

The experience left him extremely cynical about Soviet tactics and intentions, alarmed at the weakness and drift of the Carter administration's foreign policy and dismayed by the U.S.'s strategic inferiority codified by SALT

II. Currently the president of the Abington Corporation, a Washington consulting firm that serves defense contractors, Lehman plays a leading role behind the scenes on Capitol Hill in the effort to defeat SALT II. He is assisted greatly in this effort by an extremely incisive mind and a superbly honed ability to marshal facts and present them in a convincing, even eloquent, way—not an easy thing to do when you are discussing the arcana of SALT. Arguing for Senate amendment of SALT II, Lehman stated,

As an attempt to embody equality and verifiability it has been badly botched, but with serious effort the Senate can make changes sufficient to have it aid, not obstruct, stable deterrence and hence earn Senate ratification. The Soviets, after theatrics, will of course return to negotiate on the Senate changes. If they were not to, the necessary assumption underlying the entire SALT process would be proved false and our awareness of that objective fact would in itself add immeasurably to our security.

There are "three major levels of objection" to SALT II in Lehman's opinion. The first is the specific terms of the treaty:

Five major issues and several minor should be renegotiated. For example, allowing the Soviets and prohibiting the United States 308 heavy ICBMs each with seven times our Minuteman throwweight is unacceptably destabilizing. That force alone would contain more megatonnage than all of our ICBMs and SLBMs combined. Giving up an equal right to such formidable weapons makes their future reduction and elimination impossible, for as Jan Lodal has wisely written, "We cannot expect the Soviets to make major unilateral concessions simply because we have chosen unilaterally to forego certain programs on our own."

The limits banning flight testing and development of mobile ICBMs is also unacceptable. The United States must, and for stability's sake the Soviets should also, deploy at once a mobile ICBM. To ban them is absurd.

The limits banning deployment of sea-launched and ground-launched cruise missiles over 325 miles while permitting the Soviets unlimited deployments of the 3000 mile MIRVed mobile SS-20 ballistic missile must be corrected. The fact that this U.S. concession, like that of mobiles, is in the Protocol is no excuse because as Lodal points out ". . . the Protocol does set a precedent for U.S. acceptance of continuing limits on cruise missiles and mobile land-based ICBMs in SALT III."

In this agreement the method of dealing with Backfire is an affront to common sense. There is no disagreement in the intelligence community that Backfire can attack the United States unrefueled on the same profile our B-52 would use against the Soviet Union, i.e., one-way with recovery in a third country. Yet the United States accepts and sanctifies a statement embodying what it knows to be false, that Backfire does not have the capability to strike targets in the United States. SALT thus effectively exempts an entire category of perhaps 400 strategic bombers more capable than the Soviet Bison, which is counted, four-fifths as capable as our cancelled B-1, and more than twice as capable as our only medium bomber the FB-111 (of which we have 65).

Nemeses of détente *(left to right from top)*: Mark Schneider and Tidal McCoy, staff aides to Sen. Jake Garn; W. Scott Thompson, Fletcher School of Law and Diplomacy; Charles Kupperman, policy analyst, Committee on the Present Danger; William Schneider, senior fellow, Hudson Institute, and assistant to Rep. Jack Kemp; Chris Lay, legislative assistant to Rep. Steve Symms

The verification provisions are worse than inadequate because they legitimize substantial interference with U.S. national technical means. The ABM treaty in SALT I prohibits such interference. SALT II okays wholesale denial of telemetry, of production, of storage, and of testing data. Equally bad, it has placed the U.S. Government in the odious position of making sweeping claims for our intelligence capabilities that are demonstrably false. At a minimum these treaty deficiencies must be corrected in the Senate. Otherwise we face SALT III having mortgaged our theater cruise missiles and our mobile ICBM options; having legitimized the Backfire bomber and the SS-20 as exempt from limits; having legitimized Soviet interference with U.S. verification systems and having codified a unilateral Soviet right to heavy missiles.

The second level of objection, Lehman contends, is "to our conduct of the SALT process" during three administrations:

Eleven years of negotiations have seen eleven years of sustained Soviet strategic buildup emphasizing counterforce, and a substantial relative decline in U.S. capability. Dr. Brzezinki posed the question "My concern is that the Soviet leaders . . . may be deliberately exploiting SALT to attain military 'superiority' over the United States." Whether or not that is true, I can attest first hand that while Soviet defense programs seem to dictate Soviet SALT positions, U.S. SALT positions *have* effectively determined U.S. defense programs.

If therefore the eleven years of SALT have had counterproductive results, it does not necessarily follow that the process should be abandoned. It does follow that our entire approach should be changed to test directly the proposition, as yet untested, that the United States and Soviets do in fact share the same goal in SALT, i.e., *stabilizing* the strategic balance through real equality. Renegotiating Senate amendments is an ideal first step.

Lehman's third reason for objecting to ratification of SALT II without amendment is that is would legitimize a "bankrupt approach to national security" pursued by the Carter administration:

It would renew a mandate to the most narrow and stubbornly ideological group of policy officials ever assembled in an American government. For whatever reason, in the Carter transition, every sub-cabinet post of SALT importance was staffed from the foundation, Senate staff, and political law firm based anti-defense cult in Washington. Not one official is to be found in the administration SALT group drawn from the moderate or conservative wings of the Democratic Party let alone a Republican hard-liner. By contrast, Kissinger included many Democrats and disarmament advocates among his SALT advisers like Lodal, Sonnenfeldt, Hyland, Lord, Aaron, Slocombe, Newhouse and Harold Brown. SALT under Carter has been formulated and negotiated by a totally homogeneous circle of friends like Aaron at the NSC, Slocombe at Defense, Gelb at State, and Warnke at ACDA, all with lengthy records of commitment to the view that U.S. arms are the principal cause of the arms race. This single-minded focus of attention upon restraining American and Western systems has led some to conclude that these gentlemen truly believe that it is Western military institutions and Western contractors that constitute the principal threat to world stability. It is held as an act of faith by important policy makers that military superiority in the nuclear age has no consequence, and hence there should be no cause for concern as the Soviets attain it.

But the Carter disarmament chieftains know that their deformed reasoning will not sell to the American people, Lehman says, and

this has led to the ultimate corruption. The officials and institutions of government have become enmired in a spiral of disinformation wherein language is drained of meaning. The B-1 is cancelled ". . . to strengthen the air-breathing leg of the triad,' a 2 percent decline in the defense budget is described as '3 percent real growth'. The Navy's shipbuilding program is halved in the name of 'strengthening our surface fleet''; the U.S. concession not to demand compensation for a 4 to 1 Soviet advantage in forward-based systems is called a Soviet concession. Modernization limits that in fact permit deployment of a new Soviet generation of five new missiles are described as if they permit only one. Measures that cannot provide detection of violations are described as "adequate" verification.

Lehman expressed confidence from the outset that the administration's defective SALT treaty would not sell to the American people, and he will likely be proved right. If SALT II is defeated, Lehman, without question, will have been a factor in causing its demise. His competence and expertise on military affairs have already been widely noted and praised. Columnist James J. Kilpatrick, for instance, touts Lehman as an excellent choice for Secretary of the Navy in a Republican administration, and columnist George Will has named him as his favorite for Secretary of Defense.

Whether or not he gets one of these positions, there is no doubt that a major defense role will be Lehman's for the asking if the Republicans take over the White House in 1981.

Even assuming the optimum development from the standpoint of U.S. national security—which is to say, the defeat of SALT II, the election of a president in 1980 who has the correct perception of the problem facing the United States and the right program to redress it *and* a Congress receptive to enacting the necessary legislation to implement such a program—it would be several years before the benefits of such an ambitious effort could be felt. In the interim, the United States faces a parlous period in the early 1980s, a "window" in which the Soviets are theoretically capable of effecting a first strike on the United States that would disable our land-based ICBMs and leave the Soviets enough missiles left over to destroy American cities should the United States retaliate.

Faced with this harrowing prospect, a number of U.S. defense experts are convinced that the nation must energetically pursue a "quick fix" program that utilizes existing weapons systems to reduce U.S. vulnerability until the new weapons systems can be brought on line.

One of the foremost of these experts is W. Scott Thompson, 37, formerly an assistant to Secretary of Defense Donald Rumsfeld and now a professor at the Fletcher School of Diplomacy at Tufts University. Thompson is well-equipped for the task both intellectually and by pedigree (his father-in-law is Paul Nitze, a former secretary of the Navy and one of the nation's most brilliant defense analysts), and his wide-ranging expertise in national security matters is recognized in the defense community and on Capitol Hill. Thompson is a member of the National Strategy Information Center's "Strategic Alternatives Team" (SAT) and served as coeditor (along with William R. van Cleave) of the SAT monograph *Strategic Options for the Early Eighties.*

Describing the SAT's starting premises in the preface to the monograph, Thompson and Van Cleave write

The ability of the United States to meet threats projected eight or ten years in the future, given timely decisions, was not questioned. The group's concern was with a Soviet strategic threat that now seems very likely to peak relative to U.S. capabilities in the early 1980s, well before the United States could respond, given ordinary program procedures and lead times. Discussion revealed a consensus on the importance of determining if and how the United States could effectively adjust its strategic forces to such a near term threat, should there be a national will to do so.

. . . At the outset the Team restricted its efforts to the central strategic force balance between the United States and the Soviet Union, and to options that might improve the balance within—somewhat arbitrarily—1,000 days. For shorthand, these options became referred to as "quick fixes."

. . . What if, the group asked, there should be a national consensus that it is necessary to make the effort to avert in a very short period of time what would otherwise be an unacceptably dangerous strategic military situation? What options would be feasible and effective within 1,000 days?

Given these parameters, the SAT team formulated a "quick fix" program that includes the following suggested steps that could be completed within 1000 days:

—acceleration of programs already underway;
—resurrection of cancelled programs;
—adaptation of new technologies;
—truly makeshift or temporary fixes to existing capabilities;
—new basing of existing systems or the addition of other components;
—operational changes;
—ways to complicate Soviet strategic planning;
—new uses of existing systems or components;
—joint efforts with allies on some or all of the above.

The vulnerability of our land-based deterrent forces in the early 1980s is already officially acknowledged by the Secretary of Defense. In view of this threat, the first priority is to erase this major force vulnerability and to ensure the pre-launch survivability of our ICBMs, as well as other existing forces and then to establish 'essential equivalence' with Soviet strategic forces in all important measures.

. . . The cost of returning our land-based missile forces to their former effectiveness as an assured nuclear deterrent is estimated at most to be a few billion dollars per year. There are no technological, production, or operational problems which would present an insurmountable barrier to this option.

. . . Operational air breathing options include: 1) add parallel runways to existing air fields; 2) move SAC bases to central CONUS locations; 3) development of multiple aimpoint basing with shelters; and 4) increased alert rates and dispersal.

Thompson is definitely not a cheerful optimist as regards the U.S. strategic situation. "We are in frightfully bad shape due to the disasters of the Carter presidency," he says, "and it is necessary to face the fact that we are likely to be at a disadvantage compared to the Soviet Union until the MX missile is deployed near the end of the 1980s."

Under Carter, Thompson says, "The Navy's shipbuilding program has been cut in half, literally; the MX missile is still basically at the same stage of deployment it was in 1976; the B-1 bomber has been cancelled and promising programs such as the cruise missile have been slowed."

The development that will come as the biggest shock to Americans, he maintains, is that "we have lost our technological lead in many areas. Three years ago, the United States still maintained a lead in technological resources but that lead has withered in most areas. Today, the Soviets are outspending us by three-to-one in technological research related to the military." Thompson does believe, however, that there is much that can still be done to salvage the situation, given a change of administrations.

"We need a three-stage program," he says. First, we have a desperate need for bandages to staunch the bleeding. Second, we need surgery, and third we need a program to rehabilitate the patient.

"The very first thing I would do is to change the policies of the Voice of America and Radio Free Europe to make them into aggressive projectors of our point of view and aggressive critics of the Soviet system," Thompson says. "We have let the Russians have a free ride for far too long. The more dissension we can stir up inside the Soviet Union, the less capable the Soviet leaders will be in focusing on expansionist moves."

In Thompson's view, what is necessary in the short run is "to keep the waters muddied, to kick dirt in the enemy's eye, as it were, so as to keep the Soviets sufficiently off balance that they will not feel confident enough to risk everything in an all-out confrontation."

"It is essential for an American president to announce unequivocally that we are going to challenge Soviet aims around the world. Why, for instance, should we give them a free ride in Afghanistan? It is inevitable that they will win there eventually, but they should be made to pay in the process like we did in Vietnam."

Thompson also believes that the United States should vigorously push for the installation of offensive nuclear weapons in Western Europe, thus forcing the Soviets to spend billions of dollars to counteract them—money that would otherwise be spent on offensive weapons. In addition, he believes, the United States must give priority to developing its forward bases around the world in such places as South Korea, the Philippines, Morocco, and Diego Garcia.

"The Navy offers a way to fill the void in the short term," he says, "and that means the strengthening of existing forward bases and the acquisition of others. Also urgently needed is a crash program to build up the fleet."

Thompson believes in a policy of "talking loudly and carrying a big stick in present conditions of U.S. inferiority. The Soviets did it for years when they were much inferior to the United States and they scared the hell out of us. We have got to think along the same lines."

Also desperately needed, in his view, is a policy that reassures allies and provides them with the weapons and assistance they need. "The moment such a policy is enunciated," Thompson believes, "an enormous sigh of relief will be heard in about fifty capitals around the world."

A "new alliance superstructure" is also on Thompson's suggested agenda. "We have got to develop an alliance that brings together pro-Western powers around the world—from the Japanese to the Saudis so that an integrated plan can be developed for the defense of what is left to defend."

Thompson hopes devoutly that the SALT Treaty is defeated in the U.S. Senate, and even if it is ratified, he urges that it be terminated after the six-month notification period required. Without SALT, he says, we could do a number of things such as putting the Minuteman missiles in a multiple aim point configuration that would obviate the Soviet first strike capability for the near future. He also urges the abrogation of the ABM Treaty by the president on the grounds that a national emergency exists and that the Soviets have cheated. This, he says, would allow the United States to develop a point defense program for the nation's nuclear arsenal.

Thompson is convinced that the Soviets will provoke a crisis with the United States before the end of Carter's term. "I think they will find it irresistible to refrain from plucking a few choice cherries before this most inept of presidents is out of office," he says. Ironically, the great danger in such a confrontation, Thompson believes, is that "Carter may actually believe that the United States is still as strong as he says it is and take us over the brink in a confrontation with a Soviet power that is increasingly superior. The irony today is that the hawks are the doves because we have a realistic view of U.S. capabilities."

The great challenge facing the United States in the 1980s, he contends, is to effectively resist Soviet expansionism without provoking a decisive confrontation, and to buy time so that the defenses of the United States can be built up.

Thompson acknowledges that a U.S. policy of concerted rearmament might provoke the Soviet leadership to challenge the United States while the Soviets are at the apex of their superiority. "That is a real possibility," he says, "But it is a risk that must be taken, because if we don't take the necessary steps to bolster our defenses we are doomed to defeat."

Thompson thinks a program adequate to get the job done will mean an increase in defense spending in excess of six percent annually, adjusted for inflation. This represents an enormous increase for a nation confronted with the burden of inflation and recession, but Thompson thinks such a step will be palatable. "I firmly believe that in the next few years, the Soviets are going to provoke a crisis, probably on some totally unforeseen issue, and that crisis is going to bring home to the American people the gravity of our situation. Once the seriousness of the situation has sunk in, the American people will respond."

Another astute analyst of strategic affairs is Colin S. Gray, 36, a staff member of the Hudson Institute. An acute concern of Gray's is the deteriorating military defenses of Western Europe. Writing in the winter 1979 issue of the Heritage Foundation's *Policy Review,* Gray calls NATO "less than a very serious military organization." NATO's central strategic conept, "flexible response" is "bankrupt" according to Gray. This approach Gray says was designed in the mid-sixties and holds that "deterrence should be thought of as a seamless web of ever more threatening possibilities and that an aggressor in Europe would face the prospect of tripping a series of ever more destructive Western responses."

In the absence of a dramatic reversal in favor of the West in strategic and theater weapons, Gray says, the policy of flexible response is bankrupt. Unless the United States is prepared to take difficult and expensive steps to reverse this disparity, Gray says, NATO must design another strategy for dealing with a Soviet attack. A principle ingredient in such a strategy, Gray believes, would be the deployment of the neutron warhead. Carter's erratic performance on the neutron warhead, in his view, "is a candidate for the case file of classic examples of how not to approach arms control negotiations." Gray is a prolific writer on military affairs. Among his works are *The Soviet-American Arms Race* (1976), *U.S. Strategy in the Decade Ahead* (1978) and *Strategic Studies and Public Policy* (1979).

Appearing in the same issue of *Policy Review* as Gray's article was "The Soviet World View" by Charles M. Kupperman, 29, a defense analyst and research associate for the Committee on the Present Danger. A basic problem for U.S. policy makers, says Kupperman, is their failure to face the fact that the United States and the USSR have different world views. The Soviets, he says, have a goal of global dominance and all available resources and tactics are put in the service of attaining that goal. The Soviets, Kupperman says, see no inconsistency in pursuing a policy of "detente" on the one hand and engaging in history's most massive strategic buildup on the other. The Soviets, he says, see detente not as a relaxation of the struggle but, rather, as an intensification of it.

Next to Soviet aggressiveness, Kupperman sees in the United States a decline of "political will" and "strategic lethargy." It is essential that the United States undertake an urgent program to redress the strategic imbalance, Kupperman says, because the emerging Soviet superiority is "basic to all else that has happened or may happen in the way of a shift in the balance of world forces."

Kupperman is conceded by advocates and opponents of SALT alike to have done superb work for the Committee on the Present Danger in its effort to defeat the treaty. It can be presumed that he—and Colin Gray—will be offered the opportunity to serve in important defense-related positions in a Republican administration.

There is a considerable body of military affairs expertise to be found among the staff members on Capitol Hill and, in the event a conservative administration comes to power in 1980, it is likely that many of these conservatively-oriented defense experts on the Hill will be called upon to fill important policy positions in the national security complex, and to help facilitate the passage of a new defense program through Congress.

One of the foremost of these young defense experts is Dr. William Schneider, an aide to Representative Jack Kemp and a fellow at the Hudson Institute in New York. Schneider, 37, was formerly legislative assistant to Sen. James Buckley. He is well-traveled, well-connected in defense circles, and is extremely knowledgeable about the whole gamut of defense problems.

"I think a conservative administration should have three main priorities in terms of defense and foreign policy," Schneider says. "First we have got to arrive at a satisfactory definition of U.S. international interests—something we haven't had since Vietnam. Since then, there has been a steady narrowing of our interests. The Carter administration has tended to equate them with Western Europe, Japan, and possibly the eastern Mediterranean although here they have been ambiguous. Given this narrowing of interests, the Soviets have moved to fill the vacuum." What the United States has got to do, in Schneider's view, is "to make a persuasive demonstration of resolve wherever U.S. allies exist. This certainly includes the Persian Gulf region and it includes Africa." Schneider finds the Soviet capability to airlift troops (as in the case of Ethiopia) to be extremely impressive, and he believes the United States should develop a similar capability. In this connection he applauds the stated goal of the Carter administration to develop a mobile 100,000-man strike force, although he finds the steps being taken to develop such a force to be grossly inadequate.

The second priority, Schneider states, should be "the modernization of our forces and particularly of our strategic forces. These forces have essentially not been modernized since the early 1960s. We have an enormous backlog of modernization that has got to be addressed on an urgent basis." In this area the modernization of the Navy takes the highest priority in Schneider's view. "Fifteen years ago, we were building forty ships a year, and now we are building eight," he says. "Carter cut Ford's shipbuilding program in half. I think the narrowing of U.S. interests is paralleled by the shrinkage of the Navy, since it is primarily the Navy that projects U.S. power around the world."

The third priority, says Schneider, should be the modernization of U.S. ground and tactical air forces. "There is renewed anxiety in Western Europe over U.S. military capabilities in Europe," he says, "but the steps being taken to redress this are inadequate." Schneider believes that "we desperately need to update our tactical doctrine for NATO. We are essentially operating under a World War II era doctrine that assumes the use of multi-million-man armies and the deployment of massive firepower. Now our forces in Europe are considerably smaller, and they are unlikely to be augmented either by regulars or reserves. We must plan to operate in an environment where we are vastly outnumbered. The changes in the Soviet disposition of forces in Europe makes doing more of the same futile."

The Soviets, Schneider notes, "are concentrating heavily on long-range tactical nuclear weapons—weapons with ranges in excess of 600 miles. The NATO tactical nuclear weapons, on the other hand, are limited to a range of 450 miles. This Soviet advantage has got to be redressed."

Schneider recommends the deployment of longer-range missiles and of neutron warheads—the high-radiation, low-blast weapon system originally scheduled for deployment in West Germany but since sidetracked by President Carter. "The possession of this weapon would give our deterrent increased credibility," he says, "because it would impress on the Soviets that we could use a nuclear weapon to stop the advance of their troops without destroying Germany in the process. The situation now is increasingly unstable as their advantage grows."

Schneider also believes a new middle-range missile is needed in Western Europe to offset the deployment of the Soviet SS-20. "The officials I have spoken with in Western Europe realize that the SS-20 must be countered but they are skittish about publicly supporting such a move in view of their experience with the neutron warhead," he says. In that case, the leaders of

Britain and West Germany supported the deployment of the weapon in the face of vociferous opposition from the strong leftist elements in their countries only to find that having gone out on a limb, Carter sawed it off by cancelling the production of the weapon. With the firm restoration of American leadership, however, Schneider believes the NATO allies will agree to take the steps that are necessary.

He believes that of the Republican candidates Ronald Reagan shows the best appreciation of the moves that must be taken, but notes that the Republican party is much more united on the need for upgrading our defenses then it has been in many years. "Most of the Republican candidates would be dramatically better than what we have now," Schneider says.

The leading Republican opponent of SALT II in the U.S. Senate is Sen. Jake Garn of Utah. Garn is a former Air Force officer and has retained a keen interest in military affairs. He is one of the few people in the Senate who has the patience or the aptitude to master the arcana of the SALT debate. Garn *has* mastered the intricacies of SALT and has proved to be a resourceful and tenacious opponent of the treaty. Two reasons for his success are two young staff members advising him on the subject: Mark Schneider, 34, and Ty McCoy, 32.

Schneider, a graduate of the University of Southern California, has worked at the Stanford Research Institute, the BDM Corporation and, for five years, at the Department of Energy on arms control and intelligence affairs. His knowledge of the subtleties of the SALT debate is encyclopedic, but Schneider's opinion of SALT is blunt and easy to understand. "I think the whole process is counterproductive," he says. "We have subordinated our national security needs to political considerations and the result has been a disaster. The mentality behind the SALT process is that we can achieve security through arms control and that unilateral restraint on our part will produce restraint on the part of the Soviets. It's an extremely naive assumption and it has been proved to be false."

Schneider believes the United States needs a procurement program such as we had in the 1950s. "In the fifties we saw a threat and we responded rationally," he says. Given the growing superiority of the Soviets, Schneider believes a crash weapons program of the sort needed would mean a spending increase in the range of $40 billion implemented immediately, and real growth of 6 percent over the next five years. An urgent necessity in Schneider's view is a mobile or semi-mobile ICBM for the United States. The MX missile is scheduled to be based in this mode but Schneider, in the absence of SALT, would like to see the United States base the existing Minuteman missile in this configuration by constructing a number of silos for each missile and shifting the missile back and forth between them. "To do this quickly is an urgent priority and this precludes basing all or most of these missiles in the sparsely populated regions of Utah and Nevada," he maintains. "The infrastructure is not there and it would take too long to build it. What we've got to do is build most of these multiple silos near the existing bases, and some of these are near populated areas. This will mean seeking legislation to ease existing environmental protection restraints."

In addition, the Garn plan would provide for upgrading U.S. defenses and for revamping U.S. strategic doctrine, whether or not a SALT treaty is ratified. Among the changes: most U.S. ICBMs would be retargeted away from Soviet cities and onto military targets; the vulnerability of U.S. ICBMs would be reduced by measures like multiple silo sites, civil defense measures would be taken, and the U.S. bomber force modernized.

Garn's other advisor on SALT-related matters is Tidal M. ("Ty") McCoy. A native of Florida, McCoy graduated from West Point in 1967 and received his masters degree from George Washington University in 1975. For the next three years, he worked in the Pentagon as Director of Policy Research in the office of the under secretary of defense for policy and in that capacity was coeditor of the secretary of defense's annual report to Congress for fiscal years 1975, 1976, and 1978. McCoy is a skilled public speaker and frequently appears as a lecturer and seminar leader at the Naval War College, the Defense Institute School, and the CIA.

With Schneider, McCoy helped Garn to develop a comprehensive alternative to the existing SALT treaty. A complex point-for-point rewriting of the treaty, the Garn plan is the most detailed alternative to the Carter-Brezhnev treaty provided by opponents of the pact. Among the features of the Garn alternative:

(1) Each side would be allowed the same number of strategic nuclear delivery vehicles (SNDV), starting with 2,400 and gradually lowering this to 1,600 by December 1983. Within this total, there would also be sublimits, equally applied, on the number of missiles with multiple warheads allowed. In addition, the number of "heavy" missiles would also be the same for both sides, beginning at 308 and diminishing to 200 by December 1983.

(2) The Soviet Backfire bomber would be included, with each plane being counted as three-fourths of an SNDV (in recognition of its one-way capability). Our FB-111s, on the same principle, would then each be counted as one-half an SNDV. Garn would also increase the number of cruise missiles the United States is permitted, allow the transfer of this and other technology to our allies, and increase range limits on ground- and submarine-launched cruise missiles.

(3) Safeguards would be included against cheating. Destruction of old missiles would be required to preclude their storage use on reusable launchers. Technical rather than size limitations would be written in, to guard against the secret development of "new" missiles. The number of medium-

range missiles that could be converted to ICBMs would be limited. Encoding of telemetry from missile testing, permitted under the existing treaty, would be banned. And specific provision would be made for on-site inspection.

Another congressional staff member who is well-versed in military matters is Chris D. Lay, 32, special assistant to Rep. Steve Symms (R.-Ida.). Lay is a specialist in air power, and as such is extremely worried about the state of U.S. air defenses. "Right now we have very little in the way of air defenses," Lay says. Our main line of defense is the 300 F-101 and F-106 fighter interceptors we have. The F-101 is basically a mid-1950s plane and the F-106 a late-fifties plane."

These aircraft, Lay says, would provide some protection against the older Soviet bombers such as the Badger (an intermediate range plane), the Bear, and the Bison (both long-range bombers). But against the new Soviet Backfire Bomber, Lay says, these fighters would offer little protection. At the end of 1979, the Soviets had about 200 Backfire bombers with more than thirty being built per month. The Air National Guard squadrons located around the country would, in his opinion, be of some help, but in the face of a full-scale Soviet attack their usefulness would be marginal.

U.S. radar systems are also inadequate, Lay says, a contention corroborated by a number of well-publicized violations of U.S. air space. Lay would like to see much wider use of the AWACS system (Airborne Warning and Control System), a radar with a "look-down" capability—the capability to detect aircraft flying between the ground and the AWACS plane. He also favors configuring the F-14 and F-15 fighter planes, modern fighters new in the U.S. arsenal but which presently are configured for ground support activity rather than interceptor duty.

"Another area where we are heading toward disaster is our bomber force," Lay says. "In the SALT agreement, 546 U.S. B-52s are counted toward our delivery system total, but 229 of those are in the boneyard. Most of those have been cannibalized to get parts for the operating B-52s, and even those that could be rehabilitated would take thirty to ninety days to make operational." Lay states that it is estimated that, in the event of a Soviet first strike, 70 percent of the B-52s not knocked out would reach at least one of their targets in the USSR. Should the Soviets complete an integrated radar defense system, however, that percentage would fall dramatically. They are reported to be working hard on just such a system. Meanwhile, Lay says, "We are back to square one on modernizing our bomber force. With the cancellation of the B-1 we are back to where we were in the mid-sixties when options for a new bomber were being debated."

The resulting bomber, of course, was the B-1 which was cancelled just as it was ready to go into production. Now, according to Lay, the Soviets are hard at work developing a post-Backfire bomber dubbed the "Soviet B-1," a large supersonic bomber capable of hitting the United States and returning to the USSR. Lay would like to see the United States respond by reopening B-1 production. "The start-up problems would be substantial," he says, "but in three years we could have sixty-five produced."

Despite his worries about U.S. defenses, Lay says he is encouraged by the research and development trends. "Our R&D budgets sort of bottomed out in 1973," he says, "and they have been on the upswing since then. I'm encouraged by research into things such as two-stage cruise missiles, supersonic cruise missiles, work on new superstrength air frames, and communications advances."

Paralleling the decline in U.S. defense capabilities and the retrenchment of U.S. power around the globe has been a progressive constriction of the U.S. intelligence agencies, both domestic and foreign. In recent years, the House Committee on Un-American Activities has been abolished as have the Senate Internal Security Subcommittee and the Eubversive Activities Control Board. The FBI and CIA have been subjected to lengthy Congressional investigations and their charters have been rewritten in such a way as to severely circumscribe this ability to do the job they were originally established to do.

One of the most perceptive analysts of U.S. intelligence problems is Angelo Codevilla, 36, a staff analyst with the Senate Select Committee on Intelligence. Before coming to his present position, Cordevilla served as a naval intelligence officer from 1969–71, assisting in the publication of the *Fleet Intelligence Journal*, the Atlantic Fleet's intelligence publication. He also worked in the aerospace section of the Bendix Corporation and served for a time on the staff of the Hoover Institution.

The prevailing view of intelligence in the liberal foreign policy establishment, Codevilla says, is that, "The intelligence community of the United States is an extremely decentralized group of amoral, headstrong men who became used to acting beyond the law and without their lawful superiors' knowledge. These men tend to be visceral conservatives. They are either military or have a profound bias for military or violent solutions. Thus they gave the American people inflated notions of foreign and domestic threats.

"At home this meant that people innocent of any subversive or criminal conduct were deprived of their constitutional rights. Abroad, this tendency led to unconscionable interference in the internal affairs of countries such as Italy and Chile in order to thwart the fortunes of Communist movements which are of no legitimate concern to us."

In many of the celebrated cases alleging abuse by the intelligence agencies, Codevilla says, the agencies have taken a bum rap. "The touted abuses such as electronic surveillance of Martin Luther King Jr.'s womanizing took place at the direction of Cabinet officers or of the President. The CIA's investigation of the connection between domestic groups which were opposing the United States' effort in Vietnam and Communist countries followed a presidential directive."

Real reform of the intelligence establishment *is* necessary, Codevilla says, but not for the reasons given. Rather, it is necessary because "our defenses against terrorists, enemy spies and contamination of our intelligence by disinformation are weak, to say the least. The number of hostile agents working against us has increased, while the CIA's counterintelligence has been gutted and the FBI's has not kept pace. In addition, our counterintelligence and counterterrorist forces are working under unprecedented restrictions. Nor are we suffering from a surfeit of information from a net of penetrations which covers the world. Rather, we have a clandestine service which can barely be called clandestine. Other government agencies refuse to give it more than fig leaves; the names of its operatives are published with impunity."

The main scandal of our foreign intelligence service, Codevilla says, is "its gross and consistent underestimation of the size, scope and purpose of the Soviet strategic buildup over the last decade and a half. Throughout the period, those who sought to prevent the United States from staying ahead of or even abreast of the Soviets found a powerful ally in the CIA.

The officially prescribed cure for our intelligence maladies—greater centralization and political control—is, in Codevilla's mind, the opposite of the reform needed. "During the last decade and a half the military intelligence services have been much closer to the truth about the size of the Soviet buildup than the CIA, but they were only given meager roles in preparing the estimates. What we need is more decentralization, more independent centers of investigation so that the president has more options to compare."

As a means of simultaneously upholding the constitutional rights of the citizens and protecting the national security against the rampant disclosure of classified material, Codevilla recommends the following steps:

(1) Establish stricter guidelines for classifying information as important to the nation's security.

(2) Establish procedures for releasing classified information to the public.

(3) Make the unauthorized disclosure of classified information a strict-liability crime, to be tried in open court with full constitutional guarantees.

(4) Make punishment for the crime of unauthorized disclosure vary between purely nominal (e.g., a one dollar fine) and heavy penalties, depending on the disclosed information's importance to the nation and to the harm to be reasonably expected from the disclosure.

(5) Vest the right to determine harm done by the disclosure in the trial jury, meeting *in camera*, subject to security clearance and bound to secrecy. The attorneys would be similarly cleared and bound.

(6) Ensure that the two questions be handled separately in the appeals process and that the question of harm done continues to be decided *in camera*.

There are numerous other highly qualified defense analysts in congressional offices who could be expected to either enter a Republican administration or play an important part in the Congressional battle for a revitalized defense program. Probably foremost among these is Richard Perle, 38, assistant to Sen. Henry Jackson (D.-Wash.). Urbane, witty, and brilliant, Perle is perhaps the most knowledgeable—and certainly the most influential—congressional staff member when it comes to matters of military preparedness. He has an encyclopedic knowledge of defense-related arcana, is an astute and cold-blooded realist when it comes to weighing Soviet intentions and he enjoys the complete confidence of Sen. Jackson who sits on the powerful Senate Armed Services Committee. Whether or not he goes to work in a Republican administration, Perle will be extremely important in designing a defense program that has both the support of the administration and Congress.

Other important staff members include Sven Kramer, 40, an analyst with the Senate Republican Policy Committee; Michael Donly, 25, assistant to Sen. Roger Jepsen (R.-Iowa); Christopher Lehman, 29, an assistant to Sen. John Warner (R.-Va.); David Fitzgerald, 35, assistant to Sen. Gordon Humphrey (R.-N.H.); Ronald Lehman, 36, policy analyst on the Senate Armed Services Committee.

One area of great interest is that of lasers and charged particle beam weapons, weapons once relegated to the realm of science fiction but which are being discussed more and more as possibilities in the near future. The man responsible for the growing interest in this field is Maj. Gen. George Keegan, former head of Air Force intelligence. As General Keegan tells the story, it was in 1972 that he began to suspect that the Soviets might be on the way to a breakthrough in a highly advanced weapons system. Keegan, who was then chief of Air Force intelligence, says that Stephen Williams, with the Foreign Technology Division at Wright-Patterson Air Force Base near Dayton, Ohio, told him that photographs had revealed suspiciously large amounts of hydrogen emitting from the Soviet test facility in the Semipalatinsk region of the southern USSR.

In reviewing the evidence, Keegan came to the conclusion that the Soviets might be trying to build the prototype for a charged particle beam weapon— a futuristic, laserlike device, previously consigned to the *Star Wars* realm of weaponry. Keegan sought expert advice on the feasibility of building such a weapon, but his inquiries met with uniform skepticism. The United States has attempted several times to implement the charged particle beam concept, he was told, and had failed.

Undaunted, Keegan kept searching. Finally, he came upon a paper in the

March 12, 1973, issue of *Physical Review Letters* titled "Autoresonant Accelerator Concept," written by M. L. Sloan and W. E. Drummond of Austin Research Associates of Austin, Texas. In the obscure jargon of their science, the two physicists explained their concept in the abstract of their paper:

We present a new ion accelerator idea which combines the basic concepts of traveling wave and collective acceleration. The lower cyclotron made of a relativistic electron beam along a spatially decreasing magnetic field B constitutes the traveling wave, the wave phase velocity varying inversely with B. The negative energy character of the wave allows automatic extraction of energy from the electron beam for the acceleration process. Typical ion energy versus current outputs are estimated.

Relying extensively on Soviet scientific literature in the field, the two scientists concluded that it was theoretically possible to build such a device.

Pressed later by Keegan to describe the essentials for such a weapons system, Sloan sketched a prototype that corresponded closely to the Soviet Semipalatinsk facility. In an article in a confidential newsletter published in London, A. H. Stanton Candlin described the Soviet site as having the following characteristics:

At the Semipalatinsk site, known to the USAF intelligence as PNUT (possible nuclear underground test), the same place being known to the CIA as URDF 3 (unidentified research and development facility 3) there has been an intensive programme for the past ten years or more. Concurrently there has been a concentrated intelligence collection and evaluation programme to resolve the meaning of the Semipalatinsk site. The place consists of a complex of buildings with a central building 200 ft. wide and 700 ft. long with walls of reinforced concrete 10 ft. thick. It has also been made clear by high resolution photographic techniques that there have been excavations indicating the existence of a very large underground complex as well, used for testing purposes.

Evidently the purpose of the establishment is to conduct high energy tests of a directed beam system deriving its energy from nuclear explosions with appropriate energy storage systems being used. Some of the officials involved in this study in the United States have listed the technologies that can be applied to produce a beam weapon as (a) Explosive or pulsed power generation through either fission or fusion to achieve peak pulses of power; (b) Giant capacitors capable of storing extremely high levels of power for fractions of a second; (c) Electron injectors capable of generating high energy pulse streams of electrons at high velocities; (d) A collective accelerator to generate electron pulse streams or hot gas plasma necessary to accelerate other subatomic particles at high velocities; (e) Flux compression to convert energy from explosive generators to energy to produce the electron beam; (f) Switching necessary to store the energy from the generators to power stores. The lines must be cryogenically cooled because of the extreme power levels involved.

The level of energy required by a beam weapon is 10^{12} joules per pulse matched with the energy of a particle in the beam from 1 to 100 giga electron volts. These energy levels are so high that they have provoked much scepticism among some analysts.

Liquid hydrogen in large amounts is believed by some officials to be utilized to cushion the nuclear explosive generator sphere and for cryogenic pumping of large drift tubes nearly a kilometer in length through which the beams are propagated for underground testing. In both cases large amounts of gaseous hydrogen are formed and released into the atmosphere, probably carrying large amounts of nuclear debris or radioactive tritium that can be exploded at altitude and dispersed to avoid harming people below, according to some U.S. scientists.

Explosions of such gaseous hydrogen are now being detected with regularity from Soviet experients . . . and scientific studies of the gas releases and explosions have confirmed their source as being near the Semipalatinsk site.

It seems that these breakthroughs in high energy physics involving explosive generation were solved in the U.S.S.R. by Soviet academician Andrei Terletsky, formerly a KGB agent in Sweden, and Andrei Sakharov, the well-known dissident.

After an in-depth investigation, Keegan concluded that the Soviets were indeed developing a charged particle beam weapon, and he stated: "The Soviet Union is twenty years ahead of the United States in a technology which they believe will neutralize the ballistic missile." Faced with this information, Keegan determined to attempt to initiate a crash research program in the area. He enlisted Lee Sloan, then 26, to help coordinate the effort. The two of them went to see William Clements, then secretary of the army (now Governor of Texas), to appeal for funds. Clements was impressed by the arguments, and the fact that Sloan was the son of a good friend didn't hurt either. At Clements' direction, the Army appropriated a sum for research preliminary to developing a prototype beam weapon. Work on this project is still in progress at Austin Research Associates.

In the past six years the government has awarded contracts to several other defense-oriented research facilities to explore the possibilities of particle beam and laser weapons. Needless to say, the work in progress at these facilities is extremely sensitive in nature, and details are in short supply. Suffice it to say that should such a weapon be developed, current doctrine calls for it to be deployed on satellites from which they could, on command, obliterate Soviet missiles as they leave the atmosphere and while still over the Soviet Union. The rub, of course, is that the Soviets, as already mentioned, are working on such a weapon too—all of which raises the ghastly possibility that if the United States survives the threat of nuclear annihilation or blackmail at the hands of the Soviets in the 1980s, the nation may be locked in an even more deadly weapons race in the 1990s—a race in which space will be the battleground. Chilling though the prospect is, the nation would appear to have little choice other than to compete with the Soviets until such time as their leaders are prepared to negotiate real, mutual, and balanced arms control.

Bearding the bureaucrats: Donald Lambro, UPI reporter and author of *The Federal Rathole* and *Fat City*

14 | TAMING THE BUREAUCRACY

The federal bureaucracy is very much like the weather: everyone talks about it and nobody can seem to *do* anything about it. Among the most energetic flayers of the bureaucratic leviathan are the politicians of both parties—a fact that any political activist who has had to endure the indignities of the fried chicken circuit knows excruciatingly well.

In their newsletters, press releases, banquet speeches and on the hustings in the fall of an election year, members of the House and Senate from Aspin to Zorinsky can be heard (1) excoriating the malfeasance of the bureaucrats and (2) emphasizing to their constituents how much in money and services they have been able to wheedle out of the same bureaucrats.

It seems at times that the bureaucrat has replaced the village idiot, the traveling salesman and the farmer's daughter as the mother lode of the comedian's material. Ronald Reagan's bureaucratic horror stories and absurdities have become legendary. Malcolm Wallop rode to the Senate from Wyoming by lampooning the Occupational Safety and Health Administration's requirement that all farm employees, including cowboys riding the open range, have toilet facilities made available to them within 500 yards of their work place.

Each month Sen. William Proxmire regales the public and infuriates the Washington bureaucracy with the awarding of his "Golden Fleece" award, given to the federal department or agency for the most egregious waste of the taxpayers' money. Past winners include programs to study the sex habits of African tree frogs and the bossom sizes of airline stewardesses. Jimmy Carter was elected president largely on his reputation as an outsider who, as governor of Georgia, had streamlined the state bureaucracy and who would do the same in Washington.

Despite the gnashing of teeth, the speeches, the jokes and jeremiads, the federal bureaucracy, like the brook, goes on forever, the rate of growth

229

Reforming the bureaucracy *(left to right from top):* Ronald Moe, Library of Congress policy analyst; Howard Phillips, former acting director of the Office of Economic Opportunity; Jack Svahn, management consultant; Linda McMahan, staff analyst, Senate Finance Committee; Dr. Kenneth Clarkson, University of Miami; Dr. Edgar Olsen, University of Virginia

being the only variable in question. And growth there most certainly has been. In his essay, "Close Encounters with the Fourth Branch," Representative Dan Quayle sums up the growth of the federal government thus:

Today the federal government consumes 22 percent of the gross national product as compared to less than 10 percent in 1930. It employs a work force of 2.9 million people in civilian capacities. They are responsible for spending $458 billion annually and administering 1,040 domestic programs. This means one out of every six Americans works for the federal government, whereas in 1935 one out of every 204 was employed at the federal level. Since 1930 the federal payroll has increased dramatically, by 462 percent. During the same time span the entire population of the United States increased by only 71 percent.

The bureaucrats staff 11 major cabinet positions, 59 agencies, and more than 1,200 boards and advisory commissions. It is estimated that the operations of the federal government cost each man, woman, and child roughly $2,112 each year or $8,500 per average family.

Our government pays over 84,700 people to do nothing but regulate its citizens. Their job responsibility requires them to study products, situations, or conditions

which the government wants to control. Then it is the regulators' duty to write regulations to give the bureaucrats the control they desire. Bureaucrats are not interested in money, but only in the power to regulate and control. These regulations have consumed 1.2 million pages in the *Federal Register* since 1940 alone. There are so many rules and regulations that an accurate count is virtually impossible; yet, every American is responsible for knowing and complying with these laws.

When the Federal Commission on Paperwork compiled statistics, it concluded that our government pays $43 billion for paperwork. It also found that businesses which must comply with the paperwork demands must spend an additional $32 billion.

By conservative estimates, there are over 22,000 different forms required to be filed with the federal government. The Office of Mangement and Budget which accounts for only one third of all federal forms, has over 7,500 in use. Our taxing agency, the Internal Revenue Service, is not required to account for its forms and no one knows how many IRS really has.

This federal paperwork jungle required one small firm to file over 8,800 reports with 18 different agencies in one year alone.

. . . While the population of the United States has increased 60 times since the founding of the republic, the size of the bureaucracy has increased 8,170 times.

Rep. Richard Schulze (R.-Pa.) drives home the dimensions of bureaucratic growth by tracing the growth of the *Federal Register,* the publication which lists the government's new and proposed regulations. Says Schulze:

The annual number of pages published by the *Federal Register* between 1955 and 1975 increased from just over ten thousand to more than sixty thousand, making the compounded rate of growth just under five percent annually. However, between 1970 and 1975 the annual rate of growth jumped to nearly 33 percent.

. . . In 1975 there appeared in the *Federal Register* 177 proposed new rules and 2,865 proposed amendments to existing rules. In the same year 309 final rules and an additional 7,305 final rule amendments were published. Also in 1975, federal agencies alone had under consideration over 10,000 regulations—a 14 percent increase over 1974. Just to list the new regulations and interpretations in 1976 required 67,027 pages of fine print, which tally exceeds the number of pages in two complete sets of the *Encyclopedia Britannica!*

The volume of these regulations and directives affecting a single industry is astonishing. For example, over 5,000 regulations from at least 27 agencies apply to the steel industry alone.

In an attempt to dramatize the awesome size of the federal behomoth *U.S. News and World Report* pointed out that

—The federal government owns 2.5 billion square feet of building space—equal to 564 times the size of the Sears Tower in Chicago, the world's tallest building. In addition, space rented by the federal government amounts to 219 million additional square feet, equal to forty-nine Sears Towers.

—The federal work force of 2,866,657 is equal to three times the work force of AT&T, the country's largest private corporation.

—In the twelve-month period ending September 30, 1978, the General Services Administration purchased 330,752 tons of paper for use by federal agencies. This amount is equal to 66 billion sheets of eight and a half by eleven paper, or enough to reach the moon (238,857 miles away) forty-eight times.

—Land owned by the federal government is equal to the entire United States east of the Mississippi River, plus Texas and Louisiana.

All this government does not come cheap. In his book *Two Cheers for Capitalism,* Prof. Irving Kristol describes some of the costs of federal regulations. Among them:

—The steel industry's spending for pollution control equipment will total more than $1 billion per year, more than one-quarter of the industry's annual profits.

—EPA's 1983 waste pollution standards will cost U.S. industry $60 billion for capital equipment and $12 billion in annual operating and maintenance costs.

—Compliance with OSHA's noise pollution standards will mean capital costs of at least $15 billion and possibly as much as $30 billion with operating costs of $1 billion to $2 billion a year.

The situation we have gotten ourselves into would be ridiculous if it were not so critical Kristol says, adding, "We have been much exercised . . . by the fact that the OPEC monopoly has cost this country over $30 billion in increased oil prices since 1972, but in that time we have inflicted upon ourselves much larger economic costs through environmental and other regulations and will continue to do so, perhaps at an increasing rate."

The total cost to American consumers of the mass of regulations in force is, in fact, estimated conservatively at $150 billion per year. Some analysts think it could be as high as $450 billion per year. In addition, much, perhaps most, of the money spent by the federal bureaucracy is misallocated and additional billions are simply lost, as incredible as that might sound. An audit of the federal government completed in 1978 concluded that $25 billion allocated by the budget could not be accounted for.

A final indignity is that much—perhaps as much as 80 percent—of the funds appropriated for domestic programs such as welfare payments does not get to the people it was intended to help but instead goes to pay the salaries of the bureaucrats. Given this fact, it is not surprising to learn, therefore, that the two wealthiest counties in the nation are Montgomery County, Maryland, and Fairfax County, Virginia, suburban counties bordering Washington. The median income in Montgomery and Fairfax for 1976 was $26,709 and $28,500 respectively—versus $12,700 for the nation as a whole. As an article by Tom Bethel in *Harper's* noted, "While Congress lets a Thousand Taxes Bloom the Federal City Grows Sleek and Fat."

So great has the growth of government been that in 1975 outgoing director of the Office of Management and Budget, Roy Ash, gravely warned that if government spending continues to grow as fast as it has in recent years, then by the end of the century government outlays will consume two-thirds of the gross national product—and this assumes no major new initiatives such as national health insurance. The staggering dimension of this growth can be appreciated if one realizes that federal expenditures for 1929 were approximately $3 billion. For 1979 they were approximately $500 billion or an increase of 16,600 percent! The population growth during the same period was only about 70 percent.

While being appropriately grateful to Mr. Ash for his timely warning, it is necessary to emphasize that this enormous growth of government is not the fault of the Democrats exclusively. Under the Nixon and Ford administrations the federal budget grew from $178,833,000,000 to $366,439,000,000. Federal deficits during this period total an astounding $225 billion. It is, of course, argued by many Republican partisans, and by many Democrats as well, that the major part of this growth is comprised of "uncontrollables," social welfare and "income security" programs such as social security which are impossible to curb. This may be a satisfactory answer superficially, but if it is accepted as fact, it bodes disaster for the nation. The largest part of federal spending is now taken up by such programs and since these programs are increasing in size both absolutely and relative to other programs, if their growth is not arrested, there will be nothing left to do save donning our crash helmets and awaiting the collapse of our economy. This would be, perforce, the logical outcome of the course we are now on.

But such an attitude is fatuous, of course. These programs are in force because they were mandated by Congress and approved by the President. And what they did, they can undo, or at least modify. The only ingredient missing is the courage to face the facts and to take the necessary remedial action.

It should also be noted that as regards Republican administrations, several of the most pernicious regulatory agencies were established under Nixon and Ford. Among these are OSHA (1971), EPA (1970), and the Consumer Products Safety Administration (1973). As pointed out, these agencies, though not as overtly costly as some others such as HEW, are extremely damaging to the economy because of the increase in costs they force on business, much of which is passed on to the consumer in higher prices. The nation would unquestionably be far better off without these agencies, and it is only because of the acquiescence of Republican presidents that they are in operation.

Should a conservative president take office in 1981, surely the main domestic task confronting his administration will be to stop and then reverse the concentration of power in Washington—a theme proclaimed by Richard Nixon twelve years ago. Twelve years later, the problem is more acute than ever. Nixon failed in his self-proclaimed task, and one of the reasons he did was that there is lacking on the Republican-conservative side the expertise or inclination to take the tough steps that need to be taken to reform the bureaucracy.

Robert Carleson, the architect of Ronald Reagan's much praised welfare reform program in California, is one of the few people to recognize this problem. Says Carleson, "The big problem we had with reforming welfare in California was that conservatives were contemptuous of the welfare system, and because of that they wouldn't get involved with it, even to correct the abuses." Carleson adds, "Sure welfare is a disaster; sure the bureaucracy is a disaster but if the mess is ever going to be cleaned up, conservatives are going to have to roll up their sleeves and do the distasteful things that have to be done." The unfortunate truth, however, is that even after eight years of control of the executive branch by Republicans, conservatives still have a relatively small pool of expertise from which to draw the needed reformers.

One person who knows the bureaucracy and what needs to be done with it is Donald Lambro, 39, a reporter in UPI's Washington bureau. It is strange, but true, that in this era of the "investigative reporter" very few people in the media have any knowledge about or any interest in what goes on inside the vast domestic bureaus of the federal government. Lambro is an exception. Formerly assigned to the Capitol Hill beat, Lambro gradually became interested in the programs that the Congress established and funded but frequently had lost interest in or control over, as well as in the proliferating fiefdoms and the obscure people in the federal departments who made the far-reaching decisions that affected the entire country.

Lambro began devoting more of his time to a study of the bureaucracy, and he published his initial findings and impressions in a book titled *The Federal Rathole* (Arlington House), which was widely quoted in Congress and the media. Subsequently, Lambro persuaded his bureau chief to let him make the bureaucracy his primary focus, and he has since written a stream of articles on various facets of the bureaucracy that have been published in hundreds of newspapers across the country. Lambro has recently written another book about the bureaucracy titled *Fat City: How Washington Wastes Your Money*, which reviews 100 major government programs giving specific recommendations as to how they should be reformed or abolished outright.

"For over four decades we have been on a welfare state treadmill, consuming an increasing amount of individual and business earnings for an increasingly vast wasteland of public programs that have either outlived their usefulness or been greatly swollen out of proportion to the nation's problems," Lambro states.

One of Lambro's most impressive jobs was on the Social Security system, a sacrosanct American institution that few politicians dare to question let alone criticize. Writing in *Inquiry* magazine in a piece later reprinted in the Sunday *Washington Star,* Lambro puts it on the line: "With all the pious rhetoric swirling about the Social Security System, no one seems able to summon forth the courage to say out loud what a few economists have now realized, namely that for many young, middle and upper-income Americans just entering the labor force, Social Security's retirement program is a rotten investment."

Under the tax hike passed by Congress in 1977, Lambro notes, Social Security levies will consume 14 percent of all payrolls in 1987 versus 2 percent in 1940. So big has the Social Security tax bite become, in fact, that it is now second to the federal income tax in size. In addition, Lambro says, the Social Security tax will grow at an increasing rate in future years as the number of retired people increases relative to the number of working people. In the next decade alone, taxes for workers earning the maximum taxable income will triple.

The great tragedy of the system, Lambro says, is that if working people were permitted to opt out of Social Security and invest their money in private pension plans, their post-retirement income would be much larger. Using the example of a new wage earner earning $20,000, he points out that this individual will get a monthly Social Security pension of $6,209 upon retirement, but if the $209,255 he will end up paying in taxes over his working life had gone instead into a savings plan, he would have retired with a personal estate of $891,229. Such is the power of compounded interest. Assuming fifteen years of life in retirement, the value of his benefits will be 98.8 percent of taxes paid—not quite a breakeven proposition. If this worker, at age 65, were to take just his own invested payments and buy a life insurance annuity, one that leaves no money after death, he would get a yearly income of $90,030 for life—$15,572 per year more than Social Security would pay.

Of the 150 million Americans eighteen years old or older, Lambro points out, 50 million of them already have negative balances in their Social Security payments—that is, they will pay more into the system then they will get out.

If the American people really understood that Social Security is an abysmal investment, Lambro believes, most would opt out of the system—even as a growing number of *government workers'* groups have done. The fraudulent nature of Social Security is just now beginning to sink in with American workers—thanks in part to Lambro and others like him. As the extent of the fraud becomes manifest, aided by the increasingly painful Social Security tax bite, we are likely to see in the 1980s a thorough overhaul and retrenchment of the system.

One of Lambro's contributions has been his investigations into the true size of the federal work force. For years, we have been faced with the anomoly that, while the size of the federal budget has grown almost exponentially and the intrusions of federal bureaucrats have become progressively more onerous, the size of the federal bureaucracy has not appeared to change much. If you look at the figures on civilian employees in fact, it would appear that the number has even declined somewhat from a little over 3 million at the height of the Vietnam war to 2.9 million today. These figures are highly misleading, Lambro says, because they do not include a myriad of consultants and part-time workers whose salaries—or at least part of them—are paid by the federal government. "The pressure is to keep the number as low as possible," he quotes one Civil Service Commission representative as saying.

What has happened, in effect, is that in order to comply with Congressionally mandated personnel ceilings on the one hand and in order to spend all the money allotted on the other, the federal bureaucracy has resorted to hiring millions of consultants and part-time workers who are not required to be listed on the payroll. While stressing that it is impossible to know exactly how many people work for the federal government, Lambro, after a lengthy investigation, concludes that the number exceeds 7 million!

The HEW statistics are illustrative of the phenomenon. The giant department officially claims to employ 145,000 people in its agencies. Former HEW Secretary Joseph Califano has stated, however, that HEW pays part or all of the salaries of "84,600 in state government, 572,000 in local government, 87,000 in universities, 33,400 people in non-profit research institutions, 113,900 employees in private contractors and 88,000 in other areas." In other words, more than 1.1 million people in all.

As the network of "private" consultants has grown, a symbiotic relationship has been established between it and the bureaucracy. Movement back and forth between the two sectors is continuous, with the feathering of nests being not an inconsiderable aspect of the enterprise. Since consultants are not bound by federal pay ceilings it has become a common practice for bureaucrats to design a program with a consulting firm, see that the contract is signed, and then leave government to go to work for the firm. Clearly this vast, hidden network, dispersed and elusive, is a major part of the problem confronting any effort to reform the federal bureaucracy.

Another Lambro contribution has been to expose the fraudulent nature of the much-touted Carter reorganization of the federal government. Asked what he considered the leading successes of the Carter presidency, domestic policy advisor Robert Strauss placed the reorganization of the executive branch at the top of the list. Such a claim, Lambro makes plain, is clearly without justification.

In a June 3, 1979, story for UPI, Lambro took a close look at the president's much-vaunted government reorganization program, a scrutiny it did not survive intact. Noting that during the campaign Carter had said, "The challenge before the nation is to cut the bureaucracy down to size," Lambro concluded that, "despite ambitious plans only a few functioning agencies have actually been abolished, most of them representing a relatively small savings. By virtually every measurable criterion, the government continues to grow substantially."

First of all, Lambro pointed out, the federal budget had grown by $70 billion since Gerald Ford left office, reaching a total of $522 billion in 1979. The number of federal employees had likewise grown by 34,000—not counting the additional number of consultants, part-time employees and state and local employees whose salaries are paid by the government. The growth here would appear to be tens of thousands more.

A White House inventory of the bureaucracy taken at Carter's behest revealed there were 1,846 departments, bureaus, commissions, etc. in the federal government. Of this total, Carter claimed to have cut 760 units and added 348, for a net reduction of 412. Upon closer examination, Lambro states, it turns out that 677 of the agencies trimmed were informal advisory committees which met only sporadically, did not require any staff, and involved only minor costs. Even with this cut, however, the cost of advisory committees actually increased in 1978, going from $64.9 million to $74.1 million. The 677 advisory committees aside, there were a total of 83 actual Cabinet programs on the Carter cut list. Upon closer examination, however, it turns out that most of these were merged with other larger programs with their tasks and payrolls left intact—and frequently enlarged.

"In fact," Lambro says, "only about a dozen functioning governmental units or agencies have been terminated as a result of Carter's efforts. Most of them are small advisory offices or councils, some with little or no staffing. And, in most instances, the employees remain, moving to other government jobs." An example is the White House Office on Telecommunications which was merged with a similar office in the Commerce Department. The 1977 budget for the two offices was $10 million; the budget for 1978 for the one combined office was $12 million.

Other agencies abolished, such as the Energy Resources Council, were, in the words of a White House staffer, "pretty much moribund anyway." Still other agencies that Carter claimed to have disbanded turn out to have been cut by the Congress; still others *supported* by the president were cut by the Congress, and others such as the Bicentennial Administration simply reached the end of their terms and expired.

So much for reorganizing the bureaucracy.

One of the most disgraceful failures of the federal government, by Lambro's reckoning, is that of the Department of Housing and Urban Development (HUD). Since its inception in 1966, HUD has spent over $70 billion in an effort to provide every American with decent housing. Yet, fifteen years later, the program is a spectacular failure. After studying HUD's record, Lambro says, "It is difficult to determine where most of HUD's resources go and who benefits most from its multi-billion dollar programs."

Among the findings of the Lambro study:

—As of 1978, HUD had constructed approximately 1,000,000 housing units. Had the money simply been given away to purchase housing, 1,300,000 units costing $50,000 at *today's* prices could have been bought.

—"A significant chunk of HUD's money appears to be benefitting, not the poor, but the banks, private investors, consulting firms and university researchers."

—Overhead costs for community development programs run as high as 74 percent.

—In addition to an annual public relations budget of $3 million, HUD, in 1968, launched a $13 million publicity blitz to shore up its sagging reputation.

—Between 1972 and 1978, HUD had to pay out more than $7.6 billion to banks and other lenders for defaulted housing loans.

—As of June 1, 1978, HUD owned 28,658 single-family residences and 386 multi-family projects with 39,443 dwelling units—the result of default on HUD loans.

—The Department spends $22 million annually on travel—an expenditure that one HUD employee said was "rampant with unnecessary trips."

Confirming Lambro's worst assessment of HUD is Dr. Edgar Olsen, 37, a professor of economics at the University of Virginia. Olsen worked for a time as a consultant to HUD during the period when President Nixon was attempting to scale back the agency, and he returned for a year during 1978–1979 as a visiting scholar in the Division of Housing Research, a short-tenured, semi-autonomous position that gave him considerable latitude for independent thought and action.

HUD's reputation as one of the most wasteful and chaotic departments in the federal government is, in Olsen's view, richly deserved. Incompetence and ineptitude, he maintains, were rampant in the Department from the Secretary on down. To start with, he says, then-Secretary Patricia Roberts Harris was "in way over her head. Mrs. Harris is a prominent black laywer who served on a lot of boards. She didn't have any particular knowledge about housing, but when the Cabinet was being staffed and the major positions were filled Carter and his people looked at the mix and decided they needed more women and more minorities, so they picked Mrs. Harris. She has a reputation for quickness and glibness but she was absolutely incapable of analyzing policy. It was impossible to talk numbers with her."

Olsen just shakes his head when he contemplates Mrs. Harris' elevation to Secretary of HEW. "It ups the Peter Principle," he says. "They have just given her a bigger job to mess up. She has gone from a department where there is $1 billion in welfare fraud a year to a department where there is $20 billion."

The deployment of Mrs. Harris, in Olsen's view, makes sense only from a political point of view. "She is an effective campaigner with a constituency that Carter needs badly. I don't think she will have much to do with the actual running of HEW. What she will do is give lots of speeches."

(At least it can be argued that the choice of Harris for HEW Secretary makes political sense—a case that cannot be made for Gerald Ford's selection of David Matthews for the job. Matthews was then president of the University of Alabama and had spent virtually his whole adult life at the university. He had no experience with HEW, nor in fact with the federal government. Ford did not ask him for his views on what should be done at HEW nor did he tell him what he expected him to do there. Unbelievable though it seems, he apparently had met Matthews and hit it off with him and, on that basis, gave him control of the government's biggest department—spending in excess of $100 billion per year.)

A typical performance by Mrs. Harris as seen by Olsen involved the energy crisis. "Energy was the number one topic with the administration at the time, and Harris wanted to know what HUD could do about the problem so as to get in good with Carter. So she asked us to determine what the effect of rising energy costs would be on housing loan defaults—and she wanted the answer in a matter of a few days."

Olsen, given the task, demurred. "I told my boss that it would be impossible to come up with any meaningful answer within that amount of time and also that my strong feeling was that there would be very little effect—not the answer they wanted. So they assigned another visiting scholar to the question. He worked for four or five days and came up with the answer that if energy prices were lower than a certain arbitrary figure for last year there would have been forty-six fewer defaults."

The problems with Secretary Harris were magnified at the senior management positions, Olsen says, citing as one problem the pressure on subordinates to come up with "answers" to complex questions in an arbitrary amount of time—in many cases a few days or even hours. As a result, he says, underlings often gave superficial answers totally uncorroborated by facts and which were often misleading.

Much of Olsen's time at HUD was spent on the "Section 8" program, the housing subsidy program, and he renders a harsh judgement on it. "The people there were just incredibly ignorant," he says.

They did not even know the basic numbers for the program. I mean if you asked them how many people live in units with elevators—a basic statistic easily available—they didn't know. And you could go right down the list. Housing figures from the census? They didn't know.

As an example, ever since I got to HUD, I was told that there was a big discrepancy in rental costs between the suburbs and the cities, and so you had to have a special subsidy rate for suburban areas or people couldn't afford to live there. The two counties they always came up with as examples were Westchester County in New York and Fairfax in Virginia—two of the wealthiest counties in the country.

I told them the census figures showed that just wasn't correct. They show that in Fairfax and Westchester about 25 percent of the rents are in excess of the mean for the metropolitan area. The rules required that visiting scholars and their superiors both sign policy memoranda to the Secretary, and I told them I was going to point out the Census statistics if they continued special rates policy. Faced with that, they changed the policy.

The paucity of statistics given the Secretary was a major problem at HUD, Olsen believes. "Memos would start out at the lower levels giving lots of facts that would enable her to make an independent judgment," he says, "but they were usually sent back for rewriting and deletion. When the memos finally got to her, the figures were usually filtered out, and they were just vague statements and policy recommendations. It used to be a standard joke about memos to say, 'I guess it's bad enough to send now.' "

In HUD, according to Olsen, the new construction interests dominate and as a result, much of the housing built is far more expensive than necessary. "The typical rent for a HUD-financed unit is $400 per month," he says. "That's the top 5 percent of the rental market. If the taxpayers knew this, they would rebel."

Another anomaly he points out is that of the changes in policy for rejuvenating the cities. "One major goal of urban renewal used to be to lure whites back to the cities. The complaint was that the cities' tax base was eroding and it was essential to bring back higher income whites to build it back up. Now you see thousands of whites moving back into the cities, and the big worry now is the displacement of blacks who live there. It's a complete reversal of policy."

Olsen believes the problem of the bureaucracy is that it is so big and contains so many programs that the average citizen doesn't understand it or how to change it. The solution in his view is to "force the programs down to the local level where their cause and effect can be seen and where people can exert some control over them."

"A strong president with the right ideas could help, too," he says. "I think Nixon was beginning to do something before he got bogged down in Watergate. Carter also promised to reform the bureaucracy and failed, but I think it can still be done."

One of the most knowledgeable conservatives on the subject of the federal bureaucracy is Ronald Moe, 40, formerly a policy analyst with the Office of Economic Opportunity and now a senior research analyst with the Congressional Research Service of the Library of Congress. Moe places much of the blame for runaway bureaucracy on Congress. "Congress will pass a program mandating that billions be spent instantly combating unemployment, for example," he says. "One, we don't know what unemployment is, really. We do not know how to combat it; we just throw money at the problem. We don't give the Labor Department the time or personnel, so they have to form corporations to perform public functions and give them the money. They were forced to take the money, and that money is going out to these corporations, and they design the programs. They spend the money and they evaluate it."

The upshot of this frenetic, unplanned activity, Moe says is chaos and waste: "I used to ask students to come up with one program that they could defend as having succeeded without causing unanticipated problems that were equal to or exceeded the original one. I've never heard of one."

Frequently the problem, in Moe's view, is not so much bureaucratic malfeasance as it is unsound legislation. "For example," he says, "you could hire one hundred of the finest, most expensive executives in the United States and give them unlimited help, and the minimum wage program wouldn't work. In fact, the better it is administered, the more unemployment you have. Administrators are condemned for things that don't work, that are theoretically unsound. The problem with administrators is their underlying belief that there isn't anything they can't do. What we need to do is tell the people up here and downtown that there are some things which just aren't administrable—the minimum wage is one, and the Energy Security Corporation may be another. We are getting blamed as bureaucrats for stuff which just isn't administrable."

The media also comes in for its share of blame in Moe's analysis. Says he, "I start from the assumption that most bills passed are bad ones. That is an assumption that runs contrary to media perception. Just as Members of Congress perceive that they are at least making an attempt to solve problems by spending money, the media—through *Congressional Quarterly* and other means—counts how many bills are passed. Our perceptions are being formed by $12,000 a year journalists. They are the most powerful men in the country."

One of the remedial steps that needs to be taken, Moe believes, is for the government to establish a test and analysis division to experiment with program concepts on a small scale. Under such a system a concept that proved impractical could be junked before it became law and legally binding on the entire nation. Such a program was in force briefly during the Nixon Administration, Moe says, but was disbanded because of lack of support. Nevertheless, during its brief existence, the group performed a valuable service, demonstrating, among other things, the difficulty—futility is perhaps a better word—of establishing an income maintenance program. Moe relates,

I was on the team of 200 people who were designing the Family Income Maintenance program. The first thing that struck me was how complicated the administrative part of it was. Congress passed a law saying, "Have it in operation in one year." Well, everything depended on everything else. When we got up there, it had been working for two years and nothing had been decided. Whatever technology you decided to go with, you were talking about a system that was going to be larger than NASA's moon shot system. It was going to lock you in for ten years. If you went after the wrong basic system and the wrong equipment, you were finished. But the people who had to make those decisions couldn't make them until the policy input information was available. The policy people couldn't do it because the decisions weren't being made. So the training people said, "Until we know what type of equipment to base our training on, we can't do any training." It went on and on and on. Nothing was done. It was administratively beyond the capacity of anyone. A group of us went out there not knowing anything. I realized I was in the middle of a tremendous experiment, and we started something that I initially thought was a joke called Management by Objectives, although we called it something else. In planning exercises, it actually worked. We went backwards; we said, "This is the date we want the system working—what are the decisions that have to be made?"— a backward pyramid.

But, the decisions on what days decisions actually had to be made involved tremendous amounts of work. We spent six months coming up with just the roughest estimate of dates. We actually had it all down on a piece of paper. Well, it never passed for a number of reasons. As soon as it was evident it wasn't going to pass, the group disintegrated. But, in that process, we realized how complicated administration was. I only met three or four people who could understand the conceptualization of what it would require to have a three-month, quarterly moving average.

Moe's description of the computation of the "quarterly moving average" is a telling illustration of the difficulties inherent in making social programs work:

I think this is a key thing of why it is so difficult to administer today. You get Social Security by doing no more than turning a certain age. The amount that you are entitled to is a one-time decision. It is only changed once in a while. If the laws change, your stipend can be changed. But, this can be done on a mass basis on a computer, and you rarely have to furnish new information for the system. In order to have an income maintenance system, you're going to have to have the people input the information themselves. The information will have to be placed on an extremely timely basis. The bill that was originally going to be passed said that if you made $4000 in one year, you would get a check. You get your check six months later for a period covered the year before. Also, in real life, there are very few people who don't make any money. Most people who make a small amount of money, make it on a temporary basis. They've just gotten a divorce, and they go to work for part of the year . . . or they're sick. 75 percent of them are only poor once in a while and they need the money then, not a year and a half later. But, we don't want to over-give because they may be seasonal workers. The month that they make $1200, they don't need the money; the next month they only make $150 and they need it. The ideal was to have a moving quarterly average—you were only three months behind. The month that you were to receive would be determined by what you made during a three month period, three months ago. It took that much time to get the information into the system.

Well, I must have heard the explanation of how this would work five times, and I'm not a dummy. There were only two or three people out there who could really explain it and then answer questions. I could go through the rote part but once they got to the tough questions, then the whole thing fell apart. We had only two or three people who could explain the hardware questions and also understand conceptual problems. For example, can a person own a house and still collect? You would say yes, you shouldn't take the house into consideration. Well, then, how much should the house be worth? Can it be worth $200,000 and they still collect? You'd say no. Then you have to make a decision on how much it can be worth . . . how much you will allow them. But that's only the beginning of the questions on the house. It's unbelievable how much information has to be on these machines and be moving and changing every month. The computer people said we may have been pressing the ability of the computer to function without perpetual breakdown to the point where the system would break down. You're asking relatively intelligent people out in the local office in St. Louis to explain to some relatively ignorant person why they didn't get a check for the right amount. So, they'd be cursing the machinery. What I'm saying is that frequently it is beyond our capacity to do humane things.

According to economist Warren Coats the impact of the regulatory agencies is perhaps more damaging to the economy as a whole than is that of the much larger bureaucracies such as HEW. Says Coats,

I think one of the most crippling aspects of government in the economic sphere is the proliferation of regulations. I can't remember the exact figures, but I believe it's true that the capitalized value of corporate equity in this country has fallen in the last ten years more than it did during the great depression—which is probably a very accurate reassessment of profit prospects in this country as a result of regulation, both environmental (some of which I support, but not a lot) and a lot of other kinds of regulation which yield no discernable benefit to the economy as a whole. And the increased uncertainty, I think, plays a very major role. You'd have to be a fool, you know, to enter the energy field, particularly oil, and put up money when the best guess would be that if you're lucky and do something right and make money, there'll be a windfall profits tax to take it all away. So why undergo the risk?

Tremendous uncertainty has occurred because the government has become completely capricious and willing to enter into any area, change the ground rules in most any fashion, and thereby totally obliterate any foundation upon which you build or plan. That kind of uncertainty, you know, and the whole regulatory structure that is part of it, I can't help but believe most strongly is 90 percent of the problem with the economy, and the tax structure per se is less than 10 percent.

Until relatively recently not much was being done to analyze bureaucracy—how it works, how it grows, how it operates—and to study means of systemic reform. In the past half-dozen years, however, a whole school of analysis called Public Choice has arisen, dedicated to addressing the problem of bureaucracy. According to the May 7, 1979, issue of *Fortune*, Public Choice now has 700 members, half of them economists, half political scientists.

The purpose of Public Choice is to apply economic concepts to the study of political science, and in particular to the workings of government. According to *Fortune*, the leading figures in this effort are four men: Anthony Downs, a former consultant with the Rand Corporation and the author of *Inside Bureaucracy;* William Niskanen, a former policy analyst at the Defense Department, now chief economist with the Ford Motor Company and the author of *Bureaucracy and Representative Government;* Morris Fiorina, professor of political science at Cal Tech and the author of *Congress: the Keystone of the Washington Establishment;* and Gordon Tulloch of Virginia Polytechnic Institute, author of numerous books and an advocate of transferring government functions to the private sector.

The elementary assumption of the Public Choice group is that bureaucrats like everyone else act primarily on the basis of self-interest, a seemingly obvious assumption to be sure, but one that has been largely overlooked in designing models for bureaucratic reform. Whereas in the private sector money is the yardstick of success, in the public sector other rewards are paramount—rewards such as votes, power, fringe benefits, prerequisites of office, and job security. Unlike the private sector, where appetites are checked by competition, government bureaucracies are subject to few constraints, hence growth tends to proceed unchecked.

In his book *Inside Bureaucracy*, Anthony Downs points out that one compelling reason for bureaucratic growth is that growth increases chances for promotion. Another is that salaries tend to be meted out on the basis of

how many people a supervisor has under his jurisdiction—a virtual guarantee of overmanning.

In addition, Downs points out, growth engenders growth. As organizations grow, they necessarily adopt a larger and more complex command
structure to control the flow of information and authority. But as the chain
of command becomes more complex, waste and inefficiency increase and
this, in turn, inspires the hiring of more personnel to monitor the actual
working of the organization. The result is that the employees of the organization spend less and less time on carrying out the department's functions.

The Public Choice analysts also point out that government bureaucracies
have little incentive to be efficient—such as by saving money. The incentives, in fact, tend to run in the other direction: the less funds a department
spends one year, the less it is likely to get the next year. The understandable
tendency on the part of the bureaucrats thus is to spend every dime allotted
and then to ask for an augmentation.

One phenomenon of government identified by the Public Choice people
has been dubbed the "iron triangle," the incestuous relationship that exists
between Congress, the bureaucracies, and special interest groups. In ex-
ploring this relationship, Fiorina was particularly taken with the fact that the
percentage of incumbent congressmen replaced during elections has fallen
from 50 percent in the nineteenth century to about 5 percent today. The
reason for this, he argues, is that a congressman's success increasingly depends not on his voting record but on the services he provides his constituents—mainly services supplied by the bureaucracy. Pork barrel legislation
which was once restricted to such things as harbor projects and the like
now includes a bewildering array of programs covering law enforcement,
sewage treatment, hospitals, housing, etc., etc. Thus while congressmen
continue to rail against bureaucratic red tape they continue to vote for
specific pieces of legislation that will benefit their districts. These multitudinous pieces of legislation, however, tend to accumulate eventually into
a gargantuan bureaucracy.

A dangerous by-product of government growth is the growing power of
the bureaucrats at the polls. Today about one family in five has a member
working for government, and studies show that these people tend to vote
far more regularly than do other voters; so much so that public sector
employees and their families account for one out of every three votes. These
votes provide a strong impetus for more government spending.

The public interest people tend to be skeptical about many of the
bureaucracy-reform measures now in vogue—propoals such as sunset legislation which requires a program to expire after a certain period and requires that a justification be established for its continued existence. These
attempts, the Public Choice people believe, are superficial treatments that

attack the symptoms rather than the causes of bureaucratic abuses. The same holds true for consolidating similar programs in one super agency. This approach, they believe, may even be counterproductive because it eliminates competition.

Some Public Choice spokesmen advocate the contracting out of many government jobs to the private sector. Others urge changes in the appropriation system, such as requiring a two-thirds majority in Congress to pass money bills. Another suggestion is to assign congressmen to committees by drawing lots—thus breaking up the unholy alliance that exists between the members and the bureaucracies they oversee.

Another Public Choice scholar, Kenneth W. Clarkson, 37, adovcates a system in which a citizen could seek relief from bureaucratic abuses through the courts. A professor of economics at the University of Miami, Clarkson is a prolific author who has written a number of books, co-authored others, and contributed to a host of scholarly journals. An assiduous student of government and of bureaucracy, Clarkson has contributed valuable original research and analytical work on a variety of government programs, among them studies on the failure of the food stamp program, the inaccuracy of government unemployment statistics, and the deleterious effects of government regulation.

Like Warren Coats, Clarkson is of the opinion that relatively inexpensive regulatory agencies are more damaging to the economy than are the costly domestic departments—a conclusion he amplifies in a forthcoming book, *The FTC Since 1970: Economic Regulation and Bureaucratic Behavior,* written with colleague T. J. Muris.

In an article, "Regulating Chrysler Out of Business," which appeared in the September-October 1979 issue of *Regulation* magazine, published by the American Enterprise Institute, Clarkson asserts that the crush of government regulations put Chrysler on the verge of bankruptcy. "Sure there were management mistakes at Chrysler," Clarkson says, "but the cost of complying with the safety, fuel economy, and clean air regulations made it much more difficult for Chrysler to bounce back." Clarkson estimates that regulations will cost the ailing company $1 billion over the next eight years—if it survives.

As regards the social welfare transfer programs, Clarkson says they have largely failed to accomplish their original objectives. "Studies of the food stamp program show that it has not improved nutrition or the agriculture economy—its two goals," he says. "What it *has* done is cause the poor to change their buying habits and to purchase more expensive foods. For instance, instead of buying potatoes and peeling and cooking them as she did before, a housewife who gets food stamps is now more likely to buy TV dinners or other prepackaged foods." Under the food stamp program,

Clarkson says, the consumption of milk and cheese products—which are produced in the United States—has fallen, while the consumption of sugar—largely imported—has risen. "Maybe the aluminum industry bene-fitted by food stamps," he says, "but that's one of the few who have."

Yet, while food stamps have failed to accomplish the objectives set out for them, the program has grown and become firmly entrenched. The rea-son, according to Clarkson: "Food stamps do transfer income to some 17 million people, and the politicians are afraid to anger them by abolishing or reducing the program."

In Clarkson's view the main problem with bureaucracy is not the bu-reaucrats per se but rather the system of rulemaking that governs the bureaucracy. "The problem is that we as citizens have no way of challeng-ing the impact of bureaucratic programs that affect our lives," he says. "In legal terms, we lack 'standing.' As taxpayers we have no way to get at the programs that are hurting us. Oh, sure, I can talk to my congressman, but he has 125,000 other constituents talking with him, and he is engaged in making deals with his colleagues and in trading votes and so forth—so it's very difficult for one citizen to have an impact."

As a corrective for these problems, Clarkson suggests imposing standards of review on the bureaucracy such as a cost-benefit criterion which would be subject to the "reasonable man" standard used now in legal cases in-volving taxes, contracts, etc. The power to review the agencies would then be given to the courts, and any citizen could challenge the effect of an agency on him. The courts, using the reasonable man standard, would decide whether the plaintiff had been injured or not. If the determination were affirmative, the government would have to make restitution.

Another desirable remedy in Clarkson's view is the imposition of spending limits on the government so that gradually the size of the private sector will grow relative to that of the public sector.

Other experts such as Robert Carleson advocate the block granting of entire programs to the states—with a gradual transfer of taxing authority as well. This approach, Carleson says, would allow the states to experiment with the programs with the result that many of them would be phased out so the funds could be used for other more needed programs.

To Howard Phillips, 37, former acting director of the Office of Economic Opportunity in the Nixon administration, accountability to the people is the key to reform of the bureaucracy. "Important decisions of national policy and programmatic priority are too often decided in anonymity by men and women whose values and biases, however enlightened, structurally by-pass control by the electorate," Phillips maintains. "Nowhere is this more true," he says, "than in the social agencies, where decisions about whom to fund, which regulations to draft, which rules to enforce, and which priorities to put forward cannot help being rooted in the preferences and values of those who draft and 'sign off' on the bureaucratic documents which, taken together, come to shape and constitute agency, departmental and national policy."

Phillips won his spurs in fighting bureaucracy during his four-month stint as acting director of OEO, during which time he worked feverishly, though unsuccessfully in the end, to disband the agency. Following this, he led a year-long crusade to defeat the bill to create a National Legal Services Corporation to provide free legal council to minorities and the poor. Phillips argued, correctly as it turned out, that such legislation would employ thousands of leftist lawyers who would use their government salaried positions to press for their pet changes in the legal system.

Phillips applauded the rhetoric of candidate Nixon about returning power to the people, and he believes that under the Nixon presidency the management of the bureaucracy was improved. Nonetheless, he believes that on balance the Nixon effort to reform the bureaucracy was a failure, a failure based on "treating the management and budget process as inherently neutral, in terms of values."

Budget-making is anything but valueless, Phillips believes, adding, if elected officials don't make the value judgments, the bureaucrats will. Phillips contends further that, "Missing from the budget process are sufficient opportunities for assessment of (a) the worth of a program, in its own right, even without respect to competing priorities, and (b) assessment, within statutorily permissible range, of its consistency with the overall philosophy and objectives of the administration in power. If elections are to mean something, this kind of policy analysis must take its place side by side with assessments of cost-effectiveness and PPBS."

Phillips advocates a number of corrective measures to deal with the bureaucracy—including zero-based budgeting and adoption of the line-veto by Congress—a procedure in which specific items of appropriations legislation can be deleted, thereby removing the necessity for members to vote for an entire bill in order to save the good parts of it.

In the last analysis, however, Phillips believes that the only effective reform is to reduce the size and power of the bureaucracy. "Let us advance the *general* interest by reducing the size of bureaucracy, reprivatizing governmental functions, and dispersing power back to the people—through lower taxes, more authority to elected officials, and by *structurally* encouraging greater visibility for the decisions which are made."

John Svahn, 36, was administrator of Social and Rehabilitation Services at HEW during the Nixon administration—a position that required him to manage an annual budget of $30 billion. Now an executive with the firm of Haskins and Sells in Washington, he has some pungent observations on bureaucracy. "I am very much in favor of shifting functions of government back to the states," he says,

but I'm very much opposed to the Nixon decentralization—shifting things out of Washington and back to the ten federal regions. They wanted to decentralize as much as possible the decision-making authority for federal vis à vis state relationships in those regions to the regional administrator. Essentially what you were doing was setting up ten little Washington, D.C.s out there. It was more confusing to states and localities. In addition, the states were being treated much differently due to the variations in these regional offices.

I don't think decision-making authority ought to be spread out among ten different regions. To the states is an entirely different matter. Being a student of constitutional law, I think the states have a right to do a lot of the things that the federal government currently does. I think we ought to give a lot of these things back to the states, but I don't know if that's a doable thing. I've seen governors who ought to be arguing that way come in and place themselves at the mercy of the federal government in order to be able to point the blame. I also think there are a lot of conservative Governors who are very comfortable having the federal bureaucrats handle these programs. If there wasn't an OSHA, every time there was a blow-up at a steel mill there would be a governor in there trying to handle it.

In addition, I have found that members of Congress—particularly the powerful Democrats—are very much opposed to decentralization.

I think it would be very difficult for a conservative President to come in and make a very big dent in the bureaucracy. The government does not appeal to conservatives. They have trouble bringing people in. I don't think a Reagan or a Crane would be much different than Carter or Johnson.

They're going to have a cadre of people that they're going to put in no matter what. Then they are going to sit back just like everyone else and say: How many people do I have from the Northeast? How many blacks? How many Chicanos? I've got to get a woman secretary, etc., etc. The conservative philosophy becomes secondary to the need for acceptance. And the need for acceptance dicatates that there has to be a woman Cabinet member and a black Cabinet member. I saw Nixon do it and I saw Ford do it. Ford hired David Matthews. Matthews just sat up there and pontificated—he wrote a book. He was not interested in making decisions.

One of the most knowledgeable experts on bureaucracy is Robert Carleson, the chief architect of the Reagan welfare reform program in California and, later, U.S. commissioner of welfare in the Nixon administration. According to Carleson, "One thing you have to watch for in the federal government—as in all bureaucracies—is that they tend to reward with higher pay and higher-level positions based on the number of people you supervise. That's fine for an army. But for professional people, I think some other criterion should be used. If you have two people who could do a super job—one with a team of three, the other with a team of twelve, you'd be better off with the team of three. But the traditional manner of rating the level of the job involves how many people you supervise. It's a direct incentive to hire more people. Reducing the number of people you have under you could have the effect of downgrading your position. That's an example of one of the things that's wrong with the federal system."

As regards reform, Carleson says,

The only way you are going to get at the federal bureaucracy, if you're talking about numbers of people, is to reduce government programs. Efforts to reduce the staff by 10 percent or 15 percent are very difficult to achieve. If you're going to have a real impact on reducing the number of federal employees, I think you first have to look at government programs that have to be scrapped or transferred to the state or local level. Then let later attrition affect the number of employees who carried out these programs. It would have to be heavily disciplined so that when a program was phased out successfully there would be a tracking of the positions that supported that program with a strict prohibition against transferring those positions to other programs. Notice that I'm talking about positions—not people—that have to be eliminated. From a purely practical political standpoint, if you say you're going to reduce the working force by X percentage and lay people off—because there are so many more people potentially threatened—the political pressure that they can bring to bear to stop the whole program is tremendously effective. I think the least effective way to reduce the federal bureaucracy is to threaten the individuals directly.

The most promising approach to reforming the bureaucracy in Carleson's view is the block grant approach:

Take a program like Aid to Families with Dependent Children. In AFDC, you've got a federal matching policy that encourages waste and error. The more money the state spends, the more federal money it gets, whether it needs it or not, or whether the poor need it or not. You could replace this matching system which also has a lot of federal regulation with a block grant system which would be a finite amount of money.

Eventually the federal government could give up some of its income taxing authority. For example, the federal government could earmark the first 5 percent of everyone's income taxes to this kind of a program. In effect, a state could opt to levy none or all of the 5 percent. If a state found it could run its programs without having to levy any tax, the state taxpayers would pay 5 percent less federal taxes.

Carleson has been advocating block grants as a means of initiating the transfer of federal programs, and ultimately taxing power, back to the states. In early 1979, he acquired a powerful ally in this effort when he convinced Senator Russell Long, the powerful chairman of the Senate Finance Committee, of the wisdom of the approach. The result was the "Family Welfare Improvement Act," cosponsored by Long and Senator Robert Dole.

One of the people assisting Carleson in the drafting of this bill was Linda McMahon, 33, formerly the head of the welfare legislation division of the

U.S. Chamber of Commerce and then legislative aide to Representative William Dickenson (R.-Ala.), McMahon came to the Finance Committee in early 1979. She brought with her both a solid understanding of the way welfare works and a feel for the essentials of reform. "Bureaucrats work in a very isolated situation, removed from the real world and the problems that people have to deal with in working out the programs that were put together by the bureaucrats," McMahon says. "They are isolated from political concerns. And, for example, they don't understand what a small businessman has to go through to meet the paperwork requirements. They have no idea of what it is to run a business or meet a payroll. But the programs keep growing and things become more complicated and, as the government is looked to to do more and get into more areas, the members of Congress are spread so thin that what you have is government by staff."

As a result of the enormous growth in the number of bureaucracies, McMahon says, there is such a tangle of programs that they overlap and frequently undermine each other. "As an example, I recently saw a letter from a man who wrote that he was going to have to move out of the rest home he was in. He said he had a combined Social Security and pension of $480 per month. Medicaid, he said, paid the difference between that and the $1200 per month it cost him to stay in the nursing home. He got a cost-of-living increase from Social Security that put him $5 per month over the maximum income for Medicaid eligibility. So unless something happened, he was going to have to move out of his nursing home."

"Welfare," says McMahon, "is in a state of flux now. There is a great argument going on over who is worthy, who is deserving of help. It used to be that we had a pretty sound definition of who was worthy—the blind, disabled, widows, and so forth. But that's changing now. Now there is pressure to include women without husbands, and husbands with intact families. The goal on the part of the welfare establishment is to create an 'income floor,' a guaranteed income."

McMahon thinks such a system would be disastrous. "The purpose of welfare should be to bring people out of poverty and it has done that by and large, but I don't think the American people are interested in providing everyone with a minimum income."

Such a program, she believes, would be unfair to the majority and destructive to the initiative of the people receiving it. "Several years ago," she says, "HEW began a study on the effects of a guaranteed income. Over 5,000 people in Seattle were involved in the program, which tested variations of a guaranteed income plan using three-year and five-year programs. One of the most shocking findings was the effect this kind of plan had on the initiative to work. The disastrous impact is on the young people who-have not worked and who grow up with this system. In the sixteen to twenty-one age bracket, 55 percent of the males who marry do not work. We can see what the effect of a program would be if implemented on a national basis."

A national welfare program, McMahon says, would be extrmely costly and inefficient. "The country is so vast and the population is too large to make centralized decisions effective," she says. "In a national system of welfare, some eligible people are going to be missed and a whole lot of ineligible people are going to be included. The states are different enough in climate, levels of education, etc., that they should be allowed to design welfare plans that best fit their needs. The welfare advocacy groups who want to spend the welfare money want it spent at the federal level. If it were spent at the state and local level, they couldn't get away with a lot of things."

The Long-Dole bill, McMahon says, would be a superior approach. It works as follows:

(1) Beginning with fiscal year 1981, a Federal block grant system will replace the current open-ended federal matching of the state costs for Aid to Families with Dependent Children (AFDC).

(2) The Federal block grant will be: (a) a fixed amount based on the AFDC funds the State received in FY 1979, plus (b) to all states a portion of $1 billion in fiscal relief allocated on the basis of each state's population, plus (c) to the seventeen states with the lowest average per capita income, a portion of $400 million, distributed on the basis of a formula that factors in their average per capita income and population, to be used solely to increase the basic AFDC benefit.

(3) The federal block grant will be: (a) adjusted automatically so that the states will not have to bear the entire cost of inflation, (b) adjusted automatically when state population changes, and (c) temporarily augmented if the state experiences very high unemployment.

(4) The block grant may be used for social welfare purposes. Savings resulting from better administration, reduction in fraud and error, successful placement of welfare recipients in employment, and other improvements will be wholly retained by the states and may be used to reduce state welfare costs and improve benefits for the truly needy.

(5) The states will be permitted complete discretion to require work as a condition of AFDC eligibility.

(6) A five-year, eight-state demonstration project will be established to test the states' ability to create their own family welfare programs as an alternative to AFDC without regard to federal requirements and limitations. The eight states participating shall include Pennsylvania (to assure the in-

clusion of at least one northern industrial state), Mississippi (to assure the inclusion of at least one southern rural state), and six additional states to be selected by lot from among states desiring to participate.

(7) Beginning in fiscal year 1986, the block grant, after adjustments for inflation, population changes, and high unemployment, will be reduced each year by 2 percent. This permits the federal budget to share the states' anticipated reductions in waste.

The goals that would be accomplished by the plan, according to McMahon, are:

(1) Limit the growth of expenditures for the present open-ended federal family welfare program.

(2) Provide a strong incentive for the states to eliminate error, waste, and fraud in welfare programs and to reduce overall welfare spending.

(3) Provide fiscal relief to all states which may be used to reduce overall state welfare spending and to increase basic benefits for the truly needy.

(4) Encourage the states with the lowest per capita average income to increase their basic family welfare benefit levels.

(5) Permit the states complete discretion to require work as a condition of eligibility for family welfare benefits.

(6) Reverse the trend toward complete federalization of welfare by permitting some demonstration states to design and implement their own family welfare programs tailored to meet the needs of the individual state and its poor.

(7) Eliminate the need for a large federal bureaucracy to monitor the present open-ended federal matching system.

The Long-Dole bill enjoys the support of a majority of the members of the Senate Finance Committee, a fact that should guarantee its consideration by the entire Senate in 1980. If passed by the Congress and signed into law, it would be an important first step in shifting a whole series of federal programs back to the states, to be followed in time by shifting the taxing authority.

One member of Congress who has made reform of the bureaucracy a personal crusade is Rep. Mickey Edwards (R.-Okla.). Edwards was rewarded for his interest and expertise in the area by being named chairman of a Republican Congressional Task Force on reform of bureaucratic procedures. An acute concern of Edwards' is administrative law—the law that governs the procedures of federal agencies. It is, Edwards says, "an area where the doctrine of the rule of law simply does not apply—an area where hundreds of thousands of decisions that affect the lives of millions of people are made not in the courts, not in the Congress, but by administrative whim."

To correct some of the abuses of bureaucratic procedures, Edwards introduced a bill, H.R. 12333, the "Administrative Procedures Reform Act." Among other things, the bill would:

—Allow oral arguments to be made in favor of, or in opposition to any proposed rule.

—Prohibit any agency from making an inspection without a search warrant.

—Require that all agency decisions be consistent with prior decisions unless otherwise provided by law.

—Permit an agency to fine or punish a person only if that person has been given notice in writing of the reason and a period of at least 30 days to correct the violation.

—Prohibit any Federal agency from adopting new rules without first publishing them in the *Federal Register* at least 120 days before their effective date.

—Allow any person charged with violating an agency rule the opportunity to confront and cross-examine any witness and rebut all evidence being used against him.

"My bill," says Edwards, "will not eliminate or reduce the scope of government—an all important next step—but it will move toward a system in which all businessmen will have basic protections when they are summoned before a Federal agency. And that, at least, would be a good beginning."

Enactment of his bill, as the congressman points out, would be a beginning, but only that. The need to reform and reduce the size of the entrenched behemoth of the federal bureaucracy will without question be the largest and most difficult task facing a conservative president and Congress, and the degree of success in dealing with this challenge will most probably define in large degree the success of a conservative president's tenure.

PART IV | STRATEGY AND POLITICS

ALEC's Angels: Arizona State Rep. Donna Carlson, ALEC chairman; Connie Heckman, ALEC office manager; Kathleen Teague, ALEC executive director *(seated)*

15 | THE NEW THRUST IN STATE POLITICS

On October 8, 1978, the U.S. Senate adopted a resolution supporting a constitutional amendment to allot the District of Columbia representation in the Congress "as if it were a state." The vote followed a similar vote in the House and, as such, launched the nation on another controversial effort to amend the nation's organic document.

The launching festivities were reminiscent of a similar effort launched seven years before to enact the Equal Rights Amendment. The panjandrums of the liberal establishment sallied forth in support of the amendment, the *New York Times, Washington Post,* and most other leading liberal newspapers editorialized in its favor, and the leading liberal organizations such as the National League of Women Voters, Common Cause, the Urban League, etc., all united to push ratification. A coalition, "Self Determination for D.C.," was formed to coordinate the ratification drive and a flurry of activity ensued with D.C. delegate Walter Fauntroy and others flying to state capitals all over the country to testify in favor of the amendment.

But then a funny thing happened: nothing. Unlike the ERA, which had been approved by thirty states within a year after its passage by Congress, the D.C. Amendment, a year after its passage by Congress, had been ratified by only six legislatures. The D.C. Amendment ratification drive had stalled at the outset, and even the amendment's most ardent supporters were agreed that approval by the required thirty-six states was highly unlikely.

By the D.C. Amendment supporters' own admission, the organization which had done the most to kill the amendment was the American Legislative Exchange Council (ALEC), a small organization of conservative state legislators.

Founded by the American Conservative Union in Chicago in August 1974, ALEC was formed to provide a counterbalance to the monopoly on state legislators held by the established organization, the National Confer-

259

State leaders *(left to right from top):* Louisiana State Rep. Louis ("Woody") Jenkins and Louisiana State Sen. Dan Ritchey; Missouri State Rep. Paul Dietrich; Rep. William Batchelder, assistant minority leader, Ohio House of Representatives; Sen. Thomas Van Meter, assistant minority leader, Ohio Senate

More state house leaders
(left to right from top): California Lt. Gov. Mike Curb;
Iowa Lt. Gov. Terry Branstad; Oregon State Rep. Kurt Wolfer;
Georgia State Rep. James Paulk

ence of State Legislators. In the intervening five years, ALEC has grown from its founding core of twenty-five state legislators to a membership of 700 state legislators (almost one-tenth of the nationwide total of 7,552) and 300 paying associate members.

According to ALEC executive director, Kathleen Teague, 31, "Just in the last three years, ALEC membership has quadrupled and our budget has almost quadrupled as well, growing from slightly over $200,000 to $800,000 in 1979." Teague adds, "I think we are beginning to be a real force on the national scene."

Unquestionably, the coming of age of ALEC can be dated to the organization's leading role in the D.C. Amendment battle. As soon as the amendment was passed by Congress, ALEC moved with dispatch. "We were determined not to make the same mistake we made with ERA," says ALEC Chairman Donna Carlson, a state representative from Arizona. "ERA was ratified by thirty states before we ever got organized," she says.

Not so with the D.C. Amendment. Within a few weeks, ALEC had sent out a questionnaire to every state legislator in the country asking his opinion of it. Of the 15 percent who responded, 75 percent said they opposed the amendment. The results were released to the press, and the overwhelming opposition registered served to put an immediate chill on the ratification drive.

In December 1978, ALEC held a conference on the D.C. Amendment in Washington with state legislators from thirty-six states attending. A series of constitutional law experts testified that the amendment would do grave damage to the federal concept by giving Senate representation to a nonstate. Alternatives to this neither fish-nor-fowl arrangement were also discussed, including such measures as ceding the District back to Maryland or allowing representation in the House only—measures that would provide Congressional representation from District voters without undermining the federal system.

A novel approach to defeating the D.C. Amendment was also broached at the conference: having a state legislature defeat the D.C. Amendment and send a formal notification to Congress that it had done so. Utilizing this approach, it would take only thirteen states to defeat the amendment. Such a procedure would give an ironic twist to the argument used by ERA supporters that once a state had voted to ratify the ERA, it could not vote to rescind its ratification. The backers of the D.C. Amendment are in most cases also supporters of the ERA, and the ALEC strategy put them in a no-win situation.

Following the conference, ALEC sent out a comprehensive briefing book on the D.C. Amendment to all state legislators in the country, detailing the pitfalls of the amendment and urging them to study it carefully before adopting it. The briefing books became the primary source material for opponents of the amendment in the debates in the state legislatures.

The conference on the D.C. Amendment and other related ALEC activities received considerable coverage in the press around the country and did a great deal to enhance the organization's profile—and its recruitment and fund-raising programs.

The *Washington Post* reported, for instance, that in the Wisconsin legislature, Senator David G. Beyer, a liberal, relied heavily on the ALEC briefing book in grilling D.C. Delegate Walter Fauntroy about the amendment. "These were all good ALEC arguments," the *Post* quoted Fauntroy as saying, and grumbling, "I'd like to know where they're getting the money."

Fauntroy had a good reason for jealousy. The *Post* reported in another story that "the money spent by ALEC—which has a $300,000 annual budget raised from a mailing list of 23,000 conservative donors—is more than the grand total raised so far by supporters of the amendment." The *Post* added, "While opponents coalesce behind the fine-tuned leadership of ALEC, backers of the amendment flounder in disunity, bogged down by debates about who will direct the ratification effort and what is the best strategy to employ."

Under the leadership of Carlson and Teague, ALEC has developed into a vibrant organization with an ambitious and expanding program. The organization sponsors an annual conference (the fifth was held in August 1979 in Chicago) and a series of conferences on major issues of interest to state legislators. In addition to the D.C. Amendment, past conferences have focused on energy, mining, welfare reform, and tax limitation.

The organization also issued an annual book of suggested legislation for state legislators. The 1978–79 edition had model legislation on bueaucracy control, fiscal responsibility, prolife measures, criminal justice, education, civil law, welfare reform and resolutions, including suggested tests for sample bills. The ALEC book has been widely praised by conservative and moderate state legislators for providing them with alternatives to the generally liberal model legislation offered by the established organizations of state legislators.

ALEC also publishes a newsletter, *First Reading,* which covers items of interest to state legislators and reports conservative initiatives being pushed in legislatures throughout the country. In addition, the organization publishes a series of fact sheets on important issues. A recent one reported on the "Sagebrush Rebellion"—the drive developing in the western states to wrest control from Washington of the vast amounts of federal land in these states.

But probably ALEC's greatest accomplishment has been to bring conservative state legislators together for the exchange of information on topics of mutual concern. Out of these meetings have come a number of important initiatives. An example of these was the successful effort by Tennessee State Representative David Copeland to insert language into the state's new constitution to limit the state budget to a fixed percentage of the wealth of the state. Copeland got the idea at an ALEC conference. In the wake of his success, conservatives have organized similar drives in numerous other states.

Heading ALEC is Arizona State Representative Donna Carlson, 40. Despite the responsibility of raising six sons (Carlson is recently divorced) and of attending to her duties in the state legislature, Carlson has found the time to devote a considerable amount of effort to her duties at ALEC where she is now serving her second term as chairman.

"ALEC's success has been phenomenal," Carlson crows, "and I'm proudest of the fact that we did it on our own. The other national organizations of state legislators are funded by the taxpayers' money, but we've made it strictly on private funding. Those who believe in our goals and objectives have supported us. That's the way it's supposed to be in America."

Carlson believes that, after five years of struggle, the organization has really come into its own. "We're at the place where we are beginning to have influence on national events," she says. "When we began operations and put out our first book of suggested legislation, people were hesitant to use it. Now it's becoming fashionable to use it."

Carlson relates that a very effective recruiting device was a book written by California State Senator Bill Richardson, *What Makes You Think We Read the Bills?* "It was a humorous book that every state legislator could identify with, and we mailed a free copy to every state legislator in the country, along with an invitation for them to join ALEC," Carlson says. We had a very positive response. It showed that ALEC wasn't some right-wing kook operation. It was a real ice breaker."

Among the accomplishments that ALEC has had so far, in Carlson's view, is the movement to enact a constitutional amendment to require the federal government to balance its budget: "This concept was in our first book of model legislation and, if you survey the states that have passed it, you will find that in almost every case, the effort was led by ALEC members." So popular has the idea become, Carlson adds, that now the National Conference of State Legislators is supporting the amendment.

Another ALEC success has been the enactment of spending limitation legislation at the state level. "[Tennessee State Representative] Dave Copeland got this enacted in Tennessee before Proposition 13 was passed," she says, "and again it's been ALEC members who have led this effort in many of the states."

The "Sagebrush Rebellion" is another priority of ALEC under Carlson's leadership. The state of Nevada has already filed suit seeking control over its federally controlled lands, and others are preparing to follow suit.

Litigation, in fact, is one of the main concerns of Carlson. "We have developed a good rapport with the Mountain States Legal Foundation," she explains. "I'm on their board, and I suggested that they challenge the constitutionality of the ERA extension. They took my suggestion and are filing suit on behalf of Arizona and Idaho. I think this has the potential of becoming one of the great constitutional cases of the century." Pacific Legal Foundation is also working in the federal lands case for Nevada at Carlson's behest.

"The liberal groups and the ACLU have had a working relationship for years," Carlson states. "Now its time that people who want constitutional government, good government, and limited government start working together and taking their case to court."

Another function of ALEC, according to the chairman, is providing support for conservative members of Congress. "They need to know that they are being supported. And Congress in general needs to be reminded that the states have rights and that they have a role to play as well as the federal government does. One thing ALEC can do is to try to make sure that the people's needs are addressed at the proper level."

Carlson says she thinks ALEC has the potential of increasing its membership from the 10 percent of state legislators now involved to about 25 percent. It is an organization for those legislators who are conservative and who are willing to lead, she says, not for the lethargic or the timid. "ALEC is a training ground for future leaders," Carlson contends. "Our members are well respected in their parties and in their state legislatures. Many of them go on to run for Congress. They are young, vital, and electable, and they take what they've learned in ALEC and they apply it."

Carlson is justifiably proud of what ALEC has accomplished in its short life, and she can be forgiven a bit of boosterism when she claims the organization is the "wave of the future." "The liberals have only come up with temporary solutions," Carlson claims. "It's conservatives who are providing long-range answers to problems. We're the ones who are coming up with the innovative ideas and solutions."

Among the rising political stars associated with ALEC are a number of lieutenant governors. Best known among these is Mike Curb, lieutenant governor of California. At 35, Curb is the embodiment of the kind of success story one usually associates with Horatio Alger novels. Of middle class Mexican-American descent, he left college at 19 to try his luck in the music industry, and he became very lucky indeed, making it big almost immediately with a jingle, "You meet the nicest people on a Honda," which became one of the most successful television ads ever produced. The next year he formed his own record company, and four years later Curb became president of MGM records.

In that capacity, Curb has become a millionaire many times over, chalking up the incredible achievement of producing some forty gold records (more than 500,000 sales) and ten platinum discs (more than a million sales) featuring such recording stars as Debby Boone, Shaun Cassidy, and the Osmonds.

Curb became politically active in the Nixon campaign of 1972, and in 1976 he was named chairman of the California Reagan campaign. Reagan beat Gerald Ford two to one in the primary and for the general election Curb was asked to be cochairman of the Ford campaign in California. Ford carried the state. Party pros throughout the state were so impressed with Curb's performance that many began to pressure him into running for lieutenant governor. He agreed, won the primary, and went on to defeat incumbent Democrat Mervyn Dymally by 600,000 votes while Jerry Brown was winning reelection as Governor by 1.3 million votes.

Since that time, the sparks have flown in Sacramento. As Jerry Brown continued his peripatetic ways roaming the country and the globe, Curb surprised everyone by putting into practice the provision of the state Constitution that states that, when the governor is out of the state, the lieutenant governor becomes acting governor. On one occasion, Curb took advantage of Brown's absence to fill a vacancy in the state judiciary, a move that brought Brown winging back to the state in a rage. On another occasion he issued an executive order deregulating a large portion of the energy industry in the state. So tense has the situation become that Brown is extremely nervous about leaving the state—a situation that has anti-Brown partisans in the state and across the country in paroxysms of mirth.

Curb has been far more than a stunt man, however. He has moved aggressively to assert his leadership of the party in the state and to position himself for a run for the governorship in 1982. At Curb's instigation the Party now has its first Hispanic chairman and first woman leader of the Senate caucus—both of them staunch conservatives. He has also shown great sensitivity to the problems of Chicanos in California and to the "illegal aliens" who have moved into the state from Mexico by the hundreds of thousands.

According to Curb, "The major factor in the undocumented workers being here is that our current welfare system encourages so many Americans not to work that it puts many employers in a position where only the undocumented aliens will take those particular jobs. Therefore, we have to address this in terms of our overall welfare system, our overall incentive system, and, to some degree, as a human rights issue."

Curb has also taken the lead in the effort to attract industry to the state and to cut back the bureaucratic regulations that are impeding industrial development. "We are now developing test projects," Curb says. "Since the loss of the Sohio, Sun Desert, and Dow Chemical plants and numerous other plants and businesses throughout this state, the permit procedure issue has become more of a public issue. I am presently working on trying to encourage one major company to build a $1 billion methane-methanol plant in California. In the process of getting that plant built, we will study and track each step of the permit procedure process so as to define it in more exact terms and therefore be able to refine it quickly."

Curb has also been a champion of tax cuts and government spending limitations, having vigorously supported both Proposition 13 and the recently passed Gann amendment to put a ceiling on the growth of the state budget. He has also been a vigorous opponent of busing and friendly towards the idea of tuition vouchers and tax credits.

One of Curb's achievements is his proven ability to attract the youth vote while campaigning as a conservative. Commenting on that he says,

I am told that I carried the 18-to-34 vote and that I am one of the first Republicans in this state to have done so. One thing I did is go to the college campuses and to other youth groups and speak out on issues—in many cases issues that were popular with the young people and in other cases issues that were not popular.

In this day and age when Tom Hayden and Jane Fonda and people of this sort are able to so successfully utilize the media to get their point of view across, it is essential that Republicans my age, who have had a private sector experience in a business such as the music business to which young people can easily relate, get out there and speak and take issue with the Haydens and the Fondas and take issue with the Jerry Browns when we disagree—but do it in a way that young people can relate to and understand. That oftentimes means going right to those campuses and accepting the fact that there will be some organized opposition.

Iowa Lieutenant Governor Terry Branstad made it to the second highest position in his state at an even younger age than Curb: Branstad is 32. A graduate of the University of Iowa and Drake Law School, Branstad served for two years with the Army in Vietnam before beginning to practice law in his hometown of Lake Miller, Iowa, in 1969.

In 1972, he ran for the State House of Representatives, winning a seat by 59 percent of the vote. He was reelected in 1974 with 69 percent (burying the chairman of the Iowa Democratic Party in the process), and in 1976 he was reelected with 70 percent of the vote. In 1978, Branstad ran for lieutenant governor and received 58 percent of the vote statewide—only a fraction of a point behind the state's popular five-term governor, Robert Ray. In almost two-thirds of the counties, Branstad ran ahead of Ray.

Ray and Branstad have developed an effective working relationship, even though Ray is moderate-to-liberal and Branstad is a staunch conservative.

In some instances, however, Branstad has bucked the governor on philosophical positions and in others he has brought the governor around to his position. An example of this is the successful effort to enact tax reforms. Branstad says that he and other conservatives in the legislature pushed through the enactment of a 6 percent limit on personal property tax assessments and the exemption from those taxes of livestock and farm machinery. In 1980, he says, he plans to push a measure to provide property tax relief for industrial and commercial concerns.

In addition, Branstad led an effort to provide indexation of the state income tax. "The income tax revenues have increased eight-fold in the last ten years," he says, "and when the Democrats were in control of the legislature they made the tax quite progressive. We are starting to reform that by indexing the system."

Branstad explains that the governor opposed this initially, feeling it might put the state budget in deficit. As a compromise, Branstad and others came up with a plan that indexes the income tax for one-fourth the rate of inflation. In 1980, the tax will be indexed for one-half the inflation rate. In this manner, the state government will have time to make the necessary adjustments of the state's budget. In addition, the legislature has gone on record as favoring eventual 100 percent indexation of the income tax and Branstad indicates that moves are also going to be made to adjust the tax brackets to make them less progressive.

The lieutenant governor has led the fight for other tax and spending reforms. He led a successful effort to have the inheritance tax exemption doubled and was instrumental in getting the legislature to enact a petition calling for a constitutional amendment to require the federal government to balance the budget.

Branstad also led the fight to toughen the state's new criminal code, proposing some eighty amendments to it, about thirty of which were adopted. "The original draft would have tied the hands of local law enforcement officials," he says, "and I was able to get it amended to correct that." One of the changes was the adoption of mandatory sentences for certain types of crimes—including repeat offendersand crimes committed with firearms.

Branstad also won the governor's support for the effort to reform the state unemployment law so as to tighten up eligibility requirements and to increase the incentive to work, while increasing the benefits of the needy. This reform, he says, will save the state an estimated $30 million in 1979.

The lieutenant governor also supports reform of the welfare system and at the July 1979 conference of U.S. lieutenant governors, he introduced a proposal expressing support for a national block grant program in which the federal government would provide each state with an annual grant to help cover welfare costs while leaving the states free to design their own systems. This plan (essentially that originated by Robert Carleson, California's director of welfare under Governor Reagan) was bitterly opposed by the chairman of the conference, Massachusetts Lieutenant Governor O'Neil (son of Tip O'Neill, Speaker of the U.S. House of Representatives). Despite this opposition, Branstad succeeded in getting the proposal adopted. Branstad has been a member of the American Legislative Exchange Council for several years, and he credits ALEC with providing him with many of the ideas for legislation that he has introduced in the Iowa legislature.

Ohio State Senator Donald Lukens, a former chairman of ALEC, calls Branstad "one of the brightest and most innovative of the young conservatives in state government." Lukens predicts that, should Governor Ray decide to step down as governor in 1982, the next governor of Iowa unquestionably will be Terry Branstad.

Two excellent examples of the success the conservative movement has had in nurturing a new generation of political leaders can be seen in the Ohio legislature, where Thomas van Meter, 36, is assistant minority leader of the Senate and William Batchelder, 37, is assistant minority leader of the House of Representatives.

Both van Meter and Batchelder are aggressive, articulate conservatives with well-thought-out philosophies and solid principles, and both are products of conservative movement training, van Meter having gotten his in the Young Republicans and Batchelder his in YAF, in which he was Ohio chairman in 1963 and 1964. Both are also members of ALEC.

The two men are also proteges of U.S. Representative John Ashbrook, within whose congressional district they reside. For twenty years Ashbrook has been a national conservative leader, serving as national chairman of the Young Republicans and later as chairman of the American Conservative Union, and in 1972 running as the conservative protest candidate against Richard Nixon. Something of a maverick as far as state and national GOP leaders are concerned, Ashbrook has managed to be successful politically while remaining true to his conservative principles, and both van Meter and Batchelder cite the congressman's example of the principled politician as a model for their own careers. "John Ashbrook has probably had the greatest influence on me both philosophically and politically," van Meter says. Batchelder says much the same thing. "Ashbrook has had a tremendous impact on me. He has a strength and integrity that is inspiring and he has provided badly needed intellectual leadership. He has also urged young people to get involved in politics and has gone out of his way to campaign for us and support us."

For Batchelder, who has been in the Ohio House since 1968, service in the legislature has been more than a little frustrating. The once mighty

Republican machine which once dominated Ohio politics has crumbled in recent years, leaving the GOP at a nearly two-to-one disadvantage in the House. He nevertheless is optimistic, feeling that the party's decline has bottomed out. "The electorate is more conservative now," he says, "and you can see this in the Democrats in the House. They are becoming more conservative each year. Also, a new generation of Republican leadership is coming on the scene. Their impact is already being felt in the Senate, and I think it will soon be seen in the House."

Despite being in the minority in the House, Batchelder has had some successes, among them a leadership role in the rewriting of the state's criminal code which was adopted in 1971. As ranking Republican member of the House Judiciary Committee at the time, Batchelder helped push through a number of changes in the code. One of these was to adopt fairly lenient punishment for first offenders of most crimes and harsh mandatory punishment for repeat offenders. "We removed most of the arbitrary element from sentencing," he says, "and made incarceration almost automatic for repeat offenders. The prison population has grown as a result, but the public is better protected."

Batchelder has been conservative point man in the House on many of the major legislative battles—such as those over the District of Columbia amendment and the efforts to enact a state spending limitation and to ratify the amendment to require a balanced federal budget.

He has also sponsored a number of initiatives in the House, including bills to protect regulated industries such as the insurance industry from federal interference and to establish a catastrophic illness health insurance program. Batchelder has also proposed a bill that would provide loans for would-be homeowners. "I think as a conservative that it is of key importance to the maintenance of stability to assist the individual to have a stake in society," he says. Batchelder has also fought the appointment of judges believing that they should be more accountable to the people.

He gives much credit to Irving Kristol and the neoconservatives for helping conservatives to make inroads among the Democrats on social and economic issues. "They have helped us by proving that liberal programs don't work," he says. "Conservatives didn't argue like that before. We just said they're wrong, period. That may have been the right approach in terms of principle, but it didn't win many converts. Now that we can demonstrate that the liberal approach doesn't work, we're having a greater success."

Looking to the eighties, Batchelder sees the eventual reassertion of Republican dominance in the statehouse. "The candidates with fire in them are the ones who are going to win the close races," he contends, "and in most cases these candidates are going to be conservatives."

In the Ohio Senate, Democratic control is much more tenuous (the Democrats have the edge, 18–15), and minority leader van Meter believes a period of Republican ascendancy is at hand. "For a long time we were down by 21–12," he points out, "but in 1978 we picked up three seats, and I have no doubt but that in 1980 we will pick up from two to five new seats, which will give us control."

Despite his youth and unyielding conservatism—drawbacks in the minds of many political pros—van Meter has risen swiftly to a position of prominence in Ohio Republican politics. In the Senate, he has taken the lead in the usual array of liberal-conservative clashes over pulbic employee bargaining, spending limitations, instant voter registration, etc., and he believes that by doing so he has helped the party establish a distinct image that the voters have found appealing. Adding to this appeal is a procedural reform van Meter instituted as minority leader: opening the Senate Republican caucus to the public, making it the only one to be so opened to public scrutiny, and the step has brought praise from the media in all parts of the state.

Van Meter views his chief accomplishment, however, as the rebuilding of a viable two-party system in the Senate. "When I took over the Senate Republican Campaign Committee in 1975, there was really no plan in evidence for focusing resources," he says. "The money was just sort of allotted equally to the candidates without regard to chances or their need. So I tried to change that. In 1976, we won two seats and we lost two, but we learned a lot. In 1978, we targeted four races where we thought we had the best shot, and we brought in professional campaign consultants, media consultants, and so forth. In all, we spent $200,000 on these races, and we picked up three seats. In 1980, we will target from four to six additional seats."

Van Meter believes that one of the main ingredients in building a Republican State Senate is recruiting good candidates, and these, he says, exist in abundance. "With three or four exceptions, you just don't see much brain power in the Democrats in the Senate," he contends. "On the other hand, our Republican candidates tend to be of a higher caliber. They are mostly young and intelligent, and their conservative views are more in tune with the guy in the street. In the Senate today, we have a whole new breed." In van Meter's view, "Our best bet for gaining strength is to identify with the middle class—with the blue collar and white collar worker who has worked hard and who has improved his condition, and who, as a result of federal and state policies, is gradually losing what he has gained."

Should Republicans gain control of the State Senate in 1980, van Meter will in all probability become majority leader and he already has an agenda in mind. "I want to conduct a systematic review of state agencies," he says. "When I came here in 1973 there were 160 state boards, commissions, and agencies. Now there are over 400. Many of these should be eliminated. I also intend to push for property tax reform, for a bill restoring capital punishment, and for a spending limitation bill. In general, I want to try to establish a more realistic state budget, to get state government out of a lot of areas where it doesn't belong."

Van Meter is excited about the eighties, believing them to be a decade of great potential for conservatives. "In 1980 you are going to see most of the big newspapers in the state, including the two in Cleveland, backing us," he predicts. "They are really disillusioned with the Democrats."

In 1982, when Governor James Rhodes' term is up, van Meter wants to see the GOP field a slate of high caliber candidates for all statewide offices, the way it did in the days when the party dominated state politics. "With a new statewide slate, we have an opportunity to build for the next twenty years," van Meter says. Van Meter, it should be noted, is not speaking here only as a strategist; he has his sights set on leading the slate as the party's candidate for governor.

A former ALEC chairman, Louisiana state representative Louis E. ("Woody") Jenkins, 34, came to national attention in 1978 when he gave a big scare to U.S. Senator Benett Johnston who was running for reelection. Jenkins, a Democrat, took on Johnston in the state's nonpartisan primary. Despite the fact that Jenkins was little known and badly underfunded while Johnston enjoyed the backing of the state's Democratic establishment, Jenkins ran an effective race stressing Johnston's moderate-to-liberal voting record. Although he lost, Jenkins garnered 41 percent of the vote, a surprisingly good showing that marked him as a fast-rising leader in Louisiana politics.

In the state legislature, however, Jenkins has already shown himself to be a leader. His proudest achievement, he says, was in drafting a bill of rights and a limit on government authority for the state's new constitution, which was ratified in 1974. In his eight years in the legislature, Jenkins has also authored eighty major bills which have passed and been signed into law. One of them was the Government Growth Limitation Act, a bill tying future increases in state taxes to income growth in the state, which passed in 1979.

Other Jenkins accomplishments include the Teacher Proficiency Act, which requires all Louisiana public school teachers to pass a national exam stressing English grammar, and which requires them to display competence in the area they are teaching. Another education-related act drafted by Jenkins is the Free Enterprise Education Act, which requires all seniors in the state's public high schools to take a course on the fundamentals of the free enterprise system and to pass an exam on the same.

Jenkins is head of an informal alliance of seventeen conservative Democratic and Republican House members called the Independent Legislature Study Group. The group meets regularly to formulate positions on legislation and every year designs a package of legislation to be introduced in the legislature. "For the past four years, a majority of our proposals have been passed into law," he says.

Among the initiatives to come out of the group are a series of tax reductions which repealed all state property taxes, gave every home owner a $50,000 homeowner exemption from all local property taxes, reduced the state income tax by 20 percent, and established a tax credit of $25 per child for those parents who have children in private or parochial schools. ("The sum doesn't amount to much," Jenkins says, "but it establishes the principle.")

"In our legislature, the conservative members are the creative and aggressive ones," Jenkins says, "and the liberals are on the defensive and in disarray." Jenkins is not a conservative in the sense that he opposes change. "I don't want to conserve the status quo," he says. "I want to make fundamental changes." Friends and foes alike would readily concede that Woody Jenkins has certainly done that.

A likely future chairman of ALEC is Paul Dietrich, 31. A Missouri state representative, Dietrich was elected in 1976, having bested a liberal Republican in the primary. Since arriving in the state capitol he has become a force to be reckoned with. In the last four years, he has led a successful move on the House floor to defeat a public employee collective bargaining bill and the successful effort to stop the D.C. Amendment. Dietrich has also led a drive each year to enact a spending limitation bill. The move has always failed, but in 1979, Dietrich secured the support of the governor and now believes the effort will succeed.

Probably Dietrich's most impressive effort was the statewide drive he led to enact a right-to-work law. The campaign lasted almost two years and cost approximately $2 million. Although defeated in the end by a massive union campaign, Dietrich's drive has had all sorts of auxilliary benefits for the conservative movement in Missouri. During the campaign, hundreds of thousands of voters were contacted, and the names of those who expressed support for the right-to-work effort have been maintained on tape creating a pool of support for organizational and fundraising activities.

Dietrich was also instrumental in establishing nineteen business political action committees in the state, and these have been instrumental in electing conservatives to the state legislature. "We had a sizeable turnover in the state Senate and House in 1976 and 1977," Dietrich says, "and this was largely due to the support of the PACs." The PACs have also helped to insure conservative voting in the legislature. "Legislators know they can vote conservative and still be assured of adequate financial support for their campaigns," he says.

An interesting feature of the Missouri legislature is the amount of coalition politics that goes on. "The legislature is two-to-one Democrat to Republican," Dietrich says, "and about fifty-fifty conservative to liberal. More and more you see the conservative Democrats and Republicans joining together to push conservative legislation."

The Missouri legislature is becoming more conservative, Dietrich states, and after the 1980 elections should be solidly conservative.

Another Dietrich innovation has been the establishment of a seminar series for state legislators and their staffs. Speakers thus far have included Jude Winniski, formerly of the *Wall Street Journal;* Representative Jack Kemp; RKO's Frank Shakespeare; columnist Patrick Buchanan; and General Daniel Graham.

Dietrich also founded the Missouri Council for Economic Development, a foundation that has commissioned comprehensive studies on such issues as right-to-work legislation, public employee bargaining, tax legislation, welfare reform, and nuclear power. The foundation also publishes a weekly column that is carried in about 100 newspapers around the state.

Dietrich is a long-time conservative activist, having served as chairman of the American Conservative Union's Missouri affiliate and as a leader in many other conservative efforts. "The national conservative movement has helped me enormously," he says, "and I know of two other legislators who would not have won in the last election without national conservative PAC support. Conservatives have become much better campaigners as a result of the new campaign schools and other recent advances. We are now surpassing the liberals in terms of direct mail and sophisticated campaign techniques."

Paul Dietrich is a many-talented man (*Holiday* magazine once sent him to France to write a review of a specially prepared dinner the magazine touted as the most expensive meal ever ordered), and he is also aggressive and ambitious. His next goal, he quite candidly admits, is a U.S. congressional seat in 1982. The smart money in Missouri says he will make it.

Another ALEC activist is Illinois State Senator Mark Rhoads, 32. Rhoads was, perhaps more than any other legislator, the driving force behind the creation of ALEC. He was a member of the steering committee at the organization's founding meeting and has served on the organization's board of directors. Rhoads has also been an active participant in other conservative movement activities, having served as the Illinois Chairman of Young Americans for Freedom and the founder of the Illinois Conservative Union.

"The conservative movement has been of great help in orienting me in my political career," Rhoads says, adding, "The growth of conservative groups just in the time I've been active has been unbelievable. What we need to do now is to bring all these groups together in a more cohesive network. At the state level, this network should be used to build support for the conservative legislative agenda that is emerging."

Rhoads sees this agenda as based on five general themes: (1) a "tax-payers' bill of rights," to include tax limitation laws, constitutional amendments requiring balanced budgets, and "truth is spending" public notice laws; (2) human life guarantees; (3) renewed emphasis on fundamentals and a quest for excellence in the public schools; (4) free market guarantees against bureaucratic controls; and (5) "model" ALEC legislation on a wide variety of subjects.

Brad Cates is an ALEC member and Republican who was elected to the New Mexico House in 1974 and reelected in 1976 and 1978. Cates, 29, has already established himself as one of the most active members of the state legislature. Between 1974 and 1978 alone, he sponsored or cosponsored 106 measures in the House, 60 of which were passed.

Among Cates' legislative accomplishments are: a bill, enacted into law, providing mandatory sentences for crimes committed with firearms; a bill, enacted into law, requiring stricter penalties for purveyors of child pornography; and a bill requiring able-bodied welfare recipients to do public service work. He has also been a vocal supporter of a constitutional amendment to require the federal government to balance its budget.

In addition to his work with ALEC, Cates is a member of the National Conference of State Legislators Committee on Criminal Justice and Consumer Affairs. He is also the Young Republican National Federation committeeman from New Mexico and serves on the state GOP central and executive committees. Cates was elected student body president and executive vice president and president of the student Senate at New Mexico State University and obviously possesses considerable political ability. New Mexico political observers think it likely that he will be the next congressman from his district.

State Representative Steven Bisenius was elected to the Iowa House in 1976. The 32-year-old Bisenius, and ALEC member and long-time conservative activist, has taken his activism to the state capital. Leader of the Reagan forces in the state legislature in this crucial early caucus state, Bisenius has been in the forefront of conservative activity in Des Moines. He has introduced an amendment reaffirming U.S. support for Taiwan, been a leader in defeating the D.C. Voting Rights Amendment, led the effort to have property taxes limited to one percent of assessed valuation, and been in the forefront of the prolife effort and the fight to enact an amendment to the federal Constitution requiring a balanced budget.

Bisenius caused a great stir in 1978 when he led an Iowa trade delegation to South Africa. Upon its return, the delegation reported that sixty-seven Iowa firms were doing business in South Africa but that the prospects for doing more business were clouded by the open hostility of Iowa Senator Dick Clark, then chairman of the Africa Subcommittee of the Senate Committee on Foreign Relations. The group also reported that South Africa had suffered a severe drought, forcing it to buy grain from abroad. Partly because of Clark's antipathy, they said, the grain had not been purchased in the United States. Because of the trip, Bisenius says, the Iowa Farm Bureau took a stand strongly supporting trade with South Africa. In addition, the anger generated by the report of the lost grain sale badly hurt Clark, contributing to his defeat in the election.

ALEC member James Paulk was elected to the Georgia Senate in 1976. Since then Paulk, 30, has become a leader of the conservative Democrats in that body. "One of my priorities," Paulk says, "has been tax limitation. It is a popular issue among all groups of people in the state with the exception of government employees."

With Paulk in the forefront of the effort, the Georgia legislature recently passed a "taxpayers rights" amendment to the state constitution, which would limit state expenditures according to population and economic growth in the state. Paulk has also championed a measure to provide the citizens of the state with the right to place initiatives on the statewide ballot.

He has also been an effective advocate of prison reform. "Under a bill I authored the state gives a subsidy to the counties to provide prison facilities for state prisoners. This has a number of advantages. For one thing, it costs the state between twelve and fourteen dollars a day to house a prisoner in a state prison, whereas the counties can do it for five dollars. So the state saves seven to nine dollars a day for every prisoner. In return the counties use the prisoners to perform useful work. It's hard to manage the enormous state prisons efficiently and humanely. By placing the prisoners with the county systems, they receive better treatment, they are closer to their families, and it saves the state money."

Paulk is something of a rarity among conservative activists in that he is an ardent conservationist. "I think conservation, within reason, is consistent with the conservative philosophy," he says. In 1978, Paulk received the Legislative Conservationist of the Year award from the Georgia Wildlife Federation, an award given for, among other things, his bill requiring the mandatory recycling of beverage bottles. The bill, now law, requires a five cents deposit on every bottle, which can be reclaimed when the bottle is turned in. "This law helps us to clean up the state and to do it without creating another bureaucracy," he says.

Like Paulk, Oregon State Representative Kurt Wolfer, 30, is a Democrat, but he is not a very conventional one. He was, first of all, elected to the legislature in 1972 from a traditionally Republican district—a feat that surprised and chagrined the local Republicans. Now serving his fourth term in the legislature and an enormously popular figure in his district, he has become a source of considerable discomfort to the Democratic leadership. A high-rolling entrepreneur who makes a living trading commodities and drilling for oil and gas, Wolfer is also a maverick politican.

"The Democratic leadership in the state thought they had gotten another McGovernite when I was elected," he says, "but they were wrong." Wolfer proved to be a strong libertarian-conservative who voted his convictions rather than the party line. His renegade tendencies, in fact, caused him to be thrown out of the Democratic Caucus in 1973, a move the leadership came to regret. Working with other conservative Democrats and Republicans in the House, Wolfer began to work on forming a working conservative majority in the House.

By 1977, they had succeeded. ("We would have succeeded much earlier if it hadn't been for the liberal Republicans," he says.) In that year, the speaker of the House moved to strip Wolfer of his committee chairmanship. Wolfer and his conservative allies responded by stripping the Speaker of virtually all power and setting up a bipartisan six-man committee to actually run the House.

The split in the House now is twenty-six Democrats vs. twenty-four Republicans. However, in philosophical terms, Wolfer says, there are thirty-seven moderate-to-conservative members and twenty-three moderate-to-liberal ones, a situation that gives the conservatives a clear majority. Wolfer is now speaker pro tempore.

Under the leadership of the conservative majority in the House, the legislature has passed a number of bills, among them a cut in property taxes and a "truth in tax levies" bill that requires the financial impact of all tax levies to be printed on the ballot. Under Wolfer's lead, the legislature has also abolished a number of boards, commissions, and regulations. Last year, he said, "sixteen pages were deleted from the *Oregon Revised Statues*."

Wolfer is also a supporter of zero-based budgeting and sunset review legislation. Another Wolfer innovation is the "automatic destruct" clause that he has inserted in dozens of bills passed by the House. This clause requires that, at the end of a stipulated time, funding for a given program ceases. To restore it, the legislature has to enact new legislation. A number of programs have gone out of existence this way, Wolfer says, and the practice has caught on with other members of the House and Senate. Wolfer was also one of those responsible for bottling up the D.C. Amendment in committee.

One of his most novel ideas is that of replacing the tangle of government regulatory agencies with a toll-free number on which any citizen could call a central state office to voice a complaint about a business practice or whatever. The state official would then try to work out the difference between the two parties and, if this failed, the matter would be referred to the courts.

A fan of Ronald Reagan and Phil Crane, rather than Jimmy Carter and Teddy Kennedy, Kurt Wolfer is definitely out of synch with the established Democratic leadership. But he is successful nonetheless. "The folks are on our side," he says, a fact that is demonstrably true in his case. Wolfer's success, moreover, gives rise to the possibility that coalition politics may be the new wave in America.

Conservatives have come a long way at the state level in five years. "When we had that first ALEC conference I thought the few of us there were about the only conservative state legislators in the country," says Woody Jenkins, "but as we have gotten organized, I've realized that there's a whole lot of us."

As Jenkins indicates, ALEC has played a major role in increasing awareness among conservative state legislators. It has brought together formerly isolated conservative legislators from all parts of the country and made them aware of successful conservative tactics and legislation in other states. The legislators have in many cases appropriated these tactics and model legislation learned at ALEC conference or from ALEC publications and applied them in their own state legislatures. A good example of this is the movement to enact statutory limitations on state spending, a movement led in many states by ALEC members.

For many years, conservatives tended to focus their attention on Washington, leaving the state capitals to the tender mercies of the liberals. Such a one-sided focus was extremely shortsighted, in view of the fact that much legislation of importance is passed in the state legislatures. This oversight is at last being remedied, thanks in no small measure to the efforts of the American Legislative Exchange Council.

Rep. Newt Gingrich, secretary of the Republican freshman class, U.S. House of Representatives

16 | CONGRESS: YOUNG CONSERVATIVES MAKE THEIR MARK ON CAPITOL HILL

"Conservatism is Rising on Hill, ACU Study Says," read the headline in the September 2, 1979, *Washington Post*. The story reported that the American Conservative Union interim rating of the 96th Congress showed an appreciable shift to the right. The *Post* article would come as no surprise to anyone who has followed congressional affairs in the press. Rather it is merely the latest in what is now a long series of articles about the starboard tack of the national legislature.

A few samples: "Starring for the GOP, a February 20, 1978, *Newsweek* article about the impact Representative Jack Kemp is having in Congress and within the Republican Party. "The Old West's New Rightists," a March 29, 1979, *Wall Street Journal* article about newly elected conservative senators such as Utah's Orrin Hatch and Jake Garn, Wyoming's Malcolm Wallop, Nevada's Paul Laxalt, and Idaho's Jim McClure. The new crop of senators, according to the article, are more issue-oriented, aggressive, and politically astute than the older conservatives in the Senate. "Kennedys of the Right," a June 5, 1978, *Newsweek* piece about the Crane brothers, Phil, Dan, and David, who were all running for Congress (Phil was reelected, Dan won, but David lost). "Congress's 'New Right' Makes its Mark," an August 28, 1978, *U.S. News and World Report* story about the impact on the Hill that such bright young conservatives as Senators Richard Lugar and Orrin Hatch and Congressmen Phil Crane, Robert Bauman, and Jack Kemp were having. ("Despite lopsided liberal majorities in both the House and Senate, conservatives are scoring one victory after another," the article reported—victories that the magazine attributed to the organizational and tactical savvy of the "new rightists.") "The Dwindling Band of Liberals," a January 15, 1979, story in the *Wall Street Journal*, which reported that not in two decades had the few genuine liberals in Congress faced such a hostile mood toward spending programs. "In the Upper Chamber, Things Seem to

Freshman stars *(left to right from top):* Rep. Ken Kramer (R-Colo.), Rep. Dan Lungren (R-Calif.), Rep. Olympia Snowe (R-Me.), Rep. William Carney (R-N.Y.), Rep. James Sensenbrenner (R-Wisc.), Rep. Carroll Campbell (R-S.C.)

Be Going Right," a November 9, 1978, *Washington Post* article which reported that the twenty new senators elected indicated a swing to the right in the Senate.

But probably the most intriguing article was a lengthy report on the Republican freshman class in the House published in the July 7, 1979, issue of *Congressional Quarterly* magazine. Titled "House Freshman Republicans Seek Role as Power Brokers," the article stated that the thirty-seven Republicans newly elected to the House in 1978 were a different breed from their predecessors—more aggressive, more independent, and more conservative. Noted *Congressional Quarterly:* "With the 96th Congress only a quarter of the way through its two-year lifespan, it is clear that the GOP freshmen are working hard to shift the focus of attention in the House from the present liberal-to-moderate majority and award both the limelight and the power of winning votes to a newly strengthened conservative coalition."

Congressional Quarterly went on to say that, given their relatively small numbers (37 out of a total House membership of 435), it seemed unlikely that the freshmen could accomplish this in their first term. The journal noted, however, that if from ten to twenty like-minded Republicans were

Sophomore stars and U.S. senators, present and future
(clockwise covering both pages): Rep. Paul Trible (R-Va.);
Rep. David Stockman (R-Mich.); Rep. Robert Walker (R-Pa.);

Rep. Mickey Edwards (R-Okla.); Rep. Thomas Hagedorn (R-Minn.);
Sen. Gordon Humphrey (R-N.H.); Rep. Dan Quayle, GOP Senate
candidate, Indiana

elected in 1980, House conservatives would be in their strongest position in years. *Congressional Quarterly* pointed out that notwithstanding their small numbers and lack of experience in the House, the GOP freshmen had already had an impact, that by maintaining a high degree of unity and by persistently taking tough no-compromise positions, they were changing the Republican role in the House from responsible opposition to that of offering a clear-cut alternative to the Democratic majority. Having staked out this clear-cut opposition stance on the issues, the freshmen want to take their case to the voters in 1980 in hopes of making substantial gains.

One hallmark of the freshmen is their militant conservatism. The ACU interim rating for 1979 gives them an incredibly high cumulative total of 92.86, compared with the 81.68 score for all House Republicans and a 46.89 score for the entire House. Another distinguishing characteristic of the freshmen is their fidelity to their campaign pledges. Instead of succumbing to the spirit of compromise and accommodation characteristic of the House and of deferring to the entreaties of the more moderate GOP leadership, the freshmen have remained faithful to their pledges made on the campaign trail.

A case in point is the battle over a constitutional amendment to require the federal government to balance the budget. Republicans have campaigned on the theme of a balanced budget for longer than anyone can remember, but their resolve tends to falter when placed in a position to do something about it (as witness the budget deficits under the Nixon and Ford administrations which totaled an incredible $284 billion). Similarly, in the Congress, the GOP leadership has tended to accept the idea that a constitutionally mandated balanced budget would be disruptive to the legislative process, and hence have generally sided with the Democratic leadership in thwarting a constitutional amendment. This was the case with minority leader John Rhodes in the 96th Congress. Rhodes had come out against the constitutional amendment, angering many of the freshmen Republicans who had campaigned on a platform of a balanced budget. Unlike previous freshmen classes, however, the 96th freshmen refused to toe the leadership line. Instead, they went to the mat with Rhodes over the issue forcing the minority leader at length to come around to their position.

Nor is this the only issue on which Rhodes and the freshmen have clashed. Yet, the fundamental difference between the leadership and the new Congressmen would appear to be more one of tactics: the freshmen want a more combative, high profile kind of opposition that bedevils the Democratic leadership and makes the evening news; a strategy, in short, that will make the public aware that it is the Republican Party that is on the right side of the issue. In seeking leadership in this effort the freshmen have not so much fought with their leaders as gone around them to team up with the more aggressive conservatives such as Robert Bauman of Maryland and John Ashbrook of Ohio who stay on the House floor from gavel to gavel demanding roll call votes on unpopular spending bills, raising objections, invoking obscure rules to harass the leadership and offering multitudinous amendments to bills that have been steamrollered through the Democratic-controlled committees.

Although they are frequently not successful in blocking bills or amending them to fit their preference, Bauman and company do render a distinct service to their party by putting the Democrats unambiguously on record on a whole range of legislation—such as pay raises—on which they would just as soon remain obscure.

The freshmen have taken to the style of Bauman and his guerrilla compatriots, and one of them was quoted as saying that frequently Bauman and company are the de facto leadership on the floor. Comments Bauman: "This class of freshmen—and I have watched Republican classes come in every two years for twenty-five years now, both as an employee and as a member of Congress—is one of the more aggressive, one of the more articulate. They tend to be conservative as well as Republican—in contrast to some of the more senior members who tend to be Republican first. The freshmen are uniformly bright, aggressive. They've worked hard to get here and they're showing a very strong interest in not only issues but also parliamentary procedure. I'm very encouraged. I think they are good for the Party and will stimulate action."

The freshmen got an opportunity to really flex their muscles in June of 1979 when they drafted Henry Hyde, a two-term conservative from Illinois to run for the position of Conference Chairman vacated by John Anderson (also of Illinois). Hyde ended up losing to Representative Sam Devine, an old-school conservative from Ohio, by a vote of 75-72. Despite the loss, the close vote and the fact that the freshmen voted as a bloc, impressed many observers and signaled that the freshmen would be a force to be reckoned with in future elections.

That opportunity may not be far off. It is generally assumed that Rep. Rhodes will retire from Congress in 1980, and that will open the way for a full-scale reshuffling of the party's leadership in the House. Given the addition of a significant number of new Republicans in the 1980 election, the class of 1978 and their allies will be in the controlling position.

Representative of the aggressive young conservatives in the House is Representative Newt Gingrich, 37, of Georgia. Although he is secretary to the freshmen class rather than president (that position is filled by Representative Ed Bethune of Arkansas), Gingrich's aggressiveness, outspokeness, and high profile in the press have made him come to symbolize the restless freshmen class. Surprisingly for so combative a person, Gingrich is a scholar by profession. A native of Harrisburg, Pennsylvania, he grew up in Columbus, Georgia, and received his bachelor's degree from Emory University in Atlanta in 1965. In 1967, he received a master's degree in history and in 1970 a doctorate in modern European history, both from Tulane University in New Orleans. He was a professor of history at West Georgia College for seven years, has contributed to one book and is working on another about the Soviet threat to Western Europe.

Gingrich unsuccessfully ran for Congress twice against Representative John J. Flynt (D.-Ga.), finally winning the seat in 1978 when Flynt retired. Once in the House, Gingrich lost no time in making his mark. He took the lead in several legislative battles, among other things proposing a bill to require Congressmen to pay Social Security taxes and introducing a motion to expel Rep. Charles Diggs (D.-Mich.) who was convicted of stealing $60,000 in staff allotment funds. The Democratic leadership blocked Gingrich's expulsion move (the first such motion in sixty-eight years to be debated in the House), but the House did vote to censure Diggs.

Gingrich has also been a leader in the effort to enact the Kemp-Roth tax cut plan and in the effort to enact a constitutional amendment to require a balanced budget. In recognition of his leadership talents, the House GOP leadership appointed Ginrich to head the party's balanced budget task force and a task force to plan strategy for taking over the House in 1980 elections.

Newt Gingrich is that rare hybrid: the scholar-politican. And a happy combination it is in this case. He exhibits the vision of an Irving Kristol and the pugnaciousness of Muhammed Ali. Happily, he has absorbed the best of his professions: as a scholar, he eschews the cant and cliches that are all too often the hallmark of the politician's trade, and as a politician, he disdains the dry didacticism of the exegete.

Although a conservative, and thus solidy grounded in the realities of human limitations, Gingrich, like many of his young colleagues, nevertheless projects a message of optimism and hope that is light years away from the somber, defensive rhetoric that all too frequently characterizes the conservative approach.

We are at the beginning of a new era historically. We stand at a watershed like the moment when the New Deal signalled the end of laissez-faire capitalism and the emergence of the modern welfare state.

At any watershed, there's conflict which occurs—a conflict between world views—the dominanat philosophies of the two different eras. Thomas Kuhn, in *The Structure of Scientific Revolution*, explains that people who grew up with a particular philosophy or world view will refuse to see that the philosophy is decaying and no longer provides an explanation of what's happening. Those people will try to force the new facts into their old framework. That's how you know a world view is decaying and disintegrating—when poeple start defending it by shutting out new information and new ideas.

But eventually, some young person comes up with a better explanation, a better world view, and within a generation this replaces the old philosophy.

The defenders of the past now use their world view to talk about limits—limited resources, limited growth, limits on individuals, and of changes which threaten our survival.

The other world view—that of the future—talks in terms of opportunities, of possibilities, of dreams, and of change as a challenge; not a threat.

Each of those world views isn't just a collection of general concepts, but each world view will result in specific policies and political decisions—which in turn will directly affect and determine your life.

The consequences of a prolonged liberal dominance in Gingrich's view are dire indeed:

The old world view's defeatist approach means I can't be sure how I can provide for my wife and daughters in the future. Nor can I advise my daughters about saving money, or borrowing money, or on careers—or even on what type of world they can expect to live in. At an even bleaker level, this defeatist approach means those of you with sons face the possibility of them fighting in a war because we have based our foreign policy upon fear rather than strength or conviction. Of course, in the end, this approach of disappointment and despair means each of us will probably culminate our particular American dream cut off from loved ones in the dreary confines of a nursing home.

Compounding their colossal mistakes, in Gingrich's view, the liberals in command lack the ability, or the integrity at any rate, to face up to their mistakes. "The defenders of the past can't understand that it's precisely their policies of solving problems by bureaucracies and government grants which have actually caused much of our unemployment. The defenders of the past can't understand that consumers do know best—that if consumers are left enough resources to make changes—they can create jobs and start businesses. Consumers can deal with the energy crisis by switching to solar heating or alternative fuels—if they have enough after-tax take-home pay to switch."

Conservatives can right these past mistakes, Gingrich believes, by designing a budget that encourages work, savings, investment, and excellence. Such a budget, he says, would restore economic growth and prosperity to the nation and instill vibrancy and a sense of hope and confidence in its people:

The Rousselot-Armstrong amendment [requiring a balanced federal budget and tax and spending cuts] is more than a reflection of public disgust at the $200 billion deficit we've caused over the last five years. It is more than an appeal to the huge majorities that want a balanced budget. It's more than a fight against bureaucracy grown out of control. It's more than recognition that the Keynesian era of deficits, unending government growth, and rapid inflation is fast approaching an end. This amendment is an outline of the emerging beliefs of a new era. In fact, the currect economic chaos and lack of government policy that has led to inflation, shortages of goods and services, decay in productivity, and decline of job creation reflects both the death pangs of the Keynesian era of collective growth, and the birth pangs of a new era of individual opportunity.

Gingrich has sought aggressively to force this concept through a Congress that is still heavily Democratic and liberal. Testifying before the House Judiciary Committee on behalf of the Rousselot-Armstrong bill, Gingrich put his case this way,

The focus of the new era will be on individual growth rather than on Keynesian, collective growth, and this amendment helps us make the transition with speed and care. There will be no contradiction between budget-balancing and tax cutting in the new era. Balancing the budget and cutting tax rates are in reality forceful nudges from different directions toward the same destination—a more prosperous and more productive society. The Rousselot-Armstrong amendment nudges Congress towards a slower rise in federal spending, while not preventing us from acting in a crisis. And the tax cuts the amendment encourages will nudge Congress towards a smaller government sector, because the effects of continued tax-cutting on the marketplace will make government spending a smaller part of the total economy.

The public has the right idea. Balancing the budget, along with cutting taxes, is the best answer to our economic dilemma.

The country understands and is ready for the new economics of balanced federal budgets, tax cuts and indexation. And let us serve notice here and now that we want a floor vote on this issue. We should have an opportunity to go to the public in 1980 and say flatly: Yes, I stood for the past and voted for Keynesian policies or Yes, I stood for the future and its hope of expanded opportunity and a better life for all.

In addition to Gingrich, there are a number of other outstanding conservative freshman Congressmen. Among them are:

—William Carney, 37, who represents the First District of New York. Carney has the distinction of being the only registered Conservative in Congress. Originally a Republican, Carney became active in the campaign of Conservative Party candidate James Buckley for the Senate in 1970 and switched his registration to Conservative. In his successful 1978 campaign for Congress, Carney also had the endorsement of the Republican Party. Since his election, he has taken a leading position on a host of issues from the recognition of the government of Rhodesia to tax cut legislation.

—Rep. James Sensenbrenner (R.-Wisc.). "I didn't come to Congress to warm a seat," said Sensenbrenner, 36, a ten-year veteran of the Wisconsin legislature. And after a year in the House, Sensenbrenner has quite clearly kept his word. Known as an aggressive legislator in his years in the Wisconsin House, Sensenbrenner has maintained the pace since coming to Washington. He has already taken his place alongside Representatives Bauman, Ashbrook, and Rousselot as one of the small band of guerrilla fighters who camp out on the House floor monitoring legislation and objecting line by line to liberal bills. Sensenbrenner has also taken a leading role in the fight against government-subsidized elections, has called for an investigation of the scandal-ridden Small Business Administration, and urged the reform of CETA, Social Security, and the welfare system.

—Ken Kramer (R.-Colo.). Named by the American Conservative Union as one of the outstanding Congressmen of 1979, Kramer, 37, was an extremely active Congressman during his first year in the House. He had the distinction, unique for a freshman Republican, of having his first amendment adopted—an amendment that would require all U.S. weapons supplied to Taiwan to be current models, thereby allaying the fears of many defenders of Taiwan that the Carter administration would not supply Taiwan with the modern weapons needed for its defense. Another Kramer amendment approved by the House was to prohibit a reduction of U.S. capabilities at the Guantanamo Naval Base in Cuba.

Kramer also proposed the novel idea that congressional salaries be reduced by one percent every time the national debt showed a monthly rise. The move failed but did help to underscore the responsibility of the Congress for the nation's mounting indebtedness.

Kramer also exposed a charade attempted by the Democratic leadership of the House. Speaker Tip O'Neil had put out the word to House committee chairmen to request inflated budgets from their committees. Then House Democrats would call for slashes in these budget figures, thereby enabling them to pose as frugal budget cutters back home. But, as Kramer's study showed, the actual budget increases effected were still exorbitant—typically running to 40 percent or more, and in one case amounting to a 2,603 percent increase.

—Carroll Campbell (R.-S.C.). Campbell, 39, in the words of the Conservative Victory Fund's Gregg Hilton, "has been one of the most helpful new congressmen in terms of aiding conservative organizations. He regards himself as part of the conservative movement, and he has gone out of his way to help CVF, ACU, and other conservative groups."

In the House, Campbell was the leader in defeating the Obey-Railsback bill that would curtail the activities of the nation's political action committees and he also was instrumental in defeating the bill to provide public financing of Congressional elections. An advocate of the Kemp-Roth bill, he has proposed a measure to allow taxpayers' savings to be exempt from federal income taxes—a measure he believes would spur much-needed capital investment.

A Reagan delegate at the 1976 Republican convention, Campbell was named South Carolina chairman for the 1980 campaign. An aggressive campaigner and articulate speaker, Campbell will probably be the Republican nominee for the U.S. Senate in 1984 if Strom Thurmond retires as expected.

—Daniel Lungren (R.-Ca.). Lungren, 33, has the surprising distinction for a conservative Republican freshman of being praised in an editorial in the *Washington Post*. The *Post* commended Lungren for opposing the attempt of the House leadership to create a "committee on committees," a redundant and costly layer added to the congressional bureaucracy in Lungren's view. The *Post* agreed. The spat over the committee was just one of a number of incidents that have brought Lungren to public attention in his brief time in Congress.

"I campaigned on the theme of less government spending, lower taxes, and cleaning up the regulatory mess in Washington," Lungren says. "My constituents emphasized over and over to me that those were the issues that concerned them, and I pledged to try to do something about them when I got to Washington."

Lungren has kept his pledge, even when it meant angering the GOP leadership in the process. He was chosen cochairman of the Republican Committee on balanced budgets, for instance, and aggressively pushed the idea of a constitutional amendment to balance the budget, though the effort was opposed by Minority Leader Rhodes. Rhodes eventually came around.

Lungren also went against the wishes of the leadership when he introduced a resolution to expel Representative Charles Diggs for pocketing staff money. The motion lost, but only by nine votes, 197–205. Lungren also made news with his demand that Andrew Young resign following his pulbic comparison of the U.S. judicial system to that of the Ayatollah Khomeini. Young stayed on but ended up resigning two months later because of another flap.

The California freshman, a member of the House Judiciary Committee, was also in the vanguard of the effort to force the hiring of a special prosecutor to investigate the Carter peanut business. A prosecutor, Paul J. Curran, was hired.

Another Lungren initiative was a bill to require members of Congress and their staffs to be brought into the Social Security system. The Congress, of course, has a better pension plan, and refused to go along. But Lungren's effort did serve to underscore the flaws and the growing burden of Social Security. At home, Lungren won plaudits for his proposal that Mexican farm laborers once again be admitted to the United States on a system of temporary work permits.

One of the surprises of the freshmen class (and a pleasant one for conservatives) had been Congresswoman Olympia Snowe of Maine. For whatever reason, Capitol Hill watchers expected Snowe, 32, to be a liberal. Instead, she has chalked up a solidly conservative record.

A veteran of both the Maine House and Senate (she originally ran for the state House to fill the vacancy left by the death of her husband), Snowe was familiar with legislative ways and means and the modus operandi of a government bureaucracy before she hit Washington, and she thus arrived in the capital knowledgeable and rearing to go. One of her primary concerns has been the effort to rein in the federal bureaucracy. "Over the past several years," she stated, "Congress has gradually delegated substantial power and authority to the bureaucracy. It is my belief that Congress must exert more authority over the bureaucracy, and certainly the power of federal agencies to promulgate regulations is one area which must be addressed by the Congress."

To this end Snowe has been pushing legislation which she cosponsored that would provide a sixty-day period between the date of a regulation's publication and the date it goes into effect, during which Congress could veto it. In another move to trim the bureaucracy, Snowe has worked for a bill that would reduce the size of the federal work force by 2 percent a year for four years. Snowe has also been a staunch advocate of the effort to require the federal government to balance the budget and was a vigorous opponent of the new Department of Education, stating that it would add another costly layer of bureaucracy to the burdens of the taxpayers and that it would infringe on the province of local schools.

Because she is attractive, witty, and articulate—and one of only sixteen women in Congress—Snowe has been a favorite of the media. She has been the subject of profiles in *Newsweek* and on NBC News, and was mentioned by *Us* magazine as one of the women with the best chance to be president. Based on her record, a Snowe presidency would suit most conservatives just fine.

Among the Republican sophomore class, there are also a number of exceptional young conservatives. One is Representative Mickey Edwards, 40, of Oklahoma. A former editor of *Private Practice* magazine and a long-time conservative activist (Edwards has served for many years as a board member of the American Conservative Union and is now second vice-chairman of the organization), Edwards had no experience in practical politics when he decided in 1974 to run against six-term Democratic Congressman John Jarmin in Oklahoma City's Fifth District. Edwards and his wife, Ann, put on a spirited campaign and came within an eyelash of defeating Jarmin. Despite the defeat, Edwards kept right on campaigning, he and Ann going door to door to personally meet as many voters as possible. The couple gambled everything on the race, investing $50,000 of their own money in the campaign and living on the income from part-time work so that they could devote maximum time to campaigning. In 1976. Jarmin decided to retire, and Edwards went on to win the seat over the Democratic candidate by a razor-thin margin of 51 percent.

Again Edwards refused to let up, choosing instead to move quickly to consolidate his hold on the district. While maintaining a 98 percent attendance record in the House, he flew back to Oklahoma dozens of times during his first term, speaking the first year alone to more than 120 groups in his district. Edwards also did something that is all too uncharacteristic of conservatives: he made a conscientious effort to reach out to groups who traditionally did not vote Republican—people such as union members and blacks. Edwards' district is Democratic in registration by a ratio of three to one. In addition, 12 percent of the citizens are black. Without sacrificing his conservative principles (his ACU record remains a perfect 100 percent), he worked hard to establish a rapport with the blacks in his district. Edwards set up an office in the predominantly black area of the district and hired blacks for his staff. He has made it a point to treat blacks the same as white constituents, speaking before black organizations and visiting his black constituents in their homes, helping them with their problems, and explaining his philosophy and voting record to them.

As a result, when he ran for reelection in 1978, his position was so strong that the Democrats put up only token opposition to him. Edwards won by an astonishing 80 percent of the vote, carrying 74 percent of the black vote in the process. One of the Oklahoma City newspapers reported that the city's mostly all-white victory party on election night was abruptly integrated in a big way as Edwards entered the hall surrounded by a throng of cheering supporters—several dozen of them black.

The success of Mickey Edwards should be a lesson to the Republican Party. It shows conservatives skeptical of going after the vote of ethnic groups that such an effort can indeed succeed, and it gives the lie to those liberals in the party who say that minority votes can be won only by sacrificing the party's conservative principles.

Another come-from-behind success story is that of Rep. Dan Quayle, 32, elected from Fort Wayne, Indiana, in 1976. Quayle has the rare distinction of having succeeded in three difficult career enterprises by the time he was 30. In 1969, he received his law degree from Indiana University and became a practicing attorney. Soon thereafter, he became publisher of the *Huntington* (Indiana) *Herald-Press,* a family-owned newspaper and, in 1976, he was elected to Congress.

Quayle had never intended to run for Congress when, in early 1976, the party leaders of the Fourth District approached him about taking on Edward Roush, the popular four-term Democratic incumbent. It was a job no one else would take, but Quayle plunged into the race with gusto. Utilizing his good looks, excellent speaking ability, and the invaluable assistance of his attractive and bright wife Marilyn (a successful lawyer in her own right) he built a highly effective grass roots organization. A major asset was the solid grasp of the issues he had obtained during years of conservative movement activity in Indiana and the financial and organizational help he received from a number of national conservative organizations. Building on this base, Quayle was able to build a well-organized, well-financed campaign that, in the end, pulled off a major upset—defeating Roush by a hefty margin of over 19,000 votes (55 percent).

Following his election, the *Chicago Tribune* picked Quayle as one of the six most outstanding new members of Congress for 1978. Realizing his great potential, the Party leadership in the House gave him a number of important assignments, including a position on the Small Business Committee, a spot that Quayle used to become an expert on the bureaucracy and to effectively push for reform of such egregious insults as OSHA and EPA.

Quayle was also chosen by his freshmen colleagues to serve on the Republian Policy Committee and was later assigned to the prestigious Foreign Affairs Committee. In 1978, he was reelected with 64 percent of the vote. Quayle has continued his ties with the conservative movement since his election, especially with the American Conservative Union. He serves on the ACU's advisory board and has spoken many times at ACU conferences in Washington and around the country.

In June of 1979, Quayle announced that he would seek the Republican nomination for the Senate in Indiana for the opportunity of running against three-term Democratic Senator Birch Bayh. Bayh is a solid liberal of great campaigning ability, and Quayle is a strong conservative who is equally adept at campaigning. The race thus figures to be one of the most interesting battles of the 1980 campaign. Though Quayle must be rated an underdog, my bet is that he will win.

Another Republican sophomore of great potential is David Stockman, who represents the Fourth District of Michigan. Stockman, a 33-year-old bachelor, was identified by columnist George Will as "southern Michigan's contribution to intelligent government" and was chosen by *Time* as one of "50 Faces for America's Future" in the magazine's special issue on leadership. No stranger to Capital Hill, Stockman worked for five years as an assistant to Representative John Anderson, for two years as Anderson's administrative assistant, and for three years as executive director of the Republic Conference in the House, which Anderson chaired. His mentor's liberalism did not rub off on Stockman, however, as in his three years in the House, Stockman has amassed a solid conservative record (1979 ACU interim rating: 95 percent).

Stockman's official biography describes his self-appointed mission in Congress as "eliminating government waste and freeing the American economy from many of the strangling tenacles of a government grown too big." His assignment to House Administration Committee, Interstate and Foreign Commerce Committee, and Republican Policy Committee have given him considerable leverage for accomplishing that task. A tireless worker, Stockman has worked hard to master the dynamics of the subjects within the purview of his committees and the intricacies of legislation designed by the committees.

Displaying a keen analytical mind and solid grasp of complex subjects, Stockman has made a reputation for sending out detailed "Dear Colleague" letters on a number of important issues before the House. In one of these, he pointed out a $48 billion error in the energy program proposed by President Carter. Stockman was also instrumental in helping to defeat Carter's stand-by gas rationing plan and the President's hospital containment bill.

Stockman has also made good use of his developing expertise—and his ability to write—to take his views outside of Congress. In a space of less than a year, he wrote no less than four guest editorials on energy policy for the *Washington Post*—a rare achievement for a Congressman—especially one so junior. In future years as energy becomes a more and more pressing problem for the nation, Dave Stockman's expertise is likely to be more and more in demand.

Paul Trible, of Tidewater, Virginia, is another rising star in the GOP. The 33-year-old Trible was another underdog when he ran in Virginia's First District, a heavily Democratic district in registration and one with a large black population. Like his colleague Mickey Edwards, Trible made a concerted effort to break into this constituency and, like Edwards, he was successful, picking up about one-third of the black vote, a major factor in enabling him to win a narrow 1,600-vote victory. Also like Edwards, Trible set out immediately to consolidate his hold on the district. Intensive work and good constituent service also made the difference for him, as Trible was reelected in 1978 with 72 percent of the vote.

Trible, again like Edwards, has managed to win convincingly without sacrificing his conservative principles. In his successful career, he has been helped enormously by his wife, Rosemary, a 1967 national Junior Miss and formerly a television talk show hostess in Richmond, Virginia.

Following his election to Congress, Trible was assigned to the Armed Services Committee and the Merchant Marine and Fisheries Committee, both extremely important committees for his coastal district. He scored a notable victory shortly after coming to Congress when he discovered that the General Electric Company was planning to sell a dozen high technology CFG jet engines to the Soviet Union. Trible fired off a letter cosigned by fifty colleagues to President Carter protesting the sale. Three months later, GE aborted the sale citing "negative considerations." Trible also introduced a "Homemaker Retirement Bill," endorsed by 145 members of the House, which would allow the nation's 30-60 million homemakers to invest in Individual Retirement Accounts (IRAs), a personal tax-shelter plan. The idea was adopted by RNC chairman Bill Brock and promoted by the RNC on nationwide television.

While impressing his colleagues in Congress, Trible is also seen as an up-and-coming figure in Virginia. In early 1979, he accepted the cochairmanship of the Virginia Reagan campaign. Reagan carried Virginia in 1976 and is expected to do so again. If he does and goes on to win the nomination and election, his state chairman should have a leg up in future races for governor or senator.

Another young Republican Congressman to endorse Ronald Reagan early in the game is Representative Bob Walker of southeast Pennsylvania's 16th District. Walker served as aid to Rep. Edwin Eshleman for nine years until the Congressman retired in 1976. Running for the seat, Walker was elected with 63 percent of the vote, the highest of any freshman Republican of that year. In 1978, he was reelected with 78 percent of the vote.

Walker serves on the Government Operations Committee and is the ranking minority member of the Government Activities and Transportation Subcommittee. In that capacity, he has made the news with his aggressive prosecution of the corruption in the scandal-plagued General Services Administration. He is also Chairman of the Republican Task Force on Welfare, a platform he has used to push for reform of the burgeoning food stamp program and of the welfare system as a whole.

A resolute conservative, Walker has shown an interest in a wide range of issues from farm legislation to China policy. Representative Robert Bauman calls Walker one of the "best of the young congressmen," adding, "I've been most impressed by his grasp of the issues and by his willingness to fight for his position."

Tom Hagedorn, 36, is a three-term Congressman from Minnesota. A modest, yet principled man, Hagedorn has made his presence felt in the House through his persistance and competence. He is currently vice-chairman of the Republican Study Committee, the organization of House conservative Republicans; Midwest Minority Whip; and a member of the Republican Policy Task Force. Hagedorn is an active supporter of both Young Americans for Freedom and the American Conservative Union, and he is Minnesota Chairman of the Reagan campaign.

Hagedorn has received growing attention lately for his efforts to repeal the Davis-Bacom Act, a Depression-era law that requires that the prevailing local wage rate must be paid on construction projects if the federal government is financially involved. In practice, this has meant that the Labor Department has followed local union wage scales, costing American consumers an estimated $715 million in 1978 alone. Hagedorn's repeal efforts are picking up support—on one occasion garnering 178 votes in the House—and, with a slightly more conservative Congress, it is quite possible a bill repealing Davis-Bacon can be passed.

In the Senate, the higher age requirement (thirty versus twenty-five for the House) plus the greater need for experience in a candidate combine to insure that there are, perforce, fewer young Senators proportionately than is the case in the House. One exception to the rule is Gordon Humphrey, 37, the junior senator from New Hampshire. An airline pilot by profession, Humphrey's only political experience when he ran for the seat in 1978 was as state chairman of the Conservative Caucus. Given his novice status, plus a lack of organization and money, the experts gave Humphrey no chance of defeating incumbent Senator Thomas McIntyre. Humphrey had the advantage of contacts with a number of national conservative organizations, however, and they came to his aid, supplying financial and managerial assistance. The National Conservative Political Action Committee was especially helpful, providing both a campaign manager and media and organizational experts. This assistance and Humphrey's skillful exploitation of McIntyre's record—especially his vote in favor of the Panama Canal treaties—plus the incumbent's complacency resulted in Humphrey's upset victory over McIntyre by a narrow margin of 51 to 49 percent. McIntyre, bitter in defeat, blamed his loss on the diabolical forces of the New Right, and later vented his spleen in print by writing a book about his ordeal at the hands of the nightriders of the radical right. The conservative groups pilloried by McIntyre loved every page of the attack and skillfully used the ex-senator's ravings in their fundraising efforts as indications of their effectiveness.

Since his arrival in the Senate, Humphrey has proved to be a tireless defender of the conservative position and an energetic booster of conservative organizations and candidates. As he gains in experience, Humphrey promises to become one of the conservative movement's stellar leaders.

While not as young as Humphrey, the Senate's newest conservative additions have proved also to be a new breed. Men such as Paul Laxalt (R.-Nev.), Jake Garn and Orrin Hatch (R.-Utah), Richard Lugar (R.-Ind.), former Apollo astronaut Harrison Schmitt (R.-N.M.), Malcolm Wallop (R.-Wyo.), and William Armstrong (R.-Colo.) have arrived in the august upper chamber on their feet and running. Unlike some of their senior colleagues, they have shown themselves to be gifted and willing parliamentary maneuverers fighting for their positions with great skill in committee hearings and in debate on the floor. The new members have also differed in their ability to get along with members of the press and to use the media to get their positions across to the public.

On the eve of the 1980 election, the GOP holds 41 Senate seats out of a total of 100. In 1980, however, 24 of the 33 seats at stake are held by Democrats. As a result, the Republicans have their first real opportunity in many years to take control of the Senate. In addition, many of the new Senators elected promise to be young conservatives.

One great opportunity for conservatives is in Idaho, where Representative Steve Symms, 43, a leading conservative in the House, will take on Senator Frank Church, chairman of the Senate Foreign Relations Committee and one of the most prominent liberals in the country. Symms, an excellent campaigner, already represents half of Idaho's population in the House. The other district is even more conservative, and Symms is expected to make hay out of Church's liberal record. Church has never won big, even against unknown opponents, and this race promises to be his toughest. Knocking off Church will not be easy, but Symms should be able to do it.

Iowa presents another conservative opportunity. There three-term Republican Congressman Charles Grassley is challenging incumbent Democratic Senator John Culver. Grassley is not as dynamic a candidate as Symms, but his plainspoken image seems to play well in Iowa. Grassley is banking that Culver's undiluted liberalism is out of tune with the state's electorate, a hunch that would seem to be well-founded in view of the defeat in 1978 of Culver's equally liberal colleague, Dick Clark, who lost to Attorney General Roger Jepsen. Jepsen pounded on Clark's liberal voting record, including his proabortion votes, and the right-to-life organizations made his defeat a high priority. They have done so again with Culver. Culver is a principled liberal who has made no attempt to obscure his image. The Iowa Senate race should therefore be another classic liberal-conservative match and, all things considered, Grassley should win.

Another excellent opportunity for Republicans is Illinois, where conservative Lieutenant Governor David O'Neal is the GOP candidate for the seat being vacated by retiring Senator Adlai Stevenson. O'Neal is seen as the favorite in that race.

A longer-shot possibility for conservatives is in California, where Republican Congressman John Rousselot is running against two-term Senator Alan Cranston. Cranston has a more moderate image than Church, Culver, or McGovern, but his record is just as far to the left. Cranston has proved to be a highly diligent senator in terms of constituent service, however, and is generally popular throughout California. On the other hand, Rousselot is a very effective campaigner and should be well-funded. The edge has to be given to Cranston, but if the Republican national ticket is strong in California—and especially if the nominee is Reagan—Rousselot could pull off an upset.

There are also some intriguing novices among the Republican challengers. One is Dale Bell, a 30-year-old businessman from Spearfish, South Dakota, who is running against George McGovern. Although he has never held elective office, Bell has gained a great deal of experience in conservative politics working with the American Conservative Union, serving as a Conservative Caucus regional director, and worked in the campaign of Texas Representative Ron Paul and in the 1976 effort of Ronald Reagan.

Bell made it a point to study the tactics George McGovern used to retain his seat while maintaining one of the most liberal records in the Senate. He concluded that it was because McGovern's constituent services were excellent and because McGovern managed to obscure his real record in South Dakota. (In the 1974 campaign, McGovern went so far as to style himself a "new conservative.")

Bell concluded that, to defeat McGovern, it would be necessary to educate the voters about his real record well in advance of the election since, in the heat of a campaign, voters tend to view the charges of challengers as so much political boiler plate. Bell thus began campaigning a full year and a half before the primary date with a "Target McGovern" effort that set out to expose McGovern's record. Utilizing direct mail to conservative contributor lists, he was able to raise almost $100,000 in 1979, money that was used to produce and air television spots covering McGovern's stands on specific issues such as national defense, government spending, etc. Since McGovern's voting record was to be the primary issue, Bell hit on the novel idea of printing a disc-shaped flyer called "The Record of George S. McGovern." On one side, it listed McGovern's vote on ten controversial subjects such as energy rationing, gay rights, congressional junkets, etc., and on the other, it had a plug for Bell and his candidacy.

Bell and his supporters passed out over 20,000 of these "records" at the state fair, which draws almost half the voters of the state. Copies of the record were distributed to fair-goers on their way past the McGovern booth, where the senator himself was holding forth. As a result, hundreds of people read the record and then went on to question the senator about the facts it contained, which infuriated McGovern and his aides and attracted a great deal of press attention to Bell and his campaign.

Bell also gained a great deal of name recognition by his door-to-door campaigning throughout the state. Although most political professionals in South Dakota scoffed at his campaign in the beginning, by the fall of 1979 it was clear that Bell was a genuine threat. Should he win the primary in June (over Rep. James Abdnor), as I believe he will, an upset victory over McGovern is indicated.

In sum, I will go out on a limb to predict victories by Steve Symms in Idaho, Dan Quayle in Indiana, Charles Grassley in Iowa, and Dale Bell in South Dakota and David O'Neal in Illinois. This would mean the replacement of Frank Church, Birch Bayh, John Culver, George McGovern and Adlai Stevenson—five of the leading liberals in the Senate—by conservatives who could be counted on to retain their seats for many years to come.

In addition, it seems reasonable to assume that, given the law of averages, the GOP will pick up at least one more seat, for a net gain in the Senate of six. This would give the Republicans forty-seven seats, four short of a majority. Senator Harry Byrd, an independent from Virginia, votes with the Republicans most of the time, however, and many Democrats vote with the GOP on many issues. In addition, should the GOP capture the White House, there will be a Republican vice-president in the Senate who will be able to vote in case of a tie. Thus, it appears that, while the Republicans will not have official control of the Senate, they will have a working majority most of the time.

Strategists *(left to right):* Charles R. Black, former director of field operations of the Reagan campaign; Kevin P. Phillips, a leading partisan of John Connally; David A. Keene, political director of the Bush campaign

17 | "THE TECHNOLOGY OF WINNING"

We read that primitive societies ascribe great powers to the priests, witch doctors, and medicine men who are thought to be able to divine the will of the gods and who know what measures the tribe needs to propitiate them. Today, in our advanced democracy, power resides in "the people" rather than in supernatural forces, so the diviners of yore have accordingly been replaced by a new caste, the political pundits, pollsters, and strategists whose expertise is in ascertaining the mood of the people and designing a strategy that will enable a client politician to successfully appeal to this sentiment and to get elected.

Hence we see the overnight rise of a nobody like Patrick Caddell, Jimmy Carter's pollster, to the stature of national figure.

Despite the great technological advances made in the last century, however, it sometimes seems that the art of opinion analysis is not much more advanced; that the reading of chicken entrails is about as scientific as modern means of voter analysis.

The main reason for this is that the voters frequently take contradictory, or apparently contradictory, positions on the issues. They are apt to say, for instance, that they favor a treaty between the United States and the USSR that would limit nuclear weapons. Yet when asked, in another poll, whether they think the Soviets would live up to the terms of such a treaty, a majority say no.

Such anomolies have led to considerable confusion among those attempting to analyze the national mood. On the one hand, one sees articles such as that in the October 30, 1978, *U.S. News and World Report* titled, "As Liberals Dig Out From Under," which began: "Political observers are watching with interest—and considerable skepticism—as American liberals try to regroup and turn back the conservative tide sweeping the nation. Critics contend that it is too late to sidetrack what analysts agree is a massive

303

popular shift toward the political right." On the other hand, one sees articles such as that in the September 4, 1978, *Wall Street Journal*. The piece, written by reporter Alan Otten, was titled, "Opinion Analysts View Americans as Troubled and Looking-Inward." The subtitle was "No Conservative Trend."

Summing up his findings from interviews with a number of pollsters, Otten wrote: "Surprisingly, most of the experts talk down the notion of any broad conservative groundswell—a theory advanced by many politicians and journalists as citizens across the country mobilize behind efforts to cut taxes and government spending. Declares James Lindheim, senior vice president of Yankelovich, Skelly & White: 'There's been a very clear growth over a number of years in people's unhappiness with government and more recently with taxes—and that's conservative in a sense. But they also still expect a lot of benefits from government. They still want national health insurance, and the environment cleaned up, and other things usually regarded as liberal.' "

One of the areas of greatest ambivalence according to Otten is that of social issues: "Their surveys, the pollsters declare, point to a steady liberalization in personal attitudes on many social problems. There's increasing acceptance of the rights of women and minorities, of freer sexual relationships, of the use of marijuana. At the same time, however, there is a tendency to more conservative attitudes on public policies on many social issues: rising opposition to school busing, gay-rights ordinances, or special preferences on jobs and university admissions; rising support for capital punishment or tough statutes in drug-peddling or pornography."

Yet, despite the ambivalence and ample contradictions apparent in the views of the voters, the general thrust of voter sentiment would seem to be in a conservative direction. This was the consensus reached by pollsters surveyed by the *Journal* story. The "major ingredients of the national mood" were identified as follows:

—Inflation has surged forward as the overwhelming concern. The "tax revolt" is as much a protest against rising prices, sky-rocketing utility bills and high interest rates as against high taxes or big government.

—People are increasingly losing faith in government's ability to solve problems. Most believe there are so much waste and inefficiency that service levels and programs can be maintained even if taxes are cut.

—There is growing worry that the United States is falling behind the Soviet Union militarily and is increasingly vulnerable.

—People are becoming steadily more "liberal" in their personal attitudes on race relations, women's rights, sexual relations and similar matters; but, paradoxically, they are perhaps somewhat more conservative on what public policies should be in these areas.

In pursuit of victory *(left to right from top):* Karlyn Keene, assistant editor of *Public Opinion* magazine; Jeffrey Bell, policy analyst; Morton Blackwell, youth coordinator and special assistant to Sen. Gordon Humphrey; John Le Boutillier, author of *Harvard Hates America*

Among those most interested in the voters' mood—for understandable reasons—are the managers of the presidential campaigns. Charles R. Black, 30, field director of Ronald Reagan's campaign, says, "I thnk the major issue of the 1980s is going to be: Do we have to accept the decline of America?"

"We are in decline across the board," Black says, "In foreign affairs we're told we're weak and the only way we can get by is to appease our enemies. At home, we're told that we can have no economic growth, that we have to accept a decrease in energy supplies and a decline in our standard of living."

In Black's view, the Democrats are offering an essentially pessimistic view of the future. The Republicans, on the other hand, "believe the country can prosper, that the private sector can make a bigger pie that will allow everyone to benefit."

For the first time, Black argues, "Democrats are on the defensive on the economic issue. The American people believe that the future can be better, that it doesn't have to be worse and that's the message we're going to emphasize strongly."

Black figures that Senator Edward Kennedy will probably be the Democratic nominee, be he thinks he will have a tough time wresting the nomination away from Carter. "The press forgets that although the Georgia boys aren't much good running the government, they proved to be pretty good campaigners," Black says. "Also they have very few ties to the Democratic Party. Their whole game is Jimmy Carter and if he loses, they're not going to be graceful about it." Kennedy has the edge for the nomination, Black believes, but "there will be blood on the floor."

Black believes the contrast between Reagan and Carter or Kennedy will be quite stark on foreign policy and domestic policy, but he thinks Reagan's stands on the social issues would play better against Kennedy's. "Our strategy against Kennedy would be to contest every constituency," he says. "The more we demonstrate that the Northeast is not guaranteed and that it will take an all-out push by groups like Labor to carry those states for him, the less time he will have to make inroads in the South and West and the harder it will be for him to moderate his liberal positions. The goal is to keep him on the left and from making a shift to the center."

Black believes that this time around, Reagan will have a real shot at capturing a large part—perhaps a majority—of the Catholic vote. "With Teddy's stands in favor of government-funded abortions and against tax credits for parochial schools," he says, "I think we have a real chance to do well with working-class Catholics."

Black also believes Reagan will do extremely well in the South. "If Kennedy beats Carter, there are going to be a lot of angry Southern Democrats, and it's hard to see how Kennedy would do anything in the South in those circumstances. On the other hand, Carter has disillusioned a lot of southerners. He needed those people to beat Ford in 1976, but he will lose a lot of them to Reagan."

In the area of defense, Black believes there is a growing awareness of the increasing Soviet challenge and a growing unease about it. "When people hear the facts about the extent of the Soviet buildup, they will respond with the support necessary for a dramatic increase in defense spending," he contends.

On domestic issues, he says, Reagan will stress the need for tax cuts, reducing the level of government spending, and bureaucratic and regulatory reform. A major priority, Black indicates, will be the energy problem, with Reagan stressing the need for energy independence via increased domestic production of oil and coal and alternative sources such as nuclear power developed in a prudent manner.

"I think people realize the Democrats have made a mess of foreign policy," he says. "Mexico is a good example. Here is a country right next door where both countries have a real need for cooperation. There's no reason why we shouldn't have an excellent relationship with Mexico, but Carter has screwed things up. The governor [Reagan] was in Mexico last July for a meeting with President Lopez Portillo, who made it plain that he didn't care for Carter worth a damn."

Columnist and political analyst Kevin P. Phillips, 39, is not officially part of John Connally's campaign for president, but he is an enthusiastic supporter of Connally, and the strategy he posits for winning the White House is almost chapter and verse that being implemented by the Connally campaign. "I've never been an advocate of hundred-proof *Human Events* type conservatism," he says. "I've always felt that the winning combination is a conservative-populist approach."

Phillips was a strategist in the 1968 Nixon campaign and subsequently wrote a book, *The Emerging Republican Majority,* which became a bestseller, a book that argued the Republican Party could become the majority party by implementing a "Sun Belt" strategy that concentrated on the South and West. "Conservatives have blown that opportunity repeatedly since 1968," Phillips believes, but he also thinks the opportunity is at hand again in 1980.

In order to succeed, in Phillips' view, it is essential that Republicans "get off the extreme free-market, pro-business kick they have traditionally been on." He cites a Gallup poll taken in October 1979 as showing that, for the first time, big business has displaced big labor as the second most disliked power center. Big government is number one on the public's hate list, but Phillips cautions against overreacting to this finding. "In a lot of areas, the public wants more government," he contends. "They want the government to break up the oil companies; they want wage and price controls and national health insurance; and they want more regulation in some areas—mainly on such things as drugs and energy, where they distrust business."

Nevertheless, Phillips believes the issues are clearly present for a conservative victory if chosen judiciously. He recommends concentrating in two areas. "One is national defense and foreign policy. All the polls show an increasing nationalism on the part of the public. They are jingoistic about the Russian troops in Cuba, and they don't like America being pushed around. The people are ready to spend money on defense. They want to be number one again."

The second area of emphasis, Phillips believes, should be on an "institutionalized populism." Conservatives, in his views, should be pushing initiatives, constitutional amendments, and other measures to shake up the system."

Finally, Phillips believes conservatives should strongly emphasize the social issues. "Things like busing, welfare, quotas, tuition tax credits, and family issues. These are all important issues with the voters," he maintains. The abortion issue, too, is a plus for conservatives, he believes, although he thinks it is a "two-edged sword" that must be handled carefully. In Phillips' view it is important to be positioned correctly on the question—that is as antiabortion—so as to enlist the support of the prolife forces, but simultaneously, it is important not to be strident on the matter, a stance that would alienate a lot of voters who are neutral or "prochoice" on the question.

Phillips believes, unequivocally, that Connally is the Republican candidate best able to implement a conservative-populist strategy in 1980. "Reagan's age is a significant negative," he believes, "as is the fact that, as an outsider who was a governor, he suffers because of Carter's inept performance." Connally, he believes, has the advantage of being perceived as an outsider in the sense that he is not part of the Washington establishment but also as a person who has served in Washington and both knows how the establishment works and how to deal with it.

Phillips believes Kennedy probably will be the Democratic nominee and he fairly pants at the thought of a Kennedy-Connally contest. "I think either Reagan or Baker could outscore Kennedy in a debate," he says, "but I can see Connally actually delivering a knockout punch to Kennedy in that situation."

Although Phillips advocates a Sun Belt strategy against Kennedy or Carter, he believes significant inroads can be made in the ethnic vote in the industrial states. By appealing on the basis of social issues, the GOP, Phillips believes, should be able to garner at least 50 percent of the Catholic vote.

According to David Keene, "the issues of the 1980s will be our issues: they will be essentially conservative issues. Basically, we're talking about the citizen's relationship to the state and the size of government." Keene, at 32, has already had an extremely varied political career, having served as chairman of Young Americans for Freedom, special assistant to Vice President Spiro Agnew and Senator James Buckley and, in 1978, as Southern field director for the Reagan campaign. In 1979, he signed on as second in command of the George Bush campaign, in which position he has considerable say in both policy and organizational matters.

Like many other conservative strategists, Keene believes the major issue of the 1980 campaign will be the economy and national defense. "The economy is far and away the major issue," he says. "At a time when inflation is rising and real income is falling, it is understandable that the people will be preoccupied with the economy since that affects them personally in a direct way." It is a "revolutionary development of 1979," Keene believes, that "the people for the first time believe the main cause of inflation is government." This perception, he believes, gives Republicans and conservatives an advantage they have not had before in attacking the record of Democratic domestic policies.

"The social issues are important, too," he says, "although I think they're symptomatic of the same question of big government's performance. Busing, while not the national issue it was in the seventies, will be important in selected cases like Chicago, where it is a big local issue."

Like Black and Phillips, Keene also believes defense will be a major issue in the 1980 election: "Currently, it still registers last on the public's list of major issues, but there is a growing awareness of the bad shape that we're in, and there is growing support for increased spending and a tougher foreign policy."

In general, Keene sees the gelling national consensus on domestic issues to be one of a "reaction against the atomization of the sixties." Education is another social issue that Keene thinks will be important. "I don't know if you saw the survey done by [Senators] Dole and McGovern, but something like 60 percent of the high school students today don't know if their state has any senators or not. Parents are getting outraged by the ignorance and illiteracy that is coming out of the public schools, and they want something done about it."

Bush, says Keene, doesn't like labels, preferring to let his stands on the issues define his politics. But when forced to designate himself philosophically, he calls himself a conservative. Compared to his leading opponents, Reagan and Connally, Keene sees Bush as occupying a position somewhere between them. Not going as far as Reagan's undiluted free market stance but not favoring what he calls Connally's big government approach. Although he has few differences with Reagan, Keene differs sharply with Connally's views, calling him an "unregenerate advocate of big government." Connally, he says, does not favor tax cuts or spending limitations but only a one-shot tax cut.

"I'm also opposed to his idea to spend $25 billion to promote American products abroad," Keene says, and "as for his reputation as a tough guy on foreign policy I would just say that he is tough when it comes to handling little countries, but not the Soviet Union. His reaction to the Soviet troops in Cuba was very weak."

In Keene's view, Kennedy's entry into the presidential race "will tear the Democratic Party all to hell. I think he is the favorite to win the nomination but if he defeats Carter, I doubt he will carry a single southern state." Moreover, in Keene's view, the damage is likely to extend outside the South proper. The Southern parts of Illinois, Indiana, and Ohio all have large groups of transplanted Southerners, he points out, a fact that made Ford run very poorly in these areas in 1976. In 1980, Keene feels the antipathy of these voters to Kennedy will make a Republican victory in those states a real possibility.

The interviews with Black, Phillips and Keene were all conducted in October 1979 and a re-reading of their comments five months later bring home just how volatile an election year this has been. In October, a Kennedy nomination was taken as a given by just about everybody, press and pundits alike, and the three young operatives interviewed were no exception. But five months later, all had changed. The voters' distrust of Kennedy because of Chappaquiddick and his liberal political views proved to be insurmountable problems for the senator, dragging him down to defeat after defeat at the hands of an incumbent president who, himself, was increasingly unpopular—just less unpopular than Senator Kennedy.

Thus, alas, the Kennedy-Connally contest that Kevin Phillips lusted after was not to be, Kennedy having been devastated by Carter, and Connally having been knocked out of the race in South Carolina by Reagan. Meanwhile, Dave Keene's candidate, George Bush, was still in the race, but only barely, having lost repeatedly to Reagan in states from Alaska to Florida.

This left Charlie Black's candidate, Ronald Reagan, flying high—except that Black was no longer aboard to savor the triumph—having been jettisoned (along with press secretary James Lake) when Reagan fired his controversial campaign manager, John Sears. The campaign structure Black had put together continued to function well for Reagan in the caucus and primary states, however, and Black's political talents continued to be much in demand. He is currently a consultant to the Republican National Committee, the Republican Senate and House committees, and to a number of candidates.

Nowhere are the difficulties of deciphering the public mood more appreciated than at *Public Opinion,* a bimonthly magazine published by the American Enterprise Institute, where Karlyn Keene serves as associate editor. "The increase in the amount of polling done over the last ten years is just astounding," says Keene, 30. "But there is a lot of debate over just how accurate the polling is." Keene says that the magazine is publishing a retrospective about the seventies called "The Ambivalent Decade." "There are just so many conflicting trends that it is difficult to make sense out of what's happening," she says. "On matters like homosexuality, premarital sex, and so on—what we call personal morality—there has been a very definite liberalization, and on some questions, like national health insurance, the public takes the liberal position. But, on other things, such as taxes, bureaucracy, and defense, they take a conservative position."

On the issue the left is trying to make a cause celebre for the eighties, the abolition of nuclear power, Keene sees conservatives as being on the right side of the issue. "Even at the height of the Three Mile Island crisis, the ABC/Harris Poll showed the voters supported the building of more plants by a 47 to 45 percent. Two months later, the margin has increased to 52 to 42, and the trend is still moving in favor of the plants," she says. "The majority of the people clearly want nuclear power. The problem is that the elite, the Fonda-Hayden crowd, are able to generate a disproportionate amount of publicity."

As far as how the people perceive themselves philosophically, Keene says the polls show the conservative designation to be the more popular. Among the polls mentioned was the Harris poll taken in February of 1978. The finding: 32 percent called themselves conservatives, 41 percent moderates, and 18 percent liberals. The Gallup polls taken from 1973 through 1977 show an even greater edge for conservatives. The results are tabulated below:

	1973	May 1976	October 1976	October 1977
Conservative	41%	49%	42%	47%
Liberal	31	31	31	32
Middle of the road or no position	28	20	27	21

One of the leading pollsters on the conservative side is Arthur J. Finkelstein, 37, president of Arthur J. Finkelstein and Associates, a New York–based firm. In the last few years, Finkelstein has done the polling work for such conservative luminaries as Senators Thurmond, Buckley, Helms, Humphrey, Jepsen, Warner, and dozens of congressional candidates and candidates for the state legislatures.

In 1976 he did the polling for the Reagan presidential campaign. In 1978 he signed on with the campaign of Representative Phil Crane. Several months later, however, Finkelstein resigned over differences with the candidate, and now he is with the 1980 Reagan campaign. "A problem with many conservative movement leaders is that they are too logical and too consistent. The average voter is not, so they fail to identify with him and how he thinks," Finkelstein says. "I would never vote for a candidate who says, 'I'll never lie to you,' but the voters elected Jimmy Carter. I've stopped thinking rationally. Now I just react emotionally."

Finkelstein believes the voters react in contradictory ways. "They want lower taxes but they also want more government services," he says. His polls lead him to believe that there is a conservative trend running in the country in terms of economic issues but not in social issues.

"The key to conservative victory," he says, "is in presenting conservatism as a can-do philosophy, as the party of more, not less. We have to convince the voters that the election of conservatives will improve their situation. For too long, we have pushed an essentially negative austerity approach."

Finkelstein also believes that the voters have to be sold on the idea that the private sector is better able to provide economic progress than is government. "I think Proposition 13 helped us," he says. "There are wonderful things going on in California. The fact that the state has prospered since 13's passage should be a big selling point for conservatives in selling this kind of approach across the country."

Finkelstein says the voters believe that government is getting too big and is too inefficient. What they want is the spending cuts and more efficient service. "Conservative candidates have to be careful in designing their platforms," he says. "They should promise lower spending by cutting waste and fat out of the bureaucracy, but should make it clear that no essential services should be cut."

Finkelstein would like to see conservatives seize the initiative on energy. "I would like to see a referendum on energy," he says. "We should say to the American people, 'Would you like to be independent from foreign sources of oil?' If so, vote for our plan. We will deregulate oil and gas. That will mean a price rise in the short term but lower prices in the long run. We will also go all-out to develop alternate sources. This means the prudent development of nuclear energy with adequate safeguards and an aggressive research and development program on solar among other things. We should tell the voters: enact our plan and you'll have energy independence in five years."

Another key conservative strategist, Arnold Steinberg, largely agrees with Finkelstein that there is a conservative trend on economic matters which is not duplicated on social issues—with the exception of education. "There is a growing emphasis in California on returning to basics in education, and there's a growing interest in private education as an alternative to the declining public schools."

Steinberg feels that conservatives have done a poor job of selling their own issues. "The fact that Teddy Kennedy is getting credit for deregulating the airlines and trucking industry is an absolute scandal," he says. "That is a conservative issue and we should have been identified with it."

Steinberg cautions that care is needed in designing a conservative platform. "Limiting government is a popular issue but we need to pick and choose among the issues and concentrate on those with consensus appeal."

Conservatives would be well advised, in Steinberg's view, to be seen as opposing bigness: big government, big labor, and big business. "There is no reason we should be stuck defending the big oil companies. With the possible exception of Mobil, they don't even know how to defend themselves. And, in many cases, they are against the free play of the market."

"Conservatives need to be pro free market and anti big business," Steinberg says. "We should also be attacking the government regulatory agencies from a consumer angle. For instance, we should be attacking FCC regulations on entry into the media on a consumer basis, arguing tht deregulation would make it possible to buy companies."

Symbolism is also important in Steinberg's view. "In designing media advertisements, for instance, it is important to include many types of people: elderly people, minorities, and so on. Conservatives tend to think this is patronizing. They don't realize that people identify more easily with positions if they see similar people taking them. When people see some people excluded from ads, they may think they are excluded too. For example, when Jews see Chicanos or blacks excluded from a candidate's ads, they may think they are excluded too."

Steinberg, at the age of 32, has already gained a reputation as a very astute political manager. He worked in James Buckley's successful campaign for the Senate in New York and later served as Buckley's special assistant, leaving in 1975 to form his own management consulting firm in Los Angeles. There he has managed a number of successful campaigns for Congress and statewide and local offices, gathering experience in the process which he distilled into two books: *Political Campaign Management: A Systems Approach* and *The Political Campaign Handbook: Media, Scheduling and Advance.*

Like Finkelstein, Steinberg is extremely pleased by the success of Proposition 13. "That was the tax issue appealing to voters as consumers because it offered them more," he says. "We need more of that type of issue."

Perhaps the most aggressive advocate of mobilizing young people to work in conservative campaigns is Morton C. Blackwell, 39. Brought into conservative activity via the Goldwater campaign, Blackwell, at 23, was the youngest delegate at the 1964 Republican convention. He has since been an activist in YAF, an officer of the Young Republican National Federation, the editor of Richard Viguerie's *New Right Report,* and the founder of the Committee for Responsible Youth Politics (CRYP). He now serves as special assistant to Sen. Gordon Humphrey (R.-N.H.).

Having done organizational work on over 300 campuses and having put some 1,200 young people through his intense three-day long campaign schools at CRYP, Blackwell is a deep believer in organizing youth efforts. "Almost all the progress that conservatives have made in recruiting young people has come as a result of the intensive organizational efforts made during the Goldwater campaign," he says, adding, "I don't think nearly enough of this was done in the 1976 Reagan campaign. That's why it is absolutely essential that this time the Reagan campaign and others do more to recruit young people. If a constant renewal effort isn't maintained, the gains we have made will evaporate."

Blackwell emphasizes that "the crying need of the conservative movement now is for new blood." It is the young recruits that supply the bulk of the volunteers needed in a campaign. In the 1976 Reagan primary win in Indiana, for instance, it is estimated that young people comprised 90 percent of the total number of workers. In Texas, another big Reagan win, they supplied 50 percent." A big advantage of recruiting young volunteers for a campaign, Blackwell argues, is the "multiplier effect" that occurs: many of these recruits stay active and go to work in other areas of conservative activity.

Blackwell does not believe that conservatives face any disadvantages compared to liberals in recruiting on the campus. "Young people are full of energy but are basically apathetic politically," he says. "Left to their own devices, they will go streaking or cram into phone booths. But they can be organized. Traditionally, the left has been more adept at this than we have."

Where conservatives have organized on the campus, they have done well, Blackwell believes. "In the 1978 Virginia Senate campaign," he points out, "conservatives had an aggressive organizational effort on the campuses and John Warner [the GOP candidate] beat his liberal Democrat opponent in twenty-seven out of twenty-eight mock elections on college campuses."

As another example of success Blackwell points to the Right to Work Committee's campaign in Connecticut against compulsory union membership for students who worked in part-time jobs. Petitions were circulated on campus throughout the state and thousands of students signed. "Whenever conservatives have organized on the campus, they have clobbered the liberals," Blackwell says.

Blackwell also believes conservatives must pay more attention to the "technology of winning," and he sees signs that this is occurring. "I recently spoke to a right-to-life convention," he says, "and not about the virtues of the right-to-life position. I told them how to organize effectively. In a couple of weeks, I'm speaking before Phyllis Schlafly's Eagle Forum on how to become a delegate to the Republican or Democratic national convention."

Blackwell believes the Democratic coalition is on the verge of self-destructing. "You have Jesse Jackson cozying up to Yasser Arafat and threatening to widen the split between Jews and blacks, and you have a potentially disastrous fight shaping up between Kennedy and Carter."

Blackwell believes conservatives should encourage this divisiveness by running delegates for the Democratic convention. "Because of the proportional representation rules governing delegate selection, it is easily possible that conservatives could capture 10 to 15 percent of the delegates to the convention," he says. "This would further divide the Democratic ranks, and it would pull the major Democratic candidates to the right on the issues," he believes.

Some interesting ideas about revitalizing the Republican Party come from a young Harvard graduate, John Le Boutillier, 25. Le Boutillier entered Harvard in 1972 and was graduated magna cum laude in 1976, having encountered much that he did not like in the intervening period. Upon graduation, Le Boutillier expressed his dissatisfaction about the decadent liberalism of his alma mater in a book with the arresting title *Harvard Hates America.*

Only about half of the book actually deals with Harvard, however. The remainder tells of Le Boutillier's experiences as an activist in the Republican Party. (In 1974, he raised $250,000 for the candidate running against George McGovern for the Senate.) The GOP doesn't come off much better than Harvard at Le Boutillier's hands, with the author painting a picture of a party gone flabby, complacent, and totally lacking in vision or idealism.

As a corrective, Le Boutillier urges the party to back a plan called the "New Homestead." This plan would have as its aims:

(1) Helping to insure that every American family could buy a home, this being done by the establishment of a National Home Ownership Loan Fund and the integration of the private sector and local, state and federal government support.

(2) Providing health care. Here Le Boutillier draws on the plan authored by economist Martin Feldstein in which families would be responsible for the first $400 of medical bills per year, which they would be able to deduct from their federal income tax. The government would cover costs in excess of the established ceiling.

(3) Higher education. Le Boutillier urges the restructuring of the student loan program so that the nation's colleges are responsible for administering the plan and for collecting the payments. Such a system, he feels, would cut down sharply on the current high level of defaults.

(4) Revitalizing America's government by taking measures to strengthen local government and by experimenting with new "hybrid" forms of regional government and by dispersing the offices of the federal government around the country.

(5) Redesigning state-supported aid to the elderly by instituting a plan along the lines of the Oregon system, whereby the elderly stay in their ownhomes and are provided a part-time housekeeper, some meals, and regular visits by a registered nurse. This system, he says, is more humane and protective of the dignity of the elderly and more economical.

The New Homestead plan, Le Boutillier says, would act to strengthen the family and the sense of community and, hence, he believes, would be eminently saleable to the American people.

Another leading conservative strategist, Jeffrey Bell, agrees fundamentally with Kevin Phillips' southern strategy for the GOP. In a lengthy article, "The Road to Realignment," published in the September 24, 1977, *Human Events*, Bell argues, "Almost unnoticed, the South has become the pivot of American presidential politics. After nearly a century of one-party stupor, the South has become the nation's most unpredictable, volatile and hotly contested region, and our richest prize. In the post-war era, no one has won the presidency without a successful Southern strategy. In the foreseeable future no one is likely to."

In Bell's view, Senator Jesse Helms (R.-N.C.) is the cutting edge of the move toward Republican realignment, just as Hubert Humphrey was the most active catalyst toward the Democratc Party's realignment in 1948. In the 1948 Democratic Convention, Bell notes, Humphrey was the driving force behind the liberalization of the Party's platform in the guise of a strong plank on civil rights. Similarly, in 1976, Helms was the point man for conservatives at the Republican Convention, and his efforts resulted in the party's adoption of the most resolutely conservative platform in many years.

Also like Phillips, Bell believes there is major potential in the social issues for conservatives. "The prolife position, tougher punishment of crime, and moves to halt the decline in education, to the extent that these are 'social issues,' are social issues that will help conservatives," he says.

Bell also believes the defense question is one that conservatives can use profitably, and he feels that the Panama Canal fight helped conservatives last time and is continuing to help. "More voters probably knew how their senators voted on the Panama Canal treaty than on any other issue," he says. "It's still an issue that's in the back of their minds and, in some elections in 1980, it will probably be enough to make the difference."

But Bell is most enthusiastic about the tax issue. It was his advocacy of the Kemp-Roth tax cut that enabled him to defeat Senator Clifford Case in the 1978 New Jersey Republican primary, and it was the same issue, he believes, that made it possible to make a good showing in the general election against sports hero Bill Bradley, the popular Democratic candidate. "In no poll that I've ever seen has advocating a tax cut hurt a Republican candidate," Bell contends, "and I think it has helped many."

Tax cuts were the main factor in Margaret Thatcher's win in Britain, Bell claims. "The polls showed that the three main issues in the British elections were inflation, unemployment, and taxes in that order. The polls also showed that the people, by a ten to twelve point margin, felt Labor was better equipped to handle inflation and unemployment but that they felt by a margin of over 20 percent that Thatcher would do more to lower taxes. This edge on the tax question allowed her to more than compensate for the other two issues."

Bell believes that the voters want lower tax rates and improved government services, and, like many others, he believes the success of Proposition 13 has validated the tax cut approach. "The chaos that was predicted hasn't occurred," he says, "and it will be impossible for liberals to use that argument in 1980." Since the passage of Proposition 13, Bell says, tax rates have not gone up in any state, and in many, they have been reduced.

Bell believes that the nation stands on the threshold of a very activist period but that the activism is going to be very different from what we have seen in the past. "The 1970s have been a quiescent period, mainly because people are basically opposed to the status quo that the people in power are trying to maintain. In foreign policy, the status is détente and accommodation with the Soviet Union. SALT is an expression of that, which is why it's going to lose. In domestic affairs, the status quo is bureaucracy and big government. But the people don't want that. Carter basically stands for the status quo or for consolidating the status quo. If people wanted to preserve the status quo, Carter would be popular. I think the people are ready for activism and that they will support a lot of change," Bell states, "but the activism will be conservative."

18 | VOX POPULI: FRIENDLY CRITICS OF THE MOVEMENT SOUND OFF

In the course of researching this book, I mailed questionnaires to more than 100 young conservatives that I considered natural candidates for a compilation such as this. In addition to asking for biographical information, I asked for their assessment of the state of the conservative movement and for their ideas on the direction conservative activity should take. Many of the responses were extremely thoughtful, and I excerpt some of the best of them below.

Most of the respondents, quite predictably, felt that there is a conservative trend evident in the country and that the conservative movement has made considerable headway, especially in the intellectual sense. Some, however, did not feel that that progress has been paralleled in political terms. Typical of the latter is the response of Alan Reynolds, 37, a vice-president of the First National Bank of Chicago, who wrote,

The most encouraging development has been in the intellectual arena, where the opposition is now clearly in retreat. The weakest link remains the popularization of academic work to persuade a broad audience. Although there are now more and better outlets for conservative research and writing than ever before, the financial incentives draw talent into stifling positions in business and government. There is still an urgent need for better-targeted financial support to research institutions, journals and (especially) individuals with a proven track record in passing the message to new hands. Political victory will follow from providing the climate of opinion that equates good economics with good politics.

Several spoke out about the need to reject sectarianism, a sentiment evident in the following comment by Ronald Docksai, 29, a former chairman of Young Americans for Freedom and now a legislative assistant to Sen. Orrin Hatch:

A political "movement" is less the presence of organized activities and associations than it is a state of mind. There exists an unspoken political bond which unites

319

various groups of Americans, a bond which lends itself to identifying an American conservative community. No one leader or party or secondary association or even a particular ideology can be cited as a common denominator to explain the bond's cohesion. Rather, shared civic values and the affection which grows from common political experiences reveals the nature of this common uniting of what seems a spirit among American conservatives.

Conservatism will remain a living factor in American politics as long as no one leader or organization or any one ideology (i.e., party line) dominates what is perceived to be the conservative position. This is so, because leaders and organizations and ideologies are transient. They are flies of a summer against the historical continuum of American politics. As conservatives, we will usually vote for the same candidate and hold the same political position at any one time. We do so, though, for different reasons, and it is as self-destructive as it is naive for card-carrying sociologists to try to read "libertarian" or "traditionalist" tendencies into conservative voting patterns or other political behavior. Not self-destructive and naive for the sociologists, but for those conservatives who become ideologues through the adoption of libertarian or traditionalist or vegetarian labels. America, after all, is unlike France. Our nation of political pluralities is not a nation of multiple, rival ideological factions. Our nation is politically defined by a two party system, the soul of which is revealed through consensus and pluralism. Any conservatism which is to be American cannot keep these historical and cultural facts excluded.

Thoughts in a similar vein were expressed by Douglas Hallett, 30, a former White House fellow and now an attorney and author:

Much, perhaps, too much, has been written about the historic conflict within conservatism between libertarians and authoritarians. I have seen nothing on how this somewhat rarified discussion manifests itself in conservative politics to the detriment of the conservative movement. We recognize "social" conservatives and "economic" conservatives—and we also can see how these two political strains are rooted in the intellectual strains of traditionalism and libertarianism. But we do not see that both the intellectual conflict and its politic progeny are preventing conservatism from defining and articulating that "City on the Hill" which our movement needs to inspire our fellow countrymen. Too often, conservatives would rather be purists in one wing or another of the conservative movement—Ed Davis, the "social" conservative candidate in the '77 California primary; Ronald Reagan, with his $90-billion budget cut, the "economic" conservative of the 1976 Republican Presidential race—and use their purism as a way of polarizing internal Republican politics for short-term political advantage. But this purism is terribly self-defeating, and, in the case of Reagan, has often obscured what really lies behind. William Simon's new book is not particularly novel intellectually. What is novel about it, however, is that it represents the first time within memory that a mercantile, "economic" conservative has recognized the importance of defining a social and intellectual complement to his economic conservatism. If this effort is followed up and we can get behind polarizing rhetoric about balanced budgets and tax disincentives, on the one hand, and abortions, busing, and quotas, on the other, to see that all of these issues spring out of a common committment to the dignity of the individual and individual self-determination. We can use these tip-of-the-iceburg issues more effectively and give our fellow Americans a torch to follow at the same time.

Nonetheless, the libertarian and traditionalist camps still have their active champions. Speaking first for the libertarians is David Brudnoy, 38, columnist and commentator: "Economically, the society is coming to understand the conservative message. This is to the good. In some other ways, however, the nation is moving in a conservative direction that I do not find salutary—the hate campaigns of such as Anita Bryant, considered by many, even most, people a conservative, serve as an example of what I mean. The trend against libertarianism in many aspects of our personal lives, the nonsensical campaigns against 'pornography,' the revived pseudopuritanism, the born-again phenomenon, are all symptoms of what I would consider an unhealthy brand of conservatism."

Now listen to another libertarian, David Boaz, 26, former *New Guard* editor and now Executive Director, Council for a Competitive Economy: "My primary interest is in freedom. I have been active in the conservative movement because I think it offers the best opportunity for me to work for my beliefs, particularly in the areas of economic freedom. However, I am increasingly afraid that the conservative movement is not really working for freedom, that most conservatives pay lip service to economic freedom but really are most interested in other things. They want to use big government against the people they disapprove of just as liberals do, and they'd rather increase the budget for their favorite programs than cut taxes and spending across the board. I hope I'm wrong, but more and more I see conservatives getting excited about the wrong issues—anti-gay rights, anti-women's rights, trying to get control of government rather than reduce its size. I think conservative activity should be redirected toward reducing the size and power of government. Perhaps the tax revolt will provide a politically popular opportunity to do this. If so, then conservatism will have a good issue and an excellent opportunity for success. But if conservatives continue to crusade against pot-smoking and the like, I'm afraid they can write off the next generation. That may be the way to win a few elections, but it is no way to build an intellectual movement or to attract young people."

Speaking for the traditionalists is Frank Donatelli, 30, former executive director of YAF and now a field man with the Reagan campaign: "The fact that liberalism is in decline does not necessarily signal a conservative revival. Conservatives must address the real concerns of Americans with answers that go beyond recounting the horrors of state control. Liberty is not an end in itself. It is a means, indeed the only means, to the ultimate end, the virtuous society. We must, in short, speak to the spiritual crisis that threatens to paralyze the West."

The need to reach out and form new ad hoc alliances was asserted by Dr. Roger Fontaine, 38, of the Georgetown University Center for Strategic and International Studies: "Conservatism is still very far from being the nation's public philosophy. Two things need to be done: first (as always) we must keep conservatives away from the shoals of shrill sectarianism; second, we must capitalize on the revolt of the middle class. That revolt, of course, is most obvious on taxes, but there are a host of other issues as well. What the press has dubbed single-issue constituences are composed largely of middle class people who have (perhaps unwittingly) a natural conservative bent. From busing to abortion, the cry, quite literally, is NO MORE. If conservatives are to survive and prosper they must mold and meld these 'single issues' into a coherent and appealing public philosophy—the ground rules by which we will govern for the next generation as well as our electoral strategy. If we do not do so, we will remain a still loyal, but increasingly restive (that is, frustrated) opposition."

Coalition politics was also stressed by attorney John Bolton:

Intellectually, the "conservative" philosophy is now dominant in this country. Politically, it is still weak. If the history of New Deal liberalism is any indication, there is every reason to expect that our intellectual preminence can be translated into political power. I am sure that the more active politicians in this survey will discuss how this transformation will be accomplished. I propose to discuss two aspects of the general strategy, one substantive and one procedural: (1) coalition, where possible, with civil libertarians on the left; and (2) use of the judicial system.

First, as to coalitions with the left, several issues lend themselves readily to such an approach. In the areas of regulation of election campaigns and politics generally, regulation of lobbying, and intrusions on personal and business privacy, there is broad philosophical agreement among conservatives and civil libertarians. In both legislative activity and judicial proceedings, we have been able effectively to combine with groups like the ACLU and individuals like Senator McCarthy to oppose increased governmental regulation. There is every reason to believe that such coalitions can be formed in the future.

For instance, in the area of commercial advertising, both the conservative movement and the ACLU favor fewer governmental restrictions. Similarly, in the mental health field, there appears to be a growing consensus that 'social engineering' should be rejected in favor of greater individual autonomy. Freedom from union compulsion (of both members and nonmembers) is now also receiving increased attention from the left; it has always been of concern to the right, and there may be room for a joint effort. Other areas will undoubtedly emerge as new issues rise to public prominence.

In none of the areas just mentioned do we abandon any of our principles. What we do abandon are our inhibitions against collaborating with individuals and groups who oppose us on many other issues. I would argue that these kinds of coalitions represent the flexibility that we must have if we are to assume political power. This is flexibility not of ideas, but of tactics. In the past, we have too often confused these different ideas, usually to our political detriment. I think this ties in directly to your contention that our strategy cannot become synonymous solely with a rejection of the liberal approach.

The small number of women in conservative leadership positions was remarked by Kathleen Teague, executive director of the American Legislative Exchange Council: "I personally would like to see a concerted effort made in the conservative movement to encourage to run and then elect articulate, conservative women, who can express the conservative viewpoint and lead on such issues as Pro-Life, ERA, and other family and social related issues. There are a number of articulate women state legislators who are conservative, but virtually not one conservative woman leader in the Congress."

Although most respondents were optimistic about the prospects for conservative success, there were no pollyannas in evidence and most were critical of some aspect of the conservative demonstration to date. In a few instances, the criticism was harsh indeed. A case in point is the critique offered by Daniel Joy, 36, former chief legislative assistant to Senator James Buckley and an ACU Board member. Joy, as you will see, is hardly a rah-rah cheerleader for the right:

The question concerns the status of the conservative movement, so-called; but the question which precedes status is definition. Those political activists who speak of themselves as part of "the conservative movement" are in fact indicating an allegiance to certain organizations rather than in terms of political goals and values. The political viability of the conservative movement is another question.

The matter of viability is inherently intertwined with the political (policy) goals of conservatives. But the problem here is that those goals, to the extent that they exist in any cohesive fashion, are too frequently overly abstract or just plain bizarre. A goal of less government is an abstraction which at once means everything and nothing. Such a premise requires conclusions that government action is inherently inferior to nongovernment action—or government nonaction. The consequent overconfidence put in nongovernment institutions produces a rather absurd blindspot. There is no program, only reactions and defenses, as the case may be. Then there are the too-silly objectives of eliminating the regional administrative structure of the federal government, removing the United States from the United Nations, repealing the New Deal, and other goals too numerous to mention, too fatuous to consider.

In other words, American conservatism, movement or otherwise, borders on political irrelevance. Having no real social vision, as liberals do, conservatives have no program other than continuing negative reactions to liberal initiatives. In an unarticulated attitude, American conservatives seemingly conclude that business represents a force for good while the establishment represents a force for no-good. That American business constitutes a major element of the establishment is a latter day realization that is forcing numerous conservatives into an openly populist politics. But that kind of populism is fundamentally anticonservative and politically irresponsible as it seeks to take advantage of know-nothingism, at least on the part of those to whom the populism is aimed. The practitioners of a populist politics were never so silly as to believe all that drivel themselves. Populism, the most significant force today on the political right, is merely tactical, a means for securing power.

The failure of the right to come up with much of a political program and its recent move toward populist formulations suggest to me a future without any effective conservatism. Jarvis-Gann will carry conservatives only as far as the consequences are felt, at which time the population will conclude it has been lied to once again. As there are no free lunches, there are no magic formulae to undo the American acceptance of, or even commitment to, programs of government action.

For a politics to endure, there must be a genuine base of compatible interests. Politics, except for the romantic, exists outside the test tube. In today's American political life liberals intend to change things by introducing new factors (notably government programs) while conservatives react only to the failure of liberal programs. That failure is insufficient to form the basis of a continuing, relevant politics. Conservatives, by their own design, are not going anywhere.

There are other problems. The moral condition of the right is open to considerable question. The willingness of the right, including much of its grass-roots leadership, to defend Richard Nixon and its inability to understand that his integrity was nil and his leadership value gone, suggests a very limited moral imperative. After all, he was "our" crook. The relativism of the defense, "He didn't do anything that others did not do," is frightening. The relativism went further as the culprit in the whole of Watergate was not, for the right, Nixon, but the press, which "drove" Nixon from office. The mind that concocts that theory is of questionable political value.

Another problem for the American right is its apparent willingness to ignore problems on the right. Today hucksters on the right are reasonably free to operate, assured that no potent force on the right will dare to break the code of the "movement" by taking to task certain questionable practices which rightfully outrage those not subject to the political mandates of the "movement." Failure to keep one's own house in order when one thinks in terms of an organic movement reenforces a relativism of no small quantity. Critics are driven away, as divisive and thoroughly objectionable.

Lastly, John Ashbrook once asked whether conservatives, if they assumed power, would be able to handle it in a manner acceptable to the American people. What reasons are there to believe that conservatives would perform any better than Jimmy Carter has performed? Merely not supporting the Panama Canal treaty is insufficient basis for an administration of government. Kemp-Roth is Keynesian economics, embraced by the right only after the model is shattered. There must be more, much more.

What are the prospects for the conservative movement? Financially: good. Politically: fair. In other words, things should go reasonably well, at least until a conservative achieves a position of responsibility from which he can or must deliver, and doesn't know what to do or how to do it.

As to the directions for the future, I am without an opinion.

If Joy excoriates conservatives for having no "social vision," journalist Alan Crawford is scandalized that the right should even consider the notion:

I find it ironic that a political philosophy such as conservatism, which claims to take its inspiration from the past, in America takes its inspiration from an idealized future—that glorious tomorrow when a nation of energized conservative movement activists go to the polls to elect a slate of conservative movement candidates.

I don't believe this is ever going to happen, nor should it. Conservatives would be well-advised then, to stop deluding ourselves about the conservative resurgence, whatever our reading of the polls and demographics. The dominant intellectual tradition and political tradition in America is, and has always been, liberal and so are its people—liberal in the best sense of the word. Conservatives ought to recognize this fact and stop concocting strategies for coming to power. They should instead begin subjecting themselves, their organizations, and their ideas to a more rigorous intellectual and moral scrutiny, thus to build a responsible opposition. For a political movement that characterizes its liberal counterpart as "sentimental," contemporary conservatism strikes me as remarkably flabby, its advocates far too smug and complacent. In its current state, American conservatism is simply not up to the task of providing the opposition party that we need and that is the proper function of conservatism in a liberal society.

I think, too, that having to ask what our "alternative vision of the good society is" is to admit that we really don't have one. And it strikes me as the grossest liberalism to assume that we can fabricate such a thing on demand.

Finally, I would recommend that the only really responsible conservatism should heed the advice of Irving Kristol: Too many conservatives spend their time railing against the existence of the welfare state instead of trying to play a constructive role in it.

If we are to be taken seriously we must break out of the notion that the "conservative movement" has anything to do with the real world and begin to live and breathe in the latter.

Well now, how does one respond to that? I guess if I were George Wallace I would call Joy and Crawford outside agitators and offer to autograph their sandals. That option not being available, I will limit myself to the observation that both continue to associate with conservatives and to participate in conservative activities, a fact that leads me to think that they believe the conservative movement, despite is manifest shortcomings, is worthy of their support.

Among the individuals quoted in this chapter, it can be said that these are many differences, some of them sharp. Conservatism in America is obviously no monolithic force. Yet, by the same token, it is no hydra-headed being either. There is a clearly discernible thrust in conservative thought and activity in America today which makes it possible to say that a movement exists.

The sole exception to the generalization is Alan Crawford, who subscribes to the notion originally set forth by the late Clinton Rossiter that America is essentially a liberal nation and that the primary function of conservatives is to restrain the excesses of the ruling liberals—an exceedingly modest concept of the conservative mission that strains the reticence of even one so modest as I. It certainly *is* the duty of conservatives to battle liberal excesses, but a creed whose vision is no larger than that is one which consigns its adherents to the defeatism and despair of Sisyphus, the man condemned to an eternity spent rolling a boulder up a hill only to have it roll down again.

For too long, the drudgery of Rossiter's "thankless persuasion" (his appellation for American conservatism) *has* been the lot of American conservatives as they doggedly fought an endless series of liberal initiatives, winning a few rounds but going down to defeat on most.

Well, what was once the prediction of a few is now the realization of many: the liberal approach is flawed; liberal programs do not work. Conservatives have no panacea to offer as a replacement, but we do have an approach that is sounder; we have a program that will work *better*. In the 1980s for the first time, conservatives will be able to tell the country that they have a coherent program for the country and the expertise and talent to put it into effect. They will ask the voters to give them a chance. I predict they will.

19 | CONCLUSION

During my undergraduate days at Miami University, there was a lecture program named, if I recall correctly, the "W.A. Hammond Lecture Series on the American Tradition." The program was sustained by an endowment provided by Hammond, a wealthy and very elderly alumnus who was keen on the idea of exposing the students at the university to inspiring talks on "Americanism."

Hammond was a conservative, as was the alumni affairs director who managed the series, so it was not too surprising that the speakers were all conservatives—a bias that suited me fine since I thought the university had all too few conservative lecturers. Yet, I remember being embarrassed by the term *Americanism,* considering it to be unthinking, xenophobic, and essentially meaningless. Americanism, after all, is not like existentialism or communism or any of the other "isms" in the sense of incorporating some coherent body of doctrine.

Yet, the more I think about it the more I believe that W. A. Hammond was right: there is such a thing as Americanism. It does exist and it is definable. There is, first of all, the governmental legacy bequeathed to us by the founding fathers. The unique idea of a republic sustained by a system of checks and balances, a system whose virtues are taught—or should be taught—to every elementary school student in the country. The Constitution also is a masterful synthesis, balancing the need for order with the imperative of maximizing individual liberty. Having limited the maneuvering room of the federal government by counterpoising its three branches against each other, the Constitution also limits the power of the federal government itself by the Tenth Amendment stipulation that all powers not vested in the federal government are reserved to the states or to the people. As much as it is a charter outlining the functions of government, the Constitution is a codification of the limits of government. Moreover, underlying the Constitution's emphasis on limited government is the assumption that the most important aspects of life lie *outside* the province of government.

327

This is the basic view of government that most American conservatives subscribe to and the system of government that conservatives wish to "conserve." Critics of this view are certainly entitled to argue that such a view is unrealistic, or anachronistic, or misguided, or whatever, but certainly not that it is unconservative. The concept described is that of the nation's organic document and as M. Stanton Evans points out, adherence to it is inherently conservative.

Complementary to the Constitution's vision of rightly constructed government is a belief in the rightness and efficacy of the market economy. It is a coincidence of course, but a happy and appropriate one, that Adam Smith's *Wealth of Nations* was published in 1776, the year of the launching of the American Revolution. As Irving Kristol has pointed out, "it is a fact that capitalism in this country has a historical legitimacy that it does not possess elsewhere. In other lands, the nation and its fundamental institutions antedate the capitalist era; in the United States . . . capitalism and democracy have been organically linked." The founders believed, Kristol maintains, that "the system of natural liberty" in economic affairs was the complement to our system of constitutional liberty in political and civil affairs."

Capitalism has been an integral part of the American system since the founding of the Republic and as such rightfully occupies a prominent position in the scheme of conservative values. In addition to its pedigree in our system, it is also a fact of twentieth century life, and as Whittaker Chambers perceptively remarked, a conservatism that fails to come to grips with the fact of a capitalist society is a conservatism "destined to petulance and futility."

Another special attribute of America is the belief in America as an idea and ideal as well as a nation. From the very earliest days of colonization, this has been the case, whether it was the Plymouth Colony's John Winthrop and his vision of the "city on a hill; an alabaster city undimmed by human tears," or Abraham Lincoln's "new nation conceived in liberty," or the land of the golden door spoken of on the Statue of Liberty's dedicatory plaque, America has been seen by its leaders and citizens alike as somehow different, a land of opportunity where every individual could fulfill his potential to the extent that he had the desire and determination.

America is also a country animated by optimism, a legacy of the nation's experience with the frontier. As Frederick Jackson Turner noted, the explorers and settlers setting out westward confronted nature on an immense scale—vast prairies, mighty rivers, towering mountains—and they beheld the bounty of the land, the sweeping vistas, unspoiled earth, the openness and newness of the sight they surveyed. All of this made for optimism, hope, and expectation. The ingredients for success were there: the untapped riches of the land and the freedom to develop them. The pioneers felt that success was certain to come with hard work and perseverance. The frontier experiences left an indelible impression on the American psyche that endures, long after the wilderness has been conquered and the frontier has disappeared.

Another unique characteristic of America was noted by Alexis de Tocqueville, that most perceptive of observers of the American scene: "voluntary associations." Everywhere one went in America, Tocqueville wrote, one encountered voluntary associations—clubs, charities, civic groups, religious organizations, and a myriad of others organized by the local citizenry to further some need. This tradition has grown infinitely richer and stronger since Tocqueville's day. Called the "independent sector" by author Richard Cornuelle, the "third sector" by Peter Drucker, and a web of "mediating institutions" by sociologist Peter Berger, the network of voluntary associations now encompasses hundreds of thousands of organizations from tiny local fraternal clubs to such giants as the Red Cross.

As Peter Drucker wrote in the *Wall Street Journal,* "The third sector . . . includes hospitals, museums, universities, libraries and symphony orchestras; thousands of industry or trade associations, chambers of commerce, professional bodies like the Bar Association or the registered nurses', civic groups like the Boy Scouts and religious ones like the Knights of Columbus, public interest lobbies like the Naderites or Sierra Club; but also the widget plant's bowling club and foreman's association and any number of special pleaders for every conceivable (or inconceivable) cause." These third sector institutions—neither private nor public in nature—have grown to such an extent that Drucker believes they may now employ more people than government at all levels, federal, state, and local combined.

A final uniquely American characteristic is the belief that America is a nation of destiny; that the noble design of its structure of liberty, and its institutionalized notion of justice, equality and opportunity have given it an ideal that should be projected; that God has bestowed upon it both a special grace and a special responsibility; that America has a mission in the world.

It is within these broad confines, I believe, that a proper conservative public policy and agenda should be constructed. Creating a conservative program, however, presents certain difficulties that those on the left do not encounter. Since conservatives in general feel that the transcendent purposes of life are to be found in the cultivation of self and in the activities of family, church, and community—*not* in government—it follows that conservatives have no overarching political ideology to project and no societal blueprint to offer.

Since conservatives, unlike liberals, do not look to government as the agent of the first resort, they tend to expect and want less of government than do liberals, preferring to channel energy and action through the private sector. Unfortunately, the aversion to government activity has been misconstrued by critics of conservatives as an indication of selfishness and a lack of compassion. The great failure of conservative leaders in the last thirty years has been the inability to deal with this criticism. The task confronting conservatives is to reorient the public debate along terms favorable to the conservative viewpoint. This means demonstrating the superiority of the private sector as a means of providing for society's needs.

In view of the failure of the liberal domestic program manifest in the past few years, I believe that it is increasingly within the power of conservatives to do that. Over the last few decades, liberals have plugged a whole panoply of new programs, promising free health care, free education, free housing, and so forth, and since it is in the nature of voters to vote in their perceived self-interest, a majority could always be found to support these "free" programs. The liberal politicians neglected to say, of course, that these programs were actually paid for, one way or another by the "beneficiaries"— the voters. The voters have caught on, however, the lesson having been brought home by raging inflation and soaring property and social security taxes. The prevailing mood in the country today is that taxes are much too high for the return received in services. It is now possible, therefore, to ask voters "Would you prefer lower taxes even if it means fewer government services?" and have them answer, "Yes!" This is a development of great significance for conservatives, making it possible for the first time to reverse the trend toward greater government growth.

Such a reversal would be beneficial to the nation's economy by insuring a wiser deployment of resources. It would also be a move that would strengthen the nation's moral fiber by placing greater responsibility on the shoulders of the individual and on nongovernmental institutions. One of the most insidious byproducts of government centralization, in my judgment, has been the attenuation of personal responsibility and a growing reliance on government largesse. The result has been a devastating blow to a personal morality that places a high value on personal commitment, charity, and compassion. As state-supplied medical programs and homes for the aged have burgeoned, America's elderly are living longer and in greater material comfort, but more and more are consigned to lives detached from the love and concern of children who no longer feel a responsibility for them. As welfare benefits grow, steadily diminishing the necessity to work, it can be argued that poverty has been reduced but the dignity and self-regard of those able-bodied recipients has been diminished as well. As government programs to eradicate poor housing, malnutrition, and poverty have multiplied, there has been some ameliorating of the problems treated, but there has also been a lessening of personal responsibility on the part of the people.

The process, already well advanced here, is much farther along in Europe, where acts of philanthropy are viewed with suspicion and contempt as self-serving stunts on the part of the donors and as demeaning to the intended recipients. As a result, charity in the Western European democracies is on its way to extinction.

The United States has not come to this, of course, but the trend is unmistakably in that direction. Thus it is that a *Washington Post* review of a book about the Mellon and Guggenheim families can say about their legacy of foundations and museums: "The spoor of the rich is everywhere." The writer of that review and other kindred spirits would eliminate such "spoor" by taxing the rich out of existence. The kind of leveling process that this sort of mentality relishes results in the end in the obliterating of the thick forest of "mediating institutions," leaving the individual naked before the power of the state. In the society resulting from such a process, the individual's material needs are satisfied but at a terrible spiritual and psychological cost. It is an homogonized society that results, a society sapped of vitality and creative spirit.

Testifying before a House committee on government aid to the humanities, novelist John Updike (hardly a conservative) stated,

> I think a government, in time, can come to cherish a nation's cultural heritage, its creators safely dead and in perspective. But in the living present how can publicly salaried men not think in terms of respectability, of socially beneficial optimism, of wide and uncontroversial appeal? How can legislators asked to vote tax money away not begin to think of "guidelines" that insidiously edge toward censorship?
>
> If government money becomes an increasingly important presence in the financing of the humanities, is there a danger, I respectfully ask, of humanists becoming politicians?

Yes, there is such a danger and it is one that conservatives must unceasingly guard against. But to do that is not enough. A static position is doomed to failure. Some cogent comments on how to proceed were offered to me in a letter from Paul Gigot, 24, a summa cum laude graduate of Dartmouth, former editor-in-chief of the college newspaper there, and now an associate editor of *National Review*. Gigot wrote:

> I still think this *is* a time of immense possibility for conservatives. That is so because of what liberalism has become: pessimistic, coercive, negative. It has abandoned the essential optimism of, say, Franklin Roosevelt, an optimism which has always struck a powerful response in voters.
>
> . . . The opportunity for conservatives should be obvious: stress the positive; emphasize the great American values and then support them with public policy suggestions. In economic terms, that means talking about the possibilities of the free market, not about the austerity of a balanced budget; about progress, and goodness, and opportunities for minorities, not about endemic poverty. In short, we need to

get on the side of the angels; liberals have been wearing the halos for too long.

Conservatives should also support those essential institutions which have been the major victims of liberalism: family, neighborhood, church or religion, and voluntary groups. Most Americans react instinctively in support of these institutions; they are graspable, easy to deal with, just around the corner. Yet liberalism, by concentrating on abstractions like equality, has degraded them. It has fostered what sociologist Peter Berger has termed an "anomic precariousness": the superstructures of government, big business, and big labor squared off against lonely individuals. Americans resent this, as is demonstrated by the near-total opposition to forced busing by working-class blacks and whites.

The American people may not be steeped in the conservative principles, say, of a Burke, or even of a Buckley. But they will respond to certain conservative initiatives presented with positive, reassuring arguments by a confident candidate or party. That is the path to electoral dominance, a path already being constructed by young conservatives like Jack Kemp and Jeffrey Bell. It is also, by more than coincidence, an "alternative vision of the good society," our society, and not a utopian dream.

In the advice offered by this young conservative are the seeds of conservative ascendancy in America. The task confronting conservatives, in the domestic area, is to reverse the dynamics of political action so that power, in the tarnished words of Richard Nixon, begins to flow from Washington back to the people. Conservatives must pursue a diminution in the power and size of the federal government, providing the means by which the states and local governments can take up the slack as necessary. Then conservatives should endeavor to shift power and authority in general from government at all levels to the individual.

One way of doing this is to encourage citizens through tax incentives to provide for themselves many of the services government is now providing. Private initiative should be rewarded, not punished. With this in mind, conservatives should aggressively promote tax credits for private education, the care of the elderly, savings and investment, and for contributions to charities that are active in promoting the general welfare. Conservatives should also take steps to strengthen those basic institutions such as family, church and neighborhood, and to protect them from government intrusion.

The conservative vision of the good society is a humane society where those in need are adequately provided for but also one which encourages work, initiative, and self-reliance. It is one that looks to its people rather than the government as the source of strength and compassion. In such a society, people would look to figures other than politicians as heroes. Such people abound now as they always have in America. In perusing the daily press, one encounters them all the time.

I think, in this regard, of the leaders of the Citizens Committee for New York, whose *New York Self-Help Handbook* provides citizens with a wealth of advice on how they can improve their neighborhoods.

I think of Marva Collins, the black woman who organized and runs a successful basic education school in Chicago for inner-city children.

I think of producer Michael Cimino whose superb films, *The Deer Hunter* and Heaven's Gate (films about Vietnam and post–Civil War Montana respectively) celebrate the essential goodness and the idealism of the American people.

I think of Ronald Sharp and Frederick Turner, the young editors of the newly revived *Kenyon Review,* who give as the announced vision of their journal one which "will speak to the new audience that has grown up in the last few years—highly educated, dissatisfied with the cliches of the sixties, suspicious of the usual distinctions between science and art, books and life, and ready for a new direction in literature."

(Asked by the *Wall Street Journal* what cliches they intended to dispell, Sharp and Turner listed three: the notion that the bourgeoisie is society's enemy or is incapable of creativity, accepting as gospel the notion that "authenticity" and genuineness are our highest values, and believing unquestioningly that technology is disastrous and inimical to spirituality.

Turner maintains, "We tend to be optimistic about U.S. culture," hence the review "will tend to maintain and create our culture rather than expose and deflate it.")

I think of the young balloonists who crossed the Atlantic, and the University of Indiana swimming coach in his sixties, who swam the English Channel—symbols of those exceptional people among us whose adventuresome spirit and desire to excel leads them to rise above the crowd and proclaim their individuality.

I think of those who manage hospices where the dying are cared for in an atmosphere of warmth and dignity.

I think of those who selflessly contribute their time and money to support thousands of different charities.

In the end, government programs and government largesse are a cop-out from personal involvement and concern, and support for them allows an individual to salve his conscience without suffering the inconvenience occasioned by personal commitment. "Do all the good you can," Milton Friedman wisely admonishes us, "but do it with your own money."

Even though pinched badly by high taxes and inflation, the American people are doing a great deal of good, giving tens of billions of dollars to support thousands of charities. Despite manifest shortcomings, Americans are the most generous people on earth. Given back some of the 40 percent of their income taken by government, they will be more generous yet.

Having removed the intrusive hand of government from the areas of our domestic life where it does not belong, conservatives must also insure that the federal government reasserts itself in an area in which it has abdicated responsibility—that of protecting the nation from its foreign enemies. No one, or at least very few people, lust after larger defense budgets, armories bristling with nuclear weapons, and confrontations with foreign powers. But the fact is that the Soviet Union presents a clear and growing danger to the survival of the Free World and that only the United States possesses the wherewithal to counter this threat. The American people harbor no imperial desires or pretentions, but the challenge and reponsibility of leadership have been given to this country and there is no honorable or prudent way we can avoid it. The challenge facing conservatives in the area of foreign policy is to project the image and reality of America as a great nation worthy of the role Providence has assigned to it. This means developing a strategy that will insure the survival of the values of the West and their eventual ascendancy.

For too long, Americans have had to endure the ignominy of a government that has been beligerent and overweening in dealing with its own people while being vacillating and accommodating in dealing with its leading foreign foe. This cruel irony must end.

Professor Arthur Schlesinger, Jr., the historian whose self-appointed mission in life is, apparently, to laud and magnify the Kennedy family, has ventured the opinion that we are living in a "quiescent" period like that of the 1950s. The country, Schlesinger says, is exhausted after the rigors of the 1960s and is recharging its batteries. Once rested, the nation will embark upon a new period of "affirmative government" in the 1980s. Senator Edward Kennedy, the latest object of Schlesinger's generation, has taken up this theme, challenging the American people to become involved in the "great passions and issues of our times" and asking them rhetorically, "Will you give something back to America for all it has given you?"

Our obligation to America can be satisfied, of course, by helping put Teddy Kennedy in the White House, where he can realize his vision for the nation by such measures as implementing wage and price controls, national health insurance, and divestiture of the oil companies.

I think Schlesinger and Kennedy are wrong. I agree that we are now experiencing a period of transition and regrouping that will precede a new era of activism, but I believe the nature of that activism is likely to be fundamentally different from the orgy of big government that occurred during the 1960s.

The times now are fundamentally different than they were twenty years ago. Then liberalism was regnant in the intellectual circles of the country, its theories untested and full of promise. Across the nation, there was a powerful network in place, manned by optimistic people eager to embark on the challenge of making the promise of liberalism a reality. Conversely, there was then no conservative movement to speak of. Conservative activity, such as it was, consisted of a small coterie of intellectual spoil-sports, cur-mudgeons perversely trying to bring rain on the party.

Twenty years later, the situation is much different. Liberalism is no longer all alluring promise; it is a program that has been implemented and found to be a failure. Amongst the ranks of the nation's brightest young leaders, the tenets of liberalism are in disrepute. The liberal prescriptions have been implemented and found to be unworkable. At the same time, there is in place a large and growing conservative network manned by a young lead-ership brimming with confidence; the desire to get on with it and an elec-torate increasingly sympathetic to the approach they have to offer. Any attempt to reinstate a new wave of Schlesingerian "affirmative government" will find the going rough indeed.

I venture to predict that the1980s will be an era of affirmative private action. There is a wave building now that will crest in the 1980s, and the individuals introduced in this book will be riding it.

The young conservatives introduced here have no single ideology to sell, no utopian blueprint to offer. Yet, in the ideas and proposals they articulate, it is possible to glimpse the outlines of a conservative agenda for the na-tion—the kinds of reforms that would improve what is still, for all its short-comings, a very good society.

The challenge presented to American conservatives in the 1980s is awe-some but the opportunity is correspondingly great. If the challenge is met and the opportunity realized, the conservative affirmation of the 1980s will be an affirmation of the best elements of the American character. It will be a celebration of the best aspects of our national life, a celebration tapping the well springs of the American experience, burnishing the ideals of our land, making America once again a beacon of hope for all the world.

INDEX